A Thomas More Source Book

Thomas More [bottom center] at the opening of the 1523 Parliament. This is the
earliest known image of More. (See pages 228–29.)

A Thomas More Source Book

Edited by
Gerard B. Wegemer and Stephen W. Smith

The Catholic University of America Press
Washington, D.C.

The paper used in this publication meets the minimum requirements of
American National Standards for Information Science—Permanence of Paper for
Printed Library materials, ANSI Z39.48-1984.

∞

Library of Congress Cataloging-in-Publication Data

A Thomas More source book / edited by Gerard B. Wegemer and Stephen W. Smith.

p. cm.

Includes bibliographical references and index.

ISBN 0-8132-1376-2 (pbk. : alk. paper)

1. More, Thomas, Sir, Saint, 1478–1535.   2. Great Britain—History—Henry VIII,
1509–1547—Biography.   3. Henry VIII, King of England, 1491–1547—Relations with
humanists.   4. Great Britain—Politics and government—1509–1547.   5. Christian
martyrs—England—Biography.   6. Statesmen—Great Britain—Biography.
7. Humanists—England—Biography.   I. More, Thomas, Sir, Saint, 1478–1535.
Selections.   II. Wegemer, Gerard, 1950–   III. Smith, Stephen W., 1972–

DA334.M8 T455 2004

942.05'2'092—dc22

2003020136

Contents

4. Writings on Government

5. Writings on Religion

6. More's Last Days

Appendices

List of Illustrations

To our parents
whose wit and wisdom fostered a love
for merry tales of "sentence and solaas"

Acknowledgments

Expressing gratitude is a pleasant task after the many years of classes, conferences, and conversations that have given rise to this *Source Book*. For reviewing various editions of this work, we thank Drs. Elizabeth Mc-Cutcheon, Germain Marc'hadour, and Clarence H. Miller along with Catholic University of America Press readers Drs. John Gueguen and Anne O'Donnell. For invaluable suggestions and support, we thank Steven Bennett, Joseph Coleman, Myles Harrington, Charles LiMandri, and Thomas Spence, along with the many teachers and students who commented on earlier versions of this book, including Travis Curtright and Elaine Zajano. Special thanks to Tamara Marziani for her unflagging and conscientious attention to hundreds of details associated with bringing this book to print and with developing www.thomasmorestudies.org, which has been designed to accompany this book. We also thank Joshua Avery and the dedicated and patient staff at The Catholic University of America Press for their expert assistance, especially David McGonagle and Susan Needham, as well as Anne Theilgard and Peggy Russell of Kachergis Book Design.

Grateful acknowledgment is made to: Yale University Press for permission to reprint translations from volume 3.2 of *The Complete Works of St. Thomas More* and from *St. Thomas More: Selected Letters;* Toronto University Press for permission to reprint translations from volumes 7 and 8 of *Collected Works of Erasmus;* Scepter Publishers for permission to reprint modernizations of Mary Gottschalk from their editions of *Dialogue of Comfort Against Tribulation* and *The Four Last Things, The Supplication of Souls, and Di-*

alogue Concerning Conscience; Penguin Books for permission to reprint the translation from *Plutarch's Essays;* and to all the holders of art work recorded in the List of Illustrations. Every effort has been made to contact copyright holders; any omissions or errors will be rectified in any subsequent printings if notice is given to the editors.

Introduction

As the first major writer of the English Renaissance,[1] Thomas More is still surprisingly little known, despite the great success of Robert Bolt's play and the film it inspired, *A Man for All Seasons.* The only critical edition of his works was completed in 1997 by Yale University Press, one hundred years later than that for any comparable figure in English literature. In 1918, Oxford don and Erasmus scholar P. S. Allen lamented, "How little has England done to cherish More's memory."[2] In 1936, British literary scholar R. W. Chambers offered a reason for this neglect: "Public commemoration is not for the leaders of the losing side. . . . [W]hilst the works of the other great figures of English literature were being carefully edited, no scholar had been courageous enough to tackle More's *Works*. . . . More's reputation as a writer is sure to be re-established, as knowledge concerning him increases, as his writings come to be more and more widely known, and their place in the history of English prose appreciated."[3] As Chambers goes on to explain, More's reputation in England and throughout Europe was well established in More's own lifetime. One purpose of the present work is to help "re-establish" that reputation and to encourage the renewed study of More's life and writings by providing a selection of texts designed to reveal important facets of his thought on a broad range of topics.

1. Thomas More used the phrase "renascence of good letters." See *Selected Letters,* p. 16, and *Complete Works*, vol. 15, p. 18: *"bonas renasci litteras."*
2. *The Times Literary Supplement,* Dec. 26, 1918, p. 654.
3. Chambers' *The Place of Thomas More in English Literature and History*, pp. 21, 25.

Thomas More is a figure who has always invited controversy. Even the members of his own family did not agree or understand when this "Christian Socrates"[4] gave up all he possessed, even his life, in opposition to Henry VIII—for what most saw as but a "scruple" of conscience.[5] One of the earliest writers on Thomas More, the Tudor historian Edward Hall, perhaps most memorably expressed the confusion over More's character in the words: "I cannot tell whether I should call him a foolish wise man, or a wise foolish man."[6] The enigma of Thomas More has led many to avoid the complexities of his voluminous and varied body of work. Of the fifteen volumes in *The Yale Edition of the Complete Works of St. Thomas More*,[7] few readers know more than *Utopia*. Fewer still know he wrote 281 Latin poems, ten English poems, two histories,[8] four Platonic dialogues,[9] a response to Boethius' famous *Consolation of Philosophy*,[10] numerous theological reflections and polemics, along with a notable stream of letters to family and friends.[11]

A closer examination of his life and works reveals many apparent paradoxes and strengthens the sense that Thomas More is not easy to understand. How could it be, for instance, that the same person could write—within the same years—the dark and sinister study of tyranny *The History of King Richard III* (1513–1518), and the playfully suggestive *Utopia* (1515–1516)? How could it be that the same person could give the first philosophic and pragmatic arguments for freedom of speech and yet also defend

---

4. Harpsfield, p. 199. In 1536, Reginald Pole drew an extended comparison between More and Socrates in his *On the Unity of the Church*, pp. 231–32.

5. Two clear examples of strong family disagreement are given on pp. 29–30 and p. 55 of this *Thomas More Source Book*. Hereafter, all references to this book will be designated by *"TMSB."*

6. Cited in Holinshed's *Chronicles*, p. 793.

7. From 1963 to 1997, fifteen volumes were published in twenty-one books. Only ten of More's known 193 letters were included, however.

8. The English and Latin versions of More's *History of King Richard III* are so different that they seem to address two different audiences—one continental and one English—with different literary and historical designs.

9. Book 1 of *Utopia, Dialogue Concerning Heresies, Dialogue On Conscience* (i.e., "Letter of Margaret Roper to Alice Alington," August 1534), and *Dialogue of Comfort Against Tribulation*.

10. That More considered his *Dialogue of Comfort Against Tribulation* to be such a response, see the opening of book 1, chapter 1; see also *Complete Works*, vol. 12, pp. cxvii–cxix.

11. In the preface to her 1961 edition of *St. Thomas More: Selected Letters*, Elizabeth Rogers reported there to be "127 letters by More that remain, out of the thousands that he must have written" (p. xiii). Since then, H. Schulte Hergrüggen reported the discovery of sixty-six additional letters in "Seven New Letters from Thomas More," *Moreana*, no. 103 (Sept. 1990), pp. 49–66. The most recently discovered seven were translated and published by Clarence H. Miller in "Thomas More's Letters to Frans Van Cranevelt" in *Moreana*, no. 117 (March 1994), pp. 3–66.

the execution of heretics? And how could it be that a pious man presumably focused on the world to come was so immersed in the affairs and machinations of English political life? Nonetheless, More's most learned contemporary, Desiderius Erasmus, claimed that there was an integrity in More's thought and actions,[12] a claim More himself made late in his life. This *Source Book* sets forth the basic documents needed to recover and make intelligible the theory that lies behind these claims to integrity—the integrity both men saw as informing the drama of More's controversial life. This *Source Book* also attempts to give the reader some sense of the breadth and depth of the writings upon which this claim rests, and to serve as a companion to the study of More's best known works, *The History of Richard III* and *Utopia*.

The first writer to use the English word "integrity,"[13] More made his most provocative statement at the end of his life, as he stood on the scaffold facing execution on the charge of treason: "I die the King's good servant, *and* God's first."[14] That *and*, reported in the contemporary *Paris Newsletter* account of More's trial, underscores More's conviction that integrity is possible in political and personal life.[15] Just before his imprisonment, in an effort to use every possible means to protect his life and reputation, More sent a letter and the inscription for his tomb to Erasmus for publication throughout Europe. In that letter, More states clearly, "I consider it my duty to protect the integrity of my reputation," and he proceeds to report that, more than a year after his resignation from office, "no one has advanced a complaint against my integrity" and that, instead, "the King himself has pronounced on this situation at various times, frequently in private and twice in public."[16] More then goes on to recount King Henry's praise for his service—and thus the question is raised again: who exactly was this "masterful"[17] figure who addressed all of Europe with such "confidence and sense of command"[18] just months before his fall?

12. For example, *TMSB,* p. 10, where in speaking about More's work as a judge, Erasmus says of More, "[N]o one ever showed more absolute integrity." As shown later in this introduction, Erasmus maintained that—even after More's execution—"there was but one soul between us."

13. See the *Oxford English Dictionary*, but especially *Complete Works,* vol. 1, p. L, note 1, and p. 64, line 14, for an even earlier reference.

14. Emphasis added. *TMSB,* pp. 355–58.

15. The *Paris Newsletter* account was published on 4 August 1535. For examples of More's consistency with his principles, see Guy, *Thomas More,* pp. 163, 183, and 215.

16. *TMSB,* pp. 305–7.

17. See EE 3052, Sept. 1535 where Erasmus describes More as "imperiosum."

18. McConica, p. 67.

"The Christian English Cicero": Christian Humanism and the Ideal of Peace

Born in 1477/8 in the heart of London, Thomas More rose from modest beginnings to become Lord Chancellor of England in 1529, during what many now call the Early Modern Period and others the English Renaissance. More's own introduction to the "renascence of good letters"[19] was through Englishmen who had studied in Italy and were dedicated to improving the city by applying their "new learning" in useful ways. The three most notable examples were: Thomas Linacre, who translated Greek medical books, became founding president of the Royal Academy of Physicians, and endowed the first chairs of medicine at Oxford and Cambridge; John Colet, who used his family fortune to found St. Paul's School, making the new learning available to London youth; and William Grocyn, considered the most learned of all, who taught at Oxford and later in London served for a time as "the sole guide of [More's] life."[20]

More's ideals of Christian humanism, however, eventually conflicted with Henry VIII's imperial ambitions and love for chivalric glory.[21] Not only did Henry begin his reign by making imperial claims, but he soon acted upon them by waging war on France. More discreetly expressed opposition to Henry's 1513 war, intimating that the King suffered from a lust for power in his quest for glory.[22] More satirized the exalted view that kings often have of themselves, particularly in his Latin poetry, and he expressed his view that Christian princes should assist one another by pursuing peace rather than waging war.[23] More shared the common view of his fellow Christian humanists that peace is the ideal, although he recognized circumstances that would allow just war.[24] Significantly, More became known as the "Christian English Cicero,"[25] and he used a signet ring with the image of Titus, the Roman ruler who was thought to embody many of

---

19. See note 1 above.

20. *TMSB*, p. 177, line 70.

21. For a range of recent interpretations of humanism, see these authors, listed in Works Cited: Bradshaw, Elton, Fox, Guy, Hankins, Kinney, Kristeller, Logan, McConica, McCutcheon, Marc'hadour, Marius, Martz, Nauert, Skinner, Sylvester, and Wegemer.

22. Consider the juxtaposition of *Latin Poems* #243 and 244, *TMSB*, p. 239.

23. E.g., *TMSB*, p. 288, lines 18–28.

24. *TMSB*, pp. 286–90.

25 Harpsfield, p. 174; "Letter to Bugenhagen" in *Complete Works*, vol. 7, p. 6; Jonson, vol. 11, p. 591.

the ideals of humanism.[26] More's humanism was also distinctively Christian since he maintained that revelation provides clarity on issues and principles that would otherwise remain obscure to human thinking.[27]

Early Political Views

At the beginning of his career, More was well aware of what he called "kings' games . . . played upon scaffolds" and the ever-present dangers of a courtier's life.[28] In his Latin epigrams, for example, he wrote about the dangers of unchecked kingly power: "A king in his first year is always very mild indeed. . . . Over a long time a greedy king will gnaw away at his people. . . . It is a mistake to believe that a greedy king can be satisfied; such a leech never leaves flesh until it is drained."[29] The barb of the ending is typical of More's vivid and incisive approach. As this example indicates, however, the younger More wrote with less tact than the older and practiced statesman who lived in dangerous political conditions.

In his early political writings, More regularly used the word "citizen" instead of "subject," and he pointed out the dangers associated with monarchy.[30] Chief among these was flattery.[31] As he later warned Cromwell, a counselor should tell the king "what he ought to do, but never what he is able to do. So shall you show yourself a true faithful servant and a right worthy Councillor. For if a lion knew his own strength, hard were it for any man to rule him."[32] As this statement implies, More knew the dangers of one person possessing unlimited power. Indeed, his ode on Henry's coronation daringly warned that "unlimited power has a tendency to weaken good minds, and that even in the case of [the] very gifted."[33]

In contrast, Henry's model king was the chivalric warrior Henry V, the

26. Ackroyd, p. 88. As James Hankins states in the recent *Cambridge Companion to Renaissance Humanism,* "There has never been any doubt that Thomas More should be classed as a Renaissance humanist: his professional employments, cultural style, and the range of problems he addresses all clearly identify him as such" (p. 137). However, he immediately adds: "Yet More's relationship to earlier humanist political thought is even more complex and troubled than Machiavelli's." As this quotation indicates, much work remains to be done regarding More's humanist project.

27. For example, see *Confutation of Tyndale, Complete Works,* vol. 8, p. 996.

28. More's *History of King Richard III, Complete Works,* vol. 2, p. 81. See also *TMSB,* pp. 231–32 and 240–45.

29. *Latin Poems,* #198, *TMSB,* p. 238.

30. *TMSB,* pp. 235–39.

31. *TMSB,* p. 53 and esp. note 81.

32. *TMSB,* pp. 43 and 232.

33. *Latin Poems,* #19, *Complete Works,* vol. 3.2, p. 105.

historic figure that seemed to dominate Henry VIII's imagination of himself as a ruler.[34] This self-image led the new king to plan war with France almost immediately and, against the counsel of his advisors, to lead the troops himself—thus needlessly endangering his life and the stability of the English nation. This pursuit of glory through military conquest was in opposition to More's pursuit of a united and peaceful Christendom.[35] At the heart of this conflict were two radically different views of human and political excellence. Henry eventually accepted a view of divine right whereby authority over both church and state was vested in himself directly by God; More, as some of the selections in this volume show, saw church and state as having two distinct sources of authority: the state's authority arising from citizens inherently free; the church's authority arising from God, but through the agency of an established hierarchy.[36] And while Henry pursued a chivalric ideal of military conquest as part of his ultimate view of human excellence, More cherished with Erasmus the Christian humanist ideals of peace and cultural development.

"Born for Friendship"

Related to this Christian humanist ideal was the vital role of friendship—with God, with neighbor, and with other nations—in supporting and advancing the ends of human life and society. Erasmus, who knew leaders from around the world, marveled at More's affable and self-effacing manner. "Born for friendship," as Erasmus described him, More delighted in conversation and could accommodate himself to an unusually wide array of human beings.[37] More's best friend appears to have been Antonio Bonvisi, an Italian merchant-banker who risked his own reputation and safety, standing by More even in his time of disgrace. During More's imprisonment, for example, he supplied More with food, wine, and warm clothing. More's last letter in Latin is a moving tribute to this best of friends who had been a source of comfort and encouragement "for almost forty years."[38] Such a friend More considered to be the gift of a good and

---

34. Guy, pp. 77, 423–26; Adams, 17–19, 58–79; see also Holbein's portrait of Henry, *TMSB*, p. 230.

35. For More's concern, see *TMSB*, pp. 28; 27, lines 29–30; 300, lines 14–16; 308, lines 4–6; 354, lines 23–26.

36. E.g., *TMSB*, pp. 59–60, 294, 354.

37. "Born . . . for friendship" is Francis M. Nichols' vivid translation of "Ad amicitiam natus factusque videtur"; see also the translation given on p. 7 of *TMSB*. See EE, letter #999, 23 July 1519, "To Ulrich von Hutten."

38. *TMSB*, pp. 182–84.

merciful God, and such friendship More desired and prized throughout his life. Even after his trial, speaking to the judges who had just condemned him as a traitor and whom he had known for most of his professional life, More expressed the friendly hope that they might "yet hereafter in heaven merrily all meet together,"[39] despite what appeared to be the hopeless divisions of the present moment.

In one of his most original poems, "On Two Beggars," deviating from the Greek epigrams he had studied and translated, More gave striking expression to the importance of friendship.[40] He was convinced that every human being, no matter how gifted, is incomplete and thus in need of the help of others. In the perspective of this poem, the role of the statesman might be seen as ordering the "lame" and "blind," himself included, in such a way that all contribute to a just and peaceful society. "Proud kings," however, are incapable of bringing about this type of society because they entertain perilous delusions of self-sufficiency and power. The dangers posed by pride and by kings are given special attention by More throughout his life, as a number of selections in this book indicate. He also gave notable attention to friendship with God, which he often presented in metaphors of human friendship.[41]

Preparing for Public Service

Thomas More was forty-one when he finally accepted the invitation to join King Henry's service. He could have done so earlier, but he chose not to, perhaps because he knew that his young and growing family would need him most in those early years of his career; or perhaps because he knew that his own character and thought were not yet sufficiently developed to face the wiles of the court; or perhaps because he knew that Henry had tyrannical leanings. In any case, More learned service to his country as part of a long-established family tradition. On both his mother's side and his father's, civic service was a way of life. His grandfather Thomas Granger, for example, was a lawyer actively involved in London, serving as an alderman and eventually as sheriff. More's father was a well-known and respected lawyer, then a judge, ending as a judge of the King's Bench. There in London and from his family, More learned the importance of citizens' vigilant involvement in government, a lesson he would appreciate

---

39. *TMSB*, p. 61.   40. *Latin Poems*, #32, *TMSB*, p. 234.

41. E.g., *TMSB*, pp. 12, 164–72, 261–69.

even more deeply after studying the Greek and Roman philosophers, historians, and statesmen.

The elder More began early preparing his talented son for a life of service and leadership. After sending him to the best grammar school in London, St. Anthony's on Threadneedle Street, John More apprenticed his son to no less a leader than Lord Chancellor and Archbishop John Morton at Lambeth Palace. There, while waiting on tables and learning what a courtier must know, Thomas observed first hand the ways and dealings of the greatest leaders of England and their foreign guests. In the process, he impressed Morton, who predicted that "this child here waiting at the table, whosoever shall live to see it, will prove a marvelous man."[42] Morton admired, for example, how during theatre performances, More would "suddenly sometimes step in among the players and, never studying for the matter, make a part of his own there presently among them which made the lookers-on more sport than all the players beside."[43] Such "wit and towardness" led Morton to send Thomas to Oxford to study at his own Canterbury Hall (now Christ Church College).[44]

Young Thomas had studied at Oxford for two years when John More decided that his son should return to London to complete his education at the Inns of Court.[45] There Thomas would study the wider range of subjects needed for practical success later in life, particularly in the legal profession. Studies at New Inn prepared him for entry to Lincoln's Inn, where he actively participated as a student; years later he served as a lecturer and then as an officer. Even while he was Lord Chancellor his participation continued. For example, More was called upon to assist the Master of Revels in the Inn's celebrations, and he continued to participate in its professional and social events.[46]

Studies after Law School

Called to the bar around 1501, the studious More angered his father by not immersing himself in a legal career. Instead, More proceeded to master

---

42. *TMSB*, p. 19.

43. This unusual aptitude for improvisation was dramatized amusingly in *Sir Thomas More's* play-within-a-play, "The Marriage of Wit and Wisdom," *TMSB*, pp. 120ff.; see also Erasmus' comment, p. 12, lines 288ff.

44. *TMSB*, p. 19.

45. The four major Inns of Court have traditionally served not only as England's universities of the common law but as the legal societies having exclusive power to admit persons to practice at the bar.

46. Ackroyd, pp. 13–14.

Greek while pursuing liberal studies in philosophy, theology, history, and literature, and also considering a priestly vocation under the guidance of the Carthusians at the Charterhouse in London. More's friend Erasmus tells us that John More became so angry with his son that young More was almost disinherited.[47] Even in these early years, however, More seemed to realize that, whatever profession he would choose, he needed the philosopher's understanding of human nature, the historian's appreciation of his country, the theologian's perspective on eternity, and the poet's art of moving hearts.

More mastered Greek in three years, to such a degree that in 1505 he joined Erasmus in translating dialogues and orations of Lucian, the classical master of irony and satire, into Latin. So effective were these translations that they would go on to become the most popular of his works printed during his lifetime, surpassing even the *Utopia*.[48] More had a special love for these comic dialogues because Lucian "everywhere reprimands and censures, with very honest and at the same time very entertaining wit, our human frailties. And this he does so cleverly and effectively that although no one pricks more deeply, nobody resents his stinging words."[49] This same style can be seen later in many of More's own works, especially in his habit of *"ridentem dicere verum,"* or speaking the truth through laughter.[50] Or as More paraphrases Horace in the *Apology,* "a man may sometimes say full truth in jest."[51]

In these years, More carefully studied Plato, Aristotle, Cicero, and the Greek and Roman historians. He translated a wide selection of Greek epigrams and composed in Latin many of his own. When these are considered with his English poems, More's collection is one of the more comprehensive compiled in the period—ranging from humorous poems about the many forms of human folly, to daring political commentaries on monarchy in general (and on both King Henry VII and King Henry VIII in particular), to devout poems about the love of God.

More gave special attention not only to the classical authors but to the Bible and the Church Fathers, as shown in the series of public lectures he gave in 1501 on Augustine's *City of God*. These lectures (which have not survived) were given "not . . . from the theological point of view, but from

47. *TMSB,* p. 8.
48. Ackroyd, p. 94.
49. *Translations of Lucian, Complete Works,* vol. 3.1, p. 3.
50. Ackroyd, p. 94.
51. *The Apology, Complete Works,* vol. 9, p. 170, modernized.

the standpoint of history and philosophy"[52]—indicating More's efforts to think through the philosophic and historical issues facing the earthly city.

Freedom and More's Political Philosophy

More's study of the classical and Judeo-Christian authors led him to formulate a position rarely held in those days, a position that rested upon the conviction that each person is essentially free. For example, in his *History of Richard III* he states clearly that parliament—not the king—is "the supreme and absolute" authority in England.[53] In a Latin poem written before he joined King Henry's service, he expresses more fully his surprising view of political freedom and authority—i.e., that "The Consent of the People Both Bestows and Withdraws Sovereignty."[54] Such writings suggest that More's many years of study resulted in a coherent political philosophy that would guide him throughout his career in the King's service. The depth of this study can be seen in *Utopia*, which gives a playful but profound analysis of the nature and limits of political life, drawing heavily upon Greek, Roman, and Christian classics such as Plato's *Republic*, Cicero's *De Officiis*, and Augustine's *City of God*.

Education and Conscience

More's study of history and of human nature further led him to see that the struggle for peace and justice requires capacities and skills only perfectible through the hard work of education. More saw education as essential to effective leadership because the leader always and everywhere would need what More called a "good mother wit,"[55] or practiced good judgment,[56] particularly useful in sifting appearances and testing character in the often duplicitous world of experience. To achieve such a judgment, More again seemed to realize that a deep study of philosophy, literature, history, and theology was necessary—the very education he sought for himself and that he gave his daughters and son.

By providing his daughters with the same education as his son, More proved a far-sighted educational reformer in his times. He stated explicitly that men and women "are equally suited for the knowledge of learning."[57] According to Erasmus, More succeeded in this educational reform because

---

52. Stapleton, pp. 7–8.
53. *Complete Works*, vol. 15, p. 320.
54. *TMSB*, p. 237.
55. *TMSB*, p. 278.
56. See Alistair Fox's 1978 article on "'Good Mother Wit' and Creative Imitation."
57. *TMSB*, p. 199.

More himself combined "so much real wisdom with such charm of character"[58] that others came to see the advantages of such an education, an education that was later accepted among leading families not only in England, but throughout Europe and eventually the United States.

For More, a "right conscience" was one of the two principal objectives of education.[59] More understood conscience in the traditional manner: as a judgment of the practical intellect. As such, the role of conscience is to make practical judgments in light of principles and laws recognized as true and just. Conscience does not make those principles or laws; it only applies them in particular cases. Hence a "right conscience" is one that is neither lax nor scrupulous,[60] but one that accurately assesses the ethical demands of a particular situation. This conception is an important element in More's claim that integrity is indeed possible. Yet the difficulty in achieving integrity is obvious since even the best conscience—i.e., the best exercise of the practical judgment—can be mistaken and since human freedom always makes it possible to reject the indications of conscience. In this light one can understand why More considered the humble "love [of] good advice" as another end of education[61] and as an indispensable condition for the responsible use of freedom.[62]

Early Professional Life

More worked hard to acquire a broad range of experience as a young lawyer and local politician. His first cases were eminently practical. He worked, for example, as a commissioner for sewers,[63] helping with a project much needed to prevent the frequent flooding of the Thames River. He also worked closely with London's businessmen and merchants, who came to value his judgment and skills so much that they chose him as their spokesman in Parliament and as their negotiator for contracts.[64] He served in the 1504 Parliament, married in 1505, and lectured in law at Furnivall's Inn from 1503 to 1506. In 1507, he was elected Financial Secretary of Lincoln's Inn and in 1509 he became a member of the influential Mercers' Guild; in 1510, he returned to Parliament and also became undersheriff[65]

58. *TMSB*, p. 224.
59. "recti conscientia"—see *TMSB*, pp. 198–99, 212–14, and 316ff.
60. Consider the importance More gives to this issue at the end of his life: see *TMSB*, pp. 316ff.
61. *TMSB*, p. 200.   62. *TMSB*, pp. 240–41, 232, 354.
63. Ackroyd, pp. 148, 237.   64. Ackroyd, pp. 147ff.
65. As undersheriff, More would have served as chief legal counsel to the city of London.

of London. It was in this latter capacity that More received the widest range of practical experience and eventually became beloved by his fellow Londoners for being "the best friend that the poor e'er had" and for embodying the "marriage of wit and wisdom"—to use memorable phrases from the Elizabethan play *Sir Thomas More*.[66]

In 1511, he was asked to give the prestigious Autumn Lectures at Lincoln's Inn. In that same year, his wife Jane died. Deeply grieved, More had the additional difficulties of taking care of four children under the age of six. His solution went against the expectations of many, but within one month, he married widow Alice Middleton, although she may have been eight years his senior[67] and shared few of his interests. Time, however, proved More's choice a wise one; the marriage was both loving and effective.[68]

More's Political Career: From Citizen to Subject

From 1511 to 1518, More was a very active citizen of London. He continued as undersheriff throughout these years, while developing one of the largest and most lucrative law practices in the city. He took on greater responsibilities in governing Lincoln's Inn and was elected to the prestigious Doctors' Commons.[69] He also represented the country's business interests in foreign embassies, and still found time to write and to correspond with Europe's leading intellectuals.

In 1518 More joined Henry VIII's service with reluctance,[70] partly because he was aware of the "serious risks" involved in serving a powerful prince.[71] Besides the dangers and the substantial loss of income, this career change meant he would have less time for his family and for his own study and writing; it also meant he would be more subject to the king than a free citizen of London would be.

The year 1518 held new and important opportunities. In that year, both Henry and Wolsey decided to pursue a path of peace instead of war, and both seemed open to much needed reforms in church and state. Nevertheless, before joining Henry's service, More spoke with Henry about

66. *TMSB*, pp. 145 and 120.
67. Ackroyd, p. 139.
68. See Ackroyd's account of the match and marriage (pp. 138–46).
69. The Doctors' Commons was an association of the realm's leading lawyers, legislators, and foreign emissaries.
70. *Selected Letters*, "To John Fisher," p. 94.
71. *TMSB*, p. 10, line 236.

matters of conscience in a conversation which proved to be quite far-sighted and even prophetic, considering the series of events that would end in More's execution years later. As More reported this conversation, King Henry "graciously declared unto me that he would in no wise that I should do or say anything except that I should perceive my own conscience should serve me, and that I should first look unto God and after God unto him." This, More recalled, was the "first lesson . . . that ever his Grace gave me at my first coming into his noble service," and More considered it "the most virtuous lesson that ever prince taught his servant."[72]

Once engaged in the King's court, More rose rapidly in responsibilities and duties. He soon became Henry's private secretary, and Henry knighted him in 1521 in recognition of his wide range of services. The confidence of both King Henry and Cardinal Wolsey was shown when More became Speaker of the House of Commons in 1523, an important session in the history of British liberties, as will be seen below.

In the early 1520s, however, King Henry's appetite for war grew strong again. More expressed his opposition to this war policy in 1522,[73] and he famously quipped to his son-in-law that "if my head could win [the King] a castle in France, . . . it should not fail to go."[74] After Henry broke his own Treaty of Universal Peace in 1524 by invading France, More was significantly assigned to new domestic duties.

In 1525 Henry gave Sir Thomas responsibility for his extensive and lucrative Duchy of Lancaster. As its chancellor, More assumed the full scope of administrative and judicial duties of a political ruler. In 1526, he was given even greater responsibilities when Henry appointed him to his Royal Council's subcommittee of four, the four who oversaw all the major concerns of the realm, excluding matters of war. More also served as a peace ambassador to France in 1524, and these efforts came to fruition in the Peace of Cambrai in August of 1529. A few years later, when writing the epitaph for his tomb, More would briefly mention his service as king's counselor, knight, and chancellor, but he went on at surprising length about his work for peace.[75]

On October 25, 1529, Sir Thomas was chosen by Henry VIII to be Lord Chancellor of England, after Cardinal Thomas Wolsey was removed from that office on charges of treason.

---

72. *TMSB*, p. 358.

74. *TMSB*, p. 27.

73. *Correspondence*, p. 263, lines 43–44.

75. *TMSB*, pp. 307, line 35; 308 lines 1–5.

Free Speech and Equal Justice

Before turning to the events that led to More's trial and death, it is worth pausing to consider other events of particular historic importance in More's political career, specifically the "Petition for Free Speech," his defense of the liberty of the House of Commons, and his work in expanding access to the courts of justice.

More's "Petition for Free Speech" in 1523 is the first recorded argument that has come down to us defending the political necessity of free speech. Although it was sometimes the custom to ask the king not to punish members of parliament for expressing their mind, More's petition went far beyond the pragmatic question of punishment.[76] He set forth an argument indicating why it is in the best interests of both king and country to encourage free speech. More argued that good counsel requires the free exchange of ideas and public deliberation. He explained that, in discussing issues "of great importance, the mind is often so occupied with the matter" and not with the manner of expression that a proper examination of issues would not be possible unless the members of the House of Commons were "utterly discharged of all doubt and fear" about how they might express their judgments in the heat of discussion and debate.[77] In these and other words, More defended free deliberation of political issues.

More's memorable defense of the liberty of the House of Commons, which took place in 1523 as well, is commemorated by a life-size mural in England's Parliament. This painting[78]—one of eight in the "Building of Britain" series in St. Stephen's Hall of Parliament—depicts a famous incident that occurred in 1523 when, as Speaker of the House of Commons, More ingeniously and courageously resisted Lord Chancellor Wolsey's attempt to violate the Commons' tradition of free deliberation.[79]

As a judge, More was innovative, and he worked hard to expand access to justice and to ease the rigor of the common law by considering, through equity, the actual circumstances of individual persons.[80] This did not make him popular with the common law judges since he issued injunctions halting legal proceedings and requiring review by the Court of Chancery. When complaints against More increased, he invited to dinner all the judges concerned.[81] Over wine afterwards, he went through each

76. Neale, esp. pp. 157–159. Skinner (1998) gives a different interpretation, pp. 88–89.
77. *TMSB*, pp. 240–42 (modernized) and 24.   78. *TMSB*, p. 242.
79. *TMSB*, pp. 243–45.
80. For a recent summary of these innovations, see Guy, *Thomas More*, pp. 135–37.

injunction he had issued, and he explained his reasons for having done so, thus winning back the judges' good will.

As a judge, More became well respected among the people for fair and quick judgments. Although no evidence yet exists about its origin, there is a common rhyme testifying to this reputation. The poem probably refers to More's work as a judge while he was Chancellor of the Duchy of Lancaster:[82]

> When More sometime had Chancellor been,
> No more suits did remain.
> The like will never more be seen
> Till More be there again.

More's impartiality as a judge was also well-known. When, for example, his son-in-law complained that More did not favor his own family, More replied: "[S]on, I assure thee on my faith that, if the parties will at my hands call for justice, then, [although] my father stood on the one side and the devil on the other, his cause being good, the devil should have right."[83] More's reverence for the common law tradition of England and the Magna Carta, however, would soon lead him into the conflict that would cost him his life.

More's View on the Proper Spheres of Church and State

More's final conflict with Henry VIII is the most dramatic and best-known aspect of Sir Thomas's life. In this brief account, it will suffice to summarize More's understanding of the proper spheres of legitimate authority governing church and state, as shown on three different occasions.

In 1521, when editing Henry's *Defense of the Seven Sacraments*, More cautioned the King against exaggerating the temporal jurisdiction of the pope. In strong opposition, Henry insisted upon setting "forth that authority to the utmost," especially since "we received from that See our crown imperial."[84] This statement reveals the distance between Henry's understanding and More's own of the origins of political authority and indicates why Henry would be led to adopt the notorious conception of the "divine right of kings" which the English people would violently reject more than a hundred years later with the execution of Charles I. Since More conceived human beings as free by nature, he saw political authority as arising from a self-governing people. Hence, as seen above, he states boldly

---

81. *TMSB*, pp. 37–38.   82. Hastings, p. 110.
83. *TMSB*, p. 36.   84. *TMSB*, pp. 48–49.

in one of his more memorable poems that "the consent of the people both bestows and withdraws [temporal] sovereignty."

More clarified his view of this crucial issue again in 1529 when the church was accused of usurping state power and when anticlericalism was on the rise, especially among the Protestant reformers. Both William Tyndale and Simon Fish charged that the church forced King John in 1213 to make "England and Ireland tributary to the pope and the Holy See"[85] by demanding the payment of Peter's Pence. More denied this accusation, pointing out that Peter's Pence was always an alms freely given and that it was a custom which had begun before King John's time. More insisted upon the principle of proper jurisdiction: "For never could any king of England give away the realm to the pope, or make the land tributary, even if he wanted to."[86] More clearly understood there to be two orders, temporal and spiritual, whose governments were necessarily separate and distinct but, ideally, complementary and mutually supportive.[87] As Lord Chancellor, More worked to defend and advance this understanding of church and state, which led to one of the major struggles of his professional career—the prosecution of seditious heresy.

In order to understand the historical situation of the time better, one should note that heresy in More's day was not simply what we today understand by heresy. When More defended the use of legitimate force against heretics, he pointed out that he had a civic duty to do so because the actions of heretics were "seditious" in the eyes of the law.[88] Heresy was, as the history of that time showed, often accompanied by violence that sought to overthrow flawed but legitimate institutions.[89] Under these circumstances, More and rulers throughout Europe understood themselves to be obliged by the laws of their country to protect the peace and welfare of their people. More was not imagining this violence—it was occurring throughout Germany in alarming ways. As he reported, for example, 60,000 peasants were slain in the summer of 1525 in the state's effort to restore peace in that tumultuous land.[90] More, along with every Christian ruler of Europe, was concerned that such violence would spread. He cited

---

85. *TMSB*, p. 293. 86. Ibid.

87. The inscription on the Roper vault (where More's head is buried) in St. Dunston's Church, Canterbury, reiterates the importance of this stand by simply quoting the Magna Carta: "Ecclesia Anglicana Libera Sit."

88. E.g., *The Confutation of Tyndale, Complete Works*, vol. 8, pp. 28–33; *The Apology*, vol. 9, pp. 162, 167; *TMSB*, p. 298.

89. See Boyle, p. 138, and Wegemer's *Thomas More on Statesmanship*, pp. 161ff.

90. *TMSB*, p. 298 and *A Dialogue Concerning Heresies, Complete Works*, vol. 6, p. 369. More's est-

the authority of Augustine, who had begun his public career by urging leniency towards heretics, but after decades of violence, ended by urging public officials to use lawful force to defend the church against unlawful force.[91]

The dangers of Martin Luther's heresy, as More saw them, were primarily three. First, Luther's early claim that the spiritual elect had independence from all governors and from all laws except those of the Gospel was seen by More as a sure path to war.[92] Second, More foresaw disastrous effects from Luther's denial of free will: To teach people that they were not responsible for their actions and that their actions did not affect the state of their soul or the justice of their lives—these doctrines, in More's view, could not lead to civil behavior or a peaceful state.[93] Third, More strongly opposed Luther's inflammatory language which dehumanized "papists" and stirred thousands to angry violence against those "dregs of the earth."[94] Even Erasmus, one of the greatest proponents of peace of all times, eventually agreed that lawful force had to be used against Luther and his followers because of the extreme and widespread violence they were causing. Erasmus lamented that Luther had "shattered almost the whole world" with his angry attacks.[95]

More had long recognized the need for reform in both church and state, but he strongly advocated the traditional means of reformation: the gradual improvement of education and law, both civil and ecclesiastical[96]—not violent overthrow based on an ideological position whereby some were considered spiritually elect and therefore exempt from civil law.

---

imates varied: 70,000 in "Letter to Bugenhagen," *Complete Works*, vol. 7, p. 102, and 80,000 in *The Confutation of Tyndale, Complete Works,* vol. 8, p. 56.

91. *TMSB*, pp. 284–85.

92. *A Dialogue Concerning Heresies, Complete Works,* vol. 6, pp. 368–69; vol. 8, p. 57; *Responsio ad Lutherum,* vol. 5, pp. 691–93, 279, 281.

93. *A Dialogue Concerning Heresies, Complete Works,* vol. 6, p. 373; vol. 8, p. 498; *Responsio ad Lutherum,* vol. 5, pp. 269, 271, 207; "Letter to Bugenhagen," vol. 7, p. 49.

94. *Responsio ad Lutherum, Complete Works,* vol. 5, p. 35. Of course, as Louis Martz explains, More did not hesitate to employ "bad manners" himself in these religious disputes: "The justification for excesses on both sides has been well-stated by a later expert [John Milton] in religious controversy who expressly takes Luther as his model, arguing from the example of the prophets and Christ himself that there may be a 'sanctified bitterness against enemies of truth'" (20).

95. Erasmus, Letter 1670, "To Elector John of Saxony," 2 March 1526, trans. Hillerbrand. More concurs in his "Letter to Bugenhagen," *Complete Works,* vol. 7, p. 25: "You [Luther] hurled a burning torch on all of Germany. You lit the wildfire that is now consuming the world."

96. *TMSB*, pp. 295, 300, 301.

More's End

More repeated his understanding of the principle of church-state relations at his trial on July 1, 1535, when he invoked both the Magna Carta
and the king's ancient Coronation Oath to show the longstanding recognition of the important distinctions discussed above. At that trial, More respectfully but forcefully expressed his fundamental disagreement with
Henry's personal despotism, reminding the English people of their own
deeply held convictions about the sovereignty of law and the limited authority of government.[97]

Contrary to the impression given by Robert Bolt's artful *A Man for All
Seasons*, scholars have now clearly shown that after his resignation as Lord
Chancellor, Thomas More was not silent or passive in the face of what he
considered to be grave dangers facing England.[98] Instead, More waged one
of the most active writing campaigns conceivable, including *The Dialogue
Concerning Heresies, The Confutation of Tyndale's Answer, The Apology,* and *The
Debellation of Salem and Bizance.* This campaign was so effective in coun-
tering what More saw as the unjust manipulation of England's fundamental laws and institutions, that Henry VIII and Cromwell had to use the full
force of their positions to silence through imprisonment and then execution one of London's most popular citizens and one of Europe's most respected authors.

Up to the last moment of his life, More used discreet but effective
means of appealing to the conscience of his king and his country. He did
this not only at the cost of his own health and safety but at the cost of his
family's material welfare. This he did, convinced that the very principle of
just and legitimate government of both church and state was at stake. Although More's life seemed to end in failure, historians now recognize his
role in opposing a politics of unchecked power and in helping to advance
an understanding of democratic self-rule. As British historian John Guy
recently wrote, "For a former Lord Chancellor to defy the King and claim
freedom of conscience against the state was a revolutionary step by the
standards of the sixteenth century. More stood at the crossroads of history."[99]

The purpose of this *Source Book* is to provide the documents needed to

97. *TMSB,* pp. 60 and 354.
98. Guy, *Thomas More,* pp. 171–183; Bradshaw, pp. 554–55.
99. Guy, *Thomas More,* p. 183.

understand better the theory informing the drama of this man of conscience and integrity. It may also serve to explain why, more than 450 years later, More would have been elected Lawyer of the Millennium by the Law Society of Great Britain in 1999 and chosen as Patron of Statesmen and Politicians by John Paul II in 2000.[100]

Part one presents three sixteenth-century accounts of More's life, penned by different figures under widely different circumstances. Desiderius Erasmus' account of More's character was published in July 1519, three years after the publication of *Utopia*, before the dark clouds of political and religious upheaval changed the cultural landscape of Europe. This letter of Erasmus to a fellow renaissance reformer presents More as the embodiment of Erasmus' vision of rebirth and renewal. That More continued to embody that ideal—even after his execution—is suggested by Erasmus' statement that "there was but one soul between us."[101]

The Life of Sir Thomas More (c. 1556) was composed by William Roper, who married More's daughter Margaret in 1521 and lived in the More household for sixteen years. Surprisingly, there is no mention of *Utopia* or any of More's writings except for one poem on fortune composed in prison.[102] Writing at the age of sixty or so, some twenty years after Thomas More's death, Roper recounts his remembrances with a clarity and alacrity that have made this a favorite biography, although some suspect its reliability because of hagiographic intent.

No such intent has been said to inform the provocative Elizabethan play written about More at the end of the sixteenth century. *Sir Thomas More* (c. 1592) was written by several London playwrights, including Anthony Munday and (so it seems) William Shakespeare, the former being known as a principal informer against Catholic recusants in the 1580s. Because it was rejected by Queen Elizabeth's official censor, Edmund Tilney, this play was apparently not performed in that era. Why London playwrights as diverse as Munday, Shakespeare, and Henry Chettle would risk writing about such a controversial figure remains something of a mystery that historians and literary critics have not satisfactorily solved. But why such a diverse group would have agreed to present this alleged traitor to crown and country in a sympathetic light remains an even greater mystery. The play represents, for example, that More remained faithful to his con-

---

100. See the Law Society of Great Britain's *Gazette*, December 1999 and *L'Osservatore Romano*, 8 November 2000.

101. EE 3049, 31 August 1535.   102. *TMSB*, p. 55.

science even in the face of disgrace and death, but we never learn why.

Parts two and three of this *Source Book* contain many of More's most famous writings on love, friendship, and education; they provide an illuminating contrast to these themes as treated in *Utopia*. To indicate their interrelatedness in More's understanding, a section on "Conscience and Integrity" has been included at the end of part three as well as Erasmus' important letter explaining the character and influence of More's understanding of education. Excerpts from Plutarch's essay "How to Tell a Flatterer from a Friend" are given, partly because More included Plutarch in his own children's education, and partly because Erasmus twice presented his translation of this essay to Henry VIII early in his reign, but especially because More suggested that flattery was a principal reason for the drastic changes in King Henry.[103]

Part four presents some of More's writings on government, revealing his preference for representative government over monarchy and, contrary to what many have seen in *Utopia*, defending the necessity of private property as well as the importance and necessity of free speech. The *Latin Epigrams* in this section were originally published with the 1518 edition of *Utopia;* as such, they set up a striking contrast to the "best regime" exercise embodied in *Utopia*. The central question of these works—What is the best form of government?—raises in an English context the same issues Plato and Cicero each raised in his *Republic*. Continuing this same tradition, More probes the deepest questions about human life: What do human beings need to be happy? What type of government best facilitates that happiness?

Part five presents selections that show More's understanding of God, the church, the proper relations of church and state, and major problems that these two institutions faced in his day, most notably heresy. Part six makes available important writings that show More's own understanding of his last days and the issues of conscience he faced in the final drama of his life.

Most of the side glosses in this *Source Book* are the addition of the editors; a few are More's or his sixteenth-century editors. For additional texts, images, and supporting materials, you may wish to consult www.thomasmorestudies.org.

July 6, 2003

---

103. *TMSB*, p. 53, and esp. note 81.

1

Earliest Accounts of Thomas More's Life

This chalk drawing shows the care Holbein took in order to get Thomas More's fa-
cial expressions just right for the final oil version shown on the cover of *A Thomas
More Source Book*. Holbein first transferred his preliminary sketch to the prepared
surface of the painting by pricking the outlines of his sketch and then smearing
charcoal through those holes. The sketch and the portrait show Sir Thomas More in
1527, at age 50. Despite the rich garments and opulent green-velvet curtain in the
oil painting, More's disregard for finery is indicated by the hair sticking out from his
cap and by the three-days' stubble evident on his face. The finished portrait captures
the man of business who literally has work in hand, yet More's gaze and the window in the lower corner suggest that he is simultaneously open to things unseen.

Erasmus on Thomas More

This earliest biographical account of Thomas More was written by More's fellow humanist and friend Desiderius Erasmus. Erasmus (1466–1536) is also the author of the famous humanist text, Moriae Encomium (In Praise of Folly), *written while he stayed at More's house in Bucklersbury.[1] In this letter, Erasmus offers a memorable portrait of More's character, education, professional excellence, love of friendship, piety, and even some of his charming idiosyncrasies, such as his love of eggs.*

23 July 1519[2]

*Erasmus of Rotterdam to the
Honorable Ulrich von Hutten, Knight, Greetings:*

The affection—one might almost say, the passion—that you feel for that gifted man Thomas More, fired as of course you are by reading his books, which you rightly call as brilliant as they are scholarly—all this, believe me my dear Hutten, you share with many of us, and between you and More it works both ways: he in his turn is so delighted with the orig-

Shared affection for More

5

---

1. *Collected Works of Erasmus,* vol. 7, pp. 16–25. This "Letter to Ulrich von Hutten" was translated by R.A.B. Mynors. For the Latin version, see *EE*, Letter 999. Von Hutten (1488–1523) was a German poet, scholar, satirist, and humanist who eventually allied himself with Luther and turned against Erasmus.

2. More is forty-two and has completed his first year in Henry VIII's service. Erasmus and More first met in 1499, when More was twenty-two.

inality of your own work that I am almost jealous of you. Surely this is an example of that wisdom which Plato calls the most desirable of all things, which rouses far more passionate desire in mortal hearts than the most splendid physical beauty. The eyes of the body cannot perceive it, but the mind has its own eyes, so that here too we find the truth of the old Greek sayings that the eye is the gateway to the heart. They are the means through which the most cordial affection sometimes unites men who have never exchanged a word or set bodily eyes on one another. It is a common experience that for some obscure reason one man is captivated by this form of beauty and another by something different; and in the same way between one man's spirit and another's there seems to be a kind of unspoken kinship, which makes us take great delight in certain special people, and less in others.

Be that as it may, you ask me to draw a picture of More for you at full length, and I wish I were as skillful as you are eager. For me too it would be nothing but a pleasure to spend a little time thinking about the friend I love best. But there are difficulties: it is not everyone who can appreciate all More's gifts, and I doubt if he would endure to be depicted by any and every artist. It is, I suspect, no easier to produce a portrait of More than one of Alexander the Great or Achilles, nor did they deserve their immortality any more than he does. Such a sitter demands the skill of an Apelles, and I fear there is less of Apelles in me than of Fulvius or Rutuba. I will try, however, to do you not so much a picture as an outline sketch of the whole man, based on long-standing and intimate acquaintance, as far as my observation or memory will serve. Should any mission overseas eventually bring you together, you will realize what an incompetent artist you have selected for this task, and I am afraid that you will think me either envious or purblind—too blind to detect, or too envious to be willing to record more than a few of all his good qualities.

To begin with one aspect of More which is quite unknown to you, in stature and habit of body he is not tall, without being noticeably short, but the general harmony of his proportions is such that nothing seems amiss. He has a fair skin; his complexion tends to be warm rather than pale, though with no tendency to a high color, except for a very delicate flush which suffuses it all. His hair blackish-brown, or brownish-black if you prefer; beard somewhat thin; eyes rather greyish-blue, with a kind of fleck in them, the sort that usually indicates a gifted intelligence, and among the English is thought attractive, while our own people prefer dark eyes. No

The difficulty of describing More

More and Alexander the Great

Physical description

kind of eye, they say, is so immune from defects. His expression shows the
sort of man he is, always friendly and cheerful, with something of the air
of one who smiles easily, and (to speak frankly) disposed to be merry
rather than serious or solemn, but without a hint of the fool or the buf-
foon. His right shoulder looks a little higher than his left, especially when
walking, not by nature but from force of habit, like so many human tricks.
Otherwise there is nothing to criticize in his physique. Only his hands are
a trifle coarse,[3] at least if one compares them with his other bodily features. As for the care of his personal appearance, he has taken absolutely no
heed of it ever since boyhood, to the extent of devoting very little care
even to those niceties allotted to the gentlemen by Ovid. How good-
looking he was as a young man, one can guess even now by what remains—though I knew him myself when he was not more than three-
and-twenty, for even now he is scarcely past his fortieth year.

He enjoys good, but not rude, health, adequate at any rate to support
all the duties of a good citizen, and is subject to no complaints or very
few; there is every hope that he will enjoy long life, for his father is still
alive at a great age, but wonderfully active and vigorous for his years. I
have never seen a man less particular about his food. Until he reached
manhood he was content to drink nothing but water, a habit inherited
from his father. Only, for fear of causing any embarrassment in this regard,
he used to drink his beer out of a pewter tankard, so that the guests did
not know—small beer next door to water, and often just water. As for
wine, the habit in those parts being to invite your neighbor to drink in his
turn from the same cup, he sometimes barely sipped it, so as not to seem
entirely to dislike it, and at the same time to learn to follow common usage. Beef, salt fish, and coarse bread with much yeast in it he preferred to
the dishes of which most people are fond, though in other ways he was by
no means averse from all the things that bring harmless pleasure, be it only
to the body. Dairy produce and all the fruit which grows on trees have always had a great attraction for him, and he is particularly devoted to eggs.
His voice is not loud, yet not particularly soft, but of a sort to strike clearly on the ear; no music in it, no subtlety, a straightforward speaking voice,
for he does not seem framed by nature to be a singer, though he is fond of
music of all kinds. His language is remarkably clear and precise, without a
trace of hurry or hesitation.

More's habits of eating and drinking

His voice

3. Here Erasmus seems to hint at More's earthy humor.

His approach to clothes and ceremony

Simple clothes please him best, and he never wears silk or scarlet or a gold chain, except when it is not open to him to lay it aside. He sets surprisingly little store by the ceremonies which ordinary men regard as a touchstone of good breeding; these he neither demands from other people nor tenders meticulously himself either in public assemblies or in private parties, although he is familiar with them should he wish to use them. But he thinks it effeminate and unworthy of a man to waste a good part of his time in such frivolities.

More and power

Court life and the friendship of princes were formerly not to his taste, for he has always had a special hatred of absolute rule[4] and a corresponding love for equality. You will hardly find any court, however modest, that is not full of turmoil and self-seeking, of pretence and luxury, and is really free from any taint of despotic power. Even the court of Henry VIII he could not be induced to enter except by great efforts,[5] although it would be difficult to wish for anything more cultured and more unassuming than the present king. By nature he has a great love of liberty and leisure; but dearly as he loves to enjoy leisure when he can, no one displays more energy or more endurance at the call of duty.

More and the art of friendship

Friendship he seems born and designed for; no one is more openhearted in making friends or more tenacious in keeping them, nor has he any fear of that plethora of friendships against which Hesiod warns us. The road to a secure place in his affections is open to anyone. In the choice of friends he is never difficult to please, in keeping up with them the most compliant of men, and in retaining them the most unfailing. If by any chance he has picked on someone whose faults he cannot mend, he waits for an opportunity to be quit of him, loosening the knot of friendship and not breaking it off. When he finds open-hearted people naturally suited to him, he enjoys their company and conversation so much that one would

Pleasure in conversation

think he reckoned such things the chief pleasure in life. For ball games, games of chance, and cards he hates, and all the other pastimes with which the common run of grandees normally beguile their tedious hours. Besides which, though somewhat negligent in his own affairs, no one could take more trouble in furthering the business of his friends. In a word, whoever desires a perfect example of true friendship, will seek it nowhere to better purpose than in More.

---

4. See poems in chapter 4, *TMSB*. See also lines 279–80 below.
5. See *Selected Letters,* #18, p. 94.

115 In society he shows such rare courtesy and sweetness of disposition
that there is no man so melancholy by nature that More does not enliven *Manners and*
him, no disaster so great that he does not dissipate its unpleasantness. From *mirth*
boyhood he has taken such pleasure in jesting that he might seem born for
it, but in this he never goes as far as buffoonery, and he has never liked bit-
120 terness. In his youth he both wrote brief comedies and acted[6] in them.
Any remark with more wit in it than ordinary always gave him pleasure, *Pleasure in wit*
even if directed against himself; such is his delight in witty sayings that be-
tray a lively mind. Hence his trying his hand as a young man at epigrams,
and his special devotion to Lucian; in fact it was he (yes, he can make the
125 camel dance) who persuaded me to write my *In Praise of Folly*.

In fact there is nothing in human life to which he cannot look for entertainment, even in most serious moments.[7] If he has to do with educated and intelligent people, he enjoys their gifts; if they are ignorant and stupid, he is amused by their absurdity. He has no objection to professional
130 buffoons, such is the skill with which he adapts himself to the mood of
anyone. With women as a rule, and even with his wife, he confines himself
to humor and pleasantry.[8] You would think him Democritus[9] reborn, or
rather that Pythagorean philosopher who strolled unthinking through the
market-place watching the crowds of people buying and selling. Nobody
135 is less swayed by public opinion, and yet nobody is closer to the feelings of
ordinary men.

He takes a particular pleasure in contemplating the shapes, character,
and behavior of different living creatures. Thus there is hardly any kind of *Love of animals*
bird of which he does not keep one in his household, and the same with
140 any animal that as a rule is rarely seen, such as monkey,[10] fox, ferret, weasel,
and the like. Besides these, if he sees anything outlandish or otherwise remarkable, he buys it greedily, and has his house stocked with such things
from all sources, so that everywhere you may see something to attract the
eyes of the visitor; and when he sees other people pleased, his own pleas-
145 ure begins anew. In his younger days he was not averse from affairs with
young women, but always without dishonor, enjoying such things when

---

6. See Roper's *Life, TMSB*, p. 19.

7. For More's humor even on the scaffold, see *TMSB*, pp. 64 and 152–56.

8. This statement may reflect more about Erasmus than Sir Thomas, who regularly had deep
conversations with his learned daughters. See *TMSB*, p. 221, for how More helped change Erasmus' view on women's education.

9. Democritus (fifth century B.C.) was known as the laughing philosopher.

10. For a lesson More gives, using the monkey as an example, see *TMSB*, p. 30.

they came his way without going out to seek them, and attracted by the
mingling of minds rather than bodies.

More and the benefits of liberal education

A liberal education he had imbibed from his very earliest years. As a
young man he devoted himself to the study of Greek literature and philos-   150
ophy, with so little support from his father, a man in other respects of good
sense and high character, that his efforts were deprived of all outside help
and he was treated almost as if disinherited because he was thought to be
deserting his father's profession; for his father is a specialist in English law.
The law as a profession has little in common with literature truly so called;   155
but in England those who have made themselves authorities in that subject are in the first rank for eminence and distinction. Nor is it easy in that
country to find any other career more likely to lead to wealth and reputation; and in fact most of the nobility of the island owes its rank to studies
of this kind. In the law, they say, no one can perfect himself without many   160
years of hard work. So it was not surprising that, when he was a young
man, More's nature should swerve away from the law, being made for better things; but after a taste of the subjects studied at the university, he be-

Success at law

took himself to it with such good effect that there was no one whose advice was more freely sought by litigants, nor was a larger income made by   165
any of those who gave their whole time to the law. Such was the force and
quickness of his intelligence.

Piety and marriage

Besides this he devoted himself actively to reading the works of the or-
thodox Fathers. On St Augustine's *City of God* he gave public lectures before large audiences while still quite a young man;[11] priests and old men   170
were not ashamed to seek instruction in holy things from a young man
and a layman, or sorry they had done so. And all the time he applied his
whole mind to the pursuit of piety, with vigils and fasts and prayer and
similar exercises preparing himself for the priesthood. In this indeed he
showed not a little more sense than those who plunge headlong into so   175

Self-testing

exacting a vocation without first making trial of themselves. Nor did anything stand in the way of his devoting himself to this kind of life, except
that he could not shake off the desire to get married. And so he chose to
be a god-fearing husband rather than an immoral priest.[12]

Choice of a wife

However, he chose for his wife[13] an unmarried girl who was still very   180

---

11. More's teacher William Grocyn invited More to give these lectures at Grocyn's church (*c.*
1501), at St. Lawrence Jewry. See Stapleton, pp. 7–8.

12. Nicholas' translation: "Accordingly he resolved to be a chaste husband rather than a licentious priest," p. 394.

13. Jane Colt, from Netherhall, Essex.

young, of good family, and quite inexperienced as yet, having always lived in the country with her parents and her sisters, which gave him the more opportunity to mould her character to match his own.[14] He arranged for her education and made her skilled in music of every kind, and had (it is clear) almost succeeded in making her a person with whom he would gladly have shared his whole life, had not an early death removed her from the scene, after she had borne him several children. Of these there survive three daughters, Margaret, Alice, and Cecily, and one son, John. Nor did he endure to remain a widower for very long, though the advice of his friends urged a different course. A few months[15] after his wife's death, he married a widow, more to have someone to look after his household than for his own pleasure, for she was neither beautiful nor in her first youth,[16] she used to remark in jest, but a capable and watchful housewife, though they lived on as close and affectionate terms as if she had been a girl of the most winning appearance. Few husbands secure as much obedience from their wives by severity and giving them orders as he did by his kindness and his merry humor. He could make her do anything: did he not cause a woman already past the prime of life, of a far from elastic disposition, and devoted to her household affairs, to learn to play the zither, the lute, the monochord, and the recorder, and in this department to produce a set piece of work every day to please her exacting husband?[17]

Death of Jane

Marriage to Alice

He shows the same geniality in the management of his household, in which there are no troubles and no disputes. If anything should go wrong, he puts it right promptly or makes them agree; nor has he ever dismissed anyone as a result of ill feeling on either side. In fact his household seems to enjoy a kind of natural felicity, for no one has ever been a member of it without bettering his fortune later, and no one has ever earned the least shadow on his reputation. Indeed you would hardly find such close relations anywhere between a man and his mother as exists between him and his stepmother; for his father had now remarried for the second time, and he loved them both as if they had been his own mother. The father[18] has lately remarried a third time; and More solemnly swears that he has never seen a better person. Such moreover is his affection for his kinsmen, his

Governance of his home

Attitude towards stepmothers and relatives

---

14. For one interpretation on how this failed, see Erasmus' colloquy "Marriage," which is thought to be about More and his wife.

15. In fact, More married Alice Middleton thirty days after Jane's death, in the summer of 1511.

16. The Latin phrase is "nec belle . . . nec puelle."

17. Thomas More played the viol. See Stapleton, p. 14.

18. Sir John More married four times, his last wife being Alice Clerk.

children, and his sisters that his relations with them are never oppressive, nor yet does he ever fall short in his family duties. 215

Attitude towards money

From any love of filthy lucre he is absolutely free. To provide for his children he has earmarked as much of his resources as he considers sufficient for them; and the rest he spends liberally. In the days when he was

As a lawyer

still dependent on the income from his clients, he gave everyone helpful and reliable advice, thinking much more of their advantage than of his 220 own; the majority he used to persuade to settle their actions, on the ground that this would save them expense. If that was not successful, he then tried to show them how to carry on their litigation at the least cost to themselves; for some men are so made that they actually enjoy going to

Civil service as lawyer and judge

law. In the city of London, in which he was born, he has for some years 225 acted as judge in civil cases.[19] This office is by no means onerous, for the court sits only on Thursdays until dinner-time, but it carries much prestige. No one ever determined more cases, and no one showed more absolute integrity. Many people have had the money returned to them which according to precedent must be paid by litigants; for before the ac- 230 tion comes into court, the plaintiff must deposit three drachmas, and the

Loved by Londoners

defendant the same, nor is it permissible to demand any more. The result of this behavior was that his native city held him in deep affection.

He had made up his mind to be content with this station in life, which gave him quite sufficient standing and at the same time was not exposed 235

Serving the king

to serious risks. More than once he was forced to go on a diplomatic mission; and as he conducted these with great intelligence, his serene Majesty King Henry VIII would not rest until he had dragged the man to his court. I use the word "dragged" advisedly, for no man was ever more consumed with ambition to enter a court than he was to avoid it. But since 240 that excellent king had it in mind to fill his household with learned, wise, intelligent, and upright men, he summoned a great many others, and especially More; whom he keeps so close to him that he never allows him leave to go. If serious business is afoot, no better counselor than he; if the king wishes to relax his mind with more cheerful topics, no man's compa- 245 ny more gay. Often difficult issues demand an authoritative and able judge; and More can settle these in such a way that both parties are grateful. Yet

No bribes

no one has succeeded in persuading him to take a present from anybody. Happy indeed a commonwealth would be, if the prince would appoint to

19. More was undersheriff of London from 1510 to 1518.

250   each post a magistrate like More. And all the time no pride has touched him.

Amidst such masses of business he does not forget his old and ordinary friends, and returns to his beloved literature from time to time. Whatever power his station gives him, whatever his influence can do with so power- *Serving others*
255   ful a king, is all devoted to the good of the commonwealth and of his friends. His disposition was always most ready to do good unto all men, and wonderfully prone to show mercy; and he now gives it more play, because he has more power to do good. Some men he helps with money, to some he gives the protection of his authority, others he advances in life by
260   his recommendation. Those whom he cannot help in any other way he aids with good advice. He has never sent anyone away with a long face. You might call More the general resource of everyone who needs help. He thinks some great stroke of luck has come his way if he has been able to relieve the oppressed, to help the perplexed and entangled out of their
265   troubles, or to reconcile the parties to a quarrel. No one more enjoys doing a kindness or less demands gratitude for doing one. And yet, though he is very fortunate on so many counts, and though good fortune is often accompanied by self-conceit, it has never yet been my fortune to see a man more free from that fault than he.

270   But to return to tell of his literary pursuits, which have been the chief *Literary pursuits* bond between More and myself in both directions. His earlier years were exercised principally in poetry; after that came a long struggle to acquire a more supple style in prose by practicing his pen in every sort of writing. What his style is like now, I need not set down, especially for your benefit,
275   for you have his books always in your hands. He has taken delight especially in declamations, and, in that department, in paradoxical themes, as offering more lively practice to one's ingenuity. As a youth he even worked on a dialogue in which he supported Plato's doctrine of communalism, extending it even to wives. He wrote an answer to Lucian's *Tyran-*
280   *nicida*, on which topic it was his wish to have me as an opponent, to test more accurately what progress he had made in this sort of composition. *Utopia* he published with the purpose of showing the reasons for the   Utopia shortcomings of a commonwealth; but he represented the English commonwealth in particular, because he had studied it and knew it best. The
285   second book he had written earlier, when at leisure; at a later opportunity he added the first in the heat of the moment. Hence there is a certain unevenness in the style.

Rhetorical gifts   It would be difficult to find a more felicitous extempore speaker, so fertile are both his mind and the tongue that does its bidding. His mind is always ready, ever passing nimbly to the next point; his memory always at   290 his elbow, and as everything in it is held, so to say, in ready cash, it puts forward promptly and without hesitation whatever time or place demand. In disputations nothing more acute can be imagined, so that he has often taken on even the most eminent theologians in their own field and been almost too much for them. John Colet, a sensitive and experienced critic,   295 used to say sometimes in conversation that there was only one able man in the whole of England,[20] though the island is blessed with so many men of outstanding ability.

Piety and   True piety finds in him a practicing follower, though far removed from *friendship* all superstition. He has his fixed hours at which he says his prayers, and   300 they are not conventional but come from the heart. When he talks with friends about the life after death, you recognize that he is speaking from conviction, and not without good hope. And More is like this even at court. What becomes then of those people who think that Christians are not to be found except in monasteries?   305

Such are the men whom that most intelligent king admits to his household and his privy chamber; admits, yes, and invites, and even forces them to come. These are the continual spectators and witnesses of the way he lives; these form his council; these are the companions of his journeys. He rejoices to have them round him rather than young men or women   310 dissolute and vicious, or even rich men in their splendid collars, or all the *Concluding* blandishments of insincerity, where one man would divert him to aimless *remarks on* pleasures, another would heat his blood with thoughts of tyranny, another *Henry VIII* put forward fresh tricks with which to fleece his people. Had you lived in this court, my dear Hutten, I have no doubt you would quite rewrite your   315 *Aula*, and cease to be a professed enemy of court life, though you too live with as honorable a prince as you could wish, nor do you lack men who look for a better state of things, such as Stromerand Kopp. But what are the few that you have in comparison with such a company of distin-*Distinguished* guished men: Mountjoy, Linacre, Pace, Colet, Stokesley, Latimer, More,   320 *company* Tunstall, Clerk, and others like them? Whichever you choose to name, you will have mentioned in one word a world of all the virtues and all learn-

---

20. Nicholas' translation: "England has only one genius," p. 399. The Latin is "non nisi unicum esse ingenium" (*EE*, letter 999, line 269).

ing. I myself, however, have hopes of no common kind that Albert, the one ornament of our native Germany at this time, may gather more men
325 like himself into his household, and may set an important precedent for all the other princes, encouraging them too to wish to do the same, each in his own court.

There is the portrait, the best of sitters ill done by the worst of artists. You will like it less when you have the good fortune to know More bet-
330 ter. But I have done it to protect myself for the moment to stop your complaining that I have not done what you asked, and your constant ob-jections that my letters are too short. Though this has not seemed to me longer than usual in the writing, nor will you find it, I am sure, long-winded in the reading; my dear More's charm will see to that.

Farewell.
Erasmus

FAMILIA THOMÆ MORI ANGL: CANCELL:

Thomas Morus Aº 50. Alicia Thomæ Mori uxor Aº 57. Iohannes Morus pater Aº 76. Iohannes Morus Thomæ filius Aº 19. Anna Grisacria Iohannis Mori Sponsa Aº 15. Margareta Ropera Thomæ Mori filia Aº 22.
Elisabeta Damea Thomæ Mori filia Aº 21. Cæcilia Hercina Thomæ Mori filia Aº 20. Margareta Giga Clementii uxor Mori filialis Condiscipula et cognata Aº 22. Henricus Patensonus Thomæ Mori morio Aº 40.

Thomas More, His Father and His Household, by Hans Holbein the Younger (Kunstmuseum Basel, 1526–27). Hans Holbein drew this preliminary sketch for a life-size (*c.* 98 x 135 inches) family portrait, shortly after he came to stay in the More home in December 1526. This sketch was sent to Erasmus as a gift in 1528. From left to right are:

Elizabeth (21 years old), Margaret Giggs (22, adopted), Judge John More (76), Anne Cresacre (15, ward), Sir Thomas (50), John (18), Henry Patenson (family "fool"), Cecily (20), Margaret (22), Lady Alice (57), family monkey

The Family of Sir Thomas More, Hans Holbein/Rowland Lockey,
*c.*1530, 1593

Although the painting has the signature of Rowland Lockey (1565/7–1616), it is
dated 1530 and the linen canvas dates back to the 1520s. Recent studies indicate
that Holbein probably began but never finished this more permanent oil version of
the water-based painting that he had completed *c.* 1527. The water-based
("distempered") original perished in a fire in 1752. Margaret is pointing to the
word "demens" ("mad") in the chorus of Seneca's *Oedipus,* act 4. Other books
identified are Seneca's *Letters* under the arm of Elizabeth and Boethius' *Consolation
of Philosophy* on the sideboard. This painting hangs at Nostell Priory in Wakefield,
England. See Lesley Lewis's *The Thomas More Family Group Portraits After Holbein*
(Gracewing, 1998), p. 13 esp., Angela Lewi's *The Thomas More Family Group*
(London: Her Majesty's Stationery Office, 1974), pp. 5–7, and Ruth Norrington's
The Household of Sir Thomas More (Buckinghamshire, Eng: The Kylin Press, 1985).

The Life of
Sir Thomas More, Knight

c. 1556

by William Roper

William Roper lived in More's home for sixteen years, from roughly 1518 when Roper began his law studies at Lincoln's Inn until 1534 when More was arrested and imprisoned in the Tower of London. In 1521, William married Margaret More, the daughter closest to More in aspirations and gifts.

Written twenty years after More's death, as soon as the political climate allowed, this Life gives Roper's personal remembrances, although he also draws upon the materials that were soon to be published in the 1557 English Works of Sir Thomas More. *Whether Roper expected his own work to be published is not known, since he had already commissioned Nicholas Harpsfield to write More's official biography. Harpsfield refers to Roper's Life as the "Notes" which Harpsfield incorporated, often verbatim, into his longer biography. These "Notes" have been recognized, however, as perhaps the first and one of the finest biographies written in English. Regarding the* Life's *focus, two distinguished editors of this work explained:*

The key concept—the key word, in fact—is "conscience." The first time the word occurs is in the opening sentence and thereafter it appears again and again until More has reached his personal crisis. The word itself may be said to recapitulate the action of the story. More's

William Roper, 1536–40, miniature by Hans Holbein

conscience first becomes an issue when, as a "beardless boy" in Parliament, he upsets the plans of King Henry VII to exact a "three-fifteenths" subsidy from the people to promote the marriage of his daughter Margaret to James IV of Scotland. From this time on, there is not a single anecdote or episode in the book that does not reflect in some way More's conscience or integrity of character.[1]

History has shown that this account contains a few errors, all understandable given that Roper was writing from memory. Yet there are omissions that are surprising, such as no mention of More's writings. The best critical edition of this text continues to be the 1935 edition of the Early English Text Society, edited by E. V. Hitchcock, The Lyfe of Sir Thomas Moore, knight *(Oxford UP).*

The Life of Sir Thomas More, Knight
by William Roper

More's merit Forasmuch as Sir Thomas More, knight, sometime Lord Chancellor of England, a man of singular virtue and of a clear unspotted conscience, as witnesseth Erasmus, more pure and white than the whitest snow, and of such an angelical wit as England, he saith, never had the like before, nor never shall again, universally, as well in the laws of our own realm (a study in effect able to occupy the whole life of a man), as in all other sciences, right well studied, was in his days accounted a man worthy of perpetual famous memory: 5

Roper's qualification I, William Roper, though most unworthy, his son-in-law by marriage to his eldest daughter,[1] knowing at this day no one man living that of him and of his doings understood so much as myself, for that I was continually resident in his house by the space of sixteen years and more, thought it therefore my part to set forth such matters touching his life as I could at this present call to remembrance. Among which things, very many notable things (not meet[2] to have been forgotten) through negligence and long continuance of time are slipped out of my mind. Yet, to the intent the same should not all utterly perish, I have at the desire of divers worshipful   10   15

---

1. Richard S. Sylvester and Davis P. Harding, *Two Early Tudor Lives* (Yale UP, 1962), p. xvi.
1. Roper married Margaret More on July 2, 1521.
2. *meet*—proper, fitting

friends of mine (though very far from the grace and worthiness of them, nevertheless as far forth as my mean wit, memory and knowledge would serve me) declared so much thereof as in my poor judgment seemed worthy to be remembered.

5   This Sir Thomas More, after he had been brought up in the Latin tongue at St. Anthony's in London, was by his father's[3] procurement received into the house of the right reverend, wise, and learned prelate Cardinal Morton,[4] where, though he was young of years, yet would he at Christmas-tide suddenly sometimes step in among the players, and never 10 studying for the matter, make a part of his own there presently among them, which made the lookers-on more sport than all the players beside. In whose wit and towardness[5] the Cardinal, much delighting, would often say of him unto the nobles that divers times dined with him, "This child here waiting at the table, whosoever shall live to see it, will prove a mar- 15 velous man."

    Whereupon for his better furtherance in learning, he placed him at Oxford, where, when he was both in the Greek[6] and Latin tongue sufficiently instructed, he was then for the study of the law of the realm put to an Inn of Chancery called New Inn, where for his time he very well pros- 20 pered. And from thence was admitted to Lincoln's Inn, with very small allowance, continuing there his study until he was made and accounted a worthy utter barrister.

    After this, to his great commendation, he read for a good space a public lecture of St. Augustine's *De Civitate Dei,* in the Church of St. Law- 25 rence in the old Jewry, whereunto there resorted Doctor Grocyn an excellent cunning[7] man, and all the chief learned of the City of London.

    Then was he made reader at Furnival's Inn, so remaining by the space of three years and more.

    After which time he gave himself to devotion and prayer in the Char- 30 terhouse of London, religiously living there, without vow, about four years, until he resorted to the house of one Master Colt, a gentleman of Essex, that had oft invited him thither, having three daughters, whose hon-

Early education

At Morton's court, c. 1489

Skill in acting

Morton's prediction

Oxford, c. 1491

New Inn, c. 1493

Lincoln's Inn, c. 1496

Lectures on Augustine, c. 1501

Furnival's Inn

Charterhouse, c. 1501–1504

3. John More (1451?–1530)

4. Lord Chancellor of England, 1487–1500; Archbishop of Canterbury, 1486–1500; made a cardinal in 1493. More entered Morton's household in 1490, at Lambeth Palace.

5. *towardness*—natural aptitude and good disposition

6. More actually began his study of Greek later, around 1501. See *Selected Letters*, p. 2.

7. *cunning*—learned

est conversation and virtuous education provoked him there specially to set his affection. And albeit his mind most served him to the second daughter, for that he thought her the fairest and best favored, yet when he considered that it would be both great grief and some shame also to the eldest to see her younger sister in marriage preferred before her, he then 5 of a certain pity framed his fancy towards her, and soon after married her, never the more discontinuing his study of the law at Lincoln's Inn, but applying still the same until he was called to the bench, and had read[8] twice, which is as often as ordinarily any judge of the law doth read.

Marries Jane Colt, 1505

Before which time he had placed himself and his wife at Bucklersbury 10 in London, where he had by her three daughters and one son, in virtue and learning brought up from their youth, whom he would often exhort to take virtue and learning for their meat, and play for their sauce.

More's home at Bucklersbury

Who, ere ever he had been reader in Court, was in the latter time of King Henry VII made a burgess of the Parliament, wherein there were by 15 the King demanded (as I have heard reported) about three-fifteenths[9] for the marriage of his eldest daughter, that then should be the Scottish queen. At the last debating whereof he made such arguments and reasons there against, that the King's demands thereby were clean overthrown. So that one of the King's Privy Chamber named Master Tyler, being present thereat, 20 brought word to the King out of the Parliament House that a beardless boy had disappointed all his purpose. Whereupon the King, conceiving great indignation towards him, could not be satisfied until he had some way revenged it. And, forasmuch as he nothing having, nothing could lose, His Grace devised a causeless quarrel against his father, keeping him in the 25 Tower until he had made him pay to him an hundred pounds fine.

More enters Parliament, 1504

An encounter with the King

Shortly thereupon it fortuned that this Sir Thomas More, coming in a suit to Doctor Fox, Bishop of Winchester (one of the King's Privy Council), the Bishop called him aside, and, pretending great favor towards him, promised him that, if he would be ruled by him, he would not fail into the 30 King's favor again to restore him, meaning (as it was after conjectured) to cause him thereby to confess his offense against the King, whereby His Highness might with the better color have occasion to revenge his displeasure against him. But when he came from the Bishop, he fell in communication with one Master Whitford, his familiar friend, then chaplain to 35

Almost entrapped by Bishop Fox

---

8. *read*—gave series of lectures
9. This is a property tax that amounted to three-fifteenths of the property's value.

that Bishop, and after a father of Sion,[10] and showed him what the Bishop had said unto him, desiring to have his advice therein, who for the Passion of God, prayed him in no wise to follow his counsel. "For my lord, my master," quoth he, "to serve the King's turn, will not stick[11] to agree to his own father's death." So Sir Thomas More returned to the Bishop no more. And had not the King soon after died,[12] he was determined to have gone over the sea, thinking that, being in the King's indignation, he could not live in England without great danger.

After this he was made one of the under-sheriffs of London, by which office and his learning together (as I have heard him say), he gained without grief not so little as four hundred pounds[13] by the year, since there was at that time in none of the prince's courts of the laws of this realm any matter of importance in controversy wherein he was not with the one part of counsel. Of whom, for his learning, wisdom, knowledge, and experience, men had such estimation that, before he came to the service of King Henry VIII, at the suit and instance of the English merchants, he was by the King's consent made twice ambassador in certain great causes between them and merchants of the Steelyard: whose wise and discreet dealing therein, to his high commendation, coming to the King's understanding, provoked his Highness to cause Cardinal Wolsey (then Lord Chancellor) to procure him to his service. And albeit the Cardinal, according to the King's request, earnestly travailed[14] with him therefore, among many other his persuasions alleging unto him how dear his service must needs be unto his Majesty, which could not, with his honor, with less than he should yearly lose thereby, seem to recompense him. Yet he, loath to change his estate, made such means to the King, by the Cardinal, to the contrary, that his Grace, for that time, was well satisfied.

Now happened there after this, a great ship of his that then was Pope to arrive at Southampton, which the King claiming for a forfeiture, the Pope's ambassador, by suit unto His Grace, obtained that he might for his master the Pope have counsel learned in the laws of this realm, and the matter in his own presence (being himself a singular[15] civilian) in some

More appointed Under-sheriff of London, 1510–1518

Legal successes and reputation

Ambassador for English merchants, 1515 and 1517

More avoids working for the King

---

10. Sion was a Bridgettine monastery in Middlesex.
11. *stick*—delay, hesitate
12. April 1509.
13. An ordinary worker earned roughly ten pounds a year.
14. *travailed*—labored
15. *singular*—of exceptional status

public place to be openly heard and discussed. At which time there could

Counsel to Pope's
ambassador, 1517

none of our law be found so meet to be of counsel with this ambassador as
Sir Thomas More, who could report to the ambassador in Latin all the reasons and arguments by the learned counsel on both sides alleged. Upon
this the counselors of either part, in presence of the Lord Chancellor and   5
other the judges, in the Star Chamber had audience accordingly. Where
Sir Thomas More not only declared to the ambassador the whole effect of
all their opinions, but also, in defense of the Pope's side, argued so learnedly himself, that both was the aforesaid forfeiture to the Pope restored, and
himself among all the hearers, for his upright and commendable demeanor   10

Henry insists on
More's service

therein, so greatly renowned, that for no entreaty would the King from
thenceforth be induced any longer to forbear his service. At whose first
entry thereunto he made him Master of the Requests (having then no
better room[16] void[17]) and within a month after, knight and one of his
Privy Council.   15

Henry delights in
More's company

And so from time to time was he by the Prince advanced, continuing
in his singular favor and trusty service twenty years and above, a good part
whereof used the King upon holy-days, when he had done his own devo-
tions, to send for him into his travers,[18] and there sometime in matters of
astronomy, geometry, divinity, and such other faculties, and sometimes of   20
his worldly affairs, to sit and confer with him. And other whiles would he,
in the night, have him up into his leads,[19] there for to consider with him
the diversities, courses, motions, and operations of the stars and planets.
And because he was of a pleasant disposition, it pleased the King and the
Queen, after the Council had supped, at the time of their supper, for their   25
pleasure, commonly to call for him to be merry with them. Whom when

More merrier
at home

he perceived so much in his talk to delight, that he could not once in a
month get leave to go home to his wife and children (whose company he
most desired) and to be absent from the Court two days together, but that
he should be thither sent for again, he, much misliking this restraint of his   30

More dissembles

liberty, began thereupon somewhat to dissemble his nature, and so by little
and little from his former accustomed mirth to disuse[20] himself, that he was
of them from thenceforth at such seasons no more so ordinarily sent for.

16. *room*—office
17. *void*—empty
18. *travers*—small screened-off portion of a larger room
19. *leads*—flat roof covered with lead
20. *disuse*—disengage

Then died one Master Weston, Treasurer of the Exchequer, whose office, after his death, the King of his own offer, without any asking, freely gave unto Sir Thomas More.[21]

In the fourteenth year of his Grace's reign was there a Parliament holden, whereof Sir Thomas More was chosen Speaker, who, being very loath to take that room[22] upon him, made an oration (not now extant)[23] to the King's Highness for his discharge thereof; whereunto when the King would not consent, he spake unto his Grace in form following:

Appointed Speaker of the House, 1523

Since I perceive, most redoubled Sovereign, that it standeth not with your high pleasure to reform this election and cause it to be changed, but have by the mouth of the most reverend father in God, the legate, your Highness's Chancellor, thereunto given your most royal assent, and have of your benignity determined, far above that I may bear, to enable me and for this office to repute me meet[24] rather than you should seem to impute unto your Commons that they have unmeetly chosen, I am therefore, and always shall be, ready obediently to conform myself to the accomplishment of your high commandment, in my most humble wise beseeching your most noble Majesty that I may with your Grace's favor, before I farther enter thereunto, make mine humble intercession unto your Highness for two lowly petitions: the one privately concerning myself, the other the whole assembly of your Common House.

His oration

More is ready to obey

For myself, gracious Sovereign, that if it mishap me in anything hereafter that is on the behalf of your Commons in your high presence to be declared, to mistake my message, and in the lack of good utterance, by my misrehearsal,[25] to pervert or impair their prudent instructions, it may then like your most noble Majesty, of your abundant grace, with the eye of your accustomed pity, to pardon my simpleness, giving me leave to repair again to the Common House, and there to confer with them, and to take their substantial advice what thing and in what wise I shall on their behalf utter and speak before your noble Grace, to the intent their prudent devices[26] and affairs be not by my simpleness and folly hindered or impaired: which thing, if it should so mishap, as it were well likely to mishap in me, if your gracious benignity relieved not my oversight, it could not fail to be during my life a perpetual grudge and heaviness to my heart, the help and remedy whereof, in manner aforesaid remembered, is, most gracious Sovereign, my first lowly suit and humble petition unto your most noble Grace.

Request for himself

21. Here Roper errs. More was made undertreasurer of the Exchequer, and his predecessor was John Castle, not Weston.

22. *room*—office

23. See Edward Hall's summary of that speech, p. 279.

24. *repute me meet*—declare me qualified

25. *misrehearsal*—misrepresentation

26. *devices*—opinions

Request for the
Commons

Mine other humble request, most excellent Prince, is this: forasmuch as there
be of your Commons, here by your high commandment assembled for your Parliament, a great number which are, after the accustomed manner, appointed in the
Common House to treat and advise of the common affairs among themselves
apart, and albeit, most dear liege Lord, that according to your prudent advice, by   5
your honorable writs everywhere declared, there hath been as due diligence used
in sending up to your Highness's Court of Parliament the most discreet persons
out of every quarter that men could esteem meet thereunto, whereby it is not to
be doubted but that there is a very substantial assembly of right wise and politic
persons; yet, most victorious Prince, since among so many wise men neither is   10
every man wise alike, nor among so many men, like well-witted, every man like
well-spoken, and it often happeneth that, likewise as much folly is uttered with
painted polished speech, so many, boisterous and rude in language, see deep indeed, and give right substantial counsel; and since also in matters of great importance, the mind is often so occupied in the matter that a man rather studieth what   15
to say than how, by reason whereof the wisest man and the best spoken in a
whole country fortuneth among,[27] while his mind is fervent in the matter, somewhat to speak in such wise as he would afterward wish to have been uttered otherwise, and yet no worse will had when he spake it, than he hath when he would
so gladly change it; therefore, most gracious Sovereign, considering that in your   20
High Court of Parliament is nothing entreated but matter of weight and importance concerning your realm and your own royal estate, it could not fail to let[28]
and put to silence from the giving of their advice and counsel many of your discreet Commons, to the great hindrance of the common affairs, except that every

Request for
freedom of speech

of your Commons were utterly discharged of all doubt and fear how anything   25
that it should happen them to speak, should happen of your Highness to be taken.
And in this point, though your well known and proved benignity putteth every
man in right good hope, yet such is the weight of the matter, such is the reverend
dread that the timorous hearts of your natural subjects conceive toward your
High Majesty, our most redoubled King and undoubted Sovereign, that they can-   30
not in this point find themselves satisfied, except your gracious bounty therein
declared put away the scruple of their timorous minds, and animate and encourage them, and put them out of doubt. It may therefore like your most abundant
Grace, our most benign and godly King, to give to all your Commons here assembled your most gracious licence and pardon, freely, without doubt of your   35
dreadful displeasure, every man to discharge his conscience, and boldly in everything incident among us to declare his advice, and whatsoever happen any man to
say, that it may like your noble Majesty, or your inestimable goodness, to take all
in good part, interpreting every man's words, how uncunningly[29] soever they be

27. *fortuneth among*—now and then
28. *let*—hinder
29. *uncunningly*—unskillfully

couched, to proceed yet of good zeal towards the profit of your realm and honor of your royal person, the prosperous estate and preservation whereof, most excellent Sovereign, is the thing which we all, your most humble loving subjects, according to the most bounden duty of our natural allegiance, most highly desire and pray for.

At this Parliament Cardinal Wolsey found himself much grieved with the Burgesses thereof, for that nothing was so soon done or spoken therein but that it was immediately blown abroad in every alehouse. It fortuned at that Parliament a very great subsidy to be demanded, which the Cardinal fearing would not pass the Common House, determined for the furtherance thereof to be there personally present himself. Before whose coming, after long debating there, whether it were better but with a few of his lords (as the most opinion of the House was) or with his whole train royally to receive him there amongst them. *Wolsey to violate the ancient liberty of the House, 1523*

"Masters," quoth Sir Thomas More, "forasmuch as my Lord Cardinal lately, you wot[30] well, laid to our charge the lightness of our tongues for things uttered out of this House, it shall not in my mind be amiss with all his pomp to receive him, with his maces, his pillars, his pole-axes, his crosses, his hat, and Great Seal, too—to the intent, if he find the like fault with us hereafter, we may be the bolder from ourselves to lay the blame on those that his Grace bringeth hither with him." Whereunto the House wholly agreeing, he was received accordingly. *More advises the Commons*

Where, after that he had in solemn oration by many reasons proved how necessary it was the demand there moved to be granted, and further showed that less would not serve to maintain the Prince's purpose, he, seeing the company sitting still silent, and thereunto nothing answering, and contrary to his expectation showing in themselves towards his request no towardness of inclination, said unto them: "Masters, you have many wise and learned men among you, and since I am from the King's own person sent hither unto you for the preservation of yourselves and the realm, I think it meet you give me some reasonable answer." Whereat, every man holding his peace, then began he to speak to one Master Marney (after Lord Marney): "How say you," quoth he, "Master Marney?" Who making no answer neither, he severally asked the same question of divers others accounted the wisest of the company. *Wolsey's oration*

Silence

To whom, when none of them all would give so much as one word,

30. *wot*—know

being before agreed, as the custom was, by their Speaker to make answer,
"Masters," quoth the Cardinal, "unless it be the manner of your House, as

*An attempt at
intimidation* of likelihood it is, by the mouth of your Speaker, whom you have chosen
for trusty and wise, as indeed he is, in such cases to utter your minds, here
is without doubt a marvelous obstinate silence."   5

And thereupon he required an answer of Master Speaker, who first
More's response reverently upon his knees excusing the silence of the House, abashed at
the presence of so noble a personage, able to amaze the wisest and best
learned in a realm, and after by many probable arguments proving that for
them to make answer was it neither expedient nor agreeable with the an-   10
cient liberty of the House, in conclusion for himself showed that though
they had all with their voices trusted him, yet except every one of them
could put into his one head all their several wits, he alone in so weighty a
matter was unmeet to make his Grace answer.

Whereupon the Cardinal, displeased with Sir Thomas More, that had   15
not in this Parliament in all things satisfied his desire, suddenly arose and
departed.

*Wolsey seeks
revenge* And after the Parliament ended, in his gallery at Whitehall in Westminster, uttered unto him his griefs, saying, "Would to God you had been at
Rome, Master More, when I made you Speaker." "Your Grace not offend-   20
*More turns the
conversation* ed, so would I too, my lord," quoth he. And to wind such quarrels out of
the Cardinal's head, he began to talk of that gallery, and said, "I like this
gallery of yours, my lord, much better than your gallery at Hampton
Court." Wherewith so wisely brake he off the Cardinal's displeasant talk
that the Cardinal at that present, as it seemed, wist[31] not what more to say   25
*Wolsey strikes
back* to him. But for the revengement of his displeasure, counseled the King to
send him ambassador into Spain, commending to his Highness his wisdom, learning, and meetness for that voyage; and the difficulty of the cause
considered, none was there, he said, so well able to serve his Grace therein.
Which, when the King had broken to Sir Thomas More, and that he had   30
declared unto his Grace how unfit a journey it was for him, the nature of
the country and disposition of his complexion so disagreeing together that
he should never be likely to do his Grace acceptable service there, knowing right well that if his Grace sent him thither, he should send him to his
grave, but showing himself nevertheless ready, according to his duty (all   35
were it with the loss of his life), to fulfill his Grace's pleasure in that behalf,

31. *wist*—knew

the King, allowing well[32] his answer, said unto him, "It is not our meaning, Master More, to do you hurt, but to do you good would we be glad; we will this purpose devise upon some other, and employ your service otherwise."

Wolsey foiled

5 And such entire favor did the King bear him that he made him Chancellor of the Duchy of Lancaster, upon the death of Sir Richard Wingfield, who had that office before.

Chancellor of Lancaster, 1525

And for the pleasure he took in his company, would his Grace suddenly sometimes come home to his house at Chelsea, to be merry with him; 10 whither on a time, unlooked for, he came to dinner to him, and after dinner, in a fair garden of his, walked with him by the space of an hour, holding his arm about his neck. As soon as his Grace was gone, I, rejoicing thereat, told Sir Thomas More how happy he was, whom the King had so familiarly entertained, as I never had seen him to do to any other except 15 Cardinal Wolsey, whom I saw his Grace once walk with, arm in arm. "I thank our Lord, son," quoth he, "I find his Grace my very good lord indeed, and I believe he doth as singularly favor me as any subject within this realm. Howbeit, son Roper, I may tell thee I have no cause to be proud thereof, for if my head could win him a castle in France (for then 20 was there war between us) it should not fail to go."

Henry visits Chelsea

"My head . . . should not fail to go," c. 1524

This Sir Thomas More, among all other his virtues, was of such meekness that if it had fortuned him with any learned man resorting to him from Oxford, Cambridge, or elsewhere, as there did divers,[33] some for desire of his acquaintance, some for the famous report of his wisdom and 25 learning, and some for suits of the universities, to have entered into argument (wherein few were comparable unto him) and so far to have discoursed with them therein that he might perceive they could not, without some inconvenience, hold out much further disputation against him, then, lest he should discomfort them, as he that sought not his own glory, but 30 rather would seem conquered than to discourage students in their studies, ever showing himself more desirous to learn than to teach, would he by some witty device courteously break off into some other matter, and give over.

More's love for dispute . . .

in a courteous manner

Of whom, for his wisdom and learning, had the King such an opinion, 35 that at such time as he attended upon his Highness, taking his progress ei-

32. *allowing well*—accepting as satisfactory
33. *divers*—on different occasions

ther to Oxford or Cambridge, where he was received with very eloquent orations, his Grace would always assign him, as one that was prompt and ready therein, *ex tempore* to make answer thereunto. Whose manner was, whensoever he had occasion, either here or beyond the sea, to be in any university, not only to be present at the readings and disputations there commonly used, but also learnedly to dispute among them himself.

Ambassador, 1521, 1527

Who, being Chancellor of the Duchy, was made ambassador twice, joined in commission with Cardinal Wolsey, once to the Emperor Charles into Flanders, the other time to the French King into France.

Complaints against More

Not long after this, the Water-bailiff of London, sometime his servant, hearing, where he had been at dinner, certain merchants liberally to rail against his old master, waxed so discontented therewith that he hastily came to him and told him what he had heard. "And were I you, sir," quoth he, "in such favor and authority with my Prince as you are, such men surely should not be suffered so villainously and falsely to misreport and slander me. Wherefore I would wish you to call them before you, and to their shame for their lewd malice punish them."

Seeing enemies as friends

His concern for integrity

Who, smiling upon him, said, "Why, Master Water-bailiff, would you have me punish those by whom I receive more benefit than by you all that be my friends? Let them, a God's name, speak as lewdly as they list of me, and shoot never so many arrows at me, as long as they do not hit me, what am I the worse? But if they should once hit me, then would it indeed not a little trouble me. Howbeit I trust, by God's help, there shall none of them all once be able to touch me. I have more cause, I assure thee, Master Water-bailiff, to pity them than to be angry with them." Such fruitful communication had he oftentimes with his familiar friends.

So on a time, walking with me along the Thames-side at Chelsea, in talking of other things he said unto me, "Now would to our Lord, son Roper, upon condition that three things were well established in Christendom, I were put into a sack, and here presently cast into the Thames."

"What great things be those, sir," quoth I, "that should move you so to wish?"

"Wouldst thou know what they be, son Roper?" quoth he.

"Yea, marry, with good will, sir, if it please you," quoth I.

Three things desired for Christendom

"In faith, son, they be these," said he. "The first is, that where the most part of Christian princes be at mortal war, they were all at an universal peace. The second, that where the Church of Christ is at this present sore afflicted with many errors and heresies, it were settled in a perfect uniformity of religion. The third, that where the King's matter of his marriage is now come in question, it were to the glory of God and quietness of all parties brought to a good conclusion." Whereby, as I could gather, he judged that otherwise it would be a disturbance to a great part of Christendom.

Thus did it by his doings throughout the whole course of his life appear that all his travail and pains, without respect of earthly commodities, either to himself, or any of his, were only upon the service of God, the prince, and the realm, wholly bestowed and employed, whom I heard in his later time to say that he never asked the King himself the value of one penny.

No worldly ambition

As Sir Thomas More's custom was daily, if he were at home, besides his private prayers, with his children to say the Seven Psalms, litany and suffrages following, so was his guise[34] nightly, before he went to bed, with his wife, children, and household, to go to his chapel and there upon his knees ordinarily to say certain psalms and collects with them. And because he was desirous for godly purposes sometime to be solitary, and sequester himself from worldly company, a good distance from his mansion house builded he a place called the New Building, wherein there was a chapel, a library, and a gallery, in which, as his use was upon other days to occupy himself in prayer and study together, so on the Friday there usually continued he from morning till evening, spending his time only in devout prayers and spiritual exercises.

Family prayer

Personal prayer and study

And to provoke his wife and children to the desire of heavenly things, he would sometimes use these words unto them:

Desiring heavenly things

It is now no mastery[35] for you children to go to heaven, for everybody giveth you good counsel, everybody giveth you good example; you see virtue rewarded and vice punished, so that you are carried up to heaven even by the chins. But if you live the time that no man will give you good counsel, nor no man will give you good example, when you shall see virtue punished and vice rewarded, if you will then stand fast and firmly stick to God, upon pain of my life, though you be but half good, God will allow you for whole good.

If his wife or any of his children had been diseased or troubled, he would say unto them: "We may not look at our pleasure to go to heaven in featherbeds; it is not the way, for our Lord himself went thither with great pain

Of heaven and featherbeds

34. *guise*—custom
35. *mastery*—achievement, victory

and by many tribulations, which was the path wherein he walked thither, for the servant may not look to be in better case than his master."

And as he would in this sort persuade them to take their troubles patiently, so would he in like sort teach them to withstand the devil and his temptations valiantly, saying,   5

Devil as an ape

Whosoever will mark the devil and his temptations shall find him therein much like to an ape. For like as an ape, not well looked unto, will be busy and bold to do shrewd turns,[36] and contrariwise, being spied, will suddenly leap back and adventure no farther, so the devil, finding a man idle, slothful, and without resistance ready to receive his temptations, waxeth so hardy that he will not fail still to continue with him, until to his purpose he have thoroughly brought him. But on the other side, if he see a man with diligence persevere to prevent and withstand his temptations, he waxeth so weary that in conclusion he utterly forsaketh him. For as the devil of disposition is a spirit of so high a pride that he cannot abide to be mocked,[37] so is he of nature so envious that he feareth any more to assault him, lest he should thereby not only catch a foul fall himself, but also minister to the man more matter of merit.   10 ... 15

Thus delighted he evermore not only in virtuous exercises to be occupied himself, but also to exhort his wife, children and household to embrace and follow the same.   20

Daughter Margaret near death, 1528

To whom, for his notable virtue and godliness, God showed, as it seemed, a manifest miraculous token of his special favor towards him, at such time as my wife, as many other that year were, was sick of the sweating sickness; who, lying in so great extremity of that disease as by no invention or devices that physicians in such cases commonly use (of whom she had divers both expert, wise, and well-learned, then continually attendant about her) she could be kept from sleep, so that both physicians and all other there despaired of her recovery, and gave her over; her father, as he that most entirely tendered her, being in no small heaviness for her, by prayer at God's hand sought to get her remedy.   25 ... 30

More's prayer

Whereupon going up, after his usual manner, into his foresaid New Building, there in his chapel, upon his knees, with tears most devoutly besought almighty God that it would like His goodness, unto whom nothing was impossible, if it were His blessed will, at his mediation to vouchsafe graciously to hear his humble petition. Where incontinent[38] came into his   35

36. *shrewd turns*—harmful tricks
37. C. S. Lewis quotes this phrase on the frontispiece of the *Screwtape Letters*.
38. *incontinent*—all of a sudden

mind that a glister[39] should be the only way to help her. Which, when he told the physicians, they by and by[40] confessed that, if there were any hope of health, that was the very best help indeed, much marveling of themselves that they had not before remembered it.

Then was it immediately ministered unto her sleeping, which she could by no means have been brought unto waking. And albeit after that she was thereby thoroughly awaked, God's marks,[41] an evident undoubted token of death, plainly appeared upon her, yet she, contrary to all their expectations, was, as it was thought, by her father's fervent prayer miraculously recovered, and at length again to perfect health restored. Whom, if it had pleased God at that time to have taken to His mercy, her father said he would never have meddled with worldly matters after.[42]

Margaret's cure

Now while Sir Thomas More was Chancellor of the Duchy, the See of Rome chanced to be void, which was cause of much trouble. For Cardinal Wolsey, a man very ambitious, and desirous (as good hope and likelihood he had) to aspire unto that dignity, perceiving himself of his expectation disappointed, by means of the Emperor Charles so highly commending one Cardinal Adrian, sometime his schoolmaster, to the cardinals of Rome, in the time of their election, for his virtue and worthiness, that thereupon was he chosen pope, who from Spain, where he was then resident, coming on foot to Rome, before his entry into the city, did put off his hose and shoes, barefoot and barelegged passing through the streets towards his palace, with such humbleness that all the people had him in great reverence. Cardinal Wolsey, I say, waxed so wood[43] therewith, that he studied to invent all ways of revengement of his grief against the Emperor, which, as it was the beginning of a lamentable tragedy, so some part of it as not impertinent to my present purpose, I reckoned requisite here to put in remembrance.

Wolsey's desire to be pope, 1522

Wolsey plans revenge

This Cardinal therefore, not ignorant of the King's inconstant and mutable disposition, soon inclined to withdraw his devotion from his own most noble, virtuous, and lawful wife, Queen Katherine, aunt to the Emperor, upon every light occasion, and upon other, to her in nobility, wis-

---

39. *glister*—enema
40. *by and by*—immediately
41. Visible signs of the plague
42. Years after this event, More wrote, "Love no child of thine own so tenderly but that thou couldst be content so to sacrifice it to God as Abraham was ready with Isaac" (*A Treatise Upon the Passion, Complete Works*, vol. 13, p. 84).
43. *waxed so wood*—became so angry

dom, virtue, favor, and beauty, far incomparable, to fix his affection, mean-

Wolsey's responsibility for the divorce

ing to make this his so light disposition an instrument to bring about his ungodly intent, devised to allure the King (then already, contrary to his mind, nothing less looking for, falling in love with the Lady Anne Boleyn) to cast fantasy to one of the French King's sisters, which thing, because of ⁵ the enmity and war that was at that time between the French King and the Emperor (whom, for the cause afore remembered, he mortally ma-

The King's marriage

ligned) he was very desirous to procure. And for the better achieving thereof, [Wolsey] requested Longland, Bishop of Lincoln, and ghostly father to the King, to put a scruple into his Grace's head, that it was not law- ¹⁰ ful for him to marry his brother's wife, which the King, not sorry to hear of, opened it first to Sir Thomas More, whose counsel he required therein,

Henry seeks More's advice on the divorce, 1527

showing him certain places of Scripture that somewhat seemed to serve his appetite; which, when he had perused, and thereupon, as one that had never professed the study of divinity, himself excused to be unmeet many ¹⁵ ways to meddle with such matters. The King, not satisfied with this an- swer, so sore still pressed upon him therefore, that in conclusion he conde- scended to his Grace's motion. And further, foreasmuch as the case was of such importance as needed great advisement and deliberation, he be- sought his Grace of sufficient respite advisedly to consider of it. Where- ²⁰ with the King, well contented, said unto him that Tunstall and Clark, Bish- ops of Durham and Bath, with other learned of his Privy Council, should also be dealers therein.

More deliberates on the case

So Sir Thomas More departing, conferred those places of Scripture with expositions of divers of the old holy doctors, and at his coming to the ²⁵ Court, in talking with his Grace of the aforesaid matter, he said,

Why More and others are not fitting advisors

To be plain with your Grace, neither my Lord of Durham, nor my Lord of Bath, though I know them both to be wise, virtuous, learned, and honorable prelates, nor myself, with the rest of your Council, being all your Grace's own servants, for your manifold benefits daily bestowed on us so most bounden to you, be, in my ³⁰ judgment, meet counselors for your Grace herein. But if your Grace mind to un- derstand the truth, such counselors may you have devised, as neither for respect of their own worldly commodity, nor for fear of your princely authority, will be in- clined to deceive you.

To whom he named then St. Jerome, St. Augustine, and divers other old ³⁵ holy doctors, both Greeks and Latins, and moreover showed him what au- thorities he had gathered out of them, which although the King (as dis- agreeable with his desire) did not very well like of, yet were they by Sir

Thomas More, who in all his communication with the King in that matter had always most discreetly behaved himself, so wisely tempered, that he both presently took them in good part, and oftentimes had thereof conference with him again.

5 After this were there certain questions among his Council propounded, whether the King needed in this case to have any scruple at all, and if he had, what way were best to be taken to deliver him of it. The most part of whom were of opinion that there was good cause of scruple, and that for discharging of it, suit were meet to be made to the See of Rome, 10 where the King hoped by liberality to obtain his purpose, wherein, as it after appeared, he was far deceived.

Then was there for the trial and examination of this matrimony procured from Rome a commission in which Cardinal Campeggio and Cardinal Wolsey were joined commissioners, who for the determination 15 thereof, sat at the Blackfriars in London where a libel[44] was put in for the annulling of the said matrimony, alleging the marriage between the King and Queen to be unlawful. And for proof of the marriage to be lawful, was there brought in a dispensation, in which, after divers disputations thereon holden, there appeared an imperfection, which, by an instrument or brief, 20 upon search found in the Treasury of Spain, and sent to the commissioners in England, was supplied. And so should judgment have been given by the Pope accordingly, had not the King, upon intelligence thereof, before the same judgment, appealed to the next General Council. After whose application the Cardinal upon that matter sat no longer.

25 It fortuned before the matter of the said matrimony brought in question, when I, in talk with Sir Thomas More, of a certain joy commended unto him the happy estate of this realm that had so Catholic a prince that no heretic durst show his face, so virtuous and learned a clergy, so grave and sound a nobility, and so loving, obedient subjects, all in one faith 30 agreeing together.

"Troth it is indeed, son Roper," quoth he, and in commending all degrees and estates of the same went far beyond me. "And yet, son Roper, pray God," said he, "that some of us, as high as we seem to sit upon the mountains, treading heretics under our feet like ants,[45] live not the day that 35 we gladly would wish to be at league and composition with them, to let

More's art of candor

Commission appointed, 1528

King appeals to General Council

Foreseeing the growth of heresy and the breakdown of Christendom

44. *libel*—plaintiff's statement
45. Compare with "Letter to a Monk," *Complete Works*, vol. 15, p. 279, lines 11–12.

them have their churches quietly to themselves, so that they would be content to let us have ours quietly to ourselves." After that I had told him many considerations why he had no cause so to say. "Well," said he, "I pray God, son Roper, some of us live not till that day," showing me no reason why he should put any doubt therein. To whom I said, "By my troth, sir, it 5
is very desperately spoken." That vile term, I cry God mercy, did I give him. Who, by these words, perceiving me in a fume, said merrily unto me,
Sixteen years and   "Well, well, son Roper, it shall not be so, it shall not be so." Whom, in six-
never a fume   teen years and more being in house conversant with him, I could never perceive as much as once in a fume.   10

But now to return again where I left. After the supplying of the imper-fections of the dispensation sent (as before rehearsed) to the commission-ers into England, the King, taking the matter for ended, and then meaning no farther to proceed in that matter, assigned the Bishop of Durham and
Peace efforts, 1529   Sir Thomas More to go [as] ambassadors to Cambrai, a place neither Im- 15
perial nor French, to treat a peace between the Emperor, the French King, and him. In the concluding whereof Sir Thomas More so worthily han-dled himself, procuring in our league far more benefits unto this realm than at that time by the King or his Council was thought possible to be compassed, that for his good service in that voyage, the King, when he af- 20
ter made him Lord Chancellor, caused the Duke of Norfolk openly to de-clare unto the people (as you shall hear hereafter more at large) how much all England was bound unto him.

Now upon the coming home of the Bishop of Durham and Sir Thom-as More from Cambrai, the King was as earnest in persuading Sir Thomas 25
Henry again seeks   More to agree unto the matter of his marriage as before, by many and
More's approval of   divers ways provoking him thereunto. For the which cause, as it was
the divorce, 1529   thought, he the rather soon after made him Lord Chancellor, and further declaring unto him that, though at his going over sea to Cambrai he was in utter despair thereof, yet he had conceived since some good hope to 30
compass it. For albeit his marriage, being against the positive laws of the Church and the written laws of God, was helped by the dispensation, yet was there another thing found out of late, he said, whereby his marriage appeared to be so directly against the law of nature that it could in no wise by the Church be dispensable, as Doctor Stokesley (whom he then pre- 35
ferred to be Bishop of London, and in that case chiefly credited) was able to instruct him, with whom he prayed him in that point to confer. But for all his conference with him, he saw nothing of such force as could induce

him to change his opinion therein, which notwithstanding the Bishop showed in his report of him to the King's Highness so good and favorable that he said he found him in his Grace's cause very toward, and desirous to find some good matter wherewith he might truly serve his Grace to his
5 contentment.

This Bishop Stokesley, being by the Cardinal not long before in the Star Chamber openly put to rebuke and awarded[46] to the Fleet, not brooking his contumelious usage, and thinking that forasmuch as the Cardinal, for lack of such forwardness in setting forth the King's divorce as his Grace
10 looked for, was out of his Highness's favor, he had now a good occasion offered him to revenge his quarrel against him, further to incense the King's displeasure towards him, busily travailed to invent some colorable device for the King's furtherance in that behalf, which (as before is mentioned) he to his Grace revealed, hoping thereby to bring the King to the
15 better liking of himself, and the more misliking of the Cardinal, whom his Highness therefore soon after of his office displaced, and to Sir Thomas More, the rather to move him to incline to his side, the same in his stead committed.

More replaces Wolsey as Lord Chancellor, 1529

Who, between the Dukes of Norfolk and Suffolk, being brought
20 through Westminster Hall to his place in the Chancery, the Duke of Norfolk, in audience of all the people there assembled, showed that he was from the King himself straightly charged, by special commission, there openly, in the presence of them all, to make declaration how much all England was beholding to Sir Thomas More for his good service, and how
25 worthy he was to have the highest room[47] in the realm, and how dearly his Grace loved and trusted him, for which, said the Duke, he had great cause to rejoice. Whereunto Sir Thomas More, among many other his humble and wise sayings not now in my memory, answered: that although he had good cause to take comfort of his Highness's singular favor towards him,
30 that he had, far above his deserts, so highly commended him, to whom therefore he acknowledged himself most deeply bounden, yet, nevertheless, he must of his own part needs confess, that in all things by his Grace alleged he had done no more than was his duty, and further disabled himself as unmeet for that room, wherein, considering how wise and honor-
35 able a prelate had lately before taken so great a fall, he had, he said, thereof

Praise from Norfolk

More's reply

46. *awarded*—sentenced
47. *room*—office

no cause to rejoice. And as they had before, on the King's behalf, charged him uprightly to minister indifferent justice to the people, without corruption or affection,[48] so did he likewise charge them again that, if they saw him, at any time, in any thing, digress from any part of his duty in that honorable office, even as they would discharge their own duty and fidelity   5 to God and the King, so should they not fail to disclose it to his Grace, who otherwise might have just occasion to lay his fault wholly to their charge.

More's impartiality and justice

While he was Lord Chancellor, being at leisure (as seldom he was), one of his sons-in-law[49] on a time said merrily unto him, "When Cardinal   10 Wolsey was Lord Chancellor, not only divers of his privy chamber, but such also as were his doorkeepers got great gain." And since he had married one of his daughters, and gave still attendance upon him, he thought he might of reason look for some, where he indeed, because he was so ready himself to hear every man, poor and rich, and kept no doors shut   15 from them, could find none, which was to him a great discourage. And whereas else, some for friendship, some for kindred, and some for profit, would gladly have had his furtherance in bringing them to his presence, if he should now take anything of them, he knew, he said, he should do them great wrong, for that they might do as much for themselves as he   20 could do for them, which condition, although he thought in Sir Thomas More very commendable, yet to him, being his son, he found it nothing profitable.

When he had told him this tale: "You say well, son," quoth he. "I do not mislike that you are of conscience so scrupulous, but many other ways   25 be there, son, that I may both do yourself good and pleasure your friend also. For sometime may I by my word stand your friend in stead, and sometime may I by my letter help him, or if he have a cause depending before me, at your request I may hear him before another. Or if his cause be not all the best, yet may I move the parties to fall to some reasonable   30 end by arbitrament. Howbeit, this one thing, son, I assure thee on my faith, that if the parties will at my hands call for justice, then, all were it my

Justice for all, even the devil

father stood on the one side and the devil on the other, his cause being good, the devil should have right." So offered he his son, as he thought, he said, as much favor as with reason he could require.   35

48. *affection*—bias

49. William Dauncey, married to More's second daughter, Elizabeth, since Sept. 29, 1525. Cecily More and Giles Heron married on the same day during the same ceremony.

And that he would for no respect digress from justice, well appeared by a plain example of another of his sons-in-law called Master Heron.[50] For when he, having a matter before him in Chancery, and presuming too much of his favor, would by him in no wise be persuaded to agree to any indifferent order, then made he in conclusion a flat decree against him.

This Lord Chancellor used commonly every afternoon to sit in his open hall, to the intent that, if any persons had suit unto him, they might the more boldly come to his presence and there open their complaints before him, whose manner was also to read every bill himself ere he would award any subpoena, which bearing matter sufficient worthy a subpoena, would he set his hand unto or else cancel it.

More's availability to all

Whensoever he passed through Westminster Hall to his place in the Chancery by the court of the King's Bench, if his father, one of the judges thereof, had been sat ere he came, he would go into the same court, and there reverently kneeling down in the sight of them all, duly ask his father's blessing. And if it fortuned that his father and he, at readings in Lincoln's Inn, met together, as they sometimes did, notwithstanding his high office, he would offer in argument the pre-eminence to his father, though he, for his office's sake, would refuse to take it. And for the better declaration of his natural affection towards his father, he not only, while he lay on his death-bed, according to his duty, oft-times with comfortable words most kindly came to visit him, but also at his departure out of the world with tears taking him about the neck, most lovingly kissed and embraced him, commending him into the merciful hands of Almighty God, and so departed from him.

Reverence for a father

And as few injunctions as he granted while he was Lord Chancellor, yet were they by some of the judges of the law misliked, which I understanding, declared the same to Sir Thomas More, who answered me that they should have little cause to find fault with him therefore. And thereupon caused he one Master Crooke, chief of the six clerks, to make a docket containing the whole number and causes of all such injunctions as either in his time had already passed, or at that present depended in any of the King's Courts at Westminster before him. Which done, he invited all the judges to dine with him in the Council Chamber at Westminster, where, after dinner, when he had broken with them what complaints he had heard of his injunctions, and moreover showed them both the number

Dealing with disgruntled judges

50. Married to More's third daughter, Cecily.

of causes of every one of them, in order, so plainly that, upon full debating of those matters, they were all enforced to confess that they, in like case, could have done no otherwise themselves. Then offered he this unto them: that if the justices of every court (unto whom the reformation of the rigor of the law, by reason of their office, most especially appertained) would, upon reasonable considerations, by their own discretions (as they were, he thought, in conscience bound), mitigate and reform the rigor of the law themselves, there should from thenceforth by him no more injunctions be granted. Whereunto when they refused to condescend, then said he unto them, "Forasmuch as yourselves, my lords, drive me to that necessity for awarding out injunctions to relieve the people's injury, you cannot hereafter any more justly blame me." After that he said secretly unto me, "I perceive, son, why they like not so to do, for they see that they may by the verdict of the jury cast off all quarrels from themselves upon them, which they account their chief defense, and therefore am I compelled to abide the adventure of all such reports."

What judges should do (margin, line 5)

Why judges shirk responsibility (margin, lines 12–13)

And as little leisure as he had to be occupied in the study of Holy Scripture and controversies upon religion and such other virtuous exercises, being in manner continually busied about the affairs of the King and the realm, yet such watch[51] and pain in setting forth of divers profitable works, in defense of the true Christian religion, against heresies secretly sown abroad in the realm, assuredly sustained he,[52] that the bishops, to whose pastoral cure the reformation thereof principally appertained, thinking themselves by his travail, wherein by their own confession they were not able with him to make comparison, of their duties in that behalf discharged; and considering that for all his prince's favor he was no rich man, nor in yearly revenues advanced as his worthiness deserved, therefore at a convocation among themselves and other of the clergy, they agreed together and concluded upon a sum of four or five thousand pounds, at the least, to my remembrance, for his pains to recompense him. To the payment whereof every bishop, abbot, and the rest of the clergy were—after the rate of their abilities—liberal contributories, hoping this portion should be to his contentation.[53]

Reward refused from clergy (margin, lines 17–18)

Whereupon Tunstall, Bishop of Durham, Clark, Bishop of Bath, and, as far as I can call to mind, Veysey, Bishop of Exeter, repaired unto him, de-

Tunstall insists (margin)

51. *watch*—vigilance
52. *assuredly sustained he*—he maintained with assurance
53. *contentation*—satisfaction

claring how thankfully his travails, to their discharge in God's cause bestowed, they reckoned themselves bounden to consider him. And that albeit they could not, according to his deserts so worthily as they gladly would, requite him therefore, but must reserve that only to the goodness of God, yet for a small part of recompense, in respect of his estate so unequal to his worthiness, in the name of their whole convocation, they presented unto him that sum, which they desired him to take in good part.

Who, forsaking[54] it, said, that like as it was no small comfort unto him that so wise and learned men so well accepted his simple doings, for which he never intended to receive reward but at the hands of God only, to whom alone was the thanks thereof chiefly to be ascribed, so gave he most humble thanks to their honors all for their so bountiful and friendly *Thanks, but no* consideration.

When they, for all their importunate pressing upon him, that few would have went[55] he could have refused it, could by no means make him to take it, then besought they him to be content yet that they might bestow it upon his wife and children. "Not so, my lords," quoth he, "I had rather see it all cast into the Thames than I, or any of mine, should have thereof the worth of one penny. For though your offer, my lords, be indeed very friendly and honorable, yet set I so much by my pleasure and so little by my profit that I would not, in good faith, for so much, and much more too, have lost the rest of so many nights' sleep as was spent upon the same. And yet wish would I, for all that, upon condition that all heresies were suppressed, that all my books were burned and my labor utterly lost."

Thus departing, were they fain to restore unto every man his own again.

This Lord Chancellor, albeit he was to God and the world well known of notable virtue (though not so of every man considered) yet, for the avoiding of singularity, would he appear none otherwise than other men *Penance without* in his apparel and other behavior. And albeit outwardly he appeared hon- *singularity* orable like one of his calling, yet inwardly he no such vanities esteeming, secretly next his body wore a shirt of hair, which my sister More, a young gentlewoman,[56] in the summer, as he sat at supper singly in his doublet and hose, wearing thereupon a plain shirt without ruff or collar, chancing to spy it, began to laugh at it. My wife, not ignorant of his manner, per- *Meg alerts More*

54. *forsaking*—declining
55. *went*—thought
56. Anne Cresacre who married More's son, John, in 1529.

ceiving the same, privily told him of it, and he, being sorry that she saw it, presently amended it.

He used also sometimes to punish his body with whips, the cords knotted, which was known only to my wife, his eldest daughter, whom for her secrecy above all other he specially trusted, causing her, as need required, to wash the same shirt of hair.

Consulted on the divorce again

Now shortly upon his entry into the high office of the Chancellorship, the King yet eftsoons[57] again moved him to weigh and consider his great matter, who, falling down upon his knees, humbly besought his Highness to stand his gracious Sovereign, as he ever since his entry into his Grace's service had found him, saying there was nothing in the world had been so grievous unto his heart as to remember that he was not able, as he willingly would, with the loss of one of his limbs, for that matter anything to find whereby he could, with his conscience, safely serve his Grace's contentation,[58] as he that always bore in mind the most godly words that his Highness spake unto him at his first coming into his noble service, the most virtuous lesson that ever prince taught his servant, willing him first to look unto God, and after God to him, as, in good faith, he said he did, or else might his Grace well account him his most unworthy servant. To this the King answered, that if he could not therein with his conscience serve him, he was content to accept his service otherwise, and using the advice of other of his learned Council, whose consciences could well enough agree therewith, would nevertheless continue his gracious favor towards him, and never with that matter molest his conscience after.

"The most virtuous lesson that ever prince taught"

The King commands More to address Commons, 30 March 1531

More's silence

But Sir Thomas More, in process of time, seeing the King fully determined to proceed forth in the marriage of Queen Anne, and when he, with the bishops and nobles of the Higher House of the Parliament, were, for the furtherance of that marriage, commanded by the King to go down to the Common House to show unto them both what the universities, as well as of other parts beyond the seas as of Oxford and Cambridge, had done in that behalf, and their seals also testifying the same—all which matters, at the King's request, not showing of what mind himself was therein, he opened to the Lower House of the Parliament—nevertheless, doubting lest further attempts after should follow, which, contrary to his conscience, by reason of his office, he was likely to be put unto, he made

57. *eftsoons*—soon afterwards
58. *contentation*—satisfaction

suit unto the Duke of Norfolk, his singular dear friend, to be a means to
the King that he might, with his Grace's favor, be discharged of that
chargeable room[59] of the chancellorship, wherein, for certain infirmities of
his body, he pretended himself unable any longer to serve.

*More seeks
to resign*

⁵ This Duke, coming on a time to Chelsea to dine with him, fortuned to
find him at the church, singing in the choir, with a surplice on his back; to
whom, after service, as they went homeward together, arm in arm, the
Duke said, "God body! God body! My Lord Chancellor, a parish clerk,
a parish clerk! You dishonor the King and his office." "Nay," quoth Sir
¹⁰ Thomas More, smiling upon the Duke, "your Grace may not think that
the King, your master and mine, will with me, for serving of God his master, be offended, or thereby count his office dishonored."

*Norfolk chides
More for dishonor-
able singing*

When the Duke, being thereunto often solicited, by importunate suit
had at length of the King obtained for Sir Thomas More a clear discharge
¹⁵ of his office, then, at a time convenient, by his Highness's appointment, repaired he to his Grace to yield up unto him the Great Seal. Which, as his
Grace, with thanks and praise for his worthy service in that office, courteously at his hands received, so pleased it his Highness further to say unto
him that, for the service that he before had done him, in any suit which he
²⁰ should after have unto him that either should concern his honor (for that
word it liked his Highness to use unto him) or that should appertain unto
his profit, he should find his Highness good and gracious lord unto him.

*More remains in
the King's good
favor*

*Resigns, 16 May
1532*

After he had thus given over the chancellorship, and placed all his gentlemen and yeomen with bishops and noblemen, and his eight watermen
²⁵ with the Lord Audley, that in the same office succeeded him, to whom also
he gave his great barge, then, calling us all that were his children unto him
and asking our advice how we might now, in this decay of his ability (by
the surrender of his office so impaired that he could not, as he was wont,
and gladly would, bear out the whole charge[60] of them all himself) from
³⁰ thenceforth be able to live and continue together, as he wished we should;
when he saw us silent, and in that case not ready to show our opinions to
him, "Then will I," said he, "show my poor mind unto you. I have been
brought up," quoth he, "at Oxford, at an Inn of Chancery, at Lincoln's Inn
and also in the King's Court, and so forth from the lowest degree to the
³⁵ highest, and yet have I in yearly revenues at this present left me little above

Economic changes

59. *room*—office
60. *charge*—expense

Only 100 pounds a year now an hundred pounds by the year,[61] so that now must we hereafter, if we like to live together, be contented to become contributories together. But, by my counsel, it shall not be best for us to fall to the lowest fare first. We will *Oxford fare—the lowest* not therefore descend to Oxford fare, nor to the fare of New Inn, but we will begin with Lincoln's Inn diet, where many right worshipful and of good years do live full well; which, if we find not ourselves the first year able to maintain, then will we the next year go one step down to New Inn fare, wherewith many an honest man is well contented. If that exceed our ability too, then will we the next year after descend to Oxford fare, where many grave, learned and ancient fathers be continually conversant, which if our power stretch not to maintain neither, then may we yet, with bags and *Begging merrily* wallets, go a begging together, and hoping that for pity some good folk will give us their charity, at every man's door to sing *Salve Regina,* and so still keep company and be merry together."

And whereas you have heard before, he was by the King from a very worshipful living taken into his Grace's service, with whom, in all the great and weighty causes that concerned his Highness or the realm, he consumed and spent with painful cares, travels and troubles, as well beyond the seas as within the realm, in effect the whole substance of his life, yet with all the gain he got thereby, being never wasteful spender thereof, was he not able, after the resignation of his office of Lord Chancellor, for the maintenance of himself and such as necessarily belonged unto him, sufficiently to find meat, drink, fuel, apparel, and such other necessary charges. All the land that ever he purchased, which also he purchased before he was Lord Chancellor, was not, I am well assured, above the value of twenty *Only 100 pounds in goods left* marks by the year. And after his debts paid, he had not, I know, his chain excepted, in gold and silver left him the worth of one hundred pounds.

And whereas upon the holy days during his High Chancellorship, one of his gentlemen, when service at the church was done, ordinarily used to come to my lady his wife's pew and say unto her, "Madame, my lord is gone," the next holy day after the surrender of his office and departure of *"Madame, my lord is gone."* his gentleman, he came unto my lady his wife's pew himself, and making a low curtsy, said unto her, "Madame, my lord is gone."

In the time somewhat before his trouble, he would talk with his wife *Preparing the family for suffering* and children of the joys of heaven and the pains of hell, of the lives of holy martyrs, of their grievous martyrdoms, of their marvelous patience, and of

61. Sir Thomas retained his salary of 100 pounds a year as Counselor until March 1534.

their passions and deaths that they suffered rather than they would offend God. And what an happy and blessed thing it was, for the love of God, to suffer loss of goods, imprisonment, loss of lands, and life also. He would further say unto them that, upon his faith, if he might perceive his wife
5 and children would encourage him to die in a good cause, it should so comfort him that, for very joy thereof, it would make him merrily run to death. He showed unto them afore what trouble might after fall unto him, wherewith and the like virtuous talk he had so long before his trouble encouraged them, that when he after fell into trouble indeed, his trouble to
10 them was a great deal the less. *Quia spicula previsa minus laedunt.*[62]

Now upon this resignment of his office, came Master Thomas Cromwell, then in the King's high favor, to Chelsea to him with a message from the King. Wherein when they had thoroughly communed together, "Master Cromwell," quoth he, "you are now entered into the service of a most
15 noble, wise, and liberal prince. If you will follow my poor advice, you shall, in your counsel-giving unto His Grace, ever tell him what he ought to do, but never what he is able to do. So shall you show yourself a true faithful servant and a right worthy Counselor. For if a lion[63] knew his own strength, hard were it for any man to rule him."

20 Shortly thereupon was there a commission directed to Cranmer, then Archbishop of Canterbury, to determine the matter of the matrimony between the King and Queen Katherine, at St. Albans, where, according to the King's mind, it was thoroughly determined, who, pretending he had no justice at the Pope's hands, from thenceforth sequestered himself from
25 the See of Rome, and so married the Lady Anne Boleyn; which, Sir Thomas More understanding, said unto me, "God give grace, son, that these matters within a while be not confirmed with oaths." I, at that time seeing no likelihood thereof, yet fearing lest his forespeaking it would the sooner come to pass, waxed therefore for his so saying much offended
30 with him.

It fortuned not long before the coming of Queen Anne through the streets of London from the Tower to Westminster to her coronation, that he received a letter from the bishops of Durham, Bath and Winchester, requesting him both to keep them company from the Tower to the corona-
35 tion, and also to take twenty pounds that by the bearer thereof they had

Advice to Cromwell on lions

Cranmer declares marriage void, 23 May 1533

Henry marries Anne

Bishops invite More to the coronation

62. "Because spears foreseen hurt less."
63. See p. 232

sent him to buy him a gown with, which he thankfully receiving, and at home still tarrying, at their next meeting said merrily unto them:

My lords, in the letters which you lately sent me, you required two things of me, the one whereof, since I was so well content to grant you, the other therefore I thought I might be the bolder to deny you. And like as the one, because I took you for no beggars, and myself I knew to be no rich man, I thought I might the rather fulfill, so the other did put me in remembrance of an emperor that had ordained a law that whosoever committed a certain offense (which I now remember not) except it were a virgin, should suffer the pains of death, such a reverence had he for virginity. Now so it happened that the first committer of that offense was indeed a virgin, whereof the Emperor hearing was in no small perplexity, as he that by some example fain would have had that law to have been put in execution. Whereupon when his Council had sat long, solemnly debating this case, suddenly arose there up one of his Council, a good plain man, among them, and said, "Why make you so much ado, my lords, about so small a matter? Let her first be deflowered, and then after may she be devoured." And so though your lordships have in the matter of the matrimony hitherto kept yourselves pure virgins, yet take good heed, my lords, that you keep your virginity still. For some there be that by procuring your lordships first at the coronation to be present, and next to preach for the setting forth of it, and finally to write books to all the world in defense thereof, are desirous to deflower you; and when they have deflowered you, then will they not fail soon after to devour you. "Now my lords," quoth he, "it lieth not in my power but that they may devour me; but God being my good lord, I will provide that they shall never deflower me."

Of deflowered virgins

More will not be deflowered

In continuance, when the King saw that he could by no manner of benefits win him on his side, then, lo, went he about by terrors and threats to drive him thereunto. The beginning of which trouble grew by occasion of a certain nun dwelling in Canterbury, for her virtue and holiness among people not a little esteemed; unto whom, for that cause, many religious persons, doctors of divinity, and divers others of good worship[64] of the laity used to resort; who, affirming that she had revelations from God to give the King warning of his wicked life, and of the abuse of the sword and authority committed unto him by God, and understanding my Lord of Rochester, Bishop Fisher, to be a man of notable virtuous living and

Henry seeks More's indictment

The Nun of Kent

64. *worship*—renown

learning, repaired to Rochester, and there disclosed to him all her revelations, desiring his advice and counsel therein; which the Bishop perceiving
might well stand with the laws of God and His holy Church, advised her
(as she before had warning and intended) to go to the King herself, and to
let him understand the whole circumstance thereof. Whereupon she went
to the King, and told him all her revelations, and so returned home again.
And in short space after, she, making a voyage to the nuns of Sion, by
means of one Master Reynolds, a father of the same house, there fortuned
concerning such secrets as had been revealed unto her (some part whereof
seemed to touch the matter of the King's supremacy and marriage, which
shortly thereupon followed) to enter into talk with Sir Thomas More,
who, notwithstanding he might well, at that time, without danger of any
law (though after, as himself had prognosticated before, those matters were
established by statutes and confirmed by oaths) freely and safely have
talked with her therein; nevertheless, in all the communication between
them (as in process[65] appeared) had always so discreetly demeaned himself
that he deserved not to be blamed, but contrariwise to be commended
and praised.

And had he not been one that in all his great offices and doings for the
King and the realm, so many years together, had from all corruption of
wrong-doing or bribes-taking kept himself so clear that no man was able
therewith once to blemish him or make just quarrel against him, it would,
without doubt, in this troublous time of the King's indignation towards
him, have been deeply laid to his charge, and of the King's Highness most
favorably accepted, as in the case of one Parnell it most manifestly appeared; against whom, because Sir Thomas More, while he was Lord
Chancellor, at the suit of one Vaughan, his adversary, had made a decree.
This Parnell to his Highness most grievously complained that Sir Thomas
More, for making the same decree, had of the same Vaughan (unable for
the gout to travel abroad himself) by the hands of his wife taken a fair
great gilt cup for a bribe. Who thereupon, by the King's appointment, being called before the whole Council, where that matter was heinously laid
to his charge, forthwith confessed that forasmuch as that cup was, long after the aforesaid decree, brought him for a New Year's gift, he, upon her
importunate pressing upon him therefore, of courtesy, refused not to receive it.

Charges of
corruption fail

Parnell accuses
More of bribery

65. *in process*—in course of time

Then the Lord of Wiltshire[66] (for hatred of his religion preferrer of this suit) with much rejoicing said unto the lords, "Lo, did I not tell you, my lords, that you should find this matter true?" Whereupon Sir Thomas More desired their lordships that as they had courteously heard him tell the one part of his tale, so they would vouchsafe of their honors indifferently to hear the other. After which obtained, he further declared unto them that, albeit he had indeed, with much work, received that cup, yet immediately thereupon he caused his butler to fill it with wine, and of that cup drank to her, and that when he had so done, and she pledged him, then as freely as her husband had given it to him, even so freely gave her the same unto her again, to give unto her husband as his New Year's gift, which, at his instant request, though much against her will, at length yet she was fain to receive, as herself, and certain other there, presently before them deposed. Thus was the great mountain turned scant to a little molehill.

So I remember that at another time, upon a New Year's day, there came to him one Mistress Crocker, a rich widow, for whom with no small pain he had made a decree in the Chancery against the Lord Arundel, to present him with a pair of gloves, and forty pounds in angels[67] in them for a New Year's gift. Of whom he thankfully receiving the gloves, but refusing the money, said unto her, "Mistress, since it were against good manners to forsake a gentlewoman's New Year's gift, I am content to take your gloves, but as for your money I utterly refuse." So, much against her mind, enforced he her to take her gold again.

Another bribery attempt

And one Master Gresham likewise, having at the same time a cause depending in the Chancery before him, sent him for a New Year's gift a fair gilt cup, the fashion whereof he very well liking, caused one of his own (though not in his fantasy of so good a fashion, yet better in value) to be brought him out of his chamber, which he willed the messenger, in recompense, to deliver to his master, and under other conditions would he in no wise receive it.

And yet another

Many things more of like effect, for the declaration of his innocency and clearness from all corruption or evil affection, could I rehearse besides, which for tediousness omitting, I refer to the readers by these few before remembered examples, with their own judgments wisely to weigh and consider the same.

66. Sir Thomas Boleyn, who was father of Queen Anne.
67. *angels*—gold coins

At the Parliament following, was there put into the Lords' House a bill to attaint the Nun and divers other religious persons of high treason, and the Bishop of Rochester, Sir Thomas More and certain others, of misprision of treason,[68] the King presupposing of likelihood that this bill would be to Sir Thomas More so troublous and terrible that it would force him to relent and condescend to his request—wherein his Grace was much deceived. To which bill Sir Thomas More was a suitor personally to be received in his own defense to make answer. But the King, not liking that, assigned the Archbishop of Canterbury, the Lord Chancellor, the Duke of Norfolk and Master Cromwell, at a day and place appointed, to call Sir Thomas More before them. At which time, I, thinking that I had a good opportunity, earnestly advised him to labor unto those lords for the help of his discharge out of that Parliament bill. Who answered me he would.

And at his coming before them, according to their appointment, they entertained him very friendly, willing him to sit down with them, which in no wise he would. Then began the Lord Chancellor to declare unto him how many ways the King had showed his love and favor towards him, how fain he would have had him continue in his office, how glad he would have been to have heaped more benefits upon him, and finally how he could ask no worldly honor nor profit at his Highness's hands that were likely to be denied him, hoping, by the declaration of the King's kindness and affection towards him, to provoke him to recompense his Grace with the like again, and unto those things that the Parliament, the bishops and the universities had already passed, to add his consent.

To this Sir Thomas More mildly made answer, saying, "No man living is there, my lords, that would with better will do the thing that should be acceptable to the King's Highness than I, which must needs confess his manifold goodness and bountiful benefits most benignly bestowed on me. Howbeit, I verily hoped that I should never have heard of this matter more, considering that I have, from time to time, always from the beginning, so plainly and truly declared my mind unto his Grace, which his Highness to me ever seemed, like a most gracious prince, very well to accept, never minding, as he said, to molest me more therewith; since which time any further thing that was able to move me to any change could I never find, and if I could, there is none in all the world that would have been gladder of it than I."

Accused of high treason, Jan. 1534

More asks to defend himself

Roper's plea

Interrogation by members of the Privy Council, March 1534

More's reply

68. *misprision of treason*—an offense akin to treason but not liable to death

Many things more were there of like sort uttered on both sides. But in the end, when they saw they could by no manner of persuasions remove *Terror tried* him from his former determination, then began they more terribly to touch him, telling him that the King's Highness had given them in commandment, if they could by no gentleness win him, in his name with his 5 great ingratitude to charge him, that never was there servant to his sovereign so villainous, nor subject to his prince so traitorous as he, for he, by his subtle sinister slights most unnaturally procuring and provoking him to set forth a book of *The Assertion of the Seven Sacraments* and maintenance of the Pope's authority, had caused him, to his dishonor throughout all 10 Christendom, to put a sword into the Pope's hands to fight against himself.

When they had thus laid forth all the terrors they could imagine *"terrors be . . . for* against him, "My lords," quoth he, "these terrors be arguments for chil-*children"* dren, and not for me. But to answer that wherewith you do chiefly burden 15 me, I believe the King's Highness of his honor will never lay that to my charge. For none is there that can in that point say in my excuse more than his Highness himself, who right well knoweth that I never was procurer nor counselor of his Majesty thereunto. But after it was finished, by his Grace's appointment and consent of the makers of the same, only a 20 sorter-out and placer of the principal matters therein contained. Wherein *The pope's* when I found the pope's authority highly advanced and with strong argu-*authority* ments mightily defended, I said unto his Grace, 'I must put your Highness in remembrance of one thing, and that is this. The Pope, as your Grace knoweth, is a prince as you are, and in league with all other Christian 25 princes. It may hereafter so fall out that your Grace and he may vary upon some points of the league, whereupon may grow breach of amity and war between you both. I think it best therefore that that place be amended, and his authority more slenderly touched.'

" 'Nay,' quoth his Grace, 'that shall it not. We are so much bounden 30 unto the See of Rome that we cannot do too much honor unto it.'

"Then did I further put him in remembrance of the Statute of Praemunire, whereby a good part of the pope's pastoral cure[69] here was pared away.

Henry on "To that answered his Highness, 'Whatsoever impediment be to the 35 *pope's uttermost* contrary, we will set forth that authority to the uttermost. For we received *authority*

69. *cure*—charge or jurisdiction

from that See our crown imperial'—which, till his Grace with his own mouth told it me, I never heard of before. So that I trust, when his Grace shall be once truly informed of this, and call to his gracious remembrance my doing in that behalf, his Highness will never speak of it more, but clear me thoroughly therein himself."

And thus displeasantly departed they.

Then took Sir Thomas More his boat towards his house at Chelsea, wherein by the way he was very merry, and for that I was nothing sorry, *More's joy* hoping that he had got himself discharged out of the Parliament bill. When he was landed and come home, then walked we twain alone in his garden together, where I, desirous to know how he had sped, said, "I trust, sir, that all is well because you be so merry."

"It is so indeed, son Roper, I thank God," quoth he. *More speaks with Roper*

"Are you then put out of the Parliament bill?" said I.

"By my troth, son Roper," quoth he, "I never remembered it."

"Never remembered it, sir?" said I, "a case that toucheth yourself so near, and us all for your sake? I am sorry to hear it, for I verily trusted, when I saw you so merry, that all had been well."

Then said he, "Wilt thou know, son Roper, why I was so merry?"

"That would I gladly, sir," quoth I.

"In good faith, I rejoiced, son," quoth he, "that I had given the devil a foul fall, and that with those lords I had gone so far, as without great shame I could never go back again."

At which words waxed I very sad, for though himself liked it well, yet liked it me but a little.

Now upon the report made by the Lord Chancellor and the other lords to the King of all their whole discourse had with Sir Thomas More, the King was so highly offended with him that he plainly told them he was fully determined that the aforesaid Parliament bill should undoubtedly proceed forth against him. To whom the Lord Chancellor and the rest *The offended* of the lords said that they perceived the lords of the Upper House so pre- *King wants to* cisely bent to hear him, in his own defense, make answer himself, that if he *proceed against* were not put out of the bill, it would without fail be utterly an overthrow *More* of all. But, for all this, needs would the King have his own will therein, or else he said that at the passing thereof, he would be personally present himself.

Then the Lord Audley and the rest, seeing him so vehemently set *Lords on their* thereupon, on their knees most humbly besought his Grace to forbear the *knees* same, considering that if he should, in his own presence receive an over-throw, it would not only encourage his subjects forever after to condemn him, but also throughout all Christendom redound to his dishonor forever, adding thereunto that they mistrusted not in time against him to find some meeter matter to serve his turn better. For in this case of the Nun, 5 he was accounted, they said, so innocent and clear, that for his dealing therein, men reckoned him far worthier of praise then reproof. Where-

The King relents on the Nun-of-Kent charge upon at length, through their earnest persuasion, he was content to condescend to their petition.

And on the morrow, Master Cromwell, meeting me in the Parliament 10 House, willed me to tell my father that he was put out of the Parliament bill. But because I had appointed to dine that day in London, I sent the message by my servant to my wife to Chelsea. Whereof when she informed her father, "In faith, Meg," quoth he, *"Quod differtur, non aufertur."* [70]

After this, as the Duke of Norfolk and Sir Thomas More chanced to 15 fall in familiar talk together, the Duke said unto him, "By the Mass, Master More, it is perilous striving with princes. And therefore I would wish you

More unmoved by ominous threat somewhat to incline to the King's pleasure, for, by God's body, Master More, *Indignatio principis mors est."* [71]

"Is that all, my lord?" quoth he. "Then in good faith is there no more 20 difference between your Grace and me, but that I shall die today and you tomorrow."

Administering the Oath So fell it out, within a month or thereabouts after the making of the statute for the Oath of the Supremacy and Matrimony, that all the priests

The only layman summoned, 13 April 1534 of London and Westminster, and no temporal man but he, were sent for to 25 appear at Lambeth before the Bishop of Canterbury, the Lord Chancellor, and Secretary Cromwell, commissioners appointed there to tender the oath unto them.

Then Sir Thomas More, as his accustomed manner was always, ere he entered into any matter of importance, as when he was first chosen of the 30 King's Privy Council, when he was sent ambassador, appointed Speaker of the Parliament, made Lord Chancellor, or when he took any like weighty matter upon him, to go to church and be confessed, to hear Mass and be houseled[72] so did he likewise in the morning early the selfsame day that he was summoned to appear before the lords at Lambeth. And whereas he 35

70. "What is put off is not put aside."
71. "The indignation of the prince is death."
72. *be houseled*—receive the Eucharist

evermore used before at his departure from his wife and children, whom he tenderly loved, to have them bring him to his boat, and there to kiss them all, and bid them farewell, then would he suffer none of them forth of the gate to follow him, but pulled the wicket after him, and shut them all from him, and with an heavy heart, as by his countenance it appeared, with me and our four servants there took he his boat towards Lambeth. Wherein sitting still sadly a while, at last he suddenly rounded[73] me in the ear, and said, "Son Roper, I thank Our Lord, the field is won." What he meant thereby I then wist[74] not, yet loath to seem ignorant, I answered: "Sir, I am thereof glad." But as I conjectured afterwards, it was for that the love he had to God wrought in him so effectually that it conquered all his carnal affections utterly.

"The field is won"

Conscience conquers natural affection

   Now at his coming to Lambeth, how wisely he behaved himself before the commissioners, at the ministration of the oath unto him, may be found in certain letters sent to my wife remaining in a great book of his works.[75] Where, by the space of four days he was betaken to the custody of the Abbot of Westminster, during which time the King consulted with his Council what order were meet to be taken with him. And albeit in the beginning they were resolved that with an oath not to be acknowledged whether he had to the Supremacy been sworn, or what he thought thereof, he should be discharged, yet did Queen Anne, by her importunate clamor, so sore exasperate the King against him, that contrary to his former resolution, he caused the said Oath of the Supremacy to be administered unto him. Who, albeit he made a discreet qualified answer, nevertheless was forthwith committed to the Tower.

Before Privy Council, 13 April 1534

More imprisoned in the Tower, 17 April 1534

   Whom, as he was going thitherward, wearing, as he commonly did, a chain of gold about his neck, Sir Richard Cromwell, that had the charge of his conveyance thither, advised him to send home his chain to his wife, or to some of his children. "Nay, sir," quoth he, "that I will not, for if I were taken in the field by my enemies, I would they should somewhat fare the better by me."

Wears chain of gold to jail

   At whose landing Master Lieutenant at the Tower Gate was ready to receive him, where the porter demanded of him his upper garment. "Master Porter," quoth he, "here it is," and took off his cap and delivered it him

Jesting with the jailor

---

73. *rounded*—whispered
74. *wist*—knew
75. More's 1557 *English Works.*

saying, "I am sorry it is no better for you." "No, sir," quoth the porter, "I must have your gown."

And so was he by Master Lieutenant conveyed to his lodging, where he called unto him one John a Wood, his own servant, there appointed to attend upon him, who could neither write nor read, and sware him before the Lieutenant that if he should hear or see him, at any time, speak or write any manner of thing against the King, the Council, or the state of the realm, he should open it to the Lieutenant, that the Lieutenant might incontinent[76] reveal it to the Council.

Meg's first prison visit, c. May 1534

Now when he had remained in the Tower a little more than a month, my wife, longing to see her father, by her earnest suit at length got leave to go to him. At whose coming, after the Seven Psalms and litany said (which, whensoever she came to him, ere he fell in talk of any worldly matters, he used accustomably to say with her) among other communication he said unto her, "I believe, Meg, that they that put me here, ween[77] they have done me a high displeasure. But I assure thee, on my faith, my own good daughter, if it had not been for my wife and you that be my children, whom I account the chief part of my charge, I would not have failed long ere this to have closed myself in as strait a room, and straiter too. But since I am come hither without mine own desert, I trust that God

More on God's special care

of His goodness will discharge me of my care, and with His gracious help supply my lack among you. I find no cause, I thank God, Meg, to reckon myself in worse case here than in my own house. For me thinketh God maketh me a wanton,[78] and setteth me on His lap and dandleth me." Thus by his gracious demeanor in tribulation appeared it that all the troubles

Patience and profit in adversity

that ever chanced unto him, by his patient sufferance thereof, were to him no painful punishments, but of his patience, profitable exercises.

And at another time, when he had first questioned with my wife a while of the order of his wife, children, and state of his house in his absence, he asked her how Queen Anne did. "In faith, father," quoth she,

Fall of Anne Boleyn foretold

"never better." "Never better! Meg," quoth he. "Alas! Meg, alas! It pitieth me to remember into what misery, poor soul, she shall shortly come."

After this, Master Lieutenant, coming into his chamber to visit him, rehearsed the benefits and friendship that he had many ways received at his

76. *incontinent*—immediately
77. *ween*—think
78. *wanton*—spoiled child

hands, and how much bounden he was therefore friendly to entertain him and make him good cheer, which, since the case standing as it did, he could not do without the King's indignations, he trusted, he said, he would accept his good will, and such poor cheer as he had. "Master Lieu-
5 tenant," quoth he again, "I verily believe, as you may, so you are my good friend indeed, and would, as you say, with your best cheer entertain me, for the which I most heartily thank you, and assure yourself, Master Lieu-tenant, I do not mislike my cheer, but whensoever I do, then thrust me out of your doors."

More jesting with the jailor

10   Whereas the oath confirming the supremacy and matrimony was by the first statute in few words comprised, the Lord Chancellor and Master Secretary did of their own heads add more words unto it, to make it ap-pear unto the King's ears more pleasant and plausible. And that oath, so amplified, caused they to be ministered to Sir Thomas More, and to all
15 other throughout the realm. Which Sir Thomas More perceiving, said unto my wife, "I may tell thee, Meg, they that have committed me hither, for refusing of this oath not agreeable to the statute, are not by their own law able to justify my imprisonment.[79] And surely, daughter, it is great pity that any Christian prince should by a flexible Council[80] ready to follow
20 his affections, and by a weak clergy lacking grace constantly to stand to their learning, with flattery[81] be so shamefully abused." But at length the Lord Chancellor and Master Secretary, espying their own oversight in that behalf, were fain afterwards to find the means that another statute should be made for the confirmation of the oath so amplified with their addi-
25 tions.[82]

Wording of oath changed

The danger of flattery

      After Sir Thomas More had given over his office and all other worldly doings therewith, to the intent he might from thenceforth the more qui-etly settle himself to the service of God, then made he a conveyance for the disposition of all his lands, reserving to himself an estate thereof only
30 for the term of his own life, and after his decease assuring some part of the same to his wife, some to his son's wife for a jointure in consideration that

More's care in disposing of his property

79. As Reynolds points out, "Here Roper confuses the question of the Supremacy and that of the Succession," p. 41.

80. Compare this concern for good counsel with the statement reported by the *Paris Newslet-ter*, *TMSB*, p. 353.

81. About the problems associated with flattery, see also *TMSB*, pp. 55, 176, 185–86, 200, 257.

82. More could have obeyed the statute but not the "additions" to the oath by Cromwell and Audley.

she was an inheritrix in possession of more than an hundred pounds land by the year, and some to me and my wife in recompense of our marriage money, with divers remainders over. All which conveyance and assurance was perfectly finished long before that matter whereupon he was attainted was made an offense, and yet after by statute clearly avoided.[83] And so were all his lands, that he had to his wife and children by the said conveyance in such sort assured, contrary to the order of law, taken away from them, and brought into the King's hands, saving that portion which he had appointed to my wife and me, which, although he had in the foresaid conveyance reserved, as he did the rest, for term of life to himself, nevertheless, upon further consideration, two days after, by another conveyance, he gave the same immediately to my wife and me in possession. And so because the statute had undone only the first conveyance, giving no more to the King but so much as passed by that, the second conveyance, whereby it was given to my wife and me, being dated two days after, was without the compass of the statute. And so was our portion to us by that means clearly reserved.

As Sir Thomas More in the Tower chanced on a time, looking out of his window, to behold one Master Reynolds, a religious, learned, and virtuous father of Sion, and three monks of the Charterhouse, for the matters of the matrimony and supremacy, going out of the Tower to execution, he, as one longing in that journey to have accompanied them, said unto my wife, then standing there beside him, "Lo, dost thou not see, Meg, that these blessed fathers be now as cheerfully going to their deaths as bridegrooms to their marriage? Wherefore mayest thou see, mine own good daughter, what a great difference there is between such as have in effect spent all their days in a straight, hard, penitential, and painful life religiously, and such as have in the world, like worldly wretches, as thy poor father hath done, consumed all their time in pleasure and ease licentiously. For God, considering their long-continued life in most sore and grievous penance, will no longer suffer them to remain here in this vale of misery and iniquity, but speedily hence taketh them to the fruition of His everlasting deity, whereas thy silly father, Meg, that like a most wicked caitiff[84] hath passed forth the whole course of his miserable life most sinfully, God, thinking him not worthy so soon to come to that eternal felicity, leaveth

More and Meg watch as monks are led to execution, 4 May 1535

83. *avoided*—made void
84. *caitiff*—wretch

him here yet still in the world, further to be plunged and turmoiled with misery."

Within a while after, Master Secretary,[85] coming to him into the Tower from the King, pretended much friendship towards him, and for his com-
5 fort told him that the King's Highness was his good and gracious lord, and minded not with any matter wherein he should have cause of scruple, from henceforth to trouble his conscience. As soon as Master Secretary was gone, to express what comfort he conceived of his words, he wrote with a coal, for ink then had he none, these verses following:

Cromwell promises King's favor

10   Eye-flattering fortune, look thou never so fair,
          Nor never so pleasantly begin to smile,
          As though thou wouldst my ruin all repair,
          During my life thou shalt not me beguile.
          Trust I shall God, to enter in a while
15   His haven of heaven, sure and uniform;
          Ever after thy calm, look I for a storm.

More's poem on flattering fortune

When Sir Thomas More had continued a good while in the Tower, my lady, his wife, obtained license to see him, who, at her first coming, like a simple ignorant woman, and somewhat worldly too, with this manner of
20 salutation bluntly saluted him:

Lady Alice's first visit

"What the good year,[86] Master More," quoth she, "I marvel that you, that have been always hitherto taken for so wise a man, will now so play the fool to lie here in this close, filthy prison, and be content thus to be shut up amongst mice and rats, when you might be abroad at your liberty,
25 and with the favor and good will both of the King and his Council, if you would but do as all the bishops and best learned of this realm have done. And seeing you have at Chelsea a right fair house, your library, your books, your gallery, your garden, your orchard, and all other necessaries so handsome about you, where you might in the company of me your wife,
30 your children, and household be merry, I muse what, a God's name, you mean here still thus fondly[87] to tarry."

After he had a while quietly heard her, with a cheerful countenance he said unto her, "I pray thee, good Mistress Alice, tell me one thing."

"What is that?" quoth she.

More responds to Lady Alice

85. Thomas Cromwell
86. An expression that connotes impatience.
87. *fondly*—foolishly

"Is not this house," quoth he, "as nigh[88] heaven as my own?"

To whom she, after her accustomed homely fashion, not liking such talk, answered, "Tilly-vally, tilly-vally!"[89]

"How say you, Mistress Alice," quoth he, "is it not so?"

"*Bone deus, bone deus,* man, will this gear[90] never be left?" quoth she.   5

"Well then, Mistress Alice, if it be so," quoth he, "it is very well. For I see no great cause why I should much joy either of my gay house or of anything belonging thereunto, when, if I should but seven years lie buried under the ground, and then arise and come thither again, I should not fail to find some therein that would bid me get out of doors, and tell me it   10 were none of mine. What cause have I then to like such an house as would so soon forget his master?"

So her persuasions moved him but a little.

Further interrogations

Not long after came there to him the Lord Chancellor, the Dukes of Norfolk and Suffolk with Master Secretary, and certain other of the Privy   15 Council, at two several times, by all policies possible procuring[91] him, either precisely to confess the Supremacy, or precisely to deny it; whereunto, as appeareth by his examinations in the said great book,[92] they could never bring him.

Richard Rich's visit to the Tower, 12 June 1535

Shortly hereupon, Master Rich (afterwards Lord Rich), then newly   20 made the King's Solicitor, Sir Richard Southwell, and one Master Palmer, servant to the Secretary, were sent to Sir Thomas More into the Tower to fetch away his books from him. And while Sir Richard Southwell and Master Palmer were busy in the trussing up of his books, Master Rich, pretending friendly talk with him, among other things, of a set course, as it   25 seemed, said thus unto him:

"Forasmuch as it is well known, Master More, that you are a man both wise and well-learned as well in the laws of the realm as otherwise, I pray you therefore, sir, let me be so bold as of good will to put unto you this case. Admit there were, sir," quoth he, "an act of Parliament that all the   30 realm should take me for King. Would not you, Master More, take me for King?"

"Yes, sir," quoth Sir Thomas More, "that would I."

---

88. *nigh*—near
89. "An exclamation of impatience: Nonsense!" *(Oxford English Dictionary).*
90. *gear*—nonsense
91. *procuring*—endeavoring to get
92. More's 1557 *English Works.*

"I put case further," quoth Master Rich, "that there were an act of Parliament that all the realm should take me for pope. Would not you then, Master More, take me for pope?"

"For answer, sir," quoth Sir Thomas More, "to your first case, the Parliament may well, Master Rich, meddle with the state of temporal princes. But to make answer to your other cause, I will put you this case: Suppose the Parliament would make a law that God should not be God. Would you then, Master Rich, say that God were not God?"

"No, sir," quoth he, "that would I not, since no Parliament may make any such law."

"No more," said Sir Thomas More, as Master Rich reported him, "could the Parliament make the king supreme head of the Church."

Upon whose only report was Sir Thomas More indicted of treason upon the statute whereby it was made treason to deny the King to be supreme head of the Church. Into which indictment were put these heinous words—"maliciously, traitorously, and diabolically."

When Sir Thomas More was brought from the Tower to Westminster Hall to answer the indictment, and at the King's Bench bar before the judges thereupon arraigned, he openly told them that he would upon that indictment have abidden in law, but that he thereby should have been driven to confess of himself the matter indeed, that was the denial of the King's Supremacy, which he protested was untrue. Wherefore he thereto pleaded not guilty; and so reserved unto himself advantage to be taken of the body of the matter, after verdict, to avoid that indictment, and moreover added that if those only odious terms, "maliciously, traitorously, and diabolically," were put out of the indictment he saw therein nothing justly to charge him.

And for proof to the jury that Sir Thomas More was guilty of this treason, Master Rich was called forth to give evidence unto them upon his oath, as he did. Against whom thus sworn, Sir Thomas More began in this wise to say, "If I were a man, my lords, that did not regard an oath, I needed not, as it is well known, in this place, at this time, nor in this case, to stand here as an accused person. And if this oath of yours, Master Rich, be true, then pray I that I never see God in the face, which I would not say, were it otherwise, to win the whole world." Then recited he to the court the discourse of all their communication in the Tower, according to the truth, and said:

More's trial before the King's bench, 1 July 1535

More denies Rich's testimony against him

More answers
Rich's charge

In good faith, Master Rich, I am sorrier for your perjury than for my own peril. And you shall understand that neither I, nor no man else to my knowledge, ever took you to be a man of such credit as in any matter of importance I, or any other, would at any time vouchsafe to communicate with you. And I, as you know, of no small while have been acquainted with you and your conversation, who have known you from your youth hitherto. For we have long dwelled both in one parish together, where, as yourself can tell (I am sorry you compel me so to say) you were esteemed very light of your tongue, a great dicer, and of no commendable fame. And so in your house at the Temple,[93] where hath been your chief bringing up, were you likewise accounted.

Is it plausible?

Can it therefore seem likely unto your honorable lordships that I would, in so weighty a cause, so unadvisedly overshoot myself as to trust Master Rich, a man of me always reputed for one of so little truth, as your lordships have heard, so far above my Sovereign Lord the King, or any of his noble councillors, that I would unto him utter the secrets of my conscience touching the King's Supremacy, the special point and only mark at my hands so long sought for, a thing which I never did, nor never would, after the statute thereof made, reveal either to the King's Highness himself, or to any of his honorable councillors, as it is not unknown to your honors, at sundry several times sent from his Grace's own person unto the Tower unto me for none other purpose? Can this in your judgments, my lords,

Even if he did,
no malice was
involved

seem likely to be true? And yet, if I had so done indeed, my lords, as Master Rich hath sworn, seeing it was spoken but in familiar secret talk, nothing affirming, and only putting of cases, without other displeasant circumstances, it cannot justly be taken to be spoken maliciously, and where there is no malice, there can be no offense. And over this I can never think, my lords, that so many worthy bishops, so many honorable personages, and so many other worshipful, virtuous, wise, and well-learned men as at the making of that law were in Parliament assembled, ever meant to have any man punished by death in whom there could be found no malice, taking *"malitia"* for *"malevolentia."* For if *"malitia"* be generally taken for "sin," no man is there then that can thereof excuse himself. *Quia si dixerimus quod peccatum non habemus, nosmet ipsos seducimus, et veritas in nobis non est.*[94] And only

Only malicious
denial is
punishable

this word "maliciously" is in the statute material, as this term "forcible" is in the statute of forcible entries, by which statute, if a man enter peaceably, and put not his adversary out forcibly, it is no offense. But if he put him out forcibly, then by that statute it is an offense, and so shall he be punished by this term "forcibly."

The King's clear
favor to More
shows that no
malice was
involved

Besides this, the manifold goodness of the King's Highness himself, that hath been so many ways my singular good lord and gracious sovereign, that hath so dearly loved and trusted me, even at my very first coming into his noble service with the dignity of his honorable Privy Council vouchsafing to admit me, and to

93. The Middle Temple, one of the inns of court.
94. "If we say that we have no sin, we deceive ourselves, and the truth is not in us" (1 John 1:8).

offices of great credit and worship most liberally advanced me, and finally with that weighty room of his Grace's High Chancellor (the like whereof he never did to temporal man before), next to his own royal person the highest officer in this noble realm, so far above my merits or qualities able and meet therefore, of his in-
5 comparable benignity honored and exalted me, by the space of twenty years and more showing his continual favor towards me, and (until at my own poor suit, it pleased his Highness, giving me license, with his Majesty's favor, to bestow the residue of my life for the provision of my soul in the service of God, of his espe-cial goodness thereof to discharge and unburden me) most benignly heaped hon-
10 ors continually more and more upon me—all this his Highness's goodness, I say, so long thus bountifully extended towards me, were in my mind, my lords, matter sufficient to convince this slanderous surmise by this man so wrongfully imagined against me.

Master Rich, seeing himself so disproved, and his credit so foul de-
15 faced, caused Sir Richard Southwell and Master Palmer, that at the time of their communication were in the chamber, to be sworn what words had passed between them. Whereupon Master Palmer, upon his deposition, said that he was so busy about the trussing up of Sir Thomas More's books in a sack, that he took no heed to their talk. Sir Richard Southwell like-
20 wise, upon his deposition, said that because he was appointed only to look unto the conveyance of his books, he gave no ear unto them.

Southwell and Palmer refuse to support Rich

After this were there many other reasons, not now to my remem-brance, by Sir Thomas More in his own defense alleged, to the discredit of Master Rich's aforesaid evidence, and proof of the clearness of his own
25 conscience. All which notwithstanding, the jury found him guilty. And in-continent upon[95] their verdict, the Lord Chancellor, for that matter chief commissioner, beginning to proceed in judgment against him, Sir Thomas More said to him: "My lord, when I was toward the law, the manner in such case was to ask the prisoner before judgment, why judgment should
30 not be given against him." Whereupon the Lord Chancellor, staying his judgment, wherein he had partly proceeded, demanded of him what he was able to say to the contrary. Who then in this sort most humbly made answer:

More pronounced guilty

More interrupts the proceedings and argues that the indictment is invalid

"Forasmuch as, my lord," quoth he, "this indictment is grounded upon an act of
35 Parliament directly repugnant to the laws of God and His Holy Church, the supreme government of which, or of any part whereof, may no temporal prince presume by any law to take upon him, as rightfully belonging to the See of

95. *incontinent upon*—immediately after

Rome, a spiritual pre-eminence by the mouth of Our Savior himself, personally present upon the earth, only to St. Peter and his successors, bishops of the same See, by special prerogative granted, it is therefore in law amongst Christian men insufficient to charge any Christian man."

And for proof thereof, like as, among divers other reasons and authorities, he declared that this realm, being but one member and small part of the Church, might not make a particular law disagreeable with the general law of Christ's universal Catholic Church, no more than the city of London, being but one poor member in respect of the whole realm, might make a law against an act of Parliament to bind the whole realm. So farther showed he that it was contrary both to the laws and statutes of our own land yet unrepealed, as they might evidently perceive in Magna Carta, *Quod ecclesia Anglicana libera sit, et habeat omnia iura sua integra et libertates suas illaesas.*[96] And also contrary to that sacred oath[97] which the King's Highness himself and every other Christian prince always with great solemnity received at their coronations, alleging moreover that no more might this realm of England refuse obedience to the See of Rome than might a child refuse obedience to his own natural father. For as St. Paul said to the Corinthians, "I have regenerated you, my children in Christ."[98] So might St. Gregory, Pope of Rome, of whom by St. Augustine, his messenger, we first received the Christian faith, of us Englishmen truly say, "You are my children, because I have given to you everlasting salvation, a far higher and better inheritance than any carnal father can leave to his child, and by regeneration made you my spiritual children in Christ."

Then was it by the Lord Chancellor thereunto answered that seeing all the bishops, universities, and best learned of this realm had to this act agreed, it was much marveled that he alone against them all would so stiffly stick thereat, and so vehemently argue there against.

To that Sir Thomas More replied, saying, "If the number of bishops and universities be so material as your lordship seemeth to take it, then see I little cause, my lord, why that thing in my conscience should make any change. For I nothing doubt but that, though not in this realm, yet in Christendom about, of these well-learned bishops and virtuous men that

More appeals to the Magna Carta and the Coronation Oath

Audley's challenge to More

96. "That the English Church may be free, and that it may exist with all its laws uncorrupted and its liberties unviolated" is the first right listed in the Magna Carta.

97. This coronation oath required the king to confirm "especially the laws, customs, and liberties granted the clergy and the people."

98. 1 Corinthians 3:1.

are yet alive, they be not the fewer part that be of my mind therein. But if
I should speak of those which already be dead, of whom many be now
holy saints in heaven, I am very sure it is the far greater part of them that, *More claims to be*
all the while they lived, thought in this case that way that I think now. *in the majority*
5 And therefore am I not bound, my lord, to conform my conscience to the
Council of one realm against the General Council of Christendom."

Now when Sir Thomas More, for the voiding of the indictment, had
taken as many exceptions as he thought meet, and many more reasons
than I can now remember alleged, the Lord Chancellor, loath to have the *A moment of*
10 burden of that judgment wholly to depend upon himself, there openly *conscience*
asked advice of the Lord Fitz-James, then Lord Chief Justice of the King's
Bench, and joined in commission with him, whether this indictment were
sufficient or not. Who, like a wise man, answered, "My lords all, by St. Ju- *Conditional*
lian" (that was ever his oath), "I must needs confess that if the act of Parlia- *clause with triple*
15 ment be not unlawful, then is not the indictment in my conscience insuf- *negative*
ficient."

Whereupon the Lord Chancellor said to the rest of the lords: "Lo, my *The verdict against*
lords, you hear what my Lord Chief Justice saith," and so immediately gave *More*
he judgment against him.

20 After which ended, the commissioners yet further courteously offered
him, if he had anything else to allege for his defense, to grant him favorable audience. Who answered, "More have I not to say, my lords, but that
like the blessed apostle St. Paul, as we read in the Acts of the Apostles, was
present, and consented to the death of St. Stephen, and kept their clothes
25 that stoned him to death, and yet be they now both twain holy saints in
heaven, and shall continue there friends forever, so I verily trust, and shall *More hopes that*
therefore right heartily pray, that though your lordships have now here in *he and his judges*
earth been judges to my condemnation, we may yet hereafter in heaven *will be merry to-*
merrily all meet together, to our everlasting salvation." *gether in heaven.*

30 This much touching Sir Thomas More's arraignment, being not there-
at present myself, have I by credible report, partly of the right worshipful *Roper's sources*
Sir Anthony St. Leger, knight, and partly of Richard Heywood and John
Webbe, gentlemen, with others of good credit, at the hearing thereof present themselves, as far as my poor wit and memory would serve me, here
35 truly rehearsed unto you.

Now, after this arraignment, departed he from the bar to the Tower
again, led by Sir William Kingston, a tall, strong, and comely knight, Con-
stable of the Tower, and his very dear friend. Who, when he had brought

him from Westminster to the Old Swan towards the Tower, there with an
heavy heart, the tears running down by his cheeks, bade him farewell. Sir
Thomas More, seeing him so sorrowful, comforted him with as good
words as he could, saying: "Good Master Kingston, trouble not yourself,
but be of good cheer; for I will pray for you, and my good lady, your wife,   5
that we may meet in heaven together, where we shall be merry for ever
and ever."

More comforts Sir Kingston

Soon after, Sir William Kingston, talking with me of Sir Thomas More,
said, "In good faith, Master Roper, I was ashamed of myself, that, at my departing from your father, I found my heart so feeble, and his so strong, that   10
he was fain to comfort me, which should rather have comforted him."

Father and daughter meet for the last time

When Sir Thomas More came from Westminster to the Towerward
again, his daughter, my wife, desirous to see her father, whom she thought
she should never see in this world after, and also to have his final blessing,
gave attendance about the Tower Wharf, where she knew he would pass   15
by, before he could enter into the Tower, there tarrying for his coming
home. As soon as she saw him, after his blessing on her knees reverently
received, she hastening towards him, and, without consideration or care of
herself, pressing in among the midst of the throng and company of the
guard, that with halberds and bills[99] went round about him, hastily ran to   20
him, and there openly, in the sight of all, embraced him, took him about
the neck, and kissed him. Who, well liking her most natural and dear
daughterly affection towards him, gave her his fatherly blessing and many
goodly words of comfort besides. From whom after she was departed, she,
not satisfied with the former sight of him, and like one that had forgotten   25
herself, being all ravished with the entire love of her dear father, having
respect neither to herself, nor to the press of the people and multitude
that were there about him, suddenly turned back again, ran to him as before, took him about the neck, and divers times together most lovingly
kissed him, and at last, with a full heavy heart, was fain to depart from him.   30
The beholding whereof was to many of them that were present thereat
so lamentable that it made them for very sorrow thereof to mourn and
weep.

Meg's second farewell

So remained Sir Thomas More in the Tower more than a seven-night[100]
after his judgment. From whence, the day before he suffered, he sent his   35

99. *halberds and bills*—battle axes and broad swords
100. Here Roper errs. More's trial was July 1 and his execution, July 6.

shirt of hair (not willing to have it seen) to my wife, his dearly beloved daughter, and a letter written with a coal, contained in the foresaid book of his works,[101] plainly expressing the fervent desire he had to suffer on the morrow, in these words following:

Last letter to Meg

5   I cumber[102] you, good Margaret, much, but I would be sorry if it should be any longer then tomorrow, for tomorrow is St. Thomas's Even, and the Utas of St. Peter.[103] And therefore tomorrow long I to go to God; it were a day very meet and convenient for me, etc. I never liked your manner towards me better than when you kissed me last. For I like when daughterly love and dear charity have no
10   leisure to look to worldly courtesy.

More longs to die on eve of Thomas Becket's feast

And so upon the next morrow, being Tuesday, St. Thomas's Eve, and the Utas of St. Peter, in the year of Our Lord, one thousand five hundred thirty and five (according as he in his letter the day before had wished) early in the morning came to him Sir Thomas Pope, his singular friend, on
15   message from the King and his Council, that he should before nine of the clock the same morning suffer death, and that therefore forthwith he should prepare himself thereunto.

More's execution, 6 July 1535

"Master Pope," quoth he, "for your good tidings I most heartily thank you. I have been always much bounden to the King's Highness for the
20   benefits and honors that he hath still from time to time most bountifully heaped upon me, and yet more bound am I to his Grace for putting me into this place, where I have had convenient time and space to have remembrance of my end. And so help me, God, most of all, Master Pope, am I bound to his Highness that it pleaseth him so shortly to rid me out of
25   the miseries of this wretched world. And therefore will I not fail earnestly to pray for his Grace, both here and also in another world."

Grateful to the King

"The King's pleasure is further," quoth Master Pope, "that at your execution you shall not use many words."

Commanded to use few words

"Master Pope," quoth he, "you do well to give me warning of his
30   Grace's pleasure, for otherwise I had purposed at that time somewhat to have spoken, but of no matter wherewith his Grace, or any other, should have had cause to be offended. Nevertheless, whatsoever I intended, I am ready obediently to conform myself to his Grace's commandments. And I

Parting obedience

101. This is Roper's third reference to the 1557 edition of More's *English Works*.

102. *cumber*—trouble

103. July 7th was the popular feast of St. Thomas Becket and the octave of St. Peter's feast. (See Butler's *Quest for Becket's Bones* for an explanation of this anniversary of the transferring of Becket's relics from the crypt to the main floor of Canterbury Cathedral.)

beseech you, good Master Pope, to be a mean[104] unto his Highness that my daughter Margaret may be at my burial."

"The King is content already," quoth Master Pope, "that your wife, children, and other your friends shall have liberty to be present thereat."

"O, how much beholden then," said Sir Thomas More, "am I to his   5
Grace that unto my poor burial vouchsafeth to have so gracious consideration."

Comforts Sir Thomas Pope

Wherewithal Master Pope, taking his leave of him, could not refrain from weeping. Which Sir Thomas More perceiving, comforted him in this wise, "Quiet yourself, good Master Pope, and be not discomforted, for I   10
trust that we shall, once in heaven, see each other full merrily, where we shall be sure to live and love together, in joyful bliss eternally."

More plans to wear his best apparel to his death

Upon whose departure, Sir Thomas More, as one that had been invited to some solemn feast, changed himself into his best apparel, which Master Lieutenant espying, advised him to put it off, saying that he that should   15
have it was but a javel.[105]

"What, Master Lieutenant," quoth he, "shall I account him a javel that shall do me this day so singular a benefit? Nay, I assure you, were it cloth of gold, I would account it well bestowed on him, as St. Cyprian did, who gave his executioner thirty pieces of gold." And albeit at length, through   20
Master Lieutenant's importunate persuasion, he altered his apparel, yet after the example of St. Cyprian, did he, of that little money that was left him, send one angel of gold to his executioner.

And so was he by Master Lieutenant brought out of the Tower, and from thence led towards the place of execution. Where, going up the scaf-   25
fold, which was so weak that it was ready to fall, he said merrily to Master Lieutenant, "I pray you, Master Lieutenant, see me safe up, and for my coming down, let me shift for myself."

Good cheer on the scaffold

Then desired he all the people thereabout to pray for him, and to bear witness with him that he should now there suffer death in and for the   30
faith of the holy Catholic Church. Which done, he knelt down, and after his prayers said, turned to the executioner and with a cheerful countenance spake thus to him: "Pluck up thy spirits, man, and be not afraid to do thine office; my neck is very short; take heed therefore thou strike not awry, for saving of thine honesty."   35

104. *mean*—intermediary
105. *javel*—rascal; worthless person

So passed Sir Thomas More out of this world to God, upon the very same day in which himself had most desired.

Soon after whose death came intelligence thereof to the Emperor Charles. Whereupon he sent for Sir Thomas Elyot, our English ambassa- dor, and said unto him: "My Lord Ambassador, we understand that the King, your master, hath put his faithful servant and grave wise councillor, Sir Thomas More, to death." Whereunto Sir Thomas Elyot answered that he understood nothing thereof. "Well," said the Emperor, "it is too true. And this will we say, that if we had been master of such a servant, of whose doings our self have had these many years no small experience, we would rather have lost the best city of our dominions than have lost such a wor- thy councillor." Which matter was by the same Sir Thomas Elyot to my- self, to my wife, to Master Clement and his wife, to Master John Heywood and his wife, and unto divers other his friends accordingly reported.

Response of Emperor Charles

Finis. Deo gratias.

Sir Thomas More

c. 1592

by Anthony Munday, Henry Chettle, William Shakespeare, and Others

Sir Thomas More, *an Elizabethan biographical history play that survives only in the form of an unpublished prompt-book,[1] was originally written by Anthony Munday and a number of London playwrights between 1592–1595. Though it never seems to have been staged publicly before the twentieth century,* Sir Thomas More *has had a way of gaining an audience both in its own and latter days. In the 1590s, for example, the play attracted the perhaps less than desired attention of Queen Elizabeth's censor, Sir Edmund Tilney, who ordered, among other things, that the playwrights "leave out . . . wholly" their depiction of the 1517 Ill May Day riots that broke out between native Londoners and foreign merchants. Tilney then ominously concluded his remarks by reiterating on the first page of the manuscript that the scene must be replaced by a "short report and not otherwise at your own perils."[2] Difficulties with the censor and the controversy and delicacy of the subject matter during the reign of Elizabeth may be some reasons why the play was never acted. In any event, the play has become considerably more well-known since 1871,*

---

1. Hence the play is often called *The Book of Sir Thomas More.*
2. *The Book of Sir Thomas More.* Ed. W. W. Greg. Oxford: Malone Society Reprints, 1961, p. 1 (modernized slightly here).

when scholars began to debate the possibility that Shakespeare may have added some passages to the original text. Though there is a small dissenting group of critics, a general consensus has emerged that the revised depiction of Ill May Day riots in 2.3.1–147—apparently in the dramatist's own hand—and More's pensive soliloquy on greatness at 3.1.1–21 are indeed Shakespeare's.[3] *Concerning the other authors involved in the writing and revising of* Sir Thomas More, *scholars have identified Anthony Munday ("our best plotter," in fellow Elizabethan Frances Meres' words), Henry Chettle, and two others, who have sometimes been identified as Thomas Heywood and Thomas Dekker.*[4]

Textual controversies aside, the play is a fascinating depiction of the rise and fall of Sir Thomas More, and it is described by More himself as a "tragedy" at 5.4.71, perhaps of the de casibus virorum illustrium *tradition, as Walter Cohen suggests.*[5] *The three main sources of the play are Raphael Holinshed's* Chronicles, *Nicholas Harpsfield's* Life and Death of Sir Thomas More, *and Thomas Stapleton's* Vita Thomae Mori, *though the playwrights also draw on a wide array of other works, including strangely enough John Foxe's "The Life of Cromwell" and* Lusty Juventus, *an anti-Catholic work from which the morality play in act three, "The Marriage of Wit and Wisdom," is surprisingly drawn.*

As for the play itself, it has garnered praise from an array of readers for its effective structure and development. In his Shakespeare Apocrypha, *C. F. Tucker Brooke remarks that "*Sir Thomas More *ranks high among the productions of its decade" and that "it is hardly possible to withstand the conviction that if Shakespeare was ever concerned with any of the apocryphal plays, then surely it was with this."*[6] *Examining the play from a more aesthetic point of view, Charles Forker and Joseph Candido argue that "not only does the play contain some of the best verse*

---

3. These passages are now included in the most authoritative contemporary editions of Shakespeare's plays, *The Riverside Shakespeare* and the new *Oxford Shakespeare,* both of which reproduce the manuscript pages in facsimile. While there are some who deny Shakespearean involvement in the play altogether, a few on the opposite side have argued on controversial "stylometric grounds" that Shakespeare may have had a hand in up to 90% of the original play. See Thomas Merriam, "The Authorship of *Sir Thomas More*," *ALLC Bulletin* 10 (1982), 1–7, and John Velz's overview of the debate, "*Sir Thomas More* and the Shakespeare Canon: Two Approaches" in *Shakespeare and* Sir Thomas More: *Essays on the Play and Its Shakespearean Interest.* Ed. T. H. Howard-Hill. Cambridge: Cambridge UP, 1989.

4. For an exhaustive account of the manuscript and the authorship controversy, consult G. Harold Metz, "'Voice and credyt': The Scholars and *Sir Thomas More*" in *Shakespeare and* Sir Thomas More, 11–44. See also the excellent authoritative critical edition of the play, *Sir Thomas More.* Ed. Vittorio Gabrieli and Giorgio Melchiori. Manchester: Manchester UP, 1989.

5. *The Norton Shakespeare,* 2001. See also Scott McMillin, "*The Book of Sir Thomas More:* A Theatrical View," *Modern Philology* 68 (1970), p. 22.

6. C. F. Tucker Brooke, *Shakespeare Apocrypha,* Oxford: OUP, 1908, p. liv.

(even excluding those passages ascribed to Shakespeare) in all the plays of its biographical type, but it also possesses, despite its apparently unfinished state and multiple authorship, a coherence of design uncommon among such plays."[7] The design of the play is also examined by Giorgio Melchiori, who maintains that "It looks to me as if the play as a whole had been plotted with a precise intention: that of showing the abuses perpetrated under cover of the absolute power of the king."[8] In his overview of critical responses to the play, G. Harold Metz summarizes the view of many: "Most scholars consider More *theatrically the most successful of the biographical history plays."[9]*

One reason for that success is the winning portrait drawn of "merry More" throughout the play. Indeed, given the controversy surrounding More, the Reformation in England, and the Anglican settlement, this presentation of More—notably sympathetic from beginning to end—is remarkable.[10] A related facet of the play worth consideration is the playwrights' decision to minimize direct references to the religious controversies of the day, as well as their decision to treat King Henry's decisions and actions rather indirectly throughout. For example, the content of the mysterious and fateful "Articles" brought to More in act four is never specified, and the audience is presented only with his decision not to accept the Articles on the grounds of his "conscience" (4.1.74). Indeed, the playwrights intriguingly present More's drama as the struggle of his personal conscience with the authority of the King and his new laws, rather than focusing directly on the well-known controversies surrounding the Act of Succession and the Oath of Supremacy. This focus is reminiscent of Roper's emphasis throughout his Life *on the importance of conscience for More,[11] and the emphasis on conscience also anticipates some later responses to the drama of More's life, particularly John Donne's in* Biathanotos *and Shakespeare's in his last play,* Henry the Eighth. *Donne comments that More, a distant relative on his mother's side,[12] was a "man of the most tender and delicate con-*

---

7. "Wit, Wisdom, and Theatricality in *The Book of Sir Thomas More,*" *Shakespeare Studies* 13 (1980), p. 85.

8. "*The Book of Sir Thomas More:* Dramatic Unity," in T.H. Howard-Hill, *Shakespeare and* Sir Thomas More, p. 77.

9. Metz, p. 11.

10. The portrait of More is even more arresting when one considers that Anthony Munday, one of the chief authors, was known to be decidedly anti-Catholic. Walter Cohen speaks for the majority of readers when he remarks, "Throughout and especially at the end, the witty and wise protagonist is treated with almost uncritical admiration" (*Norton Shakespeare,* 2001).

11. See introduction to Roper's *Life, TMSB,* pp. 16, 18.

12. Donne's relation to More plays out as follows: Thomas More's sister, Elizabeth, married John Rastell. Their daughter Joan Rastell married the playwright John Heywood. Their daughter Elizabeth Heywood married John Donne, Sr., and their son was John Donne, the poet. See *The*

science that the world saw since Augustine,"[13] *and Shakespeare, in the words of a fallen Cardinal Wolsey, describes More in memorable lines.*

> But he's a learned man. May he continue
> Long in His Highness' favor, and do justice
> For truth's sake and his conscience, that his bones,
> When he has run his course and sleeps in blessings,
> May have a tomb of orphans' tears wept on him! (3.2.395–99)

Connected to the emphasis on conscience is the play's evident interest in depicting "the interior life of its hero" and the "unique features of More's mind and personality" which distinguished him in life, friendship, imprisonment, and death.[14] Debate over the play, as with debate over figures like More and Shakespeare, will likely continue for the foreseeable future. Regardless, Sir Thomas More *remains a revealing early work about the rise and fall of a "man for all seasons."*

❧

A Note on the Text: Our basis for this edition of the play is W.W. Greg's Book of Sir Thomas More. *We have also benefited from two other excellent editions of the play:* Sir Thomas More, *ed. John Shirley (privately printed in 1939), and* Sir Thomas More, *ed. Vittorio Gabrieli and Giorgo Melchiori. Manchester: Manchester UP, 1989. Thanks to Joshua Avery for help with the glosses and editing of this text.*

Synopsis

ACT I

Scene 1: A London Street.

The play opens in London with two upper-class foreigners attempting to take property and even a wife from lower class English folk. In response, some of the aggrieved decide to have a bill of wrongs read publicly against the foreigners.

Scene 2: The Court of Sessions

Master Sheriff Thomas More has a merry jest at the expense of Justice Suresby.

Plays of John Heywood. Ed. Richard Axton and Peter Happe. (Cambridge, UK: D.S. Brewer, 1991) xvii.

13. Donne, pp. 62–63.
14. Forker and Candido, p. 86.

Scene 3: At Court

Some English nobles remark upon the abuses of foreigners. In retaliation for these wrongs, a mob of English commoners then forms, leading to the decision by the authorities to summon More as a peacemaker.

ACT II

Scene 1: St. Martin's Lane in London

The mob, seething with anti-French sentiment, becomes violent and threatens to destroy some foreigners' homes.

Scene 2: In the Guildhall

More, Surrey, Palmer and Shrewsbury confer on how best to handle the situation, as the mob releases a number of criminals from the main London prison. More decides to attempt pacifying the crowd with diplomacy.

Scene 3: St. Martin's Lane in London

More's diplomacy succeeds, and the dissidents submit themselves to the authorities. In recognition of this capable service, the King knights More and grants him a court appointment to the Privy Council.

Scene 4: The Standard in Cheapside

More manages to obtain clemency from the King for the rioters and is thereupon appointed Lord Chancellor.

ACT III

Scene 1: Within More's House in Chelsea

More has a street-brawler shaved and plays a prank on his friend Erasmus.

Scene 2: More's Town House

More's household entertains the Mayor of London and his wife. The company enjoys a play which is marred but a little for want of a beard.

ACT IV

Scene 1: The Privy Council Chamber in Westminster

More is committed to house arrest for his refusal to sign to articles drawn up by the King.

Scene 2: The Garden at More's Chelsea Home
More informs his family of his loss of the chancellorship and enjoins them to be merry.

Scene 3: A Room in the Tower of London
Bishop John Fisher, also declining to sign the articles, retains good cheer as he is placed in the Tower.

Scene 4: Within More's Home at Chelsea
More continues to encourage his family. When Shrewsbury and Surrey arrive to arrest him, he agrees to be taken to the Tower.

ACT V

Scene 1: The Tower Gate
A poor woman laments the arrest of More. As More approaches his prison, he welcomes it as a place of comfort.

Scene 2: More's House
More's servants bewail his imprisonment.

Scene 3: More's Chamber in the Tower
More gives final farewells and injunctions to his family.

Scene 4: Tower Hill
More goes to his death with good humor.

Sir Thomas More

Dramatis Personae

More's Family and Household

Thomas More, *Sheriff of London; later Lord Chancellor*
Lady More, *More's wife*
Mistress Roper, *More's elder daughter, Margaret*
Roper, *More's son-in-law*
Elizabeth, *More's second daughter*
Catesby, *steward*
Ned, *butler*
Robin, *brewer*
Ralph, *horsekeeper*
Giles, *porter*
Randall, *servant*
Gough, *secretary*

Londoners and Foreigners

Erasmus, *humanist and friend of Thomas More*
Francis de Barde, *a Lombard*
Caveler, *a Lombard*
George Betts, *a shopkeeper*
Ralph Betts, *a Clown*
John Lincoln, *a broker*
Sherwin, *a goldsmith*
Williamson, *a carpenter*
Doll Williamson, *the carpenter's wife*
Jack Falkner, *a ruffian, Morris' servant*

Lifter, *a pickpocket*
Smart, *a plaintiff*
A poor woman

OFFICIALS

The Recorder
The Lord Mayor of London
The Lord Mayor's wife
Justice Suresby
The Earl of Shrewsbury
The Earl of Surrey
Sir Roger Cholmley
Sir John Munday
Sir Thomas Palmer
Crofts, *a Royal Messenger*
Fisher, *Bishop of Rochester*
Morris, *Secretary to Bishop of Winchester*
Gentleman Porter of the Tower
Lieutenant of the Tower
Downes, *an officer of justice*
The hangman

CHARACTERS FROM "MARRIAGE OF WIT AND WISDOM"

Inclination
Lady Vanity
Luggins
Prologue
Wit

VARIOUS CITIZENS, APPRENTICES, NOBILITY, SHERIFFS OF LONDON, OFFICERS, AND GUARDS.

Act I

Scene I. *A London Street.*

Enter at one end John Lincoln with George Betts and clown Ralph Betts together; at the other end enters Francis De Bard, a Lombard, and Doll Williamson, a lusty woman, he haling her by the arm.

Doll. Whither wilt thou hale° me?

Bard. Whither I please; thou art my prize and I plead purchase of thee.

Doll. Purchase of me? Away ye rascal! I am an honest plain carpenter's wife and though I have no beauty to like a husband, yet whatsoever is mine scorns to stoop to a stranger. Hand off then when I bid thee. 5

Bard. Go with me quietly, or I'll compel thee.

Doll. Compel me, ye dog's face? Thou thinkst thou hast the goldsmith's wife in hand, whom thou enticedst from her husband with all his plate, and when thou turnedst her home to him again, mad'st him, like an ass, pay for his wife's board. 10

Bard. So will I make thy husband too, if please me.

Enter Cavaler with a pair of doves, Williamson the carpenter and Sherwin following him.

Doll. Here he comes himself; tell him so if thou darest.

Caveler. Follow me no further; I say thou shalt not have them.

Williamson. I bought them in Cheapside,° and paid my money for them.

Sherwin. He did, sir, indeed, and you offer him wrong, both to take them 15 from him, and not restore him his money neither.

Caveler. If he paid for them, let it suffice that I possess them. Beef and brewis° may serve such hinds. Are pigeons meat for a coarse° carpenter?

Lincoln. It is hard when Englishmen's patience must be thus jetted° on by 20 strangers, and they not dare to revenge their own wrongs.

George. Lincoln, let's beat them down, and bear no more of these abuses.

---

1 *hale* pull along forcibly / 14 *Cheapside* London's main food market / 19 *brewis* broth or broth-soaked bread / 19 *coarse* common / 20 *jetted* encroached upon

74

Lincoln. We may not, Betts. Be patient and hear more.

25 *Doll.* How now, husband? What, one stranger take thy food from thee, and another thy wife? By'r Lady, flesh and blood, I think, can hardly brook that.

Lincoln. Will this gear° never be otherwise? Must these wrongs be thus endured?

30 *George.* Let us step in, and help to revenge their injury.

Bard. What art thou that talkst of revenge? My Lord Ambassador shall once more make your Mayor have a check if he punish thee not for this saucy presumption.

Williamson. Indeed, my Lord Mayor, on the Ambassador's complaint, sent 35 me to Newgate° one day because (against my will) I took the wall° of a stranger. You may do anything, the goldsmith's wife, and mine now, must be at your commandment.

George. The more patient fools are ye both to suffer it.

Bard. Suffer it? Mend it thou or he if ye can or dare; I tell thee fellow, and° 40 she were the Mayor of London's wife, had I her once in my possession, I would keep her in spite of him that durst say nay.

George. I tell thee, Lombard, these words should cost thy best cap,° were I not curbed by duty and obedience. The Mayor of London's wife? O God, shall it be thus?

45 *Doll.* Why Betts, am not I as dear to my husband as my Lord Mayor's wife to him? And wilt thou so neglectly suffer thine own shame? Hands off, proud stranger, or by Him that bought me, if men's milky hearts dare not strike a stranger, yet women will beat them down, ere they bear these abuses.

50 *Bard.* Mistress, I say you shall along with me.

Doll. Touch not Doll Williamson, lest she lay thee along on God's dear earth. *(She turns to Caveler)* And you, sir, that allow such coarse cates° to carpenters, whilst pigeons which they pay for must serve your dainty appetite: deliver them back to my husband again or I'll call so many 55 women to mine assistance, as we'll not leave one inch untorn of thee. If our husbands must be bridled by law, and forced to bear your wrongs, their wives will be a little lawless, and soundly beat ye.

---

28 *gear* business / 35 *Newgate* London's infamous main prison / 35 *I took the wall* took the privilege of walking near the wall: the cleaner and safer side of the pavement / 39 *and* if / 42 *best cap* head / 52 *cates* provisions

Caveler. Come away, de Bard, and let us go complain to my Lord Ambassador.[1]

Doll. Aye, go, and send him among us, and we'll give him his welcome too.   60
I am ashamed that freeborn Englishmen, having beaten strangers within their own bounds, should thus be braved and abused by them at home.

Sherwin. It is not our lack of courage in the cause, but the strict obedience that we are bound to: I am the goldsmith whose wrongs you talked of,   65
but how to redress yours or mine own is a matter beyond all our abilities.

Lincoln. Not so, not so, my good friends. I, though a mean man, a broker by profession and named John Lincoln, have long time winked at these vild° enormities with mighty impatience, and, as these two brethren   70
here, Bettses by name, can witness, with loss of mine own life would gladly remedy them.

George. And he is in a good forwardness,° I tell ye, if all hit right.

Doll. As how, I prithee? Tell it to Doll Williamson.

Lincoln. You know the Spital sermons[2] begin the next week. I have drawn   75
a bill of our wrongs, and the strangers' insolencies.

George. Which he means the preachers shall there openly publish in the pulpit.

Williamson. Oh, but that they would! I'faith it would tickle° our strangers thoroughly.   80

Doll. Aye, and if you men durst not undertake it, before God we women will. Take an honest woman from her husband! Why, it is intolerable!

Sherwin. But how find ye the preachers affected to it?

Lincoln. Master Doctor Standish [will not meddle with such matter in his sermon, but Master Doctor Beale promised that he will under-   85
take to][3] reform it and doubts not but happy success will ensue [the

---

70 *vild* vile / 73 *forwardness* eagerness / 79 *tickle* (a) incite (b) put an end to

    1. The tension between the foreign merchants De Bard and Cavaler and the native Londoners sets the stage for dire events of act two. This opening scene also introduces key concepts that will be developed in the play such as justice, injustice, pride, patience, duty, obedience, order, law, freedom, the common good, revenge, revolt, courage, truth, and friendship.

    2. Spital sermons: Sermons preached on Easter Monday and Tuesday from a special pulpit at St. Mary's Spital outside of Bishopsgate, London *(OED)*.

    3. This emendation follows Gabrieli and Melchiori's reconstruction. Here and occasionally throughout, a portion of the manuscript is missing or damaged.

urging of]° our wrongs. You shall perceive there's no hurt in the bill;
here's a copy of it. I pray ye hear it.

All. With all our hearts, for God's sake, read it.

90 *Lincoln (reads).* "To you all the worshipful lords and masters of this city, that
will take compassion over the poor people your neighbours, and also
of the great importable hurts, losses and hindrances, whereof pro-
ceedeth extreme poverty to all the King's subjects, that inhabit within
this city and surburbs of the same. For so it is that aliens and strangers
95 eat the bread from the fatherless children, and take the living from all
the artificers, and the intercourse from all merchants, whereby poverty
is so much increased, that every man bewaileth the misery of other, for
craftsmen be brought to beggary, and merchants to neediness. Wherefore, the premises considered, the redress must be of the commons,°
100 knit and united to one part. And as the hurt and damage grieveth all
men, so must all men set to their willing power for remedy, and not
suffer the said aliens in their wealth, and the natural born men of this
region to come to confusion."

Doll. Before God, 'tis excellent, and I'll maintain the suit to be honest.

105 *Sherwin.* Well, say 'tis read, what is your further meaning in the matter?

George. What? Marry, list to me. No doubt but this will store us with
friends enow,° whose names we will closely keep in writing, and on
May Day next in the morning we'll go forth a Maying, but make it the
worst May Day[4] for the strangers that ever they saw. How say ye? Do
110 ye subscribe, or are ye faint-hearted revolters?

Doll. Hold thee, George Betts, there's my hand and my heart; by the Lord,
I'll make a captain among ye, and do somewhat to be talk of for ever
after.°

Williamson. My masters, ere we part, let's friendly go and drink together,
115 and swear true secrecy upon our lives.

George. There spake an angel; come, let us along then.

Exeunt.

---

87 This emendation follows Shirley's reconstruction. / 99 *commons* (a) community, people as a
whole (b) lower class people / 107 *enow* enough / 112–113 *somewhat to be talk of* something to be
talked of

4. May Day: the first of May. This particular May-Day would come to be known as Ill or Evil
May-Day, as is hinted later at 2.1.70.

Scene II. *The Court of Sessions in the City.*

An arras is drawn, and behind it (as in sessions) sit the Lord Mayor,
Justice Suresby, and other justices, Sheriff More and the other sheriff sitting
by; Smart is the plaintiff, Lifter the prisoner at the bar.

Mayor. Having dispatched our weightier businesses,
    We may give ear to petty felonies.
    Master Sheriff More, what is this fellow?
More. My lord, he stands indicted for a purse,
    He hath been tried, the jury is together.   5
Mayor. Who sent him in?
Suresby.   That did I, my lord.
    Had he had right, he had been hanged ere this,
    The only captain of the cutpurse crew.
Mayor. What is his name?
Suresby. As his profession is, Lifter, my lord,   10
    One that can lift a purse right cunningly.
Mayor. And is that he accuses him?
Suresby. The same, my lord, whom, by your honour's leave,
    I must say somewhat to,° because I find
    In some respects he is well worthy blame.   15
Mayor. Good Master Justice Suresby, speak your mind.
    We are well pleased to give you audience.
Suresby. Hear me, Smart. Thou art a foolish fellow;
    If Lifter be convicted by the law,
    As I see not how the jury can acquit him,
    I'll stand to't thou art guilty of his death.   20
More. My lord, that's worth the hearing.
Mayor. Listen then, good Master More.
Suresby. I tell thee plain, it is a shame for thee
    With such a sum to tempt necessity.   25
    No less than ten pounds, sir, will serve your turn
    To carry in your purse about with ye,
    To crack and brag in taverns of your money.
    I promise ye, a man that goes abroad
    With an intent of truth,° meeting such a booty   30

---

14 *say somewhat to* say something about / 30 *an intent of truth* honest intentions

May be provoked to that he never meant.
What makes so many pilferers and felons
But such fond baits that foolish people lay
To tempt the needy miserable wretch?
35   Ten pounds odd° money, this is a pretty sum
To bear about, which were more safe at home.

Lord Mayor and More whisper.

'Fore God, 'twere well to fine ye as much more
To the relief of the poor prisoners,
To teach ye be [more mindful of]° your own.
40   *More.* Good my lord, soothe a [little jest]° for once,
Only to try conclusions in this case.
Mayor. Content, good Master More. We'll rise awhile
And till the jury can return their verdict
Walk in the garden. How say ye justices?
45   *All.* We like it well, my lord; we'll follow ye.

Exeunt Lord Mayor and justices.

More. Nay, Plaintiff, go you too: *Exit Smart.*
                    and, officers,
Stand you aside, and leave the prisoner
To me awhile. Lifter, come hither.
Lifter. What is your worship's pleasure?
50   *More.* Sirrah,° you know that you are known to me
And I have often saved ye from this place
Since first I came in office. Thou seest beside
That Justice Suresby is thy heavy friend,
For all the blame that he pretends to Smart
55   For tempting thee with such a sum of money.
I tell thee what; devise me but a means
To pick or cut his purse, and on my credit
And as I am a Christian and a man
I will procure thy pardon for that jest.[5]

---

35 *odd* plus change / 39–40 Shirley's emendation / 50 *sirrah* address to an inferior

5. More's first action in the play displays one famous facet of his character: his love for merry and wise jesting, especially when it serves to correct human folly, something Lifter grasps later in the scene. As Holinshed remarks, "This man was both learned and wise, and given much to a

Lifter. Good Master Shrieve,° seek not my overthrow.   60
　　　You know, sir, I have many heavy friends
　　　And more indictments like to come upon me.
　　　You are too deep° for me to deal withal;
　　　You are known to be one of the wisest men
　　　That is in England. I pray ye, Master Sheriff,   65
　　　Go not about to undermine my life.
More. Lifter, I am true subject to my King.
　　　Thou much mistak'st me, and for thou shalt not think
　　　I mean by this to hurt thy life at all,
　　　I will maintain° the act when thou hast done it.   70
　　　Thou knowst there are such matters in my hands
　　　As, if I pleased to give them to the jury,
　　　I should not need this way to circumvent° thee.
　　　All that I aim at is a merry jest:
　　　Perform it, Lifter, and expect my best.   75
Lifter. I thank your worship; God preserve your life.
　　　But Master Justice Suresby is gone in,
　　　I know not how to come near where he is.
More. Let me alone for that; I'll be thy setter.°
　　　I'll send him hither to thee presently   80
　　　Under the colour of thine own request
　　　Of private matters to acquaint him with.
Lifter. If ye do so, sir, then let me alone.
　　　Forty to one but then his purse is gone.
More. Well said, but see that thou diminish not   85
　　　One penny of the money, but give it me.
　　　It is the cunning act that credits thee.
Lifter. I will, good Master Sheriff; I assure ye.   *Exit More.*
　　　I see the purpose of this gentleman
　　　Is but to check the folly of the Justice   90
　　　For blaming others in a desperate case

60 *Shrieve* Sheriff / 63 *deep* profound in learning / 70 *maintain* uphold / 73 *circumvent* entrap /
79 *setter* decoy for a swindler

---

certain pleasure in merry taunts and jesting in most of his communication, which manner he forgot not at the very hour of his death" (p. 793). More also loved the pun lurking in his own last
name, Morus, which means "fool" in Greek.

Wherein himself may fall as soon as any.
To save my life it is a good adventure.°
Silence there, ho! Now doth the Justice enter.

Enter Justice Suresby.

95 *Suresby.* Now, sirrah, now what is your will with me?
 Wilt thou discharge thy conscience[6] like an honest man?
 What sayst to me, sirrah? Be brief, be brief.
Lifter. As brief, sir, as I can. *(Aside)* If ye stand fair, I will be brief anon.
Suresby. Speak out and mumble not. What sayst thou, sirrah?
100 *Lifter.* Sir, I am charged, as God shall be my comfort,
 With more than's true—
Suresby. Sir, sir, ye are indeed, "with more than's true,"
 For you are flatly charged with felony.
 You're charged with more than truth, and that is theft,
105 More than a true man should be charged withal.
 Thou art a varlet;° that's no more than true.
 Trifle not with me; do not, do not, sirrah;
 Confess but what thou knowest. I ask no more.
Lifter. There be, sir, there be, if't shall please your worship-
110 *Suresby.* There be, varlet? What be there? Tell me what there be.
 Come off or on; there be, what be there, knave?
Lifter. There be, sir, divers very cunning fellows
 That while you stand and look them in the face
 Will have your purse.
Suresby.   Th'art an honest knave.
115 Tell me what are they? Where they may be caught?
 Aye, those are they I look for.
Lifter. You talk of me, sir.-
 Alas, I am a puny.° There's one indeed,
 Goes by my name; he puts down all for purses
120 [   ]
 [   ]

---

93 *adventure* venture / 106 *varlet* rogue / 118 *puny* unimportant person

  6. The first mention of this important concept in the play. See also 4.1.74, 4.4.152, 5.1.62 and
5.3.11.

Suresby. Be as familiar as thou wilt, my knave.
    'Tis this I long to know.
Lifter (aside). And you shall have your longing ere ye go.
    This fellow, sir, perhaps will meet ye thus,   125
    Or thus, or thus, and in kind compliment

                He embraces Suresby and cuts his purse.

    Pretend acquaintance, somewhat doubtfully,
    And these embraces serve—
Suresby (shrugging gladly).   Aye, marry, Lifter,
    Wherefore serve they?
Lifter.   Only to feel
    Whether you go full under sail or no,   130
    Or that your lading be aboard your bark.°
Suresby. In plainer English, Lifter, if my purse
    Be stored° or no?
Lifter.   Ye have it, sir.
Suresby. Excellent, excellent.
Lifter. Then, sir, you cannot but for manners' sake   135
    Walk on with him, for he will walk your way,
    Alleging either you have much forgot him,
    Or he mistakes you.
Suresby. But in this time has he my purse or no?
Lifter. Not yet, sir, fie!

                Enter Lord Mayor, etc.

               No, nor I have not yours.   140
    But now we must forbear; my lords return.
Suresby. A murrain° on't! Lifter, we'll more anon.
    Aye, thou sayst true; there are shrewd knaves indeed.

                He sits down.

    But let them gull me, widgeon me, rook me, fop° me,
    I'faith, i'faith, they are too short for me.   145

---

131 *lading be aboard your bark* freight be on your vessel / 133 *stored* full / 142 *murrain* plague /
144 *gull, widgeon, rook, fop* defraud

Knaves and fools meet when purses go;
Wise men look to their purses well enow.

More. Lifter, is it done?

Lifter. Done, Master Shrieve, and there it is.

150 *More* Then build upon my word, I'll save thy life.

Recorder. Lifter, stand to the bar. The jury have returned thee guilty; thou
must die. According to the custom, look to it, Master Shrieve.

Mayor. Then gentlemen, as you are wont to do,
Because as yet we have no burial place,

155 What charity your meaning's to bestow
Toward burial of the prisoners now condemned,
Let it be given. There is first for me.

Recorder. And there's for me.

Another.   And me.

Suresby. Body of me, my purse is gone.

160 *More.* Gone, sir? What, here? How can that be?

Mayor. Against all reason, sitting on the bench?

Suresby. Lifter, I talked with you, you have not lifted me, ha?

Lifter. Suspect ye me, sir? Oh, what a world is this!

More. But hear ye, Master Suresby, are ye sure

165 Ye had a purse about ye?

Suresby. Sure, Master Shrieve? As sure as you are there,
And in it seven pounds odd money on my faith.

More. Seven pounds odd money? What, were you so mad,
Being a wise man and a magistrate,

170 To trust your purse with such a liberal sum?
Seven pounds odd money?! 'Fore God it is a shame
With such a sum to tempt necessity.
I promise ye, a man that goes abroad
With an intent of truth, meeting such a booty,

175 May be provoked to that he never thought.
What makes so many pilferers and felons,
But these fond baits that foolish people lay
To tempt the needy miserable wretch?
Should he be taken now that has your purse,

180 I'd stand to't, you are guilty of his death,
For questionless he would be cast by law.
'Twere a good deed to fine ye as much more

To the relief of the poor prisoners,

To teach ye lock your money up at home.

Suresby. Well, Master More, you are a merry man.   185

I find° ye, sir, I find ye well enough.

More. Nay, ye shall see, sir, trusting thus your money,

And Lifter here in trial for like case,

But that the poor man is a prisoner

It would be now suspected that he had it.   190

Thus may ye see what mischief often comes

By the fond carriage of such needless sums.

Mayor. Believe me, Master Suresby, this is strange.

You, being a man so settled in assurance,°

Will fall in that which you condemned in other.   195

More. Well, Master Suresby, there's your purse again,

And all your money; fear nothing of More:

Wisdom still [doth bid ye watch]° the door.   *Exeunt.*

Scene III. *At Court.*

Enter the Earls of Shrewsbury and Surrey, Sir Thomas Palmer
and Sir Roger Cholmley.

Shrewsbury. My Lord of Surrey, and Sir Thomas Palmer,

Might I with patience tempt your grave advice?

I tell ye true, that in these dangerous times

I do not like this frowning vulgar brow.

My searching eye did never entertain   5

A more distracted° countenance of grief

Than I have late observed

In the displeasèd commons of the city.

Surrey. 'Tis strange that from his princely clemency,

So well a tempered mercy and a grace   10

To all the aliens in this fruitful land,

That this high crested° insolence should spring

From them that breathe from his majestic bounty,

---

186 *find* understand / 194 *settled in assurance* self-assured / 198 Shirley's emendation / 6 *distract-ed* troubled in mind / 12 *high crested* proud

That, fattened with the traffic° of our country,
15 Already leap into his subjects' face.
Palmer. Yet Sherwin hindered to commence his suit
Against de Bard, by the Ambassador
By supplication made unto the King,
Who having first enticed away his wife
20 And got his plate, near worth four hundred pound,
To grieve some wronged citizens that found
This vile disgrace oft cast into their teeth,
Of late sues Sherwin, and arrested him
For money for the boarding of his wife.
25 *Surrey.* The more knave Bard, that, using Sherwin's goods,
Doth ask him interest for the occupation.°
I like not that, my Lord of Shrewsbury.
He's ill bestead° that lends a well paced horse
Unto a man that will not find him meat.
30 *Cholmley.* My Lord of Surrey will be pleasant still.
Palmer. I being then employed by your honours
To stay the broil° that fell about the same,
Where by persuasion I enforced the wrongs
And urged the grief of the displeasèd city,
35 He answered me, and with a solemn oath,
That, if he had the Mayor of London's wife,
He would keep her in despite of any Englishman.
Surrey. 'Tis good, Sir Thomas, then for you and me
Your wife is dead and I a bachelor.
40 If no man can possess his wife alone,
I am glad, Sir Thomas Palmer, I have none.
Cholmley. If 'a take my wife, 'a shall find her meat.
Surrey. And reason good, Sir Roger Cholmley, too.
If these hot Frenchmen needsly° will have sport,
45 They should in kindness yet defray the charge.
'Tis hard when men possess our wives in quiet
And yet leave us in to discharge their diet.°

---

14 *fattened with the traffic* enriched by the commerce / 26 *ask him interest for the occupation* demands money while getting the use of his wife / 28 *ill bestead* in a bad way / 32 *broil* quarrel / 44 *needsly* necessarily / 47 *discharge their diet* pay their room and board

Shrewsbury. My lord, our caters° shall not use the market
  For our provision, but some stranger now
  Will take the victuals from him he hath bought.   50
  A carpenter, as I was late informed,
  Who, having bought a pair of doves in Cheap,
  Immediately a Frenchman took them from him
  And beat the poor man for resisting him,
  And when the fellow did complain his wrongs,   55
  He was severely punished for his labour.
Surrey. But if the English blood be once but up,
  As I perceive their hearts already full,
  I fear me much, before their spleens be cold,
  Some of these saucy aliens for their pride   60
  Will pay for't soundly, wheresoe'er it lights.
  This tide of rage, that with the eddy strives,
  I fear me much will drown too many lives.
Cholmley. Now afore God, your honours, pardon me.
  Men of your place and greatness are to blame,   65
  I tell ye true, my lords, in that his Majesty
  Is not informal° of this base abuse,°
  And daily wrongs are offered to his subjects.
  For, if he were, I know his gracious wisdom
  Would soon redress it.   70

Enter a messenger.

Shrewsbury. Sirrah, what news?
Cholmley.   None good I fear.
Messenger. My lord, ill news, and worse I fear will follow
  If speedily it be not looked unto.
  The city is in an uproar and the Mayor
  Is threatened if he come out of his house.   75
  A number of poor artificers° [are out
  Inflamed to kill the hated aliens.
  'Twas to be]° feared what this would come unto.
  This follows on the doctor's publishing

---

48 *caters* servants in charge of ordering supplies for a household / 67 *informal* informed /
67 *abuse* deception / 76 *artificers* craftsmen / 76–78 Shirley's emendation

80   The bill of wrongs in public at the Spital.
Shrewsbury. That Doctor Beale may chance beshrew° himself
      For reading of the bill.
Palmer. Let us go gather forces to the Mayor
85   For quick suppressing this rebellious rout.
Surrey. Now I bethink myself of Master More,
      One of the sheriffs, a wise and learned gentleman,
      And in especial favour with the people.
      He, backed with other grave and sober men,
90   May by his gentle and persuasive speech
      Perhaps prevail more than we can with power.[7]
Shrewsbury. Believe me but your honour well advises.
      Let us make haste, or I do greatly fear
      Some to their graves this morning's work will bear.
                                        Exeunt.

Act II

Scene I. *St. Martin's Lane.*

*Enter Lincoln, George and Clown Bettses, Williamson, Sherwin and
other armed, Doll in a shirt of mail, a headpiece, sword
and buckler, a crew attending.*

Clown. Come come; we'll tickle their turnips; we'll butter their boxes.°
      Shall strangers rule the roost? Yes, but we'll baste the roast. Come,
      come; a flaunt, a flaunt.°
George. Brother, give place and hear John Lincoln speak.
5   *Clown.* Aye, Lincoln my leader,
      And Doll my true breeder,

---

81 *beshrew* blame / 1–2 *tickle their turnips . . . butter their boxes* beat them up / 3 *a flaunt* let us assume an arrogant, flaunting demeanor

7. As a humanist, More trained himself carefully in the arts of rhetoric and diplomacy. In his letter on More, Erasmus remarks: "It would be difficult to find a more felicitous extempore speaker, so fertile are both his mind and the tongue that does its bidding" (see p.12, *TMSB*). Erasmus also relates elsewhere that More claimed to "owe to his literary studies . . . the services the he can now render to his country, . . . his increased adaptability to court society, to life among the nobility, and to [his] whole way of life" (p. 223, *TMSB*). For a fuller account of More's rhetorical prowess, see William Nelson, "Thomas More, Grammarian and Orator." *PMLA* 58 (1943): 337–52.

        With the rest of our crew
        Shall ran tan tarra ran,
        Do all they what they can.
        Shall we be bobbed, braved?° No.   10
        Shall we be held under? No.
        We are free born
        And do take scorn
        To be used so!

Doll. Peace there, I say! Hear Captain Lincoln speak!   15
        Keep silence till we know his mind at large.

Clown. Then largely deliver! Speak bully,° and he that presumes to inter-
        rupt thee in thy oration, this for him!

Lincoln. Then, gallant bloods, you whose free souls do scorn
        To bear th'enforcèd wrongs of aliens,   20
        Add rage to resolution, fire the houses
        Of these audacious strangers. This is St Martin's,
        And yonder dwells Meautis, a wealthy Picard,
        At the Green Gate,
        De Bard, Peter van Hollock, Adrian Martin,   25
        With many more outlandish fugitives.[8]
        Shall these enjoy more privilege than we
        In our own country? Let's then become their slaves!
        Since justice keeps not them in greater awe,
        We'll be ourselves rough ministers at law.°   30

Clown. Use no more swords,
        Nor no more words,
        But fire the houses!
        Brave Captain Courageous,
        Fire me their houses!   35

Doll. Aye, for we may as well make bonfires on May-day as at midsummer;
        we'll alter the day in the calendar, and set it down in flaming letters.

Sherwin. Stay! That would much endanger the whole city whereto I
        would not the least prejudice.

---

10 *bobbed, braved* beaten, menaced / 17 *bully* comrade, mate / 30 *rough ministers at law* makeshift law enforcers; vigilantes

8. Gabrieli and Melchiori point out here that "many foreigners had taken refuge in London from religious or political persecution in their own countries, but Lincoln, in line with contemporary hostile pamphlets . . . stresses their condition as outlaws" (86).

40 *Doll.* No, nor I neither! So may mine own house be burned for company!
    I'll tell ye what: we'll drag the strangers out into Moorfields, and there
    bombast° them till they stink again.
Clown. And that's soon done, for they smell for fear already.
George. Let some of us enter the strangers' houses,
45   And if we find them there, then bring them forth.
Doll. But if ye bring them forth ere ye find them, I'll never allow of that.
Clown. Now, Mars, for thy honour,
    Dutch or French,
    So it be a wench,
50   I'll upon her.

> *Exeunt Clown, Sherwin, and others.*

Williamson. Now lads, how shall we labour in our safety?
    I hear the Mayor hath gathered men in arms
    And that Shrieve More an hour ago received
    Some of the Privy Council in at Ludgate.
55   Force now must make our peace or else we fall:
    'Twill soon be known we are the principal.°
Doll. And what of that? If thou beest afraid, husband, go home again and
    hide thy head, for by the Lord I'll have a little sport now I am at it.
George. Let's stand upon our guard, and if they come
60   Receive them as they were our enemies.

> *Enter Sherwin and the rest.*

Clown. A purchase, a purchase!° We have found, we ha' found—
Doll. What?
Clown. Nothing, not a French Fleming nor a Fleming French to be found,
    but all fled, in plain English.
65 *Lincoln.* How now, have you found any?
Sherwin. No, not one; they're all fled.
Lincoln. Then fire the houses, that the Mayor being busy
    About the quenching of them, we may 'scape.
    Burn down their kennels;° let us, straight away,
70   Lest this day prove to us an ill May-day.

---

43 *bombast* thrash / 56 *principal* chief perpetrators / 61 *purchase* acquisition / 69 *kennels* contemptuous term for dwelling places

Clown. Fire, fire! I'll be the first.
          If hanging come, 'tis welcome; that's the worst!

                                                            Exeunt.

                    Scene II. *The Guildhall*
                Enter Sheriff More and the Lord Mayor.

More. The captains of this insurrection
          Have ta'en themselves to arms, and came but now
          To both the Counters,° where they have released
          Sundry indebted prisoners, and from thence
          I hear that they are gone into St Martin's,   5
          Where they intend to offer violence
          To the amazed Lombards. Therefore, my lord,
          If we expect the safety of the city,
          'Tis time that force or parley do encounter
          With these displeasèd° men.

                    Enter a messenger.

Mayor.   How now, what news?   10
Messenger. My lord, the rebels have broke open Newgate,
          From whence they have delivered many prisoners,
          Both felons and notorious murderers,
          That desperately cleave to their lawless train.
Mayor. Up with the drawbridge; gather some forces   15
          To Cornhill and Cheapside. And, gentlemen,
          If diligence be used on every side,
          A quiet ebb will follow this rough tide.

                Enter Shrewsbury, Surrey, Palmer, Cholmley.

Shrewsbury. Lord Mayor, his Majesty, receiving notice
          Of this most dangerous insurrection,   20
          Hath sent my Lord of Surrey and myself,
          Sir Thomas Palmer and our followers
          To add unto your forces our best means

3 *Counters* prisons in London / 10 *displeasèd* angry

                For pacifying of this mutiny.
25   In God's name, then, set on with happy speed.°
                The King laments if one true subject bleed.[9]
    Surrey. I hear they mean to fire the Lombards' houses.
                O power, what art thou in a madman's eyes?
                Thou mak'st the plodding idiot° bloody wise.
30   *More.* My lords, I doubt not but we shall appease
                With a calm breath this flux° of discontent.
    Palmer. To call them to a parley questionless
                May fall out good. 'Tis well said, Master More.
    More. Let's to these simple men, for many sweat
35   Under this act that knows not the law's debt
                Which hangs upon their lives. For silly° men
                Plod° on they know not how, like a fool's pen
                That ending shows not any sentence writ,
                Linked but to common reason or slightest wit.
40   These follow for no harm,° but yet incur
                Self penalty° with those that raised this stir.
                A God's name on, to calm our private° foes
                With breath of gravity, not dangerous blows.

                                                Exeunt.

Scene III. *A London Street*[10]

Enter (at one end) Lincoln, Doll, Clown, George Betts, Sherwin,
Williamson and others; and at the other end a sergeant-at-arms, followed
by More, the other sheriff, Palmer, and Cholmley.

Lincoln. Peace, hear me! He that will not see a red herring at a Harry
    groat,° butter at elevenpence a pound, meal at nine shillings a bushel,
    and beef at four nobles° a stone, list to me.

---

25 *happy speed* good fortune / 29 *plodding idiot* mediocre incompetent / 31 *flux* flow / 36 *silly* (a) unthinking, ignorant (b) deserving of pity / 37 *plod* forge ahead thoughtlessly / 40 *follow for no harm* go along without malicious intent / 41 *Self penalty* harm to themselves / 42 *private* undistinguished / 2 *Harry Groat* a type of coin minted by Henry VIII / 3 *nobles* English gold coins

   9. Notably the King never figures directly into the action of this play, though the decision of the playwrights is perhaps understandable when one considers that they were writing during the end of his daughter Elizabeth's reign.
   10. Most critics agree that the following scene was written by Shakespeare; moreover, the

George. It will come to that pass, if strangers be suffered. Mark him!

Lincoln. Our country is a great eating country; *argo*,[11] they eat more in our   5
  country than they do in their own.

Clown. By a halfpenny loaf a day, troy weight.

Lincoln. They bring in strange° roots, which is merely to the undoing of
  our poor prentices,° for what's a sorry° parsnip to a good heart?

Williamson. Trash, trash! They breed sore eyes, and 'tis enough to infect the   10
  city with the palsy.

Lincoln. Nay, it has infected it with the palsy, for these bastards of dung—as
  you know they grow in dung—have infected us, and it is our infection
  will make the city shake, which partly comes through the eating of
  parsnips.   15

Clown. True, and pumpions° together.

Sergeant. What say you to the mercy of the King?
      Do you refuse it?

Lincoln. You would have us upon th' hip,° would you?
      No, marry, do we not. We accept of the King's mercy,   20
      but we will show no mercy upon the strangers.

Sergeant. You are the simplest° things
      That ever stood° in such a question.

Lincoln. How say you now? Prentices "simple"? Down with him!

All. Prentices simple! Prentices simple!   25

  Enter the Lord Mayor, the Earl of Surrey, and the Earl of Shrewsbury

Sheriff. Hold in the King's name! Hold!

Surrey. Friends, masters, countrymen—

Mayor. Peace ho, peace! I charge you, keep the peace!

Shrewsbury. My masters, countrymen—

---

8 *strange* foreign / 9 *prentices* apprentices / 9 *sorry* worthless / 16 *pumpions* pumpkins / 19 *upon th' hip* at a disadvantage / 22 *simplest* most foolish / 23 *stood* remained steadfast

---

manuscript of this scene appears to be in Shakespeare's own hand. The connection between More and Shakespeare is an intriguing one, particularly if one compares their visions of effective—or tragic—leadership. More served as a major literary source for Shakespeare's *Richard the Third*, and More figures indirectly yet curiously in Shakespeare's final play, *Henry VIII*.

  11. Lincoln's mangling of the Latin *ergo* (therefore) suggests that the rioters' reasoning might be less compelling logically than they believe; it also prepares for the contrast between the rioters' passionate but muddy thought and More's calm and clearer reason.

30   *Sherwin.* The noble Earl of Shrewsbury, let's hear him.
       Betts. We'll hear the Earl of Surrey.
       Lincoln. The Earl of Shrewsbury.
       Betts. We'll hear both.
       All. Both, both, both, both!
35   *Lincoln.* Peace, I say peace! Are you men of wisdom, or what are you?
       Surrey. What you will have them, but not men of wisdom.
       Some. We'll not hear my Lord of Surrey.
       Others. No, no, no, no, no! Shrewsbury, Shrewsbury!
       More. Whiles they are o'er the bank of their obedience,
40   Thus will they bear down all things.
       Lincoln. Shrieve° More speaks. Shall we hear Shrieve More speak?
       Doll. Let's hear him. 'A keeps a plentiful shrievaltry,° and 'a made my
            brother Arthur Watchins Sergeant Safe's yeoman.
       All. Shrieve More, More, More, Shrieve More![12]
45   *More.* Even by the rule you have among yourselves,
            Command still audience.
       Some. Surrey, Surrey!
       Others. More, More!
       Lincoln and Betts. Peace! Peace! Silence! Peace!
50   *More.* You that have voice and credit with the number,
            Command them to a stillness.
       Lincoln. A plague on them! They will not hold their peace.
            The devil cannot rule them.
       More. Then what a rough and riotous charge have you,
55   To lead those that the devil cannot rule.
            Good masters, hear me speak.
       Doll. Aye, by th' Mass, will we. More, thou'rt a good housekeeper, and I
            thank thy good worship for my brother Arthur Watchins.
       All. Peace, peace!
60   *More.* Look! What you do offend you cry upon,
            That is the peace.[13] Not one of you here present

---

41 *Shrieve* Sheriff / 42 *shievaltry* generous table

   12. The crowd is willing to give More a hearing, in part, as Doll indicates, because of his reputation as one who gives food and jobs to the poor.
   13. More keeps the rioters' attention by discussing the topic they are crying out for: peace. He ends this first speech with a question, a notable contrast to the way the previous leaders spoke to the mob. The pursuit of peace was a constant concern throughout More's adult life. Cf. More's

Had there such fellows lived when you were babes
That could have topped° the peace as now you would,
The peace wherein you have till now grown up
Had been ta'en from you, and the bloody times   65
Could not have brought you to the state of men.
Alas, poor things, what is it you have got,°
Although we grant you get the thing you seek?

Betts. Marry, the removing of the strangers,° which cannot choose but
much advantage the poor handicrafts° of the city.   70

More. Grant them removed, and grant that this your noise
Hath chid down all the majesty of England.
Imagine that you see the wretched strangers,
Their babies at their backs, with their poor luggage
Plodding to th' ports and coasts for transportation,   75
And that you sit as kings in your desires,
Authority quite silenced by your brawl
And you in ruff° of your opinions clothed:
What had you got? I'll tell you. You had taught
How insolence and strong hand should prevail,   80
How order should be quelled—and by this pattern
Not one of you should live an aged man,
For other ruffians as their fancies wrought—
With selfsame hand, self reasons, and self right—
Would shark° on you, and men like ravenous fishes   85
Would feed on one another.

Doll. Before God, that's as true as the Gospel.

Betts. Nay, this' a sound fellow, I tell you. Let's mark him.

More. Let me set up before your thoughts, good friends,
One supposition, which if you will mark   90
You shall perceive how horrible a shape
Your innovation° bears. First, 'tis a sin

---

63 *topped* beheaded; therefore, killed or destroyed / 67 *what is it you have got* what have you gained
/ 69 *strangers* foreigners / 70 *handicrafts* makers of handicrafts / 78 *ruff* vainglory / 85 *shark* prey
/ 92 *innovation* rebellion

---

epitaph, on which he makes special mention of his work for international peace between "the
supreme monarchs of Christendom and the restoration of a long-desired peace to the world" (see
TMSB, p. 307).

Which oft th'apostle did forewarn us of,
Urging obedience to authority;

95   And 'twere no error if I told you all
You were in arms 'gainst God.

All. Marry, God forbid that!

More. Nay, certainly you are.[14]

For, to the King, God hath his office lent

100   Of dread,° of justice, power and command,
Hath bid him rule and willed you to obey;
And to add ampler majesty to this,
He hath not only lent the King his figure,
His throne and sword, but given him his own name,

105   Calls him a god on earth.[15] What do you then,
Rising 'gainst him that God himself installs,
But rise 'gainst God? What do you to your souls
In doing this? Oh, desperate as you are,
Wash your foul minds with tears, and those same hands

110   That you like rebels lift against the peace
Lift up for peace; and your unreverent knees,
Make them your feet. To kneel to be forgiven
Is safer wars than ever you can make,
Whose discipline is riot.

115   In, in, to your obedience! Why, even your hurly°
Cannot proceed but by obedience.
Tell me but this: What rebel captain,
As mut'nies are incident,° by his name
Can still the rout? Who will obey a traitor?

120   Or how can well that proclamation sound,

---

100 *dread* respect, reverence / 115 *hurly* commotion, tumult / 118 *incident* likely to occur

14. In this speech, More provides three logical arguments against the rioters' actions and, by the time he is finished, the mob has been persuaded to stop their rioting.

15. The play seems to represent More as holding a view of kings contrary to the view given in More's works, especially in the poems on government. See epigrams 32, 121, 198, 201, and 206 in *CW* 3.2 and on page 235–239, *TMSB*. Of course, More's conscience will put him at odds with the King later in the play. Cf. Shakespeare's *Pericles*: "The blind mole casts / Copp'd hills towards heaven, to tell the earth is throng'd / By man's oppression, and the poor worm doth die for it. / Kings are earth's gods; in vice their law's their will; /And if Jove stray, who dares say Jove doth ill?" (1.1.99–104).

When there is no addition° but 'a rebel'
To qualify° a rebel? You'll put down strangers,
Kill them, cut their throats, possess their houses,
And lead the majesty of law in lyam°
To slip° him like a hound—alas, alas!   125
Say now the King,
As he is clement° if th'offender mourn,
Should so much come too short of your great trespass°
As but to banish you: whither would you go?
What country, by the nature of your error,   130
Should give you harbor? Go you to France or Flanders,
To any German province, Spain or Portugal,
Nay, anywhere that not adheres to England—
Why, you must needs be strangers. Would you be pleased
To find a nation of such barbarous temper   135
That breaking out in hideous violence
Would not afford you an abode on earth,
Whet their detested knives against your throats,
Spurn you like dogs, and like as if that° God
Owed° not nor made not you, nor that the elements   140
Were not all appropriate to your comforts,
But chartered unto° them, what would you think
To be thus used? This is the strangers' case,
And this your mountainish inhumanity.
    All. Faith, 'a says true. Let's do as we may be° done by.[16]   145
Lincoln. We'll be ruled by you, Master More,
    if you'll stand our friend° to procure our pardon.
More. Submit you to these noble gentlemen,
    Entreat their mediation to the King,
    Give up yourself to form, obey the magistrate,   150

---

121 *addition* identifying mark of one's occupation or rank / 122 *qualify* give recognized status to /
124 *lyam* a leash for hounds / 125 *slip* release a hunting animal from a leash / 127 *clement* merciful
/ 128 *come too short of your great trespass* give a punishment so much less than the crime merits /
139 *like as if that* act as though / 140 *owed* owned / 142 *chartered unto* reserved to / 145 *as we may be* as we would be / 147 *stand our friend* stand by us

   16. The rioters respond to More's words with a version of the Golden Rule. Cf. Matthew
7:12.

> And there's no doubt but mercy may be found,
> If you so seek it.
> *All.* We yield, and desire his Highness' mercy.
>
> > > > *They lay by their weapons.*
>
> *More.* No doubt his Majesty will grant it you.
155 But you must yield to go to several prisons,
> Till that his Highness' will be further known.
> *All.* Most willingly, whither you will have us.
> *Shrewsbury.* Lord Mayor, let them be sent to several prisons,
> And there in any case be well entreated.°
160 My Lord of Surrey, please you to take horse
> And ride to Cheapside, where the aldermen
> Are with their several companies in arms.
> Will them to go unto their several wards,°
> Both for the stay° of further mutiny,
165 And for the apprehending of such persons
> As shall contend.
>
> *Surrey.*   I go, my noble lord.   *Exit.*
> *Shrewsbury.* We'll straight go tell his Highness these good news.
> Withall,° Shrieve More, I'll tell him how your breath
> Hath ransomed many a subject from sad death.
>
> > > > *Exeunt Shrewsbury and Cholmley.*
>
170 *Mayor.* Lincoln and Sherwin, you shall both to Newgate, the rest unto the
> Counters.
> *Palmer.* Go, guard them hence. A little breath well spent
> Cheats expectation in his fairest event.
> *Doll.* Well, Sheriff More, thou hast done more with thy good words than
175 all they could with their weapons. Give me thy hand, keep thy promise
> now for the King's pardon, or by the Lord I'll call thee a plain cony-
> catcher.°
> *Lincoln.* Farewell, Shrieve More, and as we yield by thee,
> So make our peace; then thou dealst honestly.
180 *Clown.* Aye, and save us from the gallows, else 'a deals double honestly.°
>
> > > > *They are led away.*
>
> *Mayor.* Master Shrieve More, you have preserved the city

---

159 *entreated* treated / 163 *wards* guards / 164 *stay* prevention / 168 *withall* moreover /
176–77 *cony-catcher* cheat / 180 *double honestly* not honestly at all, as in double-dealing

From a most dangerous fierce commotion,
For if this limb of riot here in St Martin's
Had joined with other branches of the city
That did begin to kindle, 'twould have bred   185
Great rage, that rage much murder would have fed.
Palmer. Not steel but eloquence hath wrought this good.
You have redeemed us from much threatened blood.
More. My lord and brethren, what I here have spoke,
My country's love, and next the city's care,   190
Enjoined° me to, which since it thus prevails
Think God hath made weak More his instrument
To thwart sedition's violent intent.[17]
I think 'twere best, my lord, some two hours hence
We meet at the Guildhall, and there determine   195
That thorough every ward the watch be clad
In armour, but especially provide
That at the city gates, selected men,
Substantial citizens, do ward tonight,
For fear of further mischief.[18]
Mayor.   It shall be so.   200

Enter Shrewsbury

But yond methink's my Lord of Shrewsbury.
Shrewsbury. My lord, his Majesty sends loving thanks
To you, your brethren, and his faithful subjects,
Your careful° citizens. But Master More, to you
A rougher, yet as kind a salutation: 205
Your name is yet too short; nay, you must kneel.
A knight's creation is this knightly steel.
Rise up, *Sir* Thomas More.
More. I thank his Highness for thus honouring me.
Shrewsbury. This is but first taste of his princely favour,   210

---

191 *enjoined* compelled / 204 *careful* solicitous

17. More's sense of his own actions is paradoxical in quelling the riot; he has acted skillfully out of "care" and "love" for the common good, but he also attributes the success at thwarting sedition to God and characterizes himself as a "weak instrument" of heaven.
    18. Cf. Paul's Letter to the Romans, chapter 13.

        For it hath pleased his high Majesty,

        Noting your wisdom and deserving merit,

        To put this staff of honour in your hand,

        For he hath chose you of his Privy Council.[19]

215 *More.* My lord, for to deny my Sovereign's bounty

        Were to drop precious stones into the heaps

        Whence first they came, from whence they'd ne'er return;

        To urge my imperfections in excuse,

        Were all as stale as custom. No, my lord,

220   My service is my King's, good reason why,

        Since life or death hangs on our Sovereign's eye.

  Mayor. His Majesty hath honoured much the city

        In this his princely choice.

  More. My lord and brethren,

225   Though I depart for [Court]° my love shall rest

        [True to the home wherewith my youth was blessed.]°

        I now must sleep in Court; sound sleeps forbear:

        The chamberlain to state is public care.

        Yet in this rising of my private blood,°

230   My studious thoughts shall tend the city's good.[20]

                Enter Crofts.

  Shrewsbury. How now, Crofts? What news?

  Crofts. My lord, his Highness sends express command

        That a record be entered of this riot,

        And that the chief and capital offenders

235   Be thereon straight arraigned,° for himself intends

        To sit in person on the rest tomorrow

        At Westminster.[21]

  Shrewsbury.   Lord Mayor, you hear your charge.

226–227 Shirley's emendation / 229 *private blood* common origins / 236 *arraigned* tried

    19. The play here compresses events that in fact took place at different times—the quieting of the riot, the knighting of More, and the appointment to the Privy Council—for the sake of dramatic economy. The naming of More as Lord Chancellor follows with similar dramatic swiftness at 2.4.147.

    20. More's acceptance of court life despite its perils and his commitment to putting "studious thoughts" at the service of the realm are characteristic. Cf. *Utopia,* book one, *passim*, where the fictional More and the traveler Raphael Hythloday debate whether a person with philosophical gifts should enter the service of a prince or not.

    21. The fate of the prisoners is recounted by Holinshed, who relates that some 13 of the lead-

Come, good Sir Thomas More, to Court let's hie:°
You are th'appeaser of this mutiny.
More. My lord, farewell, new days begets new tides,   240
     Life whirls 'bout fate, then to a grave it slides.

                                                 Exeunt severally.

Scene IV. *Cheapside.*

Enter Sheriff and meet a messenger.

Sheriff. Messenger, what news?
Messenger. Is execution yet performed?
Sheriff. Not yet, the carts stand ready at the stairs,
     And they shall presently away to Tyburn.
Messenger. Stay, Master Shrieve, it is the Council's pleasure,   5
     For more example in so bad a case,
     A gibbet° be erected in Cheapside,
     Hard by the Standard, whither you must bring
     Lincoln and those that were the chief with him
     To suffer death, and that immediately.   10

Enter Officers.

Sheriff. It shall be done, sir.   *Exit messenger.*
          Officers, be speedy.
     Call for a gibbet, see it be erected;
     Others make haste to Newgate, bid them bring
     The prisoners hither, for they here must die.

238 *hie* go   /   7 *gibbet* gallows

ers, including Lincoln, were executed, despite More's promise of mercy (line 154). In that earlier
passage, however, More suggests that "his Highness' will" ultimately decides the fate of the prisoners, who are ordered by the King in this scene to be "straight arraigned," which does not bode
well for the leaders of the insurrection. This scene may thus contain a subtle foreshadowing of later conflicts between the King's will and More. In any case, Doll complains of what she sees as
More's violated promise later at 2.4.92–94 and 2.4.101–104, before Surrey arrives with news of a
last moment pardon worked by More—a pardon that comes too late for the hastily executed Lincoln.

15   Away, I say, and see no time be slacked.

Officers. We go, sir.   *Exeunt some severally; others set up the gibbet.*

Sheriff. That's well said, fellows; now you do your duty.

        God, for his pity, help these troublous° times.

        The street's stopped up with gazing multitudes;

20   Command our armèd officers with halberds°

        Make way for entrance of the prisoners.

        Let proclamation once again be made

        That every householder, on pain of death,

        Keep in his prentices,° and every man

25   Stand with a weapon ready at his door,

        As he will answer to the contrary.

Officer. I'll see it done, sir.   *Exit.*

                    Enter another officer.

Sheriff. Bring them away to execution.

        The writ is come above two hours since;

30   The city will be fined for this neglect.

Officer. There's such a press and multitude at Newgate,

        They cannot bring the carts unto the stairs

        To take the prisoners in.

Sheriff.   Then let them come on foot.

        We may not dally time with great command.

35 *Officer.* Some of the Bench, sir, think it very fit

        That stay be made and give it out abroad

        The execution is deferred till morning,

        And when the streets shall be a little cleared,

        To chain them up, and suddenly dispatch it.

                The prisoners are brought in well guarded.

40 *Sheriff.* Stay, in meantime methinks they come along.

        See, they are coming, so, 'tis very well.

        Bring Lincoln there, the first unto the tree.°

Clown. Aye, for I cry lag,° sir.

18 *troublous* troubled / 20 *halberds* weapons similar to battle-axes / 24 *prentices* apprentices /
42 *tree* gallows / 43 *cry lag* request to be last

Lincoln. I knew the first, sir, did belong to me.
   This the old proverb now complete doth make,   45
   That Lincoln should be hanged for London's sake.
   A° God's name, let's to work: fellow, dispatch.°

                  He goes up.

   I was the foremost man in this rebellion
   And I the foremost that must die for it.
Doll. Bravely, John Lincoln, let thy death express   50
   That as thou livedst a man, thou diedst no less.
Lincoln. Doll Williamson, thine eyes shall witness it.
   Then, to all you that come to view mine end,
   I must confess I had no ill intent,
   But against such as wronged us overmuch.   55
   And now I can perceive it was not fit
   That private men should carve out their redress,
   Which way they list. No, learn it now by me,
   Obedience is the best in each degree.
   And asking mercy meekly of my King,   60
   I patiently submit me to the law.
   But God forgive them that were cause of it,
   And, as a Christian truly from my heart,
   I likewise crave they would forgive me too.
   [ ]   65
   That others by example of the same
   Henceforth be warnèd to attempt° the like
   'Gainst any alien that repaireth° hither.
   Fare ye well, all; the next time that we meet
   I trust in heaven we shall each other greet.   70
                 He leaps off.
Doll. Farewell, John Lincoln; say all what they can:
   Thou livedst a good fellow, and diedst an honest man.
Clown. Would I were so far on my journey; the first stretch is the worst,
  methinks.
Sheriff. Bring Williamson there forward.   75

---

47 *A* In / 47 *dispatch* perform the execution / 67 *to attempt* against attempting / 68 *repaireth* comes

Doll. Good Master Shrieve, I have an earnest suit,
     And as you are a man, deny't me not.
Sheriff. Woman, what is it? Be it in my power,   ·
     Thou shalt obtain it.
80 *Doll.* Let me die next, sir; that is all I crave.
     You know not what a comfort you shall bring
     To my poor heart to die before my husband.
Sheriff. Bring her to death; she shall have her desire.
Clown. Sir, and I have a suit to you, too.
85 *Sheriff.* What is it?
Clown. That as you have hanged Lincoln first and will hang her next, so
     you will not hang me at all!
Sheriff. Nay, you set ope° the Counter gates and you must hang chiefly.°
Clown. Well then, so much for that.
90 *Doll.* Sir, your free bounty much contents my mind.
     Commend me to that good shrieve Master More,
     And tell him had't not been for his persuasion
     John Lincoln had not hung here as he does.
     We would first have locked up° in Leaden Hall
95   And there been burned to ashes with the roof.
Sheriff. Woman, what Master More did was a subject's duty,
     And hath so pleased our gracious lord the King
     That he is hence removed to higher place,
     And made of Council to his Majesty.
100 *Doll.* Well is he worthy of it, by my troth,
     An honest, wise, well-spoken gentleman;
     Yet would I praise his honesty much more
     If he had kept his word and saved our lives.
     But let that pass; men are but men, and so
105   Words are but words and pays not what men owe.
     Now, husband, since perhaps the world may say
     That through my means thou comest thus to thy end,
     Here I begin this cup of death to thee,
     Because thou shalt be sure to taste no worse
110   Than I have taken, that must go before thee.
     What though I be a woman, that's no matter;

88 *ope* open / 88 *chiefly* especially / 94 *have locked up* have been locked up

I do owe God a death, and I must pay him.
Husband, give me thy hand, be not dismayed;
This char being charred,° then all our debt is paid.
Only, two little babes we leave behind us,   115
And all I can bequeath them at this time
Is but the love of some good honest friend
To bring them up in charitable sort.
What, masters, he goes upright that never halts,
And they may live to mend their parents' faults.   120
Williamson. Why, well said, wife; i'faith thou cheerst my heart.
Give me thy hand, let's kiss, and so let's part.
                                        He kisses her on the ladder.
Doll. The next kiss, Williamson, shall be in heaven.
Now cheerly lads, George Betts, a hand with thee,
And thine too, Ralph, and thine, good honest Sherwin.   125
Now let me tell the women of this town
No stranger yet brought Doll to lying down.
So long as I an Englishman can see,
Nor French nor Dutch shall get a kiss of me.
And when that I am dead, for me yet say   130
I died in scorn to be a stranger's prey.
                                        A great shout and noise.
[*Voices*] *within.* Pardon, pardon, pardon, pardon!
Room for the Earl of Surrey! Room there, room!

                                Enter Surrey.

Surrey. Save the man's life, if it be possible.
Sheriff. It is too late, my lord; he's dead already.   135
Surrey. I tell ye, Master Sheriff, you are too forward
To make such haste with men unto their death.
I think your pains will merit little thanks
Since that his Highness is so merciful
As not to spill the blood of any subject.   140
Sheriff. My noble lord, would we so much had known.
The Council's warrant hastened our dispatch;

---

114 *this char being charred* this affair being completed

It had not else been done so suddenly.

Surrey. Sir Thomas More humbly upon his knee

145   Did beg the lives of all, since on his word

        They did so gently yield. The King hath granted it

        And made him Lord High Chancellor of England,

        According as he worthily deserves.

        Since Lincoln's life cannot be had again,

150   Then for the rest, from my dread° Sovereign's lips

        I here pronounce free pardon for them all.

All (flinging up caps). God save the King! God save the King!

        My good Lord Chancellor and the Earl of Surrey!

Doll. And Doll desires it from her very heart

155   More's name may live for this right noble part.

        And whensoe'er we talk of ill May day

        Praise More whose [word did sin and judgment stay].°

Surrey. In hope his Highness' clemency and mercy,

        Which in the arms of mild and meek compassion

160   Would rather clip° you, as the loving nurse

        Oft doth the wayward infant, than to leave you

        To the sharp rod of justice, so to draw you

        To shun such lewd° assemblies as beget

        Unlawful riots and such traitorous arts

165   That striking with the hand of private° hate

        Maim your dear country with a public wound.

        O God, that mercy, whose majestic brow

        Should be unwrinkled, and that awful justice

        Which looketh through a veil of sufferance°

170   Upon the frailty of the multitude,

        Should with the clamours of outrageous wrongs

        Be stirred and wakened thus to punishment!

        But your deservèd death he doth forgive,

        Who gives you life, pray all he long may live.

175 *All.* God save the King! God save the King!

        My good Lord Chancellor and the Earl of Surrey!

                                    Exeunt.

---

150 *dread* revered / 157 Shirley's emendation / 163 *clip* gently correct / 163 *lewd* ignorant /
165 *private* sectarian, factional / 169 *sufferance* mercy

Act III

Scene I. *A Room in More's House.*

*A table being covered with a green carpet, a state cushion on it, and the
purse and mace lying thereon, enter Sir Thomas More.*

More. It is in heaven that I am thus and thus,°
    And that which we profanely° term our fortunes
    Is the provision of the power above,
    Fitted and shaped just to that strength of nature
    Which we are born withal. Good God, good God,   5
    That I from such an humble bench° of birth
    Should step as 'twere up to my country's head
    And give the law out there. I, in my father's life,
    To take prerogative and tithe° of knees[22]
    From elder kinsmen, and him bind by my place   10
    To give the smooth and dexter° way to me
    That owe it him by nature; sure,° these things,
    Not physicked by respect,° might turn our blood°
    To much corruption. But More, the more thou hast
    Either of honour, office, wealth and calling,   15
    Which might accite° thee to embrace and hug them,
    The more do thou in serpents' natures think them.
    Fear their gay skins, with thought of their sharp state,°
    And let this be thy maxim: to be great
    Is, when the thread of hazard is once spun,   20
    A bottom° great wound up, greatly undone.[23]

Enter his man Randall attired like him.

1 *thus and thus* the way that I am / 2 *profanely* impiously / 6 *bench* situation / 9 *tithe* tribute /
11 *dexter* right hand, a position of honor / 12 *sure* surely / 13 *physicked by respect* tempered by reflection / 13 *blood* (a) sensual nature (b) family relations / 16 *accite* excite / 18 *state* i.e. stings /
21 *bottom* a ball of wound thread

22. In More's time, just as it was the custom to kneel before one's father and ask for a blessing,
it was also the custom to pay "tithe of knee" to a high official of one's fatherland. As Lord Chancellor of England and highest officer of the country, Sir Thomas would normally receive such a
sign of reverence from his own father (a judge of the King's Bench). See Roper's account on p. 37,
TMSB.

23. This speech is commonly attributed to Shakespeare on stylistic and thematic grounds. Cf.
Othello 1.3.319–20, in which Iago makes the opposite case: "Virtue? a fig! 'tis in ourselves that we
are thus or thus."

Come on, sir, are you ready?

Randall. Yes, my lord, I stand° but on a few points. I shall have° done
      presently. Before God, I have practised your lordship's shift° so well that
25   I think I shall grow proud, my lord.

More. 'Tis fit thou shouldst wax° proud, or else thou'lt ne'er
      Be near allied to greatness.[24] Observe me, sirrah:
      The learned clerk Erasmus is arrived
      Within our English Court. Last night I hear
30   He feasted with our honoured English poet
      The Earl of Surrey, and I learned today
      The famous clerk of Rotterdam will visit
      Sir Thomas More. Therefore, sir, take my seat:
      You are lord chancellor. Dress° your behaviour
35   According to my carriage,° but beware
      You talk not over much, for 'twill betray thee.
      Who prates° not much seems wise, his wit few scan,°
      While the tongue blabs tales of the imperfect man.
      I'll see if great Erasmus can distinguish
40   Merit and outward ceremony.[25]

Randall. If I do not deserve a share for playing of your lordship well, let
      me be yeoman usher to your sumpter,° and be banished from wearing
      of a gold chain for ever.

More. Well, sir, I'll hide our motion.° Act my part
45   With a firm boldness, and thou winst my heart.

Enter the Sheriff with Falkner, a ruffian, and officers.

      How now? What's the matter?

Falkner. Tug me not, I'm no bear. 'Sblood,° if all the dogs in Paris Garden

---

23 *stand* wait / 23 *have* be / 24 *shift* (a) contrivance (b) attire / 26 *wax* grow / 34 *dress* arrange
/ 35 *carriage* demeanor / 37 *prates* talks foolishly / 37 *scan* discern / 42 *let me be yeoman usher to
your sumpter* let me be demoted to serving your lowliest servant / 44 *motion* (a) show (b) true inclinations / 47 *'Sblood* God's blood

24. A typical specimen of Morean irony. The dangers of pride, particularly for the great and
gifted, figure prominently in many of More's writings, including *Utopia* and *The Dialogue of Comfort against Tribulation.* See also pp. 215–20, *TMSB.*

25. In this characteristic jest, More seeks to test Erasmus's ability to distinguish between appearance and reality. More's habit of testing character was possibly cultivated during the time he
spent as a page in Lord Chancellor Archbishop Morton's service.

hung at my tail, I'd shake 'em off with this: that I'll appear before no
king christened but my good Lord Chancellor.

Sheriff. We'll christen you, sirrah. Bring him forward.   50

More. How now, what tumults make you?

Falkner. The azured heavens protect my noble Lord Chancellor.

More. What fellow's this?

Sheriff. A ruffian, my lord, that hath set half the city in an uproar.

Falkner. My lord—   55

Sheriff. There was a fray in Paternoster Row, and because they would not
be parted, the street was choked° up with carts.

Falkner. My noble lord, Panyer Alley's throat was open.

More. Sirrah, hold your peace.

Falkner. I'll prove the street was not choked, but is as well as ever it was   60
since it was a street.

Sheriff. This fellow was a principal broacher° of the broil.

Falkner. 'Sblood, I broached° none. It was broached and half run out before I had a lick at it.

Sheriff. And would be brought before no justice but your honour.   65

Falkner. I am haled,²⁶ my noble lord.

More. No ear to choose for every trivial noise
    But mine, and in so full° a time? Away!
    You wrong me, Master Shrieve. Dispose of him
    At your own pleasure. Send the knave to Newgate.   70

Falkner. To Newgate? 'Sblood, Sir Thomas More, I appeal, I appeal! From
Newgate to any of the two worshipful Counters.°

More. Fellow, whose man are you that are thus lusty?°

Falkner. My name's Jack Falkner. I serve, next under God and my prince,
Master Morris, secretary to my Lord of Winchester.   75

More. A fellow of your hair° is very fit
    To be a secretary's follower.

Falkner. I hope so, my lord. The fray was between the Bishops' men of Ely
and Winchester, and I could not in honour but part them. I thought it
stood not with my reputation and degree° to come to my questions   80
and answers before a city justice. I knew I should to the pot.°

---

57 *choked* clogged / 62 *broacher* instigator / 63 *broached* here playing on another sense of the
word, which means to draw liquor / 68 *full* busy / 72 *Counters* prisons in London / 73 *lusty* insolent / 76 *hair* double meaning of physical hair and other sense of the word as "kind" or "type"
/ 80 *degree* position / 81 *pot* gallows

26. haled: Cf. 1.1.1.

More. Thou hast been there it seems too late already.°

Falkner. I know your honour is wise and so forth, and I desire to be only catechised° or examined by you, my noble Lord Chancellor.

85 *More.* Sirrah, sirrah, you are a busy° dangerous ruffian.

Falkner. Ruffian?

More. How long have you worn this hair?

Falkner. I have worn this hair ever since I was born.

More. You know that's not my question. But how long

90   Hath this shag fleece° hung dangling on thy head?

Falkner. How long, my lord? Why, sometimes thus long, sometimes lower, as the fates and humours please.

More. So quick,° sir, with me, ha? I see, good fellow, thou lovest plain deal-ing. Sirrah, tell me now, when were you last at barber's? How long time

95   have you upon your head worn this shag hair?

Falkner. My lord, Jack Falkner tells no Aesop's fables. Troth, I was not at barber's this three years. I have not been cut nor will not be cut upon a foolish vow which as the destinies shall direct I am sworn to keep.

More. When comes that vow out?°

100 *Falkner.* Why, when the humours are purged:° not these three years.

More. Vows are recorded in the court of heaven,

        For they are holy acts. Young man, I charge thee

        And do advise thee, start not° from that vow,

        And for° I will be sure thou shalt not shrive,°

105   Besides, because it is an odious sight

        To see a man thus hairy, thou shalt lie

        In Newgate till thy vow and thy three years

        Be full expired. Away with him.

Falkner.   My lord—

110 *More.* Cut off this fleece, and lie there but a month.

Falkner. I'll not lose a hair to be lord chancellor of Europe.

More. To Newgate then. Sirrah, great sins are bred

        In all that body where there's a foul head.

        Away with him.

                            Exeunt [all except Randall].

---

82 *been there . . . already* More plays on the sense of a pot for drinking / 84 *catechized* instructed /
85 *busy* meddlesome / 90 *shag fleece* long, unkempt hair / 93 *quick* witty / 99 *when comes that
vow out* when does the vow expire? / 100 *humours are purged* dispositions are purified / 103 *start
not from* do not break / 104 *for* in order that / 104 *shrive* go to confession

Enter Surrey, Erasmus and attendants.

Surrey. Now, great Erasmus, you approach the presence   115
       Of a most worthy learned gentleman.
       This little isle holds not a truer friend
       Unto the arts, nor doth his greatness add
       A feignèd flourish° to his worthy parts:°
       He's great in study; that's the statist's grace,°   120
       That gains more reverence than the outward place.°27
Erasmus. Report, my lord, hath crossed the narrow seas
       And to the several parts of Christendom
       Hath borne the fame of your lord chancellor.
       I long to see him whom with loving thoughts   125
       I in my study oft have visited.
       Is that Sir Thomas More?
Surrey.   It is, Erasmus.
       Now shall you view the honourablest scholar,
       The most religious° politician,
       The worthiest counsellor that tends our state.   130
       That study is the general watch of England;
       In it the prince's safety and the peace
       That shines upon our commonwealth are forged
       By loyal industry.
Erasmus.   I doubt him not
       To be as near the life of excellence   135
       As you proclaim him, when his meanest servants
       Are of some weight.° You saw, my lord, his porter
       Give entertainment to us at the gate
       In Latin good phrase. What's the master then,
       When such good parts shine in his meanest men?   140
Surrey. His lordship hath some weighty business,

---

119 *feigned flourish* pretension / 119 *parts* qualities / 120 *statist's grace* statesman's pleasing quality /
121 *outward place* visible show of one's position / 129 *religious* (a) pious (b) conscientious /
137 *weight* character

27. The poet Surrey's unusual description of statesman More's greatness ("great in study") is
developed throughout his speeches here, culminating in his claim that England's peace and safety
are defended by More's study (line 131). This exchange amounts to something like an apologia for
humanist learning and, later, for poetry in particular against "all mechanic sciences" (line 190).

For see, as yet he takes no notice of us.

Erasmus. I think 'twere best I did my duty to him

In a short Latin speech:

145   *Qui in celeberrima patria natus est et gloriosa plus habet negotii ut in*

lucem veniat quam qui—[28]

Randall. I pray thee, good Erasmus, be covered.° I have forsworn speaking

of Latin, else as I am true councillor, I'd tickle° you with a speech. Nay,

sit, Erasmus; sit, good my Lord of Surrey. I'll make my lady come to

150   you anon,° if she will, and give you good entertainment.

Erasmus. Is this Sir Thomas More?

Surrey.   Oh, good Erasmus,

You must conceive his vein:° he's ever furnished

With these conceits.

Randall. Yes, faith, my learned poet doth not lie for that matter. I am nei-

155   ther more nor less merry Sir Thomas always. Wilt sup with me? By

God, I love a parlous° wise fellow that smells of a politician better than

a long progress.°

Enter Sir Thomas More.

Surrey. We are deluded. This is not his lordship.

Randall. I pray you, Erasmus, how long will the Holland cheese in your

160   country keep without maggots?

More. Fool, painted barbarism, retire thyself

Into thy first creation.°   [*Exit Randall.*]

Thus you see,

My loving learned friends, how far respect

Waits often on the ceremonious train

165   Of base, illiterate wealth, whilst men of schools,

Shrouded in poverty, are counted fools.

Pardon, thou reverend German. I have mixed

So slight a jest to the fair entertainment

Of thy most worthy self. For know, Erasmus,

---

147 *be covered* (a) restore yourself (b) shut up / 148 *tickle* (a) delight (b) beat up (c) make an end of something / 150 *anon* presently / 152 *conceive his vein* understand his style / 156 *parlous* well-informed / 157 *long progress* a journey made by a royal personage / 162 *creation* (a) function (b) costume

28. "One born in a very renowned and glorious nation has more difficulties in becoming famous than one who—"

Mirth wrinkles up my face, and I still crave,   170
When that forsakes me, I may hug my grave.
Erasmus. Your honour's merry humour is best physic°
Unto your able body. For we learn,
Where melancholy chokes the passages
Of blood and breath, the erected spirit still   175
Lengthens our days with sportful exercise.
Study should be the saddest° time of life;
The rest, a sport exempt from thought of strife.
More. Erasmus preacheth gospel against physic.
My noble poet—
Surrey.   Oh, my lord, you tax° me   180
In that word *poet* of much idleness.
It is a study that makes poor our fate;
Poets were ever thought unfit for state.
More. Oh, give not up fair poesy,° sweet lord,
To such contempt. That I may speak my heart,   185
It is the sweetest heraldry of art
That sets a difference 'tween the tough sharp holly
And tender bay tree.
Surrey.   Yet, my lord,
It is become the very lag number°
To all mechanic sciences.°
More.   Why, I'll show° the reason.   190
This is no age for poets: they should sing
To the loud canon° *heroica facta*
Qui faciunt reges heroica carmina laudant;[29]
And as great subjects of their pen decay,
Even so unphysicked° they do melt away.   195

Enter Master Morris.

Come, will your lordship in? My dear Erasmus—

---

172 *physic* medicine / 177 *saddest* most orderly and serious / 180 *tax* blame / 184 *poesy* poetry
/ 189 *become the very lag number* has been subordinated to / 190 *mechanic sciences* non-liberal arts
disciplines / 190 *show* declare / 192 *canon* (a) musical composition (b) law or rule; standard of
judgment / 195 *unphysicked* unnurtured

29. "Epic deeds which kings perform, epic poems praise."

I'll hear you, Master Morris presently—
My lord, I make you master of my house;
We'll banquet° here with fresh and staid° delights,
200   The muses' music here shall cheer our sprites;°
The cates° must be but mean where scholars sit,
For th'are made all with courses of neat° wit.
> [*Exeunt Surrey, Erasmus and attendants.*]
How now, Master Morris?
Morris. I am a suitor to your lordship in behalf of a servant of mine.
205   *More.* The fellow with long hair? Good Master Morris, Come to me three
years hence and then I'll hear you.
Morris. I understand, your honour, but the foolish knave has submitted
himself to the mercy of a barber, and is without, ready to make a new
vow before your lordship, hereafter to live civil.
210   *More.* Nay then, let's talk with him. Pray, call him in.

> *Enter Falkner and officers.*

Falkner. Bless your honour, a new man, my lord.
More. Why, sure, this is not he.
Falkner. And° your lordship will, the barber shall give you a sample of my
head. I am he in faith, my lord, I am *ipse.*°
215   *More.* Why, now thy face is like an honest man's.
Thou hast played well at this new cut,° and won.
Falkner. No, my lord. Lost all that ever God sent me.
More. God sent thee into the world as thou art now, with short hair. How
quickly are three years run out in Newgate.
220   *Falkner.* I think so, my lord, for there was but a hair's length between my
going thither and so long time.
More. Because I see some grace° in thee, go free.
Discharge him, fellows. Farewell, Master Morris.
Thy head is for thy shoulders now more fit:
225   Thou hast less hair upon it but more wit.   *Exit.*
Morris. Did not I tell° thee always of these locks?

---

199 *banquet* have a slight repast between meals / 199 *staid* free from extravagance / 200 *sprites* spirits / 201 *cates* provisions / 202 *neat* refined, well selected / 213 *And* if / 214 *ipse* he himself, the very man / 216 *cut* (a) style (b) card game / 222 *grace* (a) virtue (b) divine favor / 226 *tell* warn

Falkner. And the locks were on again, all the goldsmiths in Cheapside
should not pick them open. 'S heart! If my hair stand not on end when
I look for my face in a glass,° I am a polecat.° Here's a lousy jest.° But
if I notch° not that rogue Tom barber that makes me look thus like a   230
Brownist,° hang me. I'll be worse to the nittical° knave than ten tooth-
drawings.° Here's a head with a pox.°

Morris. What ailst° thou? Art thou mad now?

Falkner. Mad, now? 'Nails!° If loss of hair cannot mad° a man, what can? I
am deposed;° my crown is taken from me. More had been better   235
a' scoured° Moorditch than a' notched me thus. Does he begin sheep-
shearing with Jack Falkner?

Morris. Nay, and you feed this vein, sir,° fare you well.

Falkner. Why, farewell, frost. I'll go hang myself out for the poll head. Make
a Sar'cen of Jack?   240

Morris. Thou desperate knave, for that I see the devil wholly gets hold of
thee.

Falkner. The devil's a damned rascal.°

Morris. I charge thee wait on me no more; no more call me thy master.

Falkner. Why then, a word, Master Morris.   245

Morris. I'll hear no words, sir. Fare you well.

Falkner. 'Sblood! Farewell?

Morris. Why dost thou follow me?

Falkner. Because I'm an ass. Do you set your shavers° upon me, and then
cast me off? Must I condole?° Have the fates played the fools?° Am I   250
their cut?° Now° the poor sconce° is taken, must Jack° march with bag
and baggage?

He weeps.

Morris. You coxcomb.°

---

229 *glass* mirror / 229 *polecat* vile person / 229 *jest* ludicrous event / 230 *notch* cut / 231 *Brownist* person in a political party whose members would wear short hair / 231 *nittical* lice-infested /
232 *drawings* extractions / 232 *pox* disease / 233 *ailst* troubles / 234 *'Nails* an oath; God's nails /
234 *mad* madden / 235 *deposed* dispossessed, often of kingship or authority, hence the play of
"crown" for hair / 236 *scoured* cleaned / 238 *and you feed this vein, sir* if you gratify this whim /
243 *rascal* (a) wretched man (b) person of the lower class / 249 *shavers* (a) razors (b) swindlers /
250 *condole* grieve / 250 *played the fools* the Fool of the court would entertain by mocking others
/ 251 *cut* (a) term of abuse for a person (b) blow (c) fate, lot / 251 *now* now that / 251 *sconce* (a)
hair (b) jocular term for sense, wit, ability / 251 *Jack* generic name for a commoner / 253 *coxcomb*
(a) fool (b) ludicrous term for the head

Falkner. Nay, you ha'° poached° me; you ha' given me a hair.[30] It's here,
here.°

Morris. Away, you kind° ass. Come, sir, dry your eyes. Keep your old place
and mend° these fooleries.

Falkner. I care not to be turned off,° and 'twere a ladder, so it be in my humour, or the fates beckon to me.[31] Nay, pray, sir, if the destinies spin me
a fine thread, Falkner flies another pitch. And to avoid the headache
hereafter, before I'll be a hairmonger I'll be a whoremonger.

Exeunt.

Scene II. *A Hall in More's Home.*

Enter a messenger to More.

Messenger. My honourable lord, the Mayor of London,
Accompanied with his lady and her train,
Are coming hither, and are hard at hand,
To feast with you. A sergeant's come before
To tell your lordship of their near approach.
More. Why, this is cheerful news. Friends go and come;
Reverend Erasmus, whose delicious words
Express the very soul and life of wit,
Newly took sad leave of me, with tears
Troubled the silver channel of the Thames,
Which, glad of such a burden, proudly swelled
And on her bosom bore him toward the sea.
He's gone to Rotterdam; peace go with him;
He left me heavy when he went from hence,
But this recomforts me: the kind Lord Mayor,
His brethren aldermen° with their fair wives,
Will feast this night with us. Why, so't should be;

254 *ha'* have *poached* (a) cut (b) trampled / 255 *here* variant of "hair," as well as its usual meaning / 256 *kind* (a) natural (b) ironically, well-bred, refined / 257 *mend* remedy / 258 *turned off* (a) discharged from one's position; dismissed (b) turned off the ladder to be hanged / 16 *aldermen* persons of high rank

30. hair—(a) character, type (b) variant of "hoar" which as an adj. meant a tree gray from absence of foliage. "You have made me what I am, like a defoliated tree, by allowing me only scant hair."

31. "I don't mind being dismissed, even hanged, provided it complies with my mood or the fates call me to it."

More's merry heart lives by good company.
Good gentlemen, be careful; give great charge°
Our diet be made dainty for the taste,   20
For of all people that the earth affords
The Londoners fare richest at their boards.°

Enter Master Roper and servingmen setting stools.

Come, my good fellows, stir, be diligent!
Sloth is an idle fellow; leave him now.
The time requires your expeditious° service.   25
Place me here stools to set the ladies on.
Son Roper, you have given order for the banquet?
Roper. I have, my lord, and everything is ready.

Enter Lady More.

More. Oh welcome, wife. Give you direction
How women should be placed. You know it best.   30
For my Lord Mayor, his brethren, and the rest,
Let me alone: men best can order men.
Lady. I warrant ye, my lord, all shall be well.
There's one without that stays to speak with ye,
And bade me tell ye that he is a player.   35
More. A player, wife? One of ye bid him come in.

Exit one servingman.

Nay, stir there fellows, fie; ye are too slow.
See that your lights be in a readiness;
The banquet shall be here. God's me,° madam!
Leave my Lady Mayoress? Both of us from the board?   40
And my son Roper, too? What may our guests think?
Lady. My lord, they are risen and sitting by the fire.
More. Why, yet go you and keep them company.
It is not meet° we should be absent both.   *Exit Lady.*

---

19 *give great charge* take great care / 22 *boards* meal tables / 25 *expeditious* speedy / 39 *God's me!* a general exclamation, as in "oh my!" / 44 *meet* appropriate

Enter Player.

45   Welcome, good friend. What is your will with me?
Player. My lord, my fellows and myself
         Are come to tender° ye our willing service,
         So please you to command us.
More.   What, for a play, you mean?
         Whom do you serve?
Player.   My Lord Cardinal's grace.
50   *More.* My Lord Cardinal's players? Now trust me, welcome.
         You happen hither in a lucky time,
         To pleasure me and benefit yourselves.
         The mayor of London, and some aldermen,
         His lady, and their wives, are my kind guests
55   This night at supper. Now, to have a play
         Before the banquet will be excellent.
         How think you, son Roper?
Roper.   'Twill do well, my lord,
         And be right pleasing pastime to your guests.
More. I prithee tell me, what plays have ye?
60   *Player.* Diverse, my lord: *The Cradle of Security,*
         Hit Nail o' th' Head, Impatient Poverty,
         The Play of Four Ps, Dives and Lazarus,
         Lusty Juventus, and *The Marriage of Wit and Wisdom.*
More. The Marriage of Wit and Wisdom? That, my lads!
65   I'll none but that.° The theme is very good,[32]
         And may maintain a liberal argument.
         To marry wit to wisdom asks° some cunning;
         Many have wit that may come short of wisdom.
         We'll see how master poet plays his part,
70   And whether wit or wisdom grace his art.
         Go, make him drink, and all his fellows too.
         How many are ye?

---

47 *tender* offer / 65 *I'll none but that* I'll have none but that. / 67 *asks* asks for, requires

32. The play-within-a-play that follows is an intriguing example of the Elizabethan morality play. As G. Blakemore Evans explains, the play is "based on a scene from *Lusty Juventus*, with a prologue partly derived from *The Disobedient Child*" (1777).

Player.   Four men and a boy, sir.

More. But one boy? Then I see,

  There's but few women in the play.[33]

Player. Three, my lord: Dame Science, Lady Vanity,   75

  And Wisdom, she herself.

More. And one boy play them all? By'r Lady, he's loaden.

  Well, my good fellow, get ye straight together

  And make ye ready with what haste ye may.

  Provide their supper 'gainst the play be done,°   80

  Else shall we stay our guests here overlong.

  Make haste, I pray ye.

Player.   We will, my lord.

          Exeunt Servingmen and Player.

More. Where are the waits?° Go, bid them play,

  To spend the time awhile.

       Enter Lady.

      How now, madam?

Lady. My lord, th'are coming hither.   85

More. Th'are welcome. Wife, I'll tell ye one thing:

  Our sport is somewhat mended; we shall have

  A play tonight, *The Marriage of Wit and Wisdom,*

  And acted by my good Lord Cardinal's players.

  How like ye that, wife?

Lady.   My lord, I like it well.   90

  See, they are coming.   *Waits play hautbois.*°

  Enter Lord Mayor, so many aldermen as may, the Lady Mayoress in
  scarlet, with other ladies and Sir Thomas More's daughters, servants
     carrying lighted torches by them.

More. Once again, welcome! Welcome, my good Lord Mayor,

  And brethren all, for once I was your brother

  And so am still in heart. It is not state°

---

80 *'gainst the play be done* in preparation for the play's finish / 83 *waits* musicians / 91 *hautbois*
oboe-like instruments / 94 *state* rank

  33. Young boys played the female roles on the Elizabethan stage.

95   That can our love from London separate.
            [There be, as I have oft of late espied,
            In whom Dame Fortune's gifts breed]° nought but pride,
            But they that cast an eye still whence they came,
            Know how they rose, and how to use the same.
100   *Mayor.* My lord, you set a gloss° on London's fame,
            And make it happy ever by your name.
            Needs must we say, when we remember More,
            'Twas he that drove rebellion from our door,
            With grave discretion's mild and gentle breath
105   Shielding a many subjects' lives from death.
            Oh, how our city is by you renowned,
            And with your virtues our endeavours crowned.
      More. No more, my good Lord Mayor; but thanks to all
            That on so short a summons you would come
110   To visit him that holds your kindness dear.
            Madam, you are not merry with my Lady Mayoress,
            And these fair ladies; pray ye seat them all,
            And here, my lord, let me appoint your place,
            The rest to seat themselves. Nay, I'll weary ye;
115   You will not long in haste to visit me.°
      Lady. Good madam, sit; in sooth you shall sit here.
      Mayoress. Good madam, pardon me; it may not be.
      Lady. In troth,° I'll have it so; I'll sit here by ye.
            Good ladies, sit; more stools here, ho!
120   *Mayoress.* It is your favour, madam, makes me thus
            Presume above my merit.
      Lady.   When we come to you,
            Then shall you rule us as we rule you here.
            Now must I tell ye, madam, we have a play
            To welcome ye withal;° how good soe'er°
125   That know not I; my lord will have it so.°
      More. Wife, hope the best, I am sure they'll do their best,
            They that would better° comes not at their feast.

97 Shirley's emendation / 100 *gloss* glow / 115 *You will not long in haste to visit me* you won't want
be so intent on visiting me for very long / 118 *in troth* an exclamation of "in truth," as in "by my
faith" / 124 *withal* as well / 124 *so'er* soever, meaning however / 125 I can't say how good it is,
but my lord affirms it to be good / 127 *that would better* that would demand better

My good Lord Cardinal's players, I thank them for it,
Play us a play, to lengthen out your welcome.
They say it is *The Marriage of Wit and Wisdom,*   130
A theme of some import, howe'er it prove;°
But if art fail, we'll inch it out with love.[34]
What, are they ready?
Servant. My lord, one of the players craves to speak with you.
More. With me? Where is he?   135

Enter Inclination (the Vice) ready.

Inclination. Here, my lord.
More. How now, what's the matter?
Inclination. We would desire your honour but to stay a little; one of my fel-
   lows is but run to Ogle's for a long beard for young Wit, and he'll be
   here presently.   140
More. A long beard for young Wit? Why man, he may be without a beard
   till he come to marriage, for wit goes not all by the hair. When comes
   Wit in?
Inclination. In the second scene, next to the prologue, my lord.
More. Why, play on till that scene come, and by that time Wit's beard will   145
   be grown, or else the fellow returned with it. And what part playst
   thou?
Inclination. Inclination, the Vice, my lord.
More. Gramercies,° now I may take° the vice if I list;° and wherefore hast
   thou that bridle in thy hand?   150
Inclination. I must be bridled anon, my lord.
More. And thou beest not saddled too, it makes no matter, for then Wit's
   inclination may gallop so fast that he will outstrip wisdom and fall to
   folly.
Inclination. Indeed, so he does to Lady Vanity; but we have no Folly in our   155
   play.

131 *prove* turn out / 149 *Gramercies* thank you / 149 *take* (a) assault (b) seize (c) comprehend
More may be playing on all these meanings. / 149 *list* desire to

34. More's remark here is similar to Duke Theseus's advice to Hippolyta on how to respond to
the performance of the "rude mechanicals" in act five of Shakespeare's *A Midsummer Night's Dream*
(5.1.89ff). As Gabrieli and Melchiori also point out, "Inch it out" is similar to Shakespeare's "eech
out our performance in your mind" in *Henry the Fifth*, 3.Chor.35 (p. 147). Shakespeare's gives the
same advice in the chorus of *Pericles*, 3.Chor.13: "with your fine fancies quaintly eche."

More. Then there's no wit in't, I'll be sworn: folly waits on wit as the shadow on the body, and where wit is ripest, there folly still is readiest. But
  begin, I prithee; we'll rather allow a beardless Wit, than Wit all beard to
160 have no brain.
Inclination. Nay, he has his apparel on too, my lord, and therefore he is the
  readier to enter.
More. Then, good Inclination, begin at a venture.°

Exit [Inclination].

  My Lord Mayor, Wit lacks a beard, or else they would begin.
165 I'd lend him mine, but that it is too thin.
  Silence, they come.   *The trumpet sounds.*

Enter the Prologue.

Prologue. Now, for as much as in these latter days
      Throughout the whole world in every land
      Vice doth increase and virtue decays,
170   Iniquity having the upper hand,
      We therefore intend, good gentle audience,
      A pretty short interlude to play at this present,
      Desiring your leave and quiet silence
      To show the same as is meet and expedient.
175   It is called *The Marriage of Wit and Wisdom,*
      A matter right pithy and pleasing to hear,
      Whereof in brief we will show the whole sum.
      But I must be gone, for Wit doth appear.   *Exit.*

Enter Wit ruffling° and Inclination, the Vice.

Wit. In an arbour green, asleep whereas I lay,
180   The birds sang sweetly in the midst of the day;
      I dreamed fast of mirth and play:
      In youth is pleasure, in youth is pleasure.
      Methought I walked still to and fro,
      And from her company I could not go,
185   But when I waked it was not so:
      In youth is pleasure, in youth is pleasure.
      Therefore my heart is surely plight°

---

163 *at a venture* immediately, without consideration / 178 *ruffling* swaggering / 187 *plight* pledged

Of her alone to have a sight

Which is my joy and heart's delight:

In youth is pleasure, in youth is pleasure.   190

More. Mark ye, my lord, this is Wit without a beard;° what will he be by

that time he comes to the commodity of a beard?

Inclination. Oh, sir, the ground is the better on which she doth go.

For she will make better cheer with a little she can get

Than many a one can with a great banquet of meat.   195

Wit. And is her name Wisdom?

Inclination.   Ay, sir, a wife most fit

For you, my good master, my dainty sweet Wit.

Wit. To be in her company, my heart it is set.

Therefore I prithee to let us be gone,   200

For unto Wisdom, Wit hath inclination.

Inclination. Oh, sir, she will come herself even anon,

For I told her before where we would stand,

And then she said she would beck° us with her hand.

Back with those boys and saucy great knaves!   205

Flourishing his dagger.

What! Stand ye here so big° in your braves?°

My dagger about your coxcombs° shall walk

If I may but so much as hear ye chat or talk.

Wit. But will she take pains to come for us hither?

Inclination. I warrant° ye; therefore, you must be familiar° with her.   210

When she cometh in place,°

You must her embrace

Somewhat handsomely,°

Least° she think it danger,

Because you are a stranger,   215

To come in your company.

Wit. I warrant° thee, Inclination, I will be busy.°

Oh, how Wit longs to be in Wisdom's company.

---

191 "beardless" is also used for young, immature / 204 *beck* beckon, call / 206 *big* haughty /
206 *braves* finery / 207 *coxcombs* ludicrous name for the head / 210 *warrant* assure / 210 *familiar*
courteous / 211 *in place* right there / 213 *handsomely* decently, appropriately / 214 *Least* lest /
217 *warrant* assure / 217 *busy* conscientious, careful

Enter Lady Vanity singing and beckoning with her hand.

Vanity. Come hither, come hither, come hither, come!
220   Such cheer as I have, thou shalt have some.
More. This is lady Vanity, I'll hold° my life.
          Beware, good Wit, you take not her to wife.°
Inclination. What, Unknown Honesty, a word in your ear.

                                        She offers to depart.

          You shall not be gone as yet, I swear.
225   Here's none but your friends; you need not to fray.°
          This young gentleman loves ye; therefore, you must stay.
Wit. I trust in me she will think no danger,
          For I love well the company of fair women;
          And though to you I am a stranger,
230   Yet Wit may pleasure you now and then.
Vanity. Who, you? Nay, you are such a holy man,
          That to touch one you dare not be bold.°
          I think you would not kiss a young woman
          If one would give ye twenty pound in gold.
235 *Wit.* Yes, in good sadness,° lady, that I would;
          I could find in my heart to kiss you in your smock.°
Vanity. My back is broad enough to bear that mock.
          For it hath been told me many a time
          That you would be seen in no such company as mine.
240 *Wit.* Not Wit in the company of Lady Wisdom?
          O Jove, for what do I hither come?
Inclination. Sir, she did this nothing else but to prove°
          Whether a little thing would you move
          To be angry and fret.
245   What and if one said so?
          Let such trifling matters go,
          And with a kind kiss come out of her debt.

                    Enter another player.

          Is Luggins come yet with the beard?

---

221 *hold* stake / 222 *take not her to wife* that you do not marry her / 225 *to fray* fear / 232 *not be bold* not be so bold / 235 *in good sadness* seriously, sincerely / 236 *smock* women's undergarment; also used to suggest loose morality / 242 *prove* discover

Player. No, faith, he is not come. Alas, what shall we do?

Inclination. Forsooth, we can go no further till our fellow Luggins come,   250
    for he plays Good Counsel, and now he should enter to admonish Wit
    that this is Lady Vanity and not Lady Wisdom.

More. Nay, and it be no more but so,° ye shall not tarry at a stand° for that;
    we'll not have our play marred for lack of a little good counsel: till
    your fellow come, I'll give him the best counsel that I can. Pardon me,   255
    my Lord Mayor, I love to be merry.[35]

More. O Wit, thou art now on the bow hand,°
        And blindly in thine own opinion dost stand.
        I tell thee, this naughty lewd° Inclination
        Does lead thee amiss in a very strange fashion.   260
        This is not Wisdom, but Lady Vanity,
        Therefore list° to Good Counsel, and be ruled by me.

Inclination. In troth, my lord, it is as right to Luggins's part as can be. Speak,
    Wit.

More. Nay, we will not have our audience disappointed, if I can help it.   265

Wit. Art thou Good Counsel, and wilt tell me so?
        Wouldst thou have Wit from Lady Wisdom, to go?
        Thou art some deceiver, I tell thee verily,
        In saying that this is Lady Vanity.

More. Wit, judge not things by the outward show;   270
        The eye oft mistakes, right well you do know.[36]
        Good Counsel assures thee upon his honesty
        That this is not Wisdom, but Lady Vanity.

---

253 *and it be no more but so* if that is all it is / 253 *tarry at a stand* hold off / 257 *on the bow hand*
wide of the mark / 259 *lewd* (a) wicked (b) ignorant / 262 *list* listen

35. More's extempore and merry acting here is reminiscent of his behavior as Lord Chancellor
Cardinal Morton's page when More was a young man (see *TMSB*, p. 19). George Saintsbury further observes that "the introduction of the play within the play, together with More's speeches to
the actors and his insertion into their scenes of an extempore speech of his own, is a curious anticipation of *Hamlet*" (248).

36. The difficulty of distinguishing appearance from reality is a common subject of reflection
in the plays and poetry of the era, but it is also particularly important to More, who emphasized in
his writings the need for a "good mother wit" to perceive reality accurately (p. 278, *TMSB*). As Alistair Fox explains: "Human experience, for More, was characterized by paradoxical and ironic
complexities, so that 'good mother wit' is not simply a matter of naked intelligence or reason—
these can provide the basis for sound judgment only when fertilized by an accurate perception of
the nature of things" ('78, p. 22).

Enter Luggins with the beard.

Inclination. O my lord, he is come; now we shall go forward.

275   *More.* Art thou come? Well, fellow, I have holp° to save thine honesty° a
         little. Now, if thou canst give Wit any better counsel than I have done,
         spare not. There I leave him to thy mercy.
              But by this time I am sure our banquet's ready.
              My lord and ladies, we will taste that first
280   And then they shall begin the play again,
              Which, through the fellow's absence, and by me,
              nstead of helping, hath been hindered.
              Prepare against° we come. Lights there, I say.
              Thus fools oft times do help to mar the play.

                              Exeunt all but the players.

285   *Wit.* Fie, fellow Luggins, you serve us handsomely; do ye not, think ye?

       Luggins. Why, Ogle was not within, and his wife would not let me have the
              beard, and by my troth I ran so fast that I sweat again.°

       Inclination. Do ye hear, fellows? Would not my lord° make a rare player?
              Oh, he would uphold a company beyond all ho, better than Mason
290   among the King's players. Did ye mark how extemprically he fell to°
              the matter, and spake Luggins's part almost as it is in the very book set
              down?

       Wit. Peace! Do ye know what ye say? My lord, a player? Let us not med-
              dle with any such matters. Yet I may be a little proud that my lord hath
295   answered me in my part. But come, let us go and be ready to begin the
              play again.

       Luggins. Ay, that's the best, for now we lack nothing.

Enter a Servingman to reward the players.

       Servingman. Where be these players?

       All. Here, sir.

300   *Servingman.* My lord is sent for to the Court,
              And all the guests do after supper part,
              And for he will not trouble you again,
              By me for your reward 'a sends eight angels°

---

275 *holp* helped / 275 *honesty* good name / 283 *against* for when we come [after dinner] /
287 *sweat again* sweated all the way back / 288 *my lord* referring to More / 290 *extemprically he fell*
to extemporaneously he got the gist of / 303 *angels* gold coins

With many thanks. But sup before you go:
It is his will you should be fairly entreated.   305
Follow, I pray ye.

Wit.   This, Luggins, is your negligence!
Wanting Wit's beard brought things into dislike,°
For otherwise the play had been all seen,
Where now some curious citizen disgraced it°
And, discommending it, all is dismissed.°   310

Inclination. 'Fore God, 'a says true. But hear ye, sirs, eight angels? Ha! My
lord would never give's° eight angels, more or less for twelvepence. Either it should be three pounds, five pounds or ten pounds.° There's
twenty shillings wanting, sure.°

Wit. Twenty to one 'tis so. I have a trick.°—My lord comes; stand aside.   315

Enter More with Attendants with purse and mace.

More. In haste to council! What's the business now,
That all so late his highness sends for me?
What seekst thou, fellow?

Wit.   Nay, nothing.
Your lordship sent eight angels by your man,
And I have lost two of them in the rushes.   320

More. Wit, look to that! Eight angels? I did send
Them ten. Who gave it them?

Servingman. I, my lord. I had no more about me,
But by and by they shall receive the rest.

More. Well, Wit, 'twas wisely done; thou playest Wit well indeed,   325
Not to be thus dissever'd of thy right.
Am I a man by office truly ordained
Equally to divide true right his own,
And shall I have deceivers in my house?
Then what avails my bounty,° when such servants   330
Deceive the poor of what the master gives?
Go one, and pull his coat over his ears.°

307 *dislike* discord / 309 *Where now some curious citizen disgraced it* Whereas now some exacting citizen has brought it into disrepute. / 310 *discommending it, all is dismissed* criticizing it, all is (a)
brought to an end (b) deprived of advantage / 312 *give's* give us / 314 The point is that eight angels is an odd amount for a typical reward / 314 *sure* surely / 315 *trick* contrivance / 330 *what
avails my bounty* what's the good of my wealth / 332 *pull his coat over his ears* the coat is indicative
of one's profession; hence, dismiss him

There are too many such. Give them their right.
Wit, let thy fellows thank thee; 'twas well done.
335   Thou now deservest to match° with Lady Wisdom.

> [*Exit with Attendants.*]

Inclination. God a' mercy, Wit. Sir, you had a master, Sir Thomas More.
More? but now *we* shall have more.

Luggins. God bless him. I would there were more of his mind. He loves
our quality,° and yet he's a learned man and knows what the world is.

340   *Inclination.* Well, a kind man and more loving than many other, but I think
we ha' met with the first—

Luggins. First served° his man that had our angels, and he may chance dine
with Duke Humphrey tomorrow, being turned away today. Come, let's
go.

345   *Inclination.* And many such rewards would make us all ride and horse us
with the best nags in Smithfield.

> [*Exeunt.*]

Act IV

Scene I. *The Privy Council.*

*Enter the Earls of Shrewsbury and Surrey, the Bishop of Rochester and
other lords, severally, doing courtesy to each other, the Clerk of the Council
waiting bareheaded.*

Surrey. Good morrow to my Lord of Shrewsbury.
Shrewsbury. The like unto the honoured Earl of Surrey.
        Yond comes my Lord of Rochester.
Rochester. Good morrow, my good lords.
5   *Surrey.* Clerk of the Council, what time is't of day?
Clerk. Past eight of clock, my lord.
Shrewsbury. I wonder that my good Lord Chancellor
Doth stay so long, considering there's matters
        Of high importance to be scanned upon.°
10   *Surrey.* Clerk of the Council, certify his lordship

---

335 *match with* marry / 339 *quality* people of the lower class / 342 *served* gave him what he deserved / 9 *scanned upon* examined

The lords expect him here.

Rochester.   It shall not need;

Yond comes his lordship.

Enter Sir Thomas More, with purse and mace borne before him.

More. Good morrow to this fair assembly.

Come, my good lords, let's sit.   *They sit.*

O serious square,°

Upon this little board is daily scanned   15

The health and preservation of the land.

We, the physicians, that effect this good,

Now by choice diet, anon by letting blood.

Our toil and careful watching brings the King

In league with slumbers, to which peace doth sing.   20

—Avoid the room there!

What business, lords, today?

Shrewsbury.   This, my good lord:

About the entertainment° of the Emperor

'Gainst the perfidious French into our pay.[37]

Surrey. My lords, as 'tis the custom in this place   25

The youngest should speak first, so if I chance

In this case to speak youngly, pardon me.

I will agree, France now hath her full strength,

As having new recovered the pale blood

Which war sluiced forth,° and I consent to this,   30

That the conjunction of our English forces

With arms of Germany may sooner bring

This prize of conquest in. But then, my lords,

As in the moral hunting 'twixt the lion

And other beasts, force joined [with guile]°   35

Frighted the weaker sharers from their parts,

---

14 *serious square* serious meaning "grave" or "important" and "square" for the table at which the Council sits / 23 *entertainment* support / 30 *sluiced forth* drew out / 35 Shirley's emendation

37. As in 2.3, the play here compresses events that took place over a long span of time—in this case, more than 20 years. First, the council members discuss events from *c.* 1513, when the German emperor helped the English against the French; then, the scene turns swiftly to More's resignation and his rejection of the Oath of Supremacy (along with John Fisher, Bishop of Rochester), events which actually took place in 1532 and 1534, respectively.

So if the Empire's Sovereign chance to put
His plea of partnership into war's court,
Swords should decide the difference, and our blood
40   In private tears lament his entertainment.°
Shrewsbury. To doubt° the worst is still the wise man's shield
That arms him safely; but the world knows this:
The Emperor is a man of royal faith.
His love unto our Sovereign brings him down
45   From his imperial seat, to march in pay
Under our English flag, and wear the cross
Like some high order° on his manly breast.
Thus serving, he's not master of himself,
But like a colonel, commanding other,
50   Is by the general over-awed himself.
Rochester. Yet, my good lord—
Shrewsbury.   Let me conclude my speech.
As subjects share no portion in the conquest
Of their true sovereign, other than the merit
That from the sovereign guerdons° the true subject,
55   So the good Emperor, in a friendly league
Of amity° with England, will not soil
His honour with the theft of English spoil.
More. There is no question but this entertainment
Will be most honourable, most commodious.°
60   I have oft heard good captains wish to have
Rich soldiers to attend them, such as would fight
Both for their lives and livings.° Such a one
Is the good Emperor. I would to God
We had ten thousand of such able men.
65   Ha! Then there would appear no court, no city,
But where the wars were: they would pay themselves.
Then to prevent in French wars England's loss,
Let German flags wave with our English cross.

---

40 *So if . . . lament his entertainment* The emperor may compel us to go to war with him if we ally
ourselves to him / 41 *doubt* fear / 47 *order* honor / 54 *guerdons* honors / 56 *amity* friendship /
59 *commodious* advantageous / 62 *livings* wealth

Enter Sir Thomas Palmer.

Palmer. My lords, his Majesty hath sent by me

    These Articles enclosed, first to be viewed   70

    And then to be subscribed to.° I tender° them

    In that due reverence which befits this place.

                                    With great reverence.

More. Subscribe these Articles? Stay, let us pause.

    Our conscience first shall parley° with our laws.[38]

    My Lord of Rochester, view you the paper.   75

Rochester. Subscribe to these? Now, good Sir Thomas Palmer,

    Beseech the King that he will pardon me.

    My heart will check my hand whilst I do write:

    Subscribing so, I were an hypocrite.

Palmer. Do you refuse it then, my lord?[39]

Rochester.   I do, Sir Thomas.   80

Palmer. Then here I summon you forthwith t'appear

Before his Majesty, to answer there

    This capital contempt.°

Rochester.   I rise and part,

    In lieu of this, to tender him my heart.   *He rises.*

Palmer. Will't please your honour to subscribe, my lord?   85

More. Sir, tell his Highness I entreat

    Some time for to bethink me of this task.

    In the meanwhile I do resign mine office

    Into my Sovereign's hands.

Palmer.   Then, my lord,

    Hear the preparèd order from the King.   90

    On your refusal, you shall straight depart

---

71 *subscribed to* signed / 71 *tender* offer for formal acceptance / 74 *parley* hold conference /
83 *capital contempt* act of disobedience punishable by execution

38. Cf. the present parley between conscience and law with 2.3.89ff, in which More urged obedience to the King's God-lent authority.

39. The following section (lines 79–104) was crossed out by Edmund Tilney, Queen Elizabeth's censor. There is a marginal note from Tilney along with the cross out, but it is difficult to read; Greg concludes that "the meaning, that the whole passage is to be altered, is the only certain point" (p. 42). Gabrieli and Melchiori suggest that Tilney "seems more disturbed by the sympathetic presentation of More's and Fisher's acceptance of Royal displeasure than by historical inaccuracy" (p. 166).

Unto your house at Chelsea, till you know
Our Sovereign's further pleasure.
More.   Most willingly I go.
My lords, if you will visit me at Chelsea,
95   We'll go a-fishing, and with a cunning° net,
Not like weak film, we'll catch none but the great.
Farewell, my noble lords. Why, this is right.
Good morrow to the sun, to state goodnight.[40]   *Exit.*
Palmer. Will you subscribe, my lords?
Surrey.   Instantly, good Sir Thomas.
                                       They write.
100   We'll bring the writing unto our Sovereign.
Palmer. My Lord of Rochester,
You must with me, to answer this contempt.
Rochester. This is the worst;
Who's freed from life, is from all care exempt.
                        Exeunt Rochester and Palmer.
105 *Surrey.* Now let us [bear this]° to our Sovereign.
'Tis strange that my Lord Chancellor should refuse
The duty that the law of God bequeaths
Unto the King.
Shrewsbury.   Come, let us in. No doubt
His mind will alter, and the bishop's too.
110 Error in learned heads hath much to do.°   [*Exeunt.*]

Scene II. *More's Garden at His Home in Chelsea.*
Enter the Lady More, her two Daughters, and
Master Roper, as walking.

Roper. Madam, what ails ye for to look so sad?
Lady. Troth, son, I know not what. I am not sick,

---

95 *cunning* skillfully made / 105 Shirley's emendation / 110 *hath much to do* is capable of much harm

40. Cf. *King Lear* 5.3.11–19, in which the old king reflects on his imminent imprisonment: "So we'll live, / And pray, and sing, and tell old tales, and laugh / At gilded butterflies, and hear poor rogues / Talk of court news; and we'll talk with them too— / Who loses and who wins; who's in, who's out— / And take upon 's the mystery of things / As if we were God's spies; and we'll wear out, / In a wall'd prison, packs and sects of great ones, / That ebb and flow by th' moon."

And yet I am not well; I would be merry,
But somewhat° lies so heavy on my heart,
I cannot choose but sigh. You are a scholar;   5
I pray ye tell me, may one credit° dreams?
Roper. Why ask you that, dear madam?
Lady. Because tonight I had the strangest dream
That e'er my sleep was troubled with.[41]
Methought 'twas night,   10
And that the King and Queen went on the Thames
In barges to hear music. My lord and I
Were in a little boat, methought. Lord, Lord,
What strange things live in slumbers! And being near,
We grappled° to the barge that bare the King.   15
But after many pleasing voices spent
In that still moving music-house, methought
The violence of the stream did sever us
Quite from the golden fleet, and hurried us
Unto the bridge, which with unusèd° horror   20
We entered at full tide; thence some flight shoot°
Being carried by the waves, our boat stood still
Just opposite the Tower, and there it turned
And turned about, as when a whirlpool sucks
The circled waters. Methought that we both cried   25
Till that we sunk, where arm in arm we died.[42]
Roper. Give no respect,° dear madam, to fond dreams;
They are but slight illusions of the blood.
Lady. Tell me not all are so, for often dreams
Are true diviners,° either of good or ill.   30
I cannot be in quiet° till I hear
How my lord fares.
Roper (aside).   Nor I.—Come hither, wife.

---

4 *somewhat* something   /   6 *credit* take seriously, put one's faith in   /   15 *grappled* attached our boat
/   20 *unusèd* unusual   /   21 *flight shoot* swift rush of water   /   27 *respect* regard   /   30 *diviners*
prophets, omens   /   31 *quiet* peace

41. Cf. the relation of Clarence's remarkable dream in *Richard the Third*, 1.4.9–63.
42. Lady More's dream of her and her husband's death curiously mirrors 2.4, in which Doll
and Williamson face death for their roles in the insurrection, though they go on to experience the
King's mercy through More's intercession.

I will not fright thy mother, to interpret
The nature of a dream; but trust me, sweet,
35   This night I have been troubled with thy father
Beyond all thought.

Roper's Wife.   Truly, and so have I.
Methought I saw him here in Chelsea church,
Standing upon the rood loft,° now defaced,[43]
And whilst he kneeled and prayed before the image,
40   It fell with him into the upper choir,
Where my poor father lay all stained in blood.

Roper. Our dreams all meet in one conclusion:
Fatal, I fear.

Lady. What's that you talk? I pray ye let me know it.
45   *Roper's Wife.* Nothing, good mother.

Lady. This is your fashion still;° I must know nothing!
Call Master Catesby; he shall straight to Court
And see how my lord does. I shall not rest
Until my heart lean panting on his breast.

Enter Sir Thomas More merrily, servants attending.

50   *Second Daughter.* See where my father comes, joyful and merry.

More. As seamen, having passed a troubled storm,
Dance on the pleasant shore, so I—Oh, I could speak
Now like a poet. Now, afore God, I am passing light.°
Wife, give me kind welcome; thou wast wont to blame°
55   My kissing, when my beard was in the stubble,
But I have been trimmed of late; I have had
A smooth Court shaving,° in good faith I have.

Daughters kneel.

God bless ye. Son Roper, give me your hand.

Roper. Your honour's welcome home.

---

38 *rood loft* loft forming the head of a rood screen; the rood screen separated the church's nave from the choir / 46 *your fashion still* always your way / 53 *light* light-hearted / 54 *wast wont to blame* were prone to find fault with / 57 *shaving* loss of possessions

43. Roods are crucifixes, and the apparently anachronistic statement that they are "now defaced" seems to refer to the changes made to English churches during the Reformation in England. Cf. Shakespeare's sonnet 73, which seems to allude to the destruction of the monasteries under Henry VIII: "Bare ruined choirs, where late the sweet birds sang."

More.	Honour? Ha ha.

And how dost, wife?   60

Roper.	He bears himself most strangely.
Lady. Will your lordship in?	
More.	Lordship? No, wife, that's gone.

The ground was slight that we did lean upon.

Lady. Lord, that your honour ne'er will leave these jests!

In faith, it ill becomes ye.

More.	O good wife,

Honour and jests are both together fled;   65

The merriest councillor of England's dead.

Lady. Who's that, my lord?

More. Still lord? The Lord Chancellor, wife.

Lady. That's you.

More.	Certain, but I have changed my life.

Am I not leaner than I was before?   70

The fat is gone; my title's only More.

Contented with one style,° I'll live at rest.

They that have many names are not still° best.

I have resigned mine office; countst me not wise?

Lady. O God.   75

More. Come, breed not female children in your eyes.

The King will have it so.

Lady.	What's the offence?

More. Tush, let that pass; we'll talk of that anon.

The King seems a physician to my fate;

His princely mind would train me back to state.°   80

Roper. Then be his patient, my most honoured father.

More. O son Roper,

   Ubi turpis est medicina, sanari piget.[44]

---

72 *style* title / 73 *still* always / 80 *train me back to state* persuade me back to a high position

44. More quotes Creon's words to King Oedipus from Seneca's *Oedipus,* line 517, which may be translated, "Where foul the medicine, 'tis loathsome to be healed." (trans. Frank Miller). Creon utters these words in response to Oedipus's question, "What! Wilt [thou] e'en bury revelations of the public weal?" Oedipus's ensuing exchange with Creon is relevant here: "*Oedipus.* Speak out thy tidings, or by severe suffering broken, thou shalt know what the power of an angered king can do. *Creon.* Kings hate the words whose speaking they would compel." (lines 518–20). Intriguingly, the censor Tilney crossed out this quotation, possibly because it implies that "it is better to die than to

No, wife, be merry, and be merry° all;
85   You smiled at rising; weep not at my fall.[45]
Let's in,° and here joy° like to private friends,
Since days of pleasure have repentant ends.°
The light of greatness is with triumph borne;
It sets at midday oft, with public scorn.   *Exeunt.*

Scene III. *The Tower of London, a Room.*

*Enter the Bishop of Rochester, Surrey, Shrewsbury, Lieutenant of the Tower
and warders with weapons.*

Rochester. Your kind persuasions, honourable lords,
      I can but thank ye for, but in this breast
      There lives a soul, that aims at higher things
      Than temporary pleasing earthly kings.
5   God bless his Highness, even with all my heart;
      We shall meet one day, though that now we part.
Surrey. We not misdoubt° your wisdom can discern
      What best befits it; yet in love and zeal
      We could entreat it might be otherwise.
10 *Shrewsbury.* No doubt your fatherhood will by yourself
      Consider better of the present case,
      And grow as great in favour as before.
Rochester. For that,° as pleaseth God, in my restraint
      From worldly causes, I shall better see
15   Into myself than at proud liberty.[46]

---

84 *merry* besides cheerful, it also meant contented / 86 *let's in* let's head in / 86 *here joy* here take joy / 87 *have repentant ends* eventually reverse themselves / 7 misdoubt *doubt* / 13 *for that* to that I say

---

submit," as Gabrieli and Melchiori suggest (p. 172). Perhaps also the association of More with the truth-bearing Creon and Henry with the blind tyrant, Oedipus, left Tilney uneasy. In Rowland Lockey's portrait *The Family of Sir Thomas More, c.* 1593 (roughly the date of this play), Margaret is pointing to the word "demens" [mad] in *Oedipus*, line 892. See p. 15, *TMSB.*

      45. The motion of rising and falling is the same one on which Shakespeare builds the structure of his last play, *Henry the Eighth.*

      46. Both Rochester and More express the paradoxical wisdom that their dire adversity is better than their former prosperity, especially because of the increased self-knowledge and spiritual insight that their falls provide.

The Tower and I will privately confer
Of things wherein at freedom I may err.
But I am troublesome unto your honours,
And hold ye longer than becomes my duty.
Master Lieutenant, I am now your charge,   20
And though you keep my body, yet my love
Waits on my King and you, while Fisher lives.
Surrey. Farewell, my Lord of Rochester. We'll pray
    For your release, and labour't° as we may.
Shrewsbury. Thereof assure yourself. So do we leave ye,   25
    And to your happy private thoughts bequeath ye.

Exeunt lords.

Rochester. Now, Master Lieutenant, on; a God's name, go.
    And with as glad a mind go I with you,
    As ever truant bade the school adieu.   *Exeunt.*

Scene IV. *A Room in More's Home at Chelsea.*

Enter Sir Thomas More, his Lady, daughters, Master Roper, gentlemen and
servants, as in his house at Chelsea.

More. Good morrow, good son Roper; sit, good madam,
    Upon an humble seat; the time so craves.°   *Low stools.*
    Rest your good heart on earth, the roof of graves.
    You see the floor of greatness is uneven,
    The cricket° and high throne alike near heaven.   5
    Now, daughters, you that like to branches spread
    And give best shadow to a private house,
    Be comforted, my girls, your hopes stand fair:
    Virtue breeds gentry; she makes the best heir.
Daughters. Good morrow to your honour.
More.   Nay, good night rather.   10
    Your honour's crestfall'n with your happy father.
    Roper. Oh, what formality, what square° observance
    Lives in a little room! Here, public care

24 *labour't* work for it / 2 *craves* requires / 5 *cricket* low stool / 12 *square* honorable, careful

Gags° not the eyes of slumber; here fierce riot
15   Ruffles° not proudly in a coat of trust,°
Whilst like a pawn at chess he keeps in rank
With kings and mighty fellows; yet indeed
Those men that stand on tiptoe smile to see
Him pawn his fortunes.°

More.   True, son, here['s not so,]°
20   Nor does the wanton tongue° here screw itself
Into the ear, that like a vice drinks up
The iron instrument.

Lady.   We are here at peace.

More. Then peace,° good wife.

Lady. For keeping still in compass° (a strange point
25   In time's new navigation) we have sailed
Beyond our course.°

More.   Have done.

Lady. We are exiled the Court.

More.   Still thou harpst on that.
'Tis sin for to deserve that banishment,
But he that ne'er knew° Court, courts sweet content.

Lady. Oh, but, dear husband—

30 *More.*   I will not hear thee, wife.
The winding labyrinth of thy strange discourse
Will ne'er have end. Sit still and, my good wife,
Entreat thy tongue be still, or credit me,
Thou shalt not understand a word we speak;
35   We'll talk in Latin.
Humida vallis raros patitur fulminis ictus.[47]

14 *gags* props open   /   15 *ruffles* hectors, bullies   /   15 *in a coat of trust* under a guise of loyalty   /
18–19 *Those that stand . . . pawn his fortunes* the other pretentious people enjoy watching him fall   /
19 Gabrieli and Melchiori's emendation   /   20 *wanton tongue* lawless, insolent speech   /   23 *peace*
hold your peace; be quiet   /   24 *still in compass* (a) as a metaphor, always within the guidelines of
the nautical instrument (b) literally, always within their proper sphere   /   25–26 *sailed beyond our
course* (a) metaphorically, gone beyond the charted trip of the vessel (b) literally, come to the end of
our time   /   29 *knew* (a) was familiar with (b) recognized the claims of the authority of

47. From Seneca's *Hippolytus*, lines 1132–33: "Seldom does the moist valley suffer the light-
ning's blast." (trans. Frank Miller). "The remainder of the chorus's speech resonates with themes of
the play as well: "but Caucasus the huge, and the Phrygian grove of mother Cybele, quake beneath
the bolt of high-thundering Jove. For in jealous fear Jove aims at that which neighbours on high

More rest enjoys the subject meanly bred
Than he that bears the kingdom in his head.[48]
[. . .] Great men are still musicians, else the world lies:
They learn low strains after the notes that rise.° [49]   40
Roper. Good sir, be still° yourself, and but remember
How in this general Court of short-lived pleasure,
The world, creation is the ample food
That is digested in the maw° of time.
If man himself be subject to such ruin,   45
How shall his garment then, or the loose points
That tie respect unto his awful place,
Avoid destruction?° Most honoured father-in-law,
The blood you have bequeathed these several hearts
To nourish your posterity, stands firm,   50
And as with joy you led us first to rise,
So with like hearts we'll lock preferment's eyes.°
More. Now will I speak like More in melancholy:[50]
For if grief's power could with her sharpest darts
Pierce my fierce bosom, here's sufficient cause   55
To take my farewell of mirth's hurtless laws.
Poor humbl'd lady, thou that wert of late
Plac'd with the noblest women of the land,
Invited to their angel companies,
Seeming a bright star in the courtly sphere,   60

40 *They learn . . . that rise* eventually they all fall back from their lofty states / 41 *be still* (a) be at
peace (b) remain / 44 *maw* belly / 46–48 *how shall . . . avoid destruction* if man can't even save his
life, how can he expect to retain all his honors? / 52 *lock preferment's eyes* turn away from hopes of
worldly advancement

heaven; but the low-roofed, common home ne'er feels his mighty blasts. Around thrones he thun-
ders." (1136–40) Cf. More's poems on "Two Beggars," *TMSB,* pp. 233–34.

48. See More's poem on kings and sleep, *TMSB,* p. 236. Cf. Shakespeare's *Henry the Fifth:* "Not
all these, laid in bed majestical, / Can sleep so soundly as the wretched slave" (4.3.267–68). Cf. also
Henry IV, Part Two on the burden of a crown: "O polished perturbation! golden care! / that keep'st
the ports of slumber open wide / To many a watchful night, sleep with it now! / Yet not so sound,
and half so deeply sweet, / As he whose brow with homely biggen bound / Snores out the watch
of night" (5.23–28).

49. Lines 39–40 are marked for omission on the manuscript (Greg, p. 48). Gabrieli and Melchiori suggest that the author crossed these out (p. 177).

50. Most of this passage (lines 53–122) is marked for deletion in the manuscript. Gabrieli and
Melchiori adapt an alternative text for this scene (pp. 178–80).

Why shouldst thou like a widow sit thus low
And all thy fair consorts move from the clouds
That overdrip thy beauty and thy worth?
I'll tell thee the true cause: the Court, like heaven,
65   Examines not the anger of the prince,
And being more frail compos'd of gilded earth
Shines upon them on whom the King doth shine,
Smiles if he smile, declines if he decline.
Yet seeing both are mortal, Court and King,
70   Shed not one tear for any earthly thing.
For, so God pardon me, in my saddest hour
Thou hast no more occasion to lament
Nor these, nor those, my exile from the Court,
No, nor this body's torture were't imposed—
75   As commonly disgraces of great men
As the forewarnings of a hasty death—
Than to behold me after many a toil
Honour'd with endless rest. Perchance the King,
Seeing the Court is full of vanity,
80   Has pity lest our souls should be misled,
And sends us to a life contemplative.
Oh, happy banishment from worldly pride,
When souls by private life are sanctified.
Lady. Oh, but I fear some plot against your life!
85 *More.* Why, then 'tis thus: the King of his high grace,
Seeing my faithful service to his state,
Intends to send me to the King of heaven
For a rich present, where my soul shall prove
A true rememb'rer of his Majesty.
90   Come, prithee mourn not; the worst chance is death,
And that brings endless joy for fickle breath.
Lady. Ah, but your children!
More.   Tush, let them alone.
Say they be stript from this poor painted cloth,
This outside of the earth, left houseless, bare,
95   They have minds instructed how to gather more;
There's no man that's ingenuous can be poor.
And therefore, do not weep, my little ones,

Though you lose all the earth; keep your souls even
And you shall find inheritance in heaven.
But for my servants, there's my chiefest care!   100
Come hither, faithful steward, be not griev'd
That in thy person I discharge both thee
And all thy other fellow officers,
For my great master hath discharged me.
If thou by serving me hast suffer'd loss   105
Then benefit thyself by leaving me.
I hope thou hast not, for such times as these
Bring gain to officers, whoever lese.°
Great lords have only name, but in their fall
Lord Spend-all's Steward's master, gathers all!   110
But I suspect not thee—admit thou hast,
It's good the servants save when masters waste.
But you, poor gentlemen, that had no place
T'enrich yourselves but by loath'd bribery,
Which I abhorred and never found you loved,   115
Think when an oak falls underwood shrinks down
And yet may live though bruised, I pray ye, strive
To shun my ruin, for the axe is set
Even at my root to fell me to the ground.
The best I can do to prefer you all   120
With my mean store expect, for Heaven can tell
That More loves all his followers more than well.

                    Enter a servant.

Servant. My lord, there are new-lighted° at the gate
        The Earls of Surrey and of Shrewsbury,
        And they expect you in the inner court.   125
More. Entreat their lordships come into the hall.
Lady. O God, what news with them?
More.   Why, how now, wife?
        They are but come to visit their old friend.
Lady. O God, I fear, I fear.
More.   What shouldst thou fear, fond° woman?

---

108 *lese* lose / 123 *newlighted* just dismounted / 129 *fond* foolish

130 *Iustum si fractus illabatur orbis impavidum ferient ruinae.*° 51
     Here let me live estranged from great men's looks:
     They are like golden flies on leaden hooks.

               Enter the Earls of Surrey and Shrewsbury,
               Downes with his mace, and attendants.

Shrewsbury. Good morrow, good Sir Thomas.
Surrey. Good day, good madam.   *Kind salutations.*
More.   Welcome, my good lords.
135 What ails your lordships look so melancholy?
     Oh, I know you live in Court, and the Court diet
     Is only friend to physic.°
Surrey.   Oh, Sir Thomas,
     Our words are now the King's, and our sad° looks
     The interest° of your love. We are sent to you
140 From our mild Sovereign, once more to demand
     If you'll subscribe unto those Articles
     He sent ye th'other day. Be well advised,
     For on mine honour, lord, grave Doctor Fisher
     Bishop of Rochester, at the self same instant
145 Attached° with you, is sent unto the Tower
     For the like obstinacy; his Majesty
     Hath only sent you prisoner to your house.
     But if you now refuse for to subscribe,
     A stricter course will follow.
Lady. Oh, dear husband!   *Kneeling and weeping.*
Daughters.   Dear Father!
150 *More.*   See, my lords,

130 A just man, even if a broken world falls, faces the ruin fearlessly / 137 *only friend to physic* since the court food makes one ill / 138 *sad* (a) grave (b) unhappy / 139 *interest* (a) concern for (b) claim upon / 145 *attached* arrested

51. More is quoting from Horace's *Odes* 3.3.1, 7–8, on constancy. As with the other Latin quotations in the play, the original context of this one is suggestive: "The man who knows what's right and tenacious / In the knowledge of what he knows cannot be shaken, / Not by people righteously impassioned / In a wrong cause, and not by menacings / Of tyrants' frowns, nor by the wind that roils / The stormy Adriatic, nor by the fiery / Hand of thundering Jove: the sky could fall / In pieces around him, he would not quail. / This is how Pollux and Hercules made their way up to the stars, where someday Caesar will sit, / Drinking the nectar of heaven, at the same table" (3.3.1–10, trans. David Ferry).

This partner and these subjects to my flesh
Prove rebels to my conscience. But, my good lords,
If I refuse, must I unto the Tower?[52]
Shrewsbury. You must, my lord. Here is an officer
Ready for to arrest you of high treason.   155
Lady and Daughters.   O God, O God!
Roper.   Be patient, good madam.
More. Ay, Downes, is't thou? I once did save thy life,
When else by cruel riotous assault
Thou hadst been torn in pieces. Thou art reserved
To be my summ'ner to yond spiritual court.   160
Give me thy hand, good fellow, smooth thy face;°
The diet that thou drinkst is spiced with mace,°
And I could ne'er abide it; 'twill not disgest;
'Twill lie too heavy, man, on my weak breast.
Shrewsbury. Be brief, my lord, for we are limited   165
Unto an hour.
More.   Unto an hour? 'Tis well,
The bell (earth's thunder) soon shall toll my knell.°
Lady (kneeling). Dear loving husband, if you respect° not me,
Yet think upon your daughters.
More.   Wife, stand up.
(Pondering to himself) I have bethought me,   170
And I'll now satisfy the King's good pleasure.
Daughters. Oh, happy alteration.
Shrewsbury. Come then, subscribe, my lord.
Surrey.   I am right glad
Of this your fair conversion.
More.   Oh, pardon me,
I will subscribe to go unto the Tower   175
With all submissive willingness, and thereto add
My bones to strengthen the foundation

---

161 *smooth thy face* take a calm expression / 162 *mace* (a) a nutmeg spice (b) swindling / 167 *knell*
the toll of a funeral bell; deathknell / 168 *respect* show consideration for

52. As earlier at 4.1.74, this scene presents More's struggle with Henry as one of conscience.
Despite rebellions against him by his family and servants—and by his own frailty (4.4.164)—More
presses on to the Tower and his own death.

Of Julius Caesar's palace. Now, my lord,
I'll satisfy the King even with my blood,
180   Nor will I wrong your patience. Friend, do thine office.°
Downes. Sir Thomas More, Lord Chancellor of England,
      I arrest you in the King's name of high treason.
More. Gramercies,° friend.
      To a great prison, to discharge° the strife
185   Commenced 'twixt conscience and my frailer life;
      More now must march. Chelsea, adieu, adieu.
      Strange farewell; thou shalt ne'er more see More true,
      For I shall ne'er see thee more. Servants, farewell.
      Wife, mar not thine indifferent° face; be wise;
190   More's widow's husband, he must make thee rise.
      Daughters, [. . .]° what's here, what's here?
      Mine eye had almost parted with a tear.
      Dear son, possess my virtue, that I ne'er gave.
      Grave More thus lightly walks to a quick grave.
195 *Roper. Curae leves loquuntur, ingentes stupent.*[53]
More. You that way in; mind you my course in prayer;
      By water I to prison, to heaven through air.   *Exeunt.*

Act V

Scene I. *Gateway to the Tower of London.*

Enter the Warders of the Tower with halberds.

First Warder. Ho, make a guard there!
Second Warder. Master Lieutenant gives a straight command
      The people be avoided° from the bridge.
Third Warder. From whence is he committed,° who can tell?
5 *First Warder.* From Durham House, I hear.
Second Warder. The guard were waiting there an hour ago.
Third Warder. If he stay long, he'll not get near the wharf,

---

180 *office* duty / 183 *Gramercies* thanks / 184 *discharge* relieve / 189 *indifferent* (a) unemotional
(b) of average appearance / 191 damaged ms / 3 *avoided* removed / 4 committed *imprisoned*

53. From Seneca's *Hippolytus*, line 607: "Light troubles speak; the weighty are struck dumb."
(trans. Frank Miller).

There's such a crowd of boats upon the Thames.
First Warder. Well, be it spoken without offence to any,
    A wiser or more virtuous gentleman   10
    Was never bred in England.
Second Warder. I think the poor will bury him in tears.
    I never heard a man since I was born
    So generally bewailed of everyone.[54]

Enter a Poor Woman.

Third Warder. What means this woman?—Whither dost thou press?   15
First Warder. This woman will be trod to death anon.
Second Warder. What mak'st thou here?
Woman. To speak with that good man, Sir Thomas More.
First Warder. To speak with him? He's not Lord Chancellor.
Woman. The more's the pity, sir, if it pleased God.   20
First Warder. Therefore if thou hast a petition to deliver,
    Thou mayst keep it now, for anything I know.
Woman. I am a poor woman, and have had (God knows)
    A suit this two year in the Chancery,°
    And he hath all the evidence I have,   25
    Which should I lose, I am utterly undone.
First Warder. Faith, and I fear thou'lt hardly come by 'em now.
    I am sorry for thee even with all my heart.

*Enter the Lords of Shrewsbury and Surrey with Sir Thomas More and
    attendants, and enter Lieutenant and Gentleman Porter.*

Second Warder. Woman, stand back; you must avoid this place;
    The lords must pass this way into the Tower.   30
More. I thank your lordships for your pains thus far
    To my strong house.°

---

24 *this two year in the Chancery* these two years in the court of the Lord Chancellor / 32 *strong house* stronghold

54. The Warders' praise of More, offered "without offense to any," is the first of many surprisingly sympathetic verdicts on More's character offered in act five; it also suggests something of his broad appeal to "everyone," as the Warder puts it. See also the verdicts of More's servants at Chelsea (5.2.5–20, 39–55) and the comments of the Lieutenant of the Tower on the constancy of his wisdom and merriment amidst adversity (5.3.5–9, 19).

Woman. Now, good Sir Thomas More, for Christ's dear sake,
        Deliver me my writings back again
35   That do concern my title.
More. What, my old client, art thou got hither too?
        Poor silly° wretch, I must confess indeed
        I had such writings as concern thee near,
        But the King has ta'en the matter into his own hand;
40   He has all I had; then, woman, sue to him;
        I cannot help thee; thou must bear with me.
Woman. Ah, gentle heart, my soul for thee is sad;
        Farewell, the best friend that the poor e'er had.

                                                    Exit.

Gentleman Porter. Before you enter through the Tower gate,
45   Your upper garment, sir, belongs to me.
More. Sir, you shall have it, there it is.

                                    He gives him his cap.

Gentleman Porter. The upmost on your back, sir, you mistake me.
    More. Sir, now I understand ye very well;
        But that you name my back;
50   Sure else my cap had been the uppermost.
Shrewsbury. Farewell, kind lord; God send us merry meeting.
More. Amen, my lord.
Surrey. Farewell, dear friend; I hope your safe return.
More. My lord, and my dear fellow in the Muses,
55   Farewell, farewell, most noble poet.[55]
Lieutenant. Adieu, most honoured lords.   *Exeunt Lords.*
More. Fair prison, welcome. Yet methinks,
        For thy fair building 'tis too foul a name.
        Many a guilty soul, and many an innocent,
60   Have breathed their farewell to thy hollow rooms.
        I oft have entered into thee this way,
        Yet, I thank God, ne'er with a clearer conscience
        Than at this hour.

37 *silly* pitiable

    55. More had earlier defended poets in 3.1, and here he identifies himself as one to some degree. While the other characters in act five have lamented the passing of a wise, virtuous, and kind man, here More suggests that his fall also involves the death of a poet. See also 5.4.71, where this fall is described by More as a "tragedy."

This is my comfort yet: how hard soe'er
My lodging prove, the cry of the poor suitor,   65
Fatherless orphan or distressèd widow
Shall not disturb me in my quiet sleep.
On then, a God's name, to our close° abode;
God is as strong here as he is abroad.°   *Exeunt.*

Scene II. *Thomas More's Home at Chelsea.*
Enter Butler, Brewer, Porter, and Horsekeeper
several ways.

Butler. Robin brewer, how now, man? What cheer, what cheer?

Brewer. Faith, Ned butler, sick of thy disease; and these our other fellows
here, Ralph horsekeeper and Giles porter, sad, sad; they say my lord
goes to his trial today.

Horsekeeper. To it, man? Why, he is now at it; God send him well to speed.°   5

Porter. Amen. Even as I wish to mine own soul, so speed it° with my honourable lord and master Sir Thomas More.

Butler. I cannot tell; I have nothing to do with matters above my capacity,°
but as God judge me, if I might speak my mind, I think there lives not
a more harmless gentleman in the universal world.   10

Brewer. Nor a wiser, nor a merrier, nor an honester. Go to, I'll put that in
upon mine own knowledge.

Porter. Nay, and ye bate him his due of his housekeeping,° hang ye all.
Have ye many lord chancellors comes in debt at the year's end, and for
very housekeeping?   15

Horsekeeper. Well, he was too good a lord for us, and therefore, I fear, God
himself will take him. But I'll be hanged if ever I have such another
service.°

Brewer. Soft, man, we are not discharged° yet. My lord may come home
again and all will be well.   20

Butler. I much mistrust° it; when they go to 'raigning° once, there's ever
foul weather for a great while after.

68 *close* closed up / 69 *abroad* out of doors / 5 *God send him well to speed* God bless him / 6 *so
speed it* may it be so / 8 *capacity* competence, knowledge / 13 *and ye bate him his due of his housekeeping* if you don't give him credit for his hospitality / 18 *such another service* such another good
position as a servant / 19 *Soft, man, we are not discharged* Quiet, we are not released / 21 *mistrust*
doubt / 21 *raigning* arraigning, trying; puns on raining

Enter Gough and Catesby with a paper.

But soft, here comes Master Gough and Master Catesby; now we
shall hear more.

25 *Horsekeeper.* Before God, they are very sad; I doubt° my lord is condemned.

Porter. God bless his soul, and a fig° then for all worldly condemnation.

Gough. Well said, Giles porter; I commend thee for it;
    'Twas spoken like a well affected° servant
30   Of him that was a kind lord to us all.

Catesby. Which now no more he shall be, for, dear fellows,
    Now we are masterless, though he may live
    So long as please the King. But law hath made him
    A dead man to the world, and given the axe his head,
35   But his sweet soul to live among the saints.[56]

Gough. Let us entreat ye to go call together
    The rest of your sad fellows—by the roll
    Y'are just seven score°—and tell them what ye hear
    A virtuous honourable lord hath done
40   Even for the meanest follower that he had.
    This writing found my lady in his study
    This instant° morning, wherein is set down
    Each servant's name, according to his place
    And office in the house. On every man
45   He frankly° hath bestowen twenty nobles,
    The best and worst together, all alike,
    Which Master Catesby here forth will pay ye.

Catesby. Take it, as it is meant, a kind remembrance
    Of a far kinder lord, with whose sad fall
50   He gives up house, and farewell to us all.
    Thus the fair spreading oak falls not alone,
    But all the neighbour plants and under-trees
    Are crushed down with his weight. No more of this,

---

25 *doubt* fear / 27 *a fig* term of contempt / 29 *affected* cherished / 38 *seven score* 140 / 42 *instant*
present / 45 *frankly* freely

56. An unusual line, especially considering the religious controversies of the day. More was not
canonized by the Catholic Church until 1935; since 1980 his name has been included in the Anglican calendar of saints.

Come and receive your due, and after go
Fellow-like hence, co-partners of one woe.   55

                                                   Exeunt.

Scene III. *More's Room in the Tower of London.*

*Enter Sir Thomas More, the lieutenant, and a servant attending, as in his
chamber in the Tower.*

More. Master Lieutenant, is the warrant come?
    If it be so, a God's name, let us know it.
Lieutenant. My lord, it is.
More.   'Tis welcome, sir, to me,
    With all my heart. His blessed will be done.
Lieutenant. Your wisdom, sir, hath been so well approved,°   5
    And your fair patience in imprisonment
    Hath ever shown such constancy of mind
    And Christian resolution in all troubles,
    As warrants us you are not unprepared.
More. No, Master Lieutenant, I thank my God   10
    I have peace of conscience, though the world and I
    Are at a little odds. But we'll be even now, I hope
    Ere long. When is the execution° of your warrant?
Lieutenant. Tomorrow morning.
More.   So, sir, I thank ye.
    I have not lived so ill I fear to die.   15
    Master Lieutenant, I have had a sore fit of the stone° tonight,
    But the King hath sent me such a rare receipt,°
    I thank him, as I shall not need to fear it much.
Lieutenant. In life and death, still merry Sir Thomas More.
More. Sirrah, fellow, reach me the urinal.   20

                      [The servant] gives it him.

    Ha, let me see. [There's]° gravel in the water,
    [Faith, there's no instant jeopardy in that.]°
    The man were likely to live long enough,

---

5 *approved* demonstrated / 13 *execution* issuance, with pun on its being a warrant of execution /
16 *sore fit of the stone* pain from a kidney stone, which can be excruciating / 17 *receipt* prescription
/ 21–22 Shirley's emendations

So pleased the King. Here, fellow, take it.

25 *Servant*. Shall I go with it to the doctor, sir?

More. No, save thy labour; we'll cozen° him of a fee.

       Thou shalt see me take a dram° tomorrow morning,

       Shall cure the stone I warrant, doubt it not.

       Master Lieutenant, what news of my Lord of Rochester?

30 *Lieutenant*. Yesterday morning was he put to death.

More. The peace of soul sleep with him.

       He was a learned and a reverend prelate,

       And a rich man, believe me.

Lieutenant. If he were rich, what is Sir Thomas More,

35   That all this while hath been Lord Chancellor?

More. Say ye so, Master Lieutenant? What do you think

       A man that with my time had held my place

       Might purchase?°

Lieutenant. Perhaps, my lord, two thousand pound a year.

40 *More*. Master Lieutenant, I protest to you

       I never had the means in all my life

       To purchase one poor hundred pound a year.

       I think I am the poorest chancellor

       That ever was in England, though I could wish,

45   For credit of the place, that my estate were better.

Lieutenant. It's very strange.

More.   It will be found as true.

       I think, sir, that with most part of my coin

       I have purchased as strange commodities

       As ever you heard tell of in your life.

50 *Lieutenant*. Commodities, my lord?

       Might I, without offence, enquire of them?

More. Crutches, Master Lieutenant, and bare° cloaks.

       For halting° soldiers, and poor needy scholars,

       Have had my gettings in the Chancery.

55   To think but what acheat° the Crown shall have

       By my attainder!° I prithee, if thou beest a gentleman,

       Get but a copy of my inventory.

---

26 *cozen* cheat / 27 *dram* draught of medicine / 38 *purchase* acquire / 52 *bare* simple / 53 *halting* maimed, lame / 55 *acheat* raw deal / 56 *attainder* forfeiture of property

That part of poet that was given me
Made me a very unthrift.
For this is the disease attends us all: 60
Poets were never thrifty, never shall.

Enter Lady More mourning, daughters, Master Roper.

Lieutenant. O noble More.—
       My lord, your wife, your son-in-law, and daughters.
More. Son Roper, welcome; welcome, wife and girls.
       Why do you weep? Because I live at ease?   65
       Did you not see, when I was chancellor,
       I was so cloyed° with suitors every hour
       I could not sleep, nor dine, nor sup in quiet?
       Here's none of this; here I can sit and talk
       With my honest keeper half a day together,   70
       Laugh and be merry. Why then should you weep?
Roper. These tears, my lord, for this your long restraint
       Hope had dried up with comfort that we yet,
       Although imprisoned, might have had your life.
More. To live in prison, what a life were that?   75
       The King (I thank him) loves me more than so.
       Tomorrow I shall be at liberty
       To go even whither I can,
       After I have dispatched my business.
Lady. Ah husband, husband, yet submit yourself,   80
       Have care of your poor wife and children.
More. Wife, so I have, and I do leave you all.
       To His protection hath the power to keep
       You safer than I can,
       The Father of the widow and the orphan.[57]   85
Roper. The world, my lord, hath ever held you wise,
       And 't shall be no distaste unto your wisdom

---

67 *cloyed* encumbered

57. More's position here seems to be that by remaining constant to his conscience, he provides the best "care" for his wife and children, even though that constancy leads to his death. That More's view of his situation differs profoundly from everyone else's view is evident in 5.4 as well, particularly in his cheerful conversations on the way to the "goodly" scaffold (line 48) and in his claim that his ignominious death is the means of his "birth to heaven" (lines 94ff).

To yield to the opinion of the state.
More. I have deceived myself, I must acknowledge;
90   And as you say, son Roper, to confess the same
It will be no disparagement at all.
Lady. His Highness shall be certified° thereof, immediately.

Offering to depart.

More. Nay, hear me, wife; first let me tell ye how
I thought to have had a barber for my beard.[58]
95   Now I remember that were labour lost;
The headsman° now shall cut off head and all.
Roper's Wife. Father, his Majesty upon your meek submission
Will yet, they say, receive you to his Grace
In as great credit° as you were before.
100   *More.* ['Tis so indeed]° wench. Faith, my lord the King
Has appointed me to do a little business.
If that were past, my girl, thou then shouldst see
What I would say to him about that matter.
But I shall be so busy until then, I shall not tend it.
Daughters. Ah, my dear father.
105   *Lady.*   Dear lord and husband.
More. Be comforted, good wife, to live and love my children,
For with thee leave I all my care of them.
Son Roper, for my sake that have loved thee well,
And for her virtue's sake, cherish my child.
110   Girl, be not proud, but of° thy husband's love
Ever retain thy virtuous modesty.
That modesty is such a comely garment
As it is never out of fashion: sits as fair
Upon the meaner woman as the empress.
115   No stuff that gold can buy is half so rich,
Nor ornament that so becomes a woman.[59]
Live all, and love together, and thereby

92 *certified* informed / 96 *headsman* (a) leader, therefore Henry (b) executioner / 99 *credit* favor
/ 100 Shirley's emendation. / 110 *of* on account of

58. This is another example of Morean jest, though perhaps one more exasperating than the
others, at least for his family members, who think he is having a change of heart on the Articles; in
fact, he has only decided not to have his beard barbered.
59. Cf. Thomas More's *Letter to Gonell*, pp. 197–200, *TMSB.*

You give your father a rich obsequy.°
Daughters. Your blessing, dear father.
More. I must be gone—God bless you—   120
   To talk with God, who now doth call.
Lady. Ah, my dear husband!
More.   Sweet wife, good night, good night.
   God send us all his everlasting light.
Roper. I think before this hour,
   More heavy hearts ne'er parted in the Tower.   125

              Exeunt.

Scene IV. *The Scaffold on Tower Hill.*

*Enter the sheriffs of London and their officers at one door, the warders with
their halberds at another.*

First Sheriff. Officers, what time of day is 't?
Officer. Almost eight o'clock.
Second Sheriff. We must make haste then, lest we stay too long.
First Warder. Good morrow, Master Shrieves of London; Master Lieutenant
   Wills ye repair to the limits of the Tower   5
   There to receive your prisoner.
First Sheriff. Go back, and tell his Worship we are ready.
Second Sheriff. Go bid the officers make clear the way,
   There may be passage for the prisoner.

    Enter Lieutenant and his guard with More.

More. Yet, God be thanked, here's a fair day toward°   10
   To take our journey in. Master Lieutenant,
   It were fair walking on the Tower leads.
Lieutenant. And so it might have liked my Sovereign Lord,
   I would to God you might have walked there still.°—

             He weeps.

More. Sir, we are walking to a better place.   15
   Oh, sir, your kind and loving tears
   Are like sweet odours to embalm your friend.

---

118 *obsequy* (a) obedience to my will (b) funeral rite / 10 *toward* in store / 14 *still* always

    Thank your good lady, since I was your guest
    She has made me a very wanton,°—in good sooth.
20 *Lieutenant.* Oh, I had hoped we should not yet have parted.
 More. But I must leave ye for a little while.
    Within an hour or two you may look for me,
    But there will be so many come to see me
    That I shall be so proud I will not speak.[60]
25   And sure my memory is grown so ill
    I fear I shall forget my head behind me.
 Lieutenant. God and his blessed angels be about ye.
    Here, Master Shrieves, receive your prisoner.
 More. Good morrow, Master Shrieves of London, to ye both.
30   I thank ye that ye will vouchsafe° to meet me.
    I see by this you have not quite forgot
    That I was in times past as you are now:
    A sheriff of London.
 First Sheriff. Sir, then you know our duty doth require it.
35 *More.* I know it well, sir, else I would have been glad
    You might have saved a labour at this time.
    Ah, Master Sheriff, you and I have been of old acquaintance.
    You were a patient auditor° of mine
    When I read the divinity lecture at Saint Lawrence's.[61]
40 *Second Sheriff.* Sir Thomas More, I have heard you oft, as many other did,
    To our great comfort.
 More.   Pray God, you may so now,
    With all my heart. And, as I call to mind,
    When I studied the law in Lincoln's Inn,
    I was of counsel° with ye in a cause.

---

19 *wanton* spoilt child / 30 *that ye will vouchsafe* for being willing to condescend / 38 *auditor* listener / 44 *of counsel* worked together in a legal capacity with

  60. More jokingly intimates that his severed head will soon be displayed on Tower Bridge after the execution for all to see.
  61. The line refers to More's lectures on Augustine's *City of God*, delivered at St. Lawrence Jewry in 1501 at the invitation of William Grocyn. These lost lectures, focusing on a work well-known for its argument that all efforts at securing earthly peace and justice will inevitably come up short, presumably provided More with an opportunity for reflection on the hopes and dreams of the Renaissance. Stapleton mentions in his biography that More decided to "treat this great work [not] from the theological point of view, but from the standpoint of history and philosophy" (pp. 7–8).

[First] Sheriff. I was about to say so, good Sir Thomas.   45
    [   ]°
More. Oh, is this the place?
    I promise ye, it is a goodly scaffold.
    In sooth, I am come about a headless° errand,
    For I have not much to say, now I am here.   50
    Well, let's ascend, a God's name.
    In troth, methinks your stair is somewhat weak.
    I prithee, honest friend, lend me thy hand
    To help me up. As for my coming down,
    Let me alone, I'll look to that myself.[62]   55

    As he is going up the stairs, enter the Earls of Surrey and Shrewsbury.

More. My Lords of Surrey and of Shrewsbury, give me your hands yet before we part. Ye see, though it pleaseth the King to raise me thus high, yet I am not proud, for the higher I mount, the better I can see my friends about me. I am now on a far voyage, and this strange wooden horse must bear me thither; yet I perceive by your looks you like my   60
bargain so ill, that there's not one of ye all dare venture with me. *(Walking)* Truly, here's a most sweet gallery; I like the air of it better than my garden at Chelsea. By your patience, good people that have pressed thus into my bedchamber, if you'll not trouble me, I'll take a sound sleep here.   65
Shrewsbury. My lord, 'twere good you'd publish to the world
    Your great offence° unto his Majesty.
More. My lord, I'll bequeath this legacy to the hangman, and do it instantly *(gives him his gown)*. I confess his Majesty hath been ever good to me, and my offence to his Highness makes me of a state pleader a stage   70
player° (though I am old, and have a bad voice) to act this last scene of my tragedy. I'll send him for my trespass a reverent head, somewhat bald, for it is not requisite any head should stand covered to so high majesty. If that content him not, because I think my body will then do

---

46 This line was lost due to manuscript damage. / 49 *headless* aside from the obvious literal meaning, headless meant (a) senseless and (b) subject to no ecclesiastical authority; all three senses of the word apply to More's current position. / 66–67 *publish . . . your great offence* formally acknowledge your crime / 70–71 *of a state pleader a stage player* from a lawyer of the state into a play actor

62. One of More's most famous jests. For other specimens of scaffold humor, see 5.4.78–79 and 5.4.88–92.

75   me small pleasure, let him but bury it, and take it.

Surrey. My lord, my lord, hold conference with your soul.
        You see, my lord, the time of life is short.

More. I see it, my good lord; I dispatched° that business the last night.[63] I
        come hither only to be let blood;° my doctor here tells me it is good
80   for the headache.

Hangman. I beseech ye, my lord, forgive me.

More. Forgive thee, honest° fellow? Why?

Hangman. For your death, my lord.

More. Oh, my death? I had rather it were in thy power to forgive me, for
85   thou hast the sharpest action against me: the law, my honest friend, lies
        in thy hands now. Here's thy fee (*his purse*), and, my good fellow, let my
        suit° be dispatched presently; for 'tis all one pain to die a lingering
        death and to live in the continual mill of a law-suit. But I can tell thee,
        my neck is so short that if thou shouldst behead an hundred noblemen
90   like myself, thou wouldst ne'er get credit° by it. Therefore look ye, sir,
        do it handsomely,° or of my word thou shalt never deal with me here-
        after.

Hangman. I'll take an order for that°, my lord.

More. One thing more, take heed thou cutst not off my beard. Oh, I for-
95   got; execution passed upon that last night, and the body of it lies
        buried in the Tower.—Stay! Is't not possible to make a scape° from all
        this strong guard? It is.
            There is a thing within me, that will raise
            And elevate my better part 'bove sight
100   Of these same weaker eyes. And, Master Shrieves,
            For all this troop of steel that tends° my death,
            I shall break from you, and fly up to heaven.
            Let's seek the means for this.

Hangman. My lord, I pray ye, put off your doublet.°

105 *More.* Speak not so coldly to me; I am hoarse already;
            I would be loath, good fellow, to take more.°

---

78 *dispatched* finished up / 79 *let blood* releasing blood was a common prescription for ill patients
/ 82 *honest* general term of appreciation to an inferior / 87 *suit* as in a lawsuit, a legal proceedings
/ 90 *credit* (a) payment (b) appreciation / 91 *handsomely* properly / 93 *take an order for that* take
the proper measures / 96 *scape* escape / 101 *tends* (a) awaits for (b) prepares / 104 *doublet* close-
fitting body garment / 106 *take more* take off more clothing

63. More seems to refer to his final sacramental confession the night before his execution.

Point me the block; I ne'er was here before.
Hangman. To the east side, my lord.
More.   Then to the east,
　　We go to sigh; that o'er, to sleep in rest.
　　Here More forsakes all mirth, good reason why: 110
　　The fool of flesh must with her frail life die.
　　No eye salute my trunk° with a sad tear;
　　Our birth to heaven should be thus: void of fear.   *Exit.*
Surrey. A very learned worthy gentleman
　　Seals error with his blood.[64] Come, we'll to Court.   115
　　Let's sadly hence to perfect° unknown fates,
　　Whilst he tends progress° to the state of states.°

　　　　　　　　　　　　　　　　　　　　[Exeunt.]

　　　　　　　　Finis.

---

112 *trunk* headless body / 116 *perfect* already prepared / 117 *tends progress* makes his way /
117 *state of states* (a) best possible mode of existence (b) greatest kingdom (heaven)

64. Surrey's words are perhaps intended to appease the censor, but they seem a touch ambiguous as well. What or whose error is sealed with More's blood? Also, Surrey's decision to return to court and his reference to "our perfect unknown fates" may foreshadow his own death for treason against King Henry on January 13, 1547. If so, this last speech only reinforces the play's subtle emphasis on the dangerous relationship between kings and poets, with the latter literally losing their heads.

2

Writings on Love and Friendship

Desiderus Erasmus, by Quentin Matsys, 1517

In the portrait above, Erasmus is wearing a ring given to him by More. The books marked on the shelves are his edition of St. Jerome, his Greek edition of the New Testament, Lucian, and his *In Praise of Folly* ("folly" in Greek is *Moria*—playing upon More's name). Erasmus is writing his *Paraphrase of the Epistle of St. Paul to the Romans;* on the facing page is written "Gratia" in Erasmus' hand.

Peter Giles, by Quentin Matsys, 1517

The books identified on Giles' bookshelves are Plutarch, Seneca, Erasmus' *Education of a Christian Prince,* and Suetonius. Giles has a letter from More in his hand.

The preceding two portraits were given to More as a gift commemorating his friendship with Erasmus and Peter Giles. Giles is "shown as the epitome of the active humanist life" (Campbell *et al*, p. 718). He holds a letter from More and is pointing to a book he and Erasmus also shared, since the book seems to be *Utopia*. More began writing *Utopia* in Antwerp, and both Giles and Erasmus helped with its publication. These two portraits were lost by the More family after More's execution. When More received these paintings, he wrote two Latin poems to express his thanks. One is given here in a prose translation:

"The Picture Speaks"

I show Erasmus and Giles, friends as dear to each other as were Castor and Pollux of old. More grieves to be absent from them in space, since in affection he is united with them so closely that a man could scarcely be closer to himself. They arranged to satisfy their absent friend's longing for them: a loving letter represents their minds, I their bodies. *(Latin Poems, #276, Complete Works*, vol. 3.2)

Contrasting Poems

In addition to his voluminous prose writings, More also wrote poetry. In the first selection, More reflects on the power that emotion wields, especially in matters of love. The second poem sets forth a view of love, both human and supernatural. The third selection, written while More was imprisoned in the Tower of London, reveals how More's life-long effort to govern his emotions assisted him in the midst of great adversity.

On His First Love[1]

You are really still alive, Elizabeth, dearer to me in my early years than I was myself, and once again my eyes behold you. What bad luck has kept you from me all these many years! When I was just a boy, I saw you first; now when I am almost an old man, I see you again. Sixteen years I had
5 lived—you were about two years younger—when your face inspired me with innocent devotion. That face is now no part of your appearance; where has it gone? When the vision I once loved comes before me, I see, alas, how utterly your actual appearance fails to resemble it. The years, always envious of young beauty, have robbed you of yourself but have not
10 robbed me of you. That beauty of countenance to which my eyes so often

*Latin Poem #263
c. 1518*

Love at 16

1. *Latin Poems*, #263, *Complete Works*, vol. 3.2. The original title of this poem is "He Expresses His Joy at Finding Safe and Sound Her Whom He Had Once Loved as a Mere Boy." It was probably written in 1518–1519.

Sir Thomas More, by Hans Holbein, 1527

This sketch, so different from the one on page 2, is now thought to be the preliminary sketch for the strikingly informal family portrait (pp. 14, 15), not for the stately
portrait of More as Lord Chancellor (see cover of this volume and p. 2).

clung now occupies my heart. It is natural for a dying fire, though buried
in its own cold ashes, to flare up when a gust of air blows on it. And however much you are changed from what you were, you make the old flame[2] *His old flame*
glow by giving me this new reminder. There comes now to my mind that
distant day which first revealed you to me as you enjoyed yourself amid a
band of dancing maidens. Your yellow hair enhanced the pure white of
your neck; your cheeks looked like snow, your lips like roses; your eyes,
like two stars, dazed our eyes and through my eyes made their way into my
heart: I was helpless, as though stunned by a lightning-stroke, when I
gazed and continued to gaze upon your face. Then, too, our comrades and
yours laughed at our love, so awkward, so frank and so obvious. Thus did
your beauty take me captive. Either yours was perfect beauty, or I lent it
more perfection than it had; perhaps the stirrings of adolescence and the
ardor which accompanies the approach of manhood were the reason, or
perhaps certain stars we shared at birth had influenced both our hearts. For
a gossipy companion of yours who was in on the secret revealed that your
heart, too, was moved. On this account a chaperon was imposed upon us,
and a door strong enough to thwart our very destiny kept apart a pair
whom the stars wished to bring together. And then that notable day after
so many years brought us together, far separated though we were in the
pursuit of our different destinies, that day propitious in my finding you
alive and well—seldom in my life have I met a happier day. Once upon a
time you innocently stole my heart; now too, and innocently still, you are
dear to me. Our love was blameless; if duty could not keep it so, that day
itself would be enough to keep love blameless still. Well, I beg the saints
above, who, after twenty-five years, have kindly brought us together in
good health, that I may be preserved to see you safe and sound again at the
end of twenty-five years more.

2. See Virgil's *Aeneid* 4.23, "flamma vetusta."

Twelve Properties of a Lover[1]

As part of his first published book, More took a standard list of Petrarchan qualities of love (see the sidenotes below) and wrote the following love ballad of thirteen parts. Each part has two stanzas: the first develops a quality that characterizes a youthful and fervent love; the second applies that quality to one's love of God.

The First Property

1. To love one alone and condemn all others for that one.

The first point is to love but one alone,
And for that one all other to forsake:
For whoso loveth many loveth none:
The flood that is in many channels take
In each of them shall feeble streamès make: 5
The love that is divided among many
Uneath[2] sufficeth that any part have any.

So thou that hast thy love set unto God
In thy remembrance this imprint and grave:
As He in sovereign dignity is odd,[3]   10
So will He in love no parting fellows have:
Love Him therefore with all that He thee gave:
For body, soul, wit, cunning, mind and thought,
Part will He none, but either all or naught.

The Second Property

2. To think himself unhappy if he is not with his love.

Of his love, lo, the sight and company   15
To the lover so glad and pleasant is,
That whoso hath the grace to come thereby
He judgeth him in perfect joy and bliss:
And whoso of that company doth miss,

1. The sidenotes give Pico della Mirandola's version of these conventional qualities of a lover. More expanded on these to create this unique love ballad, and he appended it to his translation of *The Life of John Picus* (c. 1510). See *Complete Works*, vol. 1, pp. 113–20.
2. *uneath*—hardly
3. *odd*—unique

20 Live he in never so prosperous estate,
He thinketh him wretched and infortunate.

So should the lover of God esteem that he
Which all the pleasure hath, mirth and disport,
That in this world is possible to be,
25 Yet till the time that he may once resort
Unto that blessed, joyful, heavenly port
Where he of God may have the glorious sight,
Is void of perfect joy and sure delight.

The Third Property

The third point of a perfect lover is
30 To make him fresh to see that all thing been
Appointed well and nothing set amiss
But all well fashioned, proper, goodly, clean:
That in his person there be nothing seen
In speech, apparel, gesture, look or pace
35 That may offend or diminish any grace.

3. To adorn himself for the pleasure of his love.

So thou that wilt with God get into favour
Garnish thyself up in as goodly wise
As comely be, as honest in behaviour,
As it is possible for thee to devise:
40 I mean not hereby that thou shouldest arise
And in the glass upon thy body prowl,[4]
But with fair virtue to adorn thy soul.

The Fourth Property

If love be strong, hot, mighty and fervent,
There may no trouble, grief, or sorrow fall,
45 But that the lover would be well content
All to endure and think it eke too small,
Though it were death, so he might therewithal
The joyful presence of that person get
On whom he hath his heart and love yset.

4. To suffer all things, even death, in order to be with his love.

4. *prowl*—search eagerly

Thus should of God the lover be content   50
Any distress or sorrow to endure,
Rather than to be from God absent,
And glad to die, so that he may be sure
By his departing hence for to procure,
After this valley dark, the heavenly light,   55
And of his love the glorious blessed sight.

The Fifth Property

Not only a lover content is in his heart
But coveteth eke and longeth to sustain
Some labour, incommodity, or smart,
Loss, adversity, trouble, grief, or pain: 60
And of his sorrow joyful is and fain,
And happy thinketh himself that he may take
Some misadventure for his lover's sake.

Thus shouldest thou, that lovest God also,
In thine heart wish, covet and be glad   65
For Him to suffer trouble, pain and woe:
For Whom if thou be never so woe bestead,
Yet thou ne shalt sustain (be not adread)
Half the dolour, grief and aversity
That He already suffered hath for thee.   70

The Sixth Property

The perfect lover longeth for to be
In presence of his love both night and day,
And if it haply so befall that he
May not as he would, he will yet as he may
Ever be with his love, that is to say,   75
Where his heavy body nil⁵ be brought
He will be conversant in mind and thought.

Lo in like manner the lover of God should,
At the least in such wise as he may,
If he may not in such wise as he would,   80

5. To desire also to suffer harm for his love, and to think that hurt sweet.

6. To be with his love ever as he may; if not in deed, yet in thought.

5. *nil*—will not

Be present with God and conversant alway;
For certes, whoso list, he may purvey,
Though all the world would him therefrom bereaven,
To bear his body in earth, his mind in heaven.

The Seventh Property

85   There is no page or servant, most or least,
That doth upon his love attend and wait,
There is no little worm, no simple beast,
Ne none so small a trifle or conceit,
Lace, girdle, point,[6] or proper glove strait,
90   But that if to his love it have been near,
The lover hath it precious, lief and dear.

So every relic, image or picture[7]
That doth pertain to God's magnificence,
The lover of God should with all busy cure[8]
95   Have it in love, honour and reverence
And specially give them pre-eminence
Which daily done His blessed body wurche,[9]
The quick relics, the ministers of His Church.[10]

7. To love all things that pertain to his love.

The Eighth Property

A very lover above all earthly thing
100   Coveteth and longeth evermore to hear
The honour, laud, commendation and praising,
And everything that may the fame clear
Of his love: he may in no manner
Endure to hear that therefrom mighten vary
105   Or anything sound into the contrary.

8. To covet that his love be praised, and not to suffer any dispraise.

6. *point*—fastening

7. As Anthony Edwards points out, More gives "a similar defense of images" in *Complete Works,*
vol. 6 p. 47, lines 19–31 (*Complete Works*, vol. 1, p. 249).

8. *cure*—care

9. *wurche*—works

10. Anthony Edwards explains this line as meaning that "priests are left behind by Christ, but
unlike ordinary relics, they are alive" (*Complete Works*, vol. 1, p. 249).

The lover of God should covet in like wise
To hear His honour, worship, laud and praise,
Whose sovereign goodness no heart may comprise,
Whom hell, earth, and all the heaven obeys,
Whose perfect lover ought by no manner ways   110
To suffer the cursed words of blasphemy
Or anything spoken of God unreverently.

The Ninth Property

*9. To believe of
his love all things
excellent, and to
desire that all
should think the
same.*

A very lover believeth in his mind
On whomsoever he hath his heart ybent,
That in that person men may nothing find   115
But honourable, worthy and excellent,
And eke surmounting far in his entent
All other that he hath known by sight or name:
And would that every man should think the same.

Of God likewise so wonderful and high   120
All thing esteem and judge his lover ought,
So reverence, worship, honour and magnify,
That all the creatures in this world ywrought
In comparison should he set at nought,
And glad be if he might the mean devise   125
That all the world would thinken in like wise.

The Tenth Property[11]

*10. To languish
ever, and ever to
burn in desire of
his love.*

The lover is of colour dead and pale;
There will no sleep into his eyes stalk;
He favoureth neither meat, wine, nor ale;
He mindeth no what men about him talk;   130
But eat he, drink he, sit, lie down or walk,
He burneth ever as it were with a fire
In the fervent heat of his desire.

Here should the lover of God ensample take
To have Him continually in remembrance,   135
With him in prayer and meditation wake,

---

11. Here More changes the order of #10 and #11 in Pico's list.

While other play, revel, sing, and dance:
None earthly joy, disport, or vain plesance
Should him delight, or anything remove
His ardent mind from God, his heavenly love.

140

The Eleventh Property

Diversely passioned is the lover's heart:
Now pleasant hope, now dread and grievous fear,
Now perfect bliss, now bitter sorrow smart;
And whether his love be with him or elsewhere,
Oft from his eyes there falleth many a tear,—
For very joy, when they together be;
When they be sundered, for adversity.

145

Like affections feeleth eke the breast
Of God's lover in prayer and meditation:
When that his love liketh in him rest
With inward gladness of pleasant contemplation,
Out break the tears for joy and delectation;
And when his love list eft to part him fro,
Out break the tears again for pain and woe.

150

*11. To weep
often with his
love: in presence,
for joy; in absence,
for sorrow.*

The Twelfth Property

A very lover will his love obey:
His joy it is and all his appetite
To pain himself in all that ever he may,
That person in whom he set hath his delight
Diligently to serve both day and night
For very love, without any regard
To any profit, guerdon or reward.

155

160

So thou likewise that hast thine heart yset
Upward to God, so well thyself endeavour,
So studiously that nothing may thee let
Not for His service any wise dissever:
Freely look eke thou serve that thereto never
Trust of reward or profit do thee bind,
But only faithful heart and loving mind.

165

*12. To serve
his love, never
thinking of any
reward or
profit.*

❦

Wageless to serve, three things may us move:[12]
First, if the service [it]self be desirable: 170
Second, if they whom that we serve and love
Be very good and very amiable:
Thirdly, of reason be we serviceable
Without the gaping after any more
To such as have done much for us before.   175

Serve God for love, then, not for hope of meed:[13]
What service may so desirable be
As where all turneth to thine own speed?
Who is so good, so lovely eke as He
Who hath already done so much for thee,   180
As he that first thee made, and on the rood[14]
Eft thee redeemèd with His precious blood?

---

12. This stanza could be paraphrased in this way: If we were to receive no wage for our work, three things might motivate us to work anyway: First, if the work itself were desirable; second, if those we worked for were people we loved and enjoyed; third, if we were serving those who have done much for us, we would not reasonably be grasping for more in terms of wages.

13. *meed*—reward

14. *rood*—cross

More's Psalm on Detachment

This poem More wrote in the margins of his Psalter while imprisoned in the Tower of London, 1534–35. For the critical edition, see Instructions and Prayers, Complete Works, *vol. 13, pp. 226–27.*

Give me thy grace, good Lord:
To set the world at nought;

To set my mind fast upon thee,
And not to hang upon the blast of men's mouths;

5   To be content to be solitary,
Not to long for worldly company;

Little and little utterly to cast off the world,
And rid my mind of all the business thereof;

Not to long to hear of any worldly things,
10   But that the hearing of worldly phantasies may be to me displeasant;

Gladly to be thinking of God,
Piteously to call for his help;

To lean unto the comfort of God,
Busily to labor to love him;

15   To know mine own vility and wretchedness,
To humble and meeken myself under the mighty hand of God;

To bewail my sins passed,
For the purging of them patiently to suffer adversity;

Gladly to bear my purgatory here,
20   To be joyful of tribulations;

To walk the narrow way that leadeth to life,
To bear the cross with Christ;

This first page from More's prayer book has, in More's own hand,
lines 1 and 2 of his Psalm on Detachment

Ad sextam de cruce.

Hora sexta ie=
sus est cruci co=
clauatus. Atq; cum
latronibus pendens
deputatus. Pre tor=
mentis sitiens felle
saturatus. Agn⁹ cri
men diluit sic ludifi=
catus. V⁹. Adoram⁹
te christe: et benedici
mus tibi. R; z. Quia
per sanctam crucem
tuam redemisti mu=
dum. Oremus.   Oratio.

Omine iesu christe fili dei viui: pone
passione cruce et morte tua inter iu=
diciu tuu & aias nostras nunc & in hora mor
tisnostre:et largiri digneris viuis misericor
dia et gratia / defunctis requie et venia / ec=
clesie tue pace et concordia / et nobis pctori=
busvita & gloria sempiterna. Qui cu patre
et spu sancto viuis et regnas deus. Per oia
secula seculor. Ame. O loriosa passio dni no
stri iesu xpi eruat nos a dolore tristi / & pdu=
cat nos ad gaudia paradisi. Ame. Pater no=
ster. Aue maria gratia.

Another page from More's prayer book, with lines 36–38 of
his Psalm on Detachment

To have the last thing in remembrance,
To have ever afore mine eye my death that is ever at hand;

To make death no stranger to me,   25
To foresee and consider the everlasting fire of hell;

To pray for pardon before the judge come,
To have continually in mind the passion that Christ suffered for me;

For his benefits uncessantly to give him thanks,
To buy the time again that I before have lost;   30

To abstain from vain confabulations,
To eschew light foolish mirth and gladness;

Recreations not necessary—to cut off;
Of worldly substance, friends, liberty, life and all, to set the loss at right
        nought for the winning of Christ;   35

To think my most enemies my best friends,
For the brethren of Joseph could never have done him so much good
        with their love and favor as they did him with their malice and
        hatred.

These minds are more to be desired of every man   40
than all the treasure of all the princes and kings, Christian and heathen,
        were it gathered and laid together all upon one heap.

Contrasting Letters

To John Colet

In this letter[1] to his fellow English humanist John Colet (1467?–1519), More offers his observations on city life and on the challenges of pursuing virtue. Even in this early letter, More shows his preoccupation with the questions evident in Utopia: What is the best way of life, and can it be achieved in a fallen world?

LONDON
23 OCTOBER 1504

Thomas More to His John Colet,[2] Greetings.

As I was walking in the law courts the other day, unbusy where everybody else was busy, I met your servant. I was delighted to see him, both because he has always been dear to me, and especially because I thought he would not have come without you. But when I heard from him not *More on his* only that you had not returned, but that you would not return for a long *friend's absence* time, I cannot tell you from what rejoicing I was cast into what dejection. For what could be more grievous to me than to be deprived of your most pleasant companionship, whose prudent advice I enjoyed, by whose most

---

1. *Selected Letters,* #2, pp. 4–6. Translated from the Latin.
2. Dean of St. Paul's Cathedral and founder of St. Paul's School.

delightful intimacy I was refreshed, by whose powerful sermons I was stirred, by whose example and life I was guided, in fine, in whose very countenance and nod I was accustomed to find pleasure? And so when encompassed by these defenses I felt myself strengthened; now that I am deprived of them I seem to languish and grow feeble. By following your footsteps I had escaped almost from the very gates of hell, and now, driven by some force and necessity, I am falling back again into gruesome darkness. I am like Eurydice, except that she was lost because Orpheus looked back at her, but I am sinking because you do not look back at me. 5

City life—its dangers   For in the city what is there to move one to live well? But rather, when a man is straining in his own power to climb the steep path of virtue, it turns him back by a thousand devices and sucks him back by its thousand enticements. Wherever you betake yourself, on one side nothing but feigned love and the honeyed poisons of smooth flatterers resound; on the other, fierce hatreds, quarrels, the din of the forum murmur against you. Wherever you turn your eyes, what else will you see but confectioners, fishmongers, butchers, cooks, poulterers, fishermen, fowlers, who supply the materials for gluttony and the world and the world's lord, the devil? Nay even houses block out from us I know not how large a measure of the light, and do not permit us to see the heavens. And the round horizon does not limit the air but the lofty roofs. I really cannot blame you if you 10 15 20

Country life—its advantages   are not yet tired of the country where you live among simple people, unversed in the deceits of the city; wherever you cast your eyes, the smiling face of the earth greets you, the sweet fresh air invigorates you, the very sight of the heavens charms you. There you see nothing but the generous gifts of nature and the traces of our primeval innocence. 25

More urges Colet to return   But yet I do not wish you to be so captivated by these delights as to be unwilling to fly back to us as soon as possible. For if the inconveniences of the city so displease you, your country parish of Stepney (of which you should have no less care) will afford you hardly less advantages than where you now dwell, whence you can sometimes turn aside, as to an inn, to the city (where there is so much that needs your service). For in the country, where men are of themselves either almost innocent, or at least not ensnared in great sins, the services of any physician can be useful. But in the city because of the great numbers that congregate there, and because of their long-standing habits of vice, any physician will have come in vain unless he be the most skillful. Certainly there come from time to time into the pulpit at St. Paul's preachers who promise health, but although they 30 35 seem to have spoken very eloquently, their life is in such sharp contrast to their words that they irritate rather than soothe. For they cannot bring men to believe that though they are themselves obviously in direst need of the physician's help, they are yet fit to be entrusted with the cure of other men's ailments. And thus when men see that their diseases are being pre- *City dwellers need* scribed for by physicians who are themselves covered with ulcers, they im- *gifted physicians* mediately become indignant and obstinate. But if (as observers of human nature assert), he is the best physician in whom the patient has the greatest confidence, who can doubt that you are the one who can do most for the cure of all in the city? Their readiness to allow you to treat their wounds, their trust, their obedience, you have yourself proved in the past, and now the universal desire and anticipation of you proclaim it all again.

Come then, my dear Colet, for Stepney's sake, which mourns your *Closing remarks* long absence as children their mother's; for the sake of your native place which should be no less dear to you than are your parents. Finally (though this will be a weak force for your return), let regard for me, who am entirely devoted to you and hang anxiously upon your coming, move you.

Meanwhile, I shall pass my time with Grocyn, Linacre, and our dear friend Lily, the first as you know the sole guide of my life (in your absence), the second my master in learning, the third the dearest partner of my endeavors.

Farewell, and love me ever as now.
Thomas More

To His Children

More is widely recognized as a gifted statesman and a man of rare intellect. What is less known about him, however, is the great love and care which characterized his relationship with his family. Even in the midst of his many and weighty travels on affairs of state, he never forgot his family. The care he exercised on their behalf is abundantly evident in More's Latin poem to his children. Writing home during a difficult journey, More reflects on the natural bond of love existing between father and children, and on how that love may increase. The poem is offered here in a prose translation.[1]

C. 1518

Thomas More Greets His Beloved Children, Margaret, Elizabeth, Cecilia and John

Occasion of the letter

I hope that a single letter to all four of you may find my children in good health and that your father's good wishes may keep you so. In the meantime, while I am making a long journey, drenched by a soaking rain, and while my mount, too frequently, is bogged down in the mud, I compose these verses for you in the hope that, although unpolished, they may 5 give you pleasure. From these verses you may gather an indication of your father's feelings for you—how much more than his own eyes he loves you; for the mud, the miserably stormy weather, and having to urge a small horse through deep waters have not been able to distract his thoughts from you or to prevent his proving that, wherever he is, he thinks of you. 10 For instance, when—and it is often—his horse stumbles and threatens to fall, your father is not interrupted in the composition of his verses. Many

The natural bond between father and child

people can hardly write poetry even when their hearts are at ease, but a father's love duly provides verses even when he is in distress. It is not so strange that I love you with my whole heart, for being a father is not a tie 15 which can be ignored. Nature in her wisdom has attached the parent to the child and bound their minds together with a Herculean knot. Thence

More as father

comes that tenderness of a loving heart that accustoms me to take you so often into my arms. That is why I regularly fed you cake and gave you ripe

---

1. *Latin Poems, #264, Complete Works,* vol. 3.2.

apples and fancy pears. That is why I used to dress you in silken garments and why I never could endure to hear you cry. You know, for example, how often I kissed you, how seldom I whipped you.

My whip was never anything but a peacock's tail. Even this I wielded
5   hesitantly and gently so as not to mark your tender backsides with painful welts. Ah, brutal and unworthy to be called father is he who does not himself weep at the tears of his child. How other fathers act I do not know, but you know well how soft and kind I am by temperament, for I have always intensely loved the children I begot, and I have always been (as a father
10 should be) easy to win over. But now my love has grown so much that it seems to me I did not love you at all before. This is because you combine *How natural love* the wise behavior of old age with the years of childhood, because your *increases* hearts have been informed with genuine learning,[2] because you have learned to speak with grace and eloquence, weighing each word carefully.
15 These accomplishments[3] tug at my heart so wonderfully, they bind me to my children so closely, that what, for many fathers, is the only reason for their affection—I mean the fact that they begot their children—has almost nothing to do with my love for you. Therefore, most dear little troop of children, continue to endear yourselves to your father and, by those same
20 accomplishments [*virtutibus*] which make me think that I had not loved you before, make me think hereafter (for you can do it) that I do not love you now.

2. The Latin here is "Artibus hoc faciunt pectora culta bonis."
3. The Latin here is "virtutibus."

To His Wife

This letter,[1] written to his wife, Lady Alice, at a time of grave economic crisis for the family, gives us an unusual glimpse into the mind of Thomas More. It has been said to show that More was a Christian Job in facing adversity.

This letter was written the month before he was appointed Lord Chancellor, and circumstances behind the letter were these: The harvest at More's Chelsea estate had just been completed, a harvest greatly anticipated after a year of famine so great that More had fed one hundred people a day at his home. Suddenly, a fire broke out that destroyed all of More's barns, part of More's home, and several of the neighbors' barns as well. This was an economic loss so great that, as More indicates in this letter, he and Alice realized that they might have to sell their estate. Since More was away accompanying the King when this occurred, Lady Alice immediately sent son-in-law Giles Heron to inform her husband. While Heron waited, More wrote this quick response. Given the spontaneity of its composition, this letter has special value in revealing More's true character when faced with a crippling loss.

WOODSTOCK

3 SEPTEMBER 1529

Lady Alice, in my most hearty way, I commend me to you.

And as I am informed by our son Heron of the loss of our barns and our neighbors' also with all the corn that was in them, except if it were not God's pleasure, it would be a great pity that so much good corn was lost. Yet since it has pleased him to send us such a chance, we must, and are

More's response to adversity

bound, not only to be content, but also to be glad of his visitation. He sent   5 us all that we have lost, and since he has by such a chance taken it away again, his pleasure be fulfilled; let us never grudge at it, but take it in good worth, and heartily thank him as well for adversity as for prosperity.

Giving thanks

And perhaps we have more cause to thank him for our loss than for our winning, for his wisdom better sees what is good for us than we do   10 ourselves. Therefore, I pray you, be of good cheer and take all the household with you to church; and there thank God both for what he has given us, and for what he has taken from us, and for what he has left us, which if

---

1. The original non-modernized version of this letter can be found in *Selected Letters*, #42, pp. 170–71. Thanks to Travis Curtright for help in modernizing the English of this letter.

it please him, he can increase when he will, and if it please him to leave us yet less, at his pleasure so be it.

I pray you to make some good inquiry into what my poor neighbors have lost, and bid them take no thought of it for, even if I should not leave *Care for his neighbors* myself a spoon, there shall be no poor neighbor of mine who bears any loss because of an accident that happened in my house.

I pray you, be merry in God with my children and your household, *Care for his family* and consider with your friends what way would be the best to make provision for corn for our household, and for seed this year coming. If you think it good that we keep the land still in our hands or not, yet I think it would not be best, whether you think it good that we shall do so or not, suddenly thus to give it all up and to put away our folk off our farm till we have advised ourselves somewhat on that; however, if we have more servants now than you shall need, and who can get themselves other masters, you may then discharge them, but I would not that any man were suddenly sent away he knows not where.

At my coming here, I thought it necessary that I should remain with the King's Grace, but now I shall, I think, because of this accident get leave this next week to come home and see you, and then we shall further consider together all things about what steps shall be best to take.

And thus, as heartfelt as you can wish, farewell to you with all our children. At Woodstock the third day of September by the hand of

Your loving husband,
Thomas More, Knight

Letter to Antonio Bonvisi

This personal and moving letter[1] was one of the last written by Thomas More. Antonio Bonvisi, an Italian merchant and banker, seems to have been More's closest friend. Despite the dangers involved, Bonvisi cared for More during his imprisonment in the Tower, sending him such gifts as a warm camlet gown,[2] wine, and food. After More's execution, Bonvisi fell into permanent disfavor with Henry VIII; he fled from England in 1544, and his property in England was confiscated.

TOWER OF LONDON
1535

To the most friendly of friends, and deservedly dearest to me, greetings.

Presentiments   Since my mind has a presentiment (perhaps a false one, but still a presentiment) that before very long I will be unable to write to you, I have decided, while I may, to show by this little letter, at least, how much I am refreshed by the pleasantness of your friendship now that fortune has abandoned me.   5

To be sure, most excellent sir, in the past I have always been wonderfully delighted by this love of yours for me, but when I remembered that for almost forty years now I have been, not a guest, but a continual habitué of the Bonvisi household, and that in all this time I have not proven to be a *On debts between* friend in repaying my debt to you, but only a barren lover, my sense of   10 *friends* shame truly made that genuine sweetness, which I otherwise enjoyed in thinking about the friendship of the Bonvisis, turn a little bit sour because I felt somehow awkward and ashamed, as if I had neglected to do my part. But certainly I now console myself with the thought that there never arose any opportunity for me to pay you back, since your fortune was so   15 large that there was no way left for me to do anything for you. And so I am aware that I did not fail to pay you back through any neglect of my duty towards you, but because there was no opportunity. But now that even the hope of recompense is taken away, when I see you persist in loving and obliging me, nay rather, when I see you push on in your friend-   20

---

1. Translated by Elizabeth McCutcheon in *Moreana* 71–72 (Nov. 1981), pp. 55–56.
2. Dr. McCutcheon explains this as "a soft, warm gown made of the finest angora yarn . . . resembl[ing] cashmere."

ship and run the race unwearied, so that few men court their fortunate
friends as much as you favor, love, cherish, and regard your More—over- *Bonvisi's steadfast*
thrown as he is, cast aside, struck down, and sentenced to prison—then I *friendship despite*
not only absolve myself from whatever bitter shame I felt before but also *circumstances*
5 find peace in the sweetness of this wonderful friendship of yours. And my
good fortune in having such a faithful friend as you seems somehow—I
don't know how—almost to counterbalance this unfortunate shipwreck of
my fleet. Certainly, apart from the indignation of the Prince, whom I love
no less than I ought to fear him, for the rest, your friendship almost out-
10 weighs my losses, since they, after all, are to be counted among the evils of
fortune.

But if I were to count the possession of such a constant friendship— *On the great good*
which such an unfavorable fall of fortune has not snatched away, but rather *of constant friend-*
cemented more strongly—among the fleeting goods of fortune, truly I *ship*
15 should be out of my mind. For the happiness of a friendship so faithful,
and so constant against the contrary blast of fortune, is a rare favor, and
without a doubt is a higher good, and a more exalted one, arising from a
certain special loving-kindness of God. Certainly I do not otherwise accept or understand it than as something arranged by the unparalleled mer-
20 cy of God, that among my poor little friends, a person such as you, so great
a friend, was prepared so long beforehand, who might assuage and lighten
by your consolation a great part of that distress which the weight of fortune rushing headlong against me has brought upon me. Therefore, my
dear Antonio, dearest of all mortals to me, with all my strength I pray (the *Friendship, present*
25 only thing I can do) to Almighty God, who provided you for me, that, *and future*
since he gave you such a debtor, who will never be able to discharge his
debt, he himself for his loving-kindness vouchsafe to requite you for those
deeds of kindness of yours which you daily expend so profusely upon me;
then that he bring us, for his great mercy, from this wretched and stormy
30 world to his peace, where there will be no need for letters, where no wall
will separate us, where no porter will prevent us from talking together, but
with God the Father unbegotten, and his only-begotten Son, our Lord
and Redeemer Jesus Christ, and the Holy Spirit of them both, the Comforter proceeding from them both, we shall fully enjoy eternal joy. Mean- *Joy to come*
35 while may Almighty God bring it about that you, my dear Antonio, and I,
and would that all mortals, and everyone everywhere, may hold cheap all
the riches of this world, all the glory of the whole universe, and even the
sweetness of life itself, for the ardent desire of that joy. Most trusty of all

friends, and most beloved by me, and (as I am now long accustomed to
call you) the apple of my eye: goodbye. May Christ keep unharmed your
whole household, so very like the head of the family in their affection for
me.

T. More: If I put down "yours," I'll have done so in vain. For you can-   5
not now not know this, when you have bought it by so many deeds of
kindness. Nor am I now such, that it matters whose I am.

Plutarch's Essay and More's Poem

---

*Plutarch (*A.D. *46–120) was a Greek writer whose major works include* The Parallel Lives, *incisive critical biographies of Greek and Roman leaders such as Alexander the Great and Julius Caesar, and the* Moralia, *or* Moral Essays, *from which the following is taken.*[1] *Erasmus dedicated his translation of this essay to King Henry VIII in 1513 and again in 1517. Both Queen Katherine and Thomas More believed that King Henry was adversely affected by flattery. The humanists, however, were not alone in their esteem for Plutarch. His shrewd studies of human nature have influenced many artists and political leaders, including Shakespeare and Abraham Lincoln. More's sympathy with the ideas expressed in Plutarch's essay is evident in his poem "On a False Friend" (c. 1516), which follows the essay.*

"How to Tell a Flatterer from a Friend"

[1] . . . Plato says a high degree of self-love is universally forgiven; but he also says that it engenders a very serious flaw (not to mention the multitude of lesser flaws)—namely, there is no way that a person in love with himself can make a fair and impartial assessment of himself. Unless educa- *Self-love and self-flattery*

---

1. Plutarch, *Essays*, pp. 60–68, 94–100, 107–112.

185

tion has accustomed one to prefer goodness, and to make this one's goal, rather than what is inbred and innate, then "Love is blind where the beloved is concerned." This lays the domain of love or friendship wide open to the flatterer; self-love provides him with a perfect base camp against us, since self-love makes each person his own primary and chief self-flatterer, and makes it easy for us to allow someone else under our guard—someone else to testify to and corroborate and support us in our beliefs and aspirations. To call anyone, as an insult, "fond of flattery" is to say that he is excessively in love with himself, since his fondness for himself leads him not just to aspire to everything, but to believe that he already has everything: the aspiration is not odd, but the belief is treacherous and needs a great deal of caution.

Self-love and self-knowledge

If truth is indeed divine and is the source, in Plato's words, "of all good things for gods and all for men," then the flatterer is likely to be inimical to the gods . . . , since a flatterer is perpetually ranged in opposition to the saying "Know yourself": he instills in everyone self-deceit and ignorance both of oneself and of those things which are good and bad for oneself— he makes the former impossible to achieve and accomplish, and the latter impossible to rectify.

[2] Now, if a flatterer were like most other bad things and exclusively or largely seized on the dregs and dross of mankind, he would not be so terrible or hard to resist; but just as it is soft, sweet woods that woodworms prefer to penetrate, so it is generous, good and fair characters which admit and nourish the parasitic flatterer [48e–49c]. . . .

The flatterer's preferred diet

At precisely the time when one needs friends, [to discover that flatterers] are no friends is hard to endure, since there is no chance then of exchanging the unreliable, counterfeit friend for one who is good and reliable. No, the friend that you have, just like the coin in your pocket, should have been examined and tried before the need arises, rather than being tested by the need when it arises. The realization ought not to occur because we have been hurt; we ought to have already acquainted ourselves with and observed the flatterer, and so avoid being hurt. Otherwise, our experience will be no different from that of people who realize the facts about lethal drugs by sampling them first: death by suicide is the price they pay for their conclusion.

Examining acquaintances

There is no possible explanation why the flatterer disguises himself in pleasing masks, except that he has noticed that friendship never excludes pleasure. But just as fool's gold and counterfeits imitate only gold's gleam

The flatterer's approach

and sheen, so the flatterer can be seen as imitating the pleasant and attractive aspects of friendship, always putting on a cheerful, vivacious face and never being negative or recalcitrant. But it is false to conclude from this that people who praise others are immediately to be suspected simply of flattering them: when either is called or, approval and disapproval are equally appropriate within friendship—or rather, although captiousness and disparagement are inevitably inimical to friendship and compatibility, we are still perfectly content to put up with criticism and someone speaking their mind, provided there have been earlier manifestations of kindliness unstintingly and enthusiastically expressing approval of deeds well done; and the reason we are content to do this is because we trust—with no hint of anxiety—that anyone who is happy to express approval expresses disapproval only when compelled to do so.

[3] At this point someone might comment that it is difficult to distinguish the flatterer and the friend, since they both equally provide pleasure and express approval; in fact, it is noticeable that flattery often outdoes friendship in favors and acts of service. . . . *The subtlety of flattery*

As Plato says, "The ultimate dishonesty is the false appearance of honesty": it is not overt, light-hearted flattery that must be regarded as problematic, but the covert, straight-faced version, which can corrupt even true friendship if we do not watch out, because its behavior coincides to a large extent with that of friendship [49e–50f]. . . .

[5] However, it is because friendship is the most gratifying thing in the world and nothing affords one more pleasure, that the flatterer's domain is pleasure and pleasure is what he uses as bait. And it is because goodwill and service are inseparable from friendship (hence the saying that a friend is more essential than fire and water), that the flatterer undertakes tasks and tries hard always to appear well-meaning, determined and enthusiastic. And since the chief factor in forging friendship at the beginning is similarity of interests and attitudes, and enjoying and avoiding the same things is usually the initial bond which brings people together, through affinity, then because the flatterer is well aware of all this, he patterns and forms himself as if he were some kind of material, in an attempt to match and mirror whoever he plans to beset by means of imitation; and he is so malleable nd plausible in his mimicry that he provokes the comment: "You are no son of Achilles, but the man himself!" However, the most iniquitous aspect of all his iniquity is that, because he has noticed that speaking one's mind is both claimed and believed to be a mode of speech specific to *The flatterer: tactics and techniques*

friendship—just as animals make specific sounds—and that someone who avoids speaking his mind is held to be unfriendly and unforthcoming, then he proceeds to imitate this too; just as skillful cooks use sharp and bitter flavors as seasonings to get rid of the cloying nature of sweet foods, so flatterers employ a candor which is false and does no good [51b–d]. . . .   5

[6] So, because the flatterer knows that if people enjoy the same things they are bound to form a relationship and take pleasure in each other's *The analogy of* company, his first tactic for getting close to a given individual and pitching *breaking animals* tent near him is as follows: he treats it like an exercise in breaking in animals, and patiently makes his approach (by means of the same interests,   10 pastimes, pursuits and occupations) and finally strokes his quarry, and keeps at it until the other submits and becomes docile and accustomed to his touch. The flatterer criticizes the activities, ways of life and people he sees the subject disliking, and is extravagant in his praise for whatever the other likes, to ensure that he is seen to express more than his share of as- 15 tonishment and incredulity; and he insists that his likes and dislikes are carefully thought out rather than being emotional reactions.

[7] So, given that we are dealing with no actual similarity or even po-
Snaring a flatterer tential similarity, and that this is all just camouflage, how can we put the flatterer to the test? What actual discrepancies are there, in which he can   20 be ensnared? Above all, one should see whether his intention is consistent and constant, whether he always enjoys the same things, approves of the same things and guides and organizes his life with regard to a single model, which is proper behavior for someone who is autonomous and who desires friendship and familiarity with a like-minded person. If he does all   25 this, he is a friend. On the other hand, since the flatterer has no single foundation for his attitudes as a source of stability and his way of life is not of his own choosing but is derived from someone else, and since he molds and adjusts himself by reference to someone else, then he is not straight-
A memorable forward or single, but complex and multifaceted; he is always streaming   30 *image* from one place to another (like water in the process of being poured) and the only form he has is given by the vessels that receive him [51e–52b].

[25] This is why I now repeat the advice I gave at the beginning of this discourse—that we should eliminate self-love and self-importance from ourselves, because it prepares the ground for external flatterers by flatter-   35 ing us first and softening us up for them. However, if we trust the god and appreciate how extremely precious for each of us is the precept "Know yourself," and if we also survey our character, upbringing, and condition-

ing to see how in countless respects they fall short of goodness and include bad, unchosen behavior, speech, and moods, then we will make it hard for flatterers to trample on us. . . . If we observe how often and in how many respects our own attributes are disgraceful, distressing, imperfect and wrong, we will constantly discover that we do not need a friend to commend and compliment us, but to take us to task and speak candidly—yes, and even critically too—about our misdeeds.

The need for true friends and candor

This need arises because there are few who have the courage to speak candidly rather than gratifyingly to friends, and again, even among the few, it is far from easy to find people who really know how to do this, rather than those who think they are using candor when they are merely being rude and critical. In fact, however, candor is no different from any other medicine: if it is not administered at the right time, the result is distress and disturbance with no benefit, and its effects are in a sense only a painful version of the pleasant effects of flattery. Inopportune criticism is just as harmful as inopportune praise, and is a prime factor in making people susceptible, easy targets for flattery, when they flow like water off the forbidding slopes and towards the undemanding valleys. This is why candor must be tempered by tact and must be rational, so that it is not overdone and so that its impact is diluted, as if it were bright light: otherwise, because people are upset and hurt by those who criticize everything and disparage everyone, they turn for shelter to the shadow of the flatterer and incline towards freedom from distress [65E–66B]. . . .

Candor as medicine

[26] Candor, therefore, is plainly beset by rather a lot of fatal defects, and the first one to remove from it is self-love: we must make absolutely sure that no one could think that we were merely being rude because of some personal reason such as unfair or hurtful treatment. For any words spoken for personal reasons are assumed to be provoked not by goodwill but by anger, and to constitute disparagement rather than rebuke—the difference being that candor is altruistic and high-minded, while disparagement is self-centered and petty,[2] which is why candor earns respect and admiration, while disparagement earns recrimination and contempt [66e]. . . .

The art of candor and possible misuses

[27] The second defect to remove from candor—in order to purify it, as it were—is any trace of insolence and mockery and ridicule and sar-

---

2. Frank Babbitt's translation is: "For frankness is friendly and noble, but fault-finding is selfish and mean" (*Moralia* 1, p. 355. London: William Heinemann, 1927).

casm, which spice up candor in a contemptible way. For just as when a doctor performs an operation, it is important that a certain delicacy and precision inform his actions, and that his hand is free of the superfluous suppleness suitable for a dancer or for wild and random gestures, so candor admits cleverness and wit (as long as this charm preserves the dignity of 5 the candor), but perishes and is utterly destroyed at the approach of belligerence, sarcasm and insolence [67e–f]. . . .

Jocularity and humor are all right to use among friends on the odd occasion, but candor must preserve its seriousness and its own character; and if it is focusing on rather important matters, then your words must be 10 made convincing and stirring by your use of emotion, gesture, and tone.

Bad timing is always extremely harmful, and never more so than when it destroys the point of candor [68c]. . . .

Why the successful have particular need of true friends

[28] Many people do not think it right—or do not have the courage—to try to [advise] friends whose affairs are going well: they regard success as 15 completely beyond the reach of rebuke. However, when a friend stumbles and trips, they oppress and ride roughshod over him, now that he has been humbled and brought low: they release their candor upon him all in a rush, like a stream which had been unnaturally dammed, and because of his former superciliousness and their former weakness, they relish the op- 20 portunity to take advantage of his change of fortune. It follows that it is rather important to discuss this matter too, and to find a reply to Euripides when he says, "When God grants success, what need is there of friends?"

The answer is that successful people have a particular need of friends who speak their minds and deflate any excessive pride, since success and 25 sound judgment rarely go together: in the majority of cases, while luck is inflating and destabilizing people, sense needs to be imported and rationality to be forced on them from outside. On the other hand, when God lays them low and divests them of their pretensions, events themselves contain all inherent rebuke and a stimulus to remorse; so there is at that time noth- 30 ing for friendly candor or serious, caustic words to do, but on occasions of change of fortune of that order, it is really "pleasing to look into the eyes of a kindly man," if he is being supportive and encouraging. Clearchus was a case in point: according to Xenophon, the sight of his kind and considerate face during battles or when danger was imminent used to put heart 35 into his threatened men.

However, the employment of candid and caustic speech on someone out of luck is like applying a stimulant to an afflicted and inflamed eye: it

does not cure anything or alleviate the pain, but adds to the pain the extra element of anger and makes the sufferer worse off. At any rate, there is no way that a healthy person gets cross or fierce with a friend for criticizing the company he keeps and his drinking, or his laziness, unfitness, constant
5   bathing and excessive eating at the wrong times of day; but it is not just intolerable for someone who is ill, but even increases his illness, to be told that his present condition is due to his indulgence, [disordered] lifestyle, rich food, and womanizing [68c–69b]. . . .

[33] A bright light should not be brought close to an inflamed eye, and   *The art of criticism*
10   neither can a mind which has been taken over by the emotions submit to candor and undiluted reproof. Therefore, one of the most useful ways to be of assistance is to blend in a pinch of praise, as in the following lines: "You are the best men in the army, so you can no longer do well by refraining from fierce heroism. . . ."
15   Speaking like that not only softens the harshness and bossiness of the criticism, but also sets up an internal rivalry: he is made to feel shame for his disgraceful aspects by being reminded of his fine aspects and by making himself an example of better conduct. However, comparisons with others (of the same age, for example, or country or family) aggravate and
20   exacerbate the contentiousness which accompanies any flaw, and which invariably retorts angrily: "So why don't you shove off to my betters, and leave me in peace?" [72b–e]. . . .

[34] The most unsuitable behavior of all is to repay a rebuke with a rebuke and candor with candor, because it makes tempers rapidly flare and
25   provokes argumentativeness, and in general this kind of bickering can give the impression of stemming not from an attempt to retort with candor but from an inability to abide candor. It is preferable, therefore, to let a friend get away with it, when he seems to be telling you off because if at a later date he goes wrong himself and needs telling off, then the situation itself
30   in a sense allows candor to be candid: if, without bearing a grudge, you remind him that he himself has tended not to stand idly by when his friends go wrong, but rather to censure them and take them in hand, he is more likely to submit and be open to correction, and will see it as repayment stemming not from angry recrimination, but from charitable goodwill.
35   [35] It is correct for a friend to put up with the hostility his reprimands   *Further advice*
generate, when crucially important issues are involved. However, if he gets   *on candor*
irate at everything, whatever the situation, and relates to his acquaintances as if they were his pupils rather than his friends, then when very important

issues arise and he tries to deliver a reprimand, he will be feeble and ineffective—he has used up his candor, like a doctor who dispenses in many minor and unessential cases medicine which, though harsh and bitter, is essential and valuable. . . . The point is that leniency over minor matters makes a friend's candor about more important matters not unwelcome, 5 whereas constant harassment, continual severity and ill-humor, and making it one's business to know everything and to interfere in everything, are not only more than flesh and blood can stand, but are intolerable even to slaves.

Some examples of [36] We must observe our friends when they do right as well as when 10
effective candor they do wrong; and our starting-point should certainly be to be ready to praise them. Cooling contracts iron and hardens it into steel, provided it has first been made tractable and fluid by heat; similarly, friends who have been relaxed and warmed by praise must later be calmly treated to a cooling bath, so to speak, of candor. Given the opportunity, we must say, "Do 15 you think there is any comparison between these two types of behavior? Can you see what kind of harvest goodness yields? We who are your friends demand that behavior from you: it is proper to you, it is your birthright. But you must banish the other kind 'into the mountains or into the waves of the roaring sea.'" 20

The analogy A considerate doctor would rather use sleep and diet than [harsh med
of a doctor icines] to relieve a patient of illness, and by the same token a good friend, a conscientious father and a teacher enjoy using praise rather than criticism as a means of moral improvement. The one thing above all which makes candor hurt as little as possible, and be as remedial as possible, is to 25 deal in a tactful and kindly fashion, without any trace of rancor, with people who are making mistakes. That is why it is important not to criticize them harshly if they deny their faults, or to stop them defending themselves: one should even help them in some way to come up with plausible excuses and should make room for a more moderate reason by distancing 30 oneself from the worse one. This is what Hector did when he said to his brother, "What are you up to? It is wrong of you to have stored up this anger in your heart"—as if his withdrawal from the battle was not [an act of cowardice], but was prompted by anger. In the same vein, Nestor said to Agamemnon, "You succumbed to your proud hearted temper." 35

The point is that it is more likely to have an effect on someone's character to say "It didn't occur to you" and "You didn't know," rather than "That was a criminal act" and "You acted disgracefully"; "You shouldn't

emulate your brother," rather than "You shouldn't be jealous of your brother"; and "You should avoid the corrupting influence of that woman," rather than "You should stop corrupting that woman." But although this is the path candor looks for when it is trying to remedy a defect, nevertheless when its goal is preventive, it takes the contrary route. When what is necessary is to divert people who are poised to go wrong, or when we want to energize and motivate people who are being won over when faced with some powerful impulse which is tending in a direction oppo-site to what is required, or who are being weak and disconsolate with regard to correct conduct, then we must attribute the situation to motives which are out of character and discreditable. Thus, when Odysseus is incit-ing Achilles in Sophocles' play, he says that it is not the case that the meal has made him angry, but "As soon as you caught sight of the buildings of Troy, you were afraid"; and again, when Achilles is livid at this and an-
nounces his intention to sail away, Odysseus says, "I know what you're running away from, and it's not slander: Hector is close—you're right not to stay." In other words, threatening to let it be known that a courageous hero is a coward, or that a restrained and disciplined man is a libertine, or that a generous and munificent person is petty and avaricious, inspires
them towards correct conduct and deters them from contemptible con-duct, provided that one is demonstrably moderate in irremediable circum-stances and distressed and sympathetic—rather than critical—when speak-ing candidly, but forceful, implacable, and unwavering when trying to prevent errors and when resisting emotions, since this is the right time for
unquenchable goodwill and true candor.

Candor as preventative medicine

It is noticeable that enemies too use criticism of past behavior against one another—and so Diogenes used to say that for safety's sake no one ought to have either good friends (to take one in hand) or fervent enemies (to tell one off). However, heeding advice and consequently taking care
not to make mistakes are preferable to being berated and consequently re-gretting one's mistakes. That is why one should apply oneself to candor with the dedication due to a craft, to the extent that it is the most impor-tant and effective medicine available to friendship; but it constantly re-quires accuracy of timing, above all, and also dilution to prevent it being
too strong.

Learning the craft of candor

[37] So since, as we have said before, candor inevitably often hurts the person undergoing the treatment, medical practice provides an important model: when doctors perform an operation, they do not abandon the part

that has been operated on and leave it aching and sore, but they apply
soothing lotions and poultices; and tactful critics do not run away either,
after they have employed their harsh and painful treatment, but they use
conversation of a different kind, consisting of tempered words, to allay and
disperse the hurt, as sculptors smooth and polish the arts of their statues   5
where tools have been used, and bits of stone broken off. If someone has
been marked by having the tool of candor used on him, and is left with
rough edges, bumps and uneven surfaces, he will be angry and therefore
The importance unresponsive and recalcitrant at a later date. It follows that this is another
of follow-up thing—one of the most important—for critics to watch out for: they   10
conversations should not leave too soon, or make anything hurtful and provocative the
conclusion of their association and relationship with their acquaintances
[72b–74e].

Thomas More's "On a False Friend"

The man who admits his hatred does less harm than he who pretends
unqualified affection. When I am warned, I avoid the man who hates me,
but how can I avoid one who pretends to be my friend? Undoubtedly,
one's worst enemy is he who in the guise of a friend deceitfully works
mischief by unsuspected guile.[3]

3. *Latin Poems*, #9, *Complete Works*, vol. 3.2

3

Writings on Education

Letter to William Gonell, the Teacher of More's Children

In this letter[1] to one of the teachers he hired for his children, More explains his vision of education. At the heart of the letter is More's reflection on the relation between learning and virtue. The letter also reflects More's serious interest in the education of his daughters.

COURT

22 MAY *c.* 1518

I have received, my dear Gonell, your letter, elegant and full of affection as always. Your devotion to my children[2] I perceive from your letter, your diligence from theirs. Everyone's letter pleased me greatly, but above all that I notice Elizabeth shows a modesty of character in the absence of her mother, which not every girl would show in her mother's presence. Let her understand that such conduct delights me more than all the learning in the world. Though I prefer learning joined with virtue to all the treasures of kings, yet renown for learning, if you take away moral probity, brings nothing else but notorious and noteworthy infamy, especially in a woman.

Learning and virtue

---

1. Selected Letters, #20, pp. 103–107.
2. Margaret (1505–1544), Elizabeth (1506–1564), Cecily (1507–1540?), John (1509–1547). Adopted: Margaret Giggs (1505–July 6, 1570), Anne Cresacre (1512–1577).

Since erudition in women is a new thing and a reproach to the sloth of men, many will gladly assail it, and impute to learning what is really the fault of nature, thinking from the vices of the learned to get their own ignorance esteemed as virtue. On the other hand, if a woman (and this I desire and hope with you as their teacher for all my daughters) to eminent virtue of mind should add even moderate skill in learning, I think she will gain more real good than if she obtain the riches of Croesus and the beauty of Helen. Not because that learning will be a glory to her, though learn-

Benefits of wisdom ing will accompany virtue as a shadow does a body, but because the reward of wisdom is too solid to be lost with riches or to perish with beauty, since it depends on the inner knowledge of what is right,[3] not on the talk of men, than which nothing is more foolish or mischievous.

On glory-seeking   For as it becomes a good man to avoid infamy, so to lay oneself out for renown is the sign of a man who is not only arrogant, but ridiculous and miserable. A mind must be uneasy which ever wavers between joy and sadness because of other men's opinions. Among all the benefits that learning bestows on men, I think there is none more excellent than that by study we are taught to seek in that very study not praise, but utility. Such has been the teaching of the most learned men, especially of philosophers, who are the guides of human life, although some may have abused learning, like other good things, simply to court empty glory and popular renown.

I have written at length on not pursuing glory, my dear Gonell, because of what you say in your letter, that Margaret's lofty and exalted character of mind should not be debased. In this judgment I quite agree with you; but to me, and, no doubt, to you also, that man would seem to debase a generous character of mind who would accustom it to admire what is vain and low. He, on the contrary, raises it who rises to virtue and true

On false and goods, and who looks down with contempt from the contemplation of
true goods the sublime, on those shadows of good things which almost all mortals, through ignorance of truth, greedily snatch at as if they were true goods.

Therefore, my dearest Gonell, since I thought we must walk by this road, I have often begged not you only, who, out of your exceptional affection for all my family, would do it of your own accord, nor only my wife, who is sufficiently urged by her truly maternal love for them, which has been proved to me in many ways, but absolutely all my friends, contin-

---

3. *inner knowledge of what is right*—the Latin phrase here is "recti conscientia."

ually to warn my children to avoid as it were the precipices of pride and *On pride*
haughtiness, and to walk in the pleasant meadows of modesty: not to be
dazzled at the sight of gold; not to lament the lack of what they erro-
neously admire in others; not to think more of themselves for gaudy trap-
pings, nor less for the want of them; not to deform the beauty that nature
has given them by neglect, nor to try to heighten it by artifice; to put
virtue in the first place among goods, learning in the second; and in their *Ordering the*
studies to esteem most whatever may teach them piety towards God, char- *goods*
ity to all, and modesty and Christian humility in themselves. By such
means they will receive from God the reward of an innocent life, and in
the assured expectation of it will view death without dread, and meanwhile possessing solid joy will neither be puffed up by the empty praise of *On solid joy*
men, nor dejected by evil tongues. These I consider the real and genuine
fruits of learning, and though I admit that all literary men do not possess
them, I would maintain that those who give themselves to study with such
intent will easily attain their end and become perfect.

   Nor do I think that the harvest is much affected whether it is a man or
a woman who does the sowing. They both have the name of human being *Learning and*
whose nature reason differentiates from that of beasts; both, I say, are *women*
equally suited for the knowledge of learning by which reason is cultivated,
and, like plowed land, germinates a crop when the seeds of good precepts
have been sown. But if the soil of a woman be naturally bad, and apter to
bear fern than grain, by which saying many keep women from study, I
think, on the contrary, that a woman's wit is the more diligently to be cultivated, so that nature's defect may be redressed by industry. This was the
opinion of the ancients, both the wisest and the most saintly. Not to speak
of the rest, Jerome and Augustine not only exhorted excellent matrons and
honorable virgins to study, but also, in order to assist them, diligently explained the abstruse meanings of the Scriptures, and wrote for tender girls
letters replete with so much erudition that nowadays old men who call
themselves doctors of sacred literature can scarcely read them correctly,
much less understand them. Do you, my learned Gonell, have the kindness
to see that my daughters thoroughly learn these works of saintly men.
From them they will learn in particular what goal they should set for their *The goal of*
studies, and the whole fruit of their endeavors should consist in the testi- *learning*
mony of God and a good conscience.[4] Thus they will be inwardly calm

---

4. *a good conscience*—"conscientia recti"

and at peace and neither stirred by praise of flatterers nor stung by the follies of unlearned mockers of learning.

But I fancy that I now hear you object that these precepts, though
true, are beyond the tender years of my daughters, since you will scarcely
find a man, however old and advanced in study, whose mind is so fixed   5
and firm as not to be tickled sometimes with desire of glory. But, dear
Gonell, the more do I see the difficulty of getting rid of this pest of pride,
the more do I see the necessity of getting to work at it from childhood.
For I find no other reason why this inescapable evil so clings to our hearts,
than that almost as soon as we are born, it is sown in the tender minds of   10
children by their nurses, it is cultivated by their teachers, it is nourished
Mistaken and brought to maturity by their parents; while no one teaches anything,
approaches to even the good, without bidding them always to expect praise as the rec-
learning and ompense and prize of virtue. Thus long accustomed to magnify praise,
virtue they strive to please the greater number (that is, the worse) and end by be-   15
ing ashamed to be good. That this plague of vainglory may be banished far
from my children, may you, my dear Gonell, and their mother and all their
friends, sing this song to them, and repeat it, and beat it into their heads,
that vainglory is despicable, and to be spit upon, and that there is nothing
more sublime than that humble modesty so often praised by Christ; and   20
this your prudent charity will so enforce as to teach virtue rather than re-
prove vice, and make them love good advice instead of hating it. To this
purpose nothing will more conduce than to read to them the lessons of
the ancient Fathers, who, they know, cannot be angry with them; and, as
they honor them for their sanctity, they must needs be much moved by   25
their authority. If you will read something of this sort, besides their reading
of Sallust[5]—to Margaret and Elizabeth, who are more mature than John
and Cecily—you will bind me and them, already in your debt, still more
to you. And besides you will make my children who are dear to me first by
the law of nature, and then dearer by learning and virtue, most dear by   30
such advancement in knowledge and good character. Farewell.

From the Court, on the vigil of Pentecost.
Thomas More

5. See his *War with Catiline* and his *War with Jugurtha.* Augustine calls Sallust "an historian of
distinguished veracity" ("nobilitatae veritatis historicus," *City of God* 1.5)

Letters to His Children

Despite the press of his professional duties, More exercised considerable care over his children's education and development, as is evidenced by these affectionate and playful—and serious—letters written from the King's Court.

Thomas More to His Whole School, Greeting.

See what a compendious salutation I have found, to save both time and   *More's economy*
paper, which would otherwise have been wasted in listing the names of
each one of you in salutation, and my labor would have been to no purpose, since, though each of you is dear to me by some special title, of
5   which I could have omitted none in an ingratiating salutation, no one is
dearer to me by any title than each of you by that of scholar. Your zeal for
knowledge binds me to you almost more closely than the ties of blood. I
rejoice that Master Drew has returned safe, for I was anxious, as you know,
about him. If I did not love you so much I should be really envious of
10   your happiness in having so many and such excellent tutors. But I think
you have no longer any need of Master Nicholas,[2] since you have learned

---

1. *Selected Letters,* #29, pp. 146–47.
2. Nicholas Kratzer (c. 1486–1550) was the king's astronomer at that time; later, he taught at Oxford.

whatever he had to teach you about astronomy. I hear you are so far advanced in that science that you can not only point out the polar star or the dog star, or any of the ordinary stars, but are able also—which requires the skill of an absolute Astronomer—among the special and principal heavenly bodies, to distinguish the sun from the moon! Onward then in that new and admirable science by which you ascend to the stars! But while you gaze on them assiduously, consider that this holy time of Lent warns you, and that beautiful and holy poem[3] of Boethius keeps singing in your ears, teaching you to raise your mind also to heaven, lest the soul look downwards to the earth, after the manner of brutes, while the body is raised aloft.

Farewell, all my dearest,
Thomas More

FROM COURT[4]
3 SEPTEMBER *c.* 1522

Thomas More to His Dearest Children and to Margaret Gyge,
Whom He Numbers Among His Children, Greeting.

The Bristol merchant brought me your letters the day after he left you, with which I was extremely delighted. Nothing can come from your workshop, however rude and unfinished, that will not give me more pleasure than the most meticulous writing of anyone else. So much does my affection for you commend whatever you write to me. Indeed, without any recommendation, your letters are capable of pleasing by their own merits, the charm and pure Latinity of their style. There has not been one of your letters that did not please me extremely. But to confess ingenuously what I feel, the letter from my son John pleased me the best, both because it was longer than the others and because he seems to have given it a bit more labor and study. For he not only put out his matter prettily and composed in fairly polished language, but he plays with me both pleasantly and cleverly, and turns my jokes on myself wittily enough. And this he does not only merrily, but with due moderation, showing that he does not forget that he is joking with his father, whom he is eager to delight and yet is cautious not to give offense.

3. See Boethius' *Consolation of Philosophy*, Book 5, Poem 5.
4. *Selected Letters*, #32, pp. 150–51.

Now I expect from each of you a letter almost every day. I will not admit excuses (for John makes none) such as want of time, sudden departure
of the letter carrier, or want of something to write about. No one hinders
you from writing, but, on the contrary, all are urging you to it. And that
5 you may not keep the letter carrier waiting, why not anticipate his coming, and have your letter written and sealed, ready two days before a carrier is available? How can a subject be wanting when you write to me, who
am glad to hear of your studies or of your games, and whom you will
please most if, when there is nothing to write about, you write just that at
10 great length? Nothing can be easier for you, especially for girls, loquacious
by nature and always doing it.

Practice makes perfect

One thing, however, I admonish you, whether you write serious matters or the merest trifles, it is my wish that you write everything diligently
and thoughtfully. It will do no harm if you first write the whole in En-
15 glish, for then you will have much less trouble and labor in turning it into
Latin; not having to look for the matter, your mind will be intent only on
the language. That, however, I leave to your own choice, whereas I strictly
enjoin you that whatever you have composed you carefully examine before writing it out clean; and in this examination first scrutinize the whole
20 sentence and then every part of it. Thus, if any solecisms have escaped you,
you will easily detect them. Correct these, write out the whole letter
again, and even then do not grudge to examine it once more, for sometimes, in rewriting, faults slip in again that one had expunged. By this diligence you will soon make your little trifles seem serious matters; for while
25 there is nothing so neat and witty that will not be made insipid by silly
and careless loquacity, so also there is nothing in itself so insipid that you
cannot season it with grace and wit if you give a little thought to it.

Parting advice on the art of writing

Farewell, my dearest children,
Thomas More.

Letter to Oxford University

In his new office as Royal Counselor, More writes to the directors of Oxford University about a serious danger there.[1] *At that time, Greek studies were new to England and one faction at Oxford denounced those engaged in Greek and caused great hostility on campus. This faction even formed a society called the "Trojans" set on eradicating the "Greeks." More addresses the difficulties at Oxford in masterful rhetoric that employs all three means of persuasion—ethos, pathos, and* logos.

ABINGDON
29 MARCH 1518

Thomas More to the Reverend Fathers, the Commissory, Proctors, and Others of the Guild of Masters of Oxford University, Greetings.

I. Introduction (Exordium)

I have been wondering, gentlemen, whether I might be permitted to communicate to scholars of your distinction certain conclusions to which I have recently come. Yet I have hesitated in approaching so brilliant a group, not so much on the ground of my style as on that of seeming to give an exhibition of pride and arrogance. Who am I, the possessor of little prudence and less practice, a scholar of mediocre proportions, to arrogate to myself the right to advise you in anything? And how can I dare to offer

A humble, though perhaps witty, opening

5

---

1. *Selected Letters,* #19, pp. 94–103. A different translation appears in *Complete Works,* vol. 15, pp. 130–149.

advice in the field of letters especially, when any one of you is fitted by his wisdom and erudition to give advice in that field to thousands?

At first sight, Venerable Fathers, I was therefore deterred by your unique wisdom. But, on second thought, I was encouraged; for it occurred *More encouraged* to me that only ignorant and arrogant fools would disdain to give a man a hearing, and that the wiser and more learned you were, the less likely you would be to think highly of yourselves or to scorn the advice of others. I was further emboldened by the thought that no one was ever harmed by just judges, such as you are above all, simply on the ground that he offered advice without thinking of the consequences. On the contrary, loyal and affectionate advice, even if imprudent, has always deserved praise and thanks.

Finally, when I consider that, with God's help, I ought to offer you whatever slight learning I have acquired, since it was at your University that my education began, it seems the duty of a loyal friend not to pass *More speaks as* over in silence what I deem it serviceable to bring to your attention. *friend* Since, then, the only danger in putting my pen to paper seemed to lie in the fact that a few might deem me too audacious, while I know that my silence would be condemned by many as ingratitude, I have preferred that the whole world should condemn my audacity rather than that anyone should have the chance to say that I showed myself ungrateful to your University, the honor of which I feel myself bound to defend to the uttermost. Moreover, no situation has, I believe, arisen in recent years, which, if you desire to maintain the honor of that institution, more urgently requires your serious attention.

The matter is as follows: when I was in London recently, I rather fre- *II. Statement of* quently heard that some members of your teaching body, either because *Facts (Narratio)* they despised Greek or were simply devoted to other disciplines, or most likely because they possessed a perverse sense of humor, had proceeded to form a society named after the Trojans. The senior sage christened himself Priam; others called themselves Hector, Paris, and so forth; the idea, whether as a joke or a piece of anti-Greek academic politics, being to pour ridicule on those devoted to the study of Greek. And I hear that things have come to such a pass that no one can admit in public or private that he enjoys Greek, without being subjected to the jeers of these ludicrous "Trojans," who think Greek is a joke for the simple reason that they don't know what good literature is. To these modern "Trojans" applies the old saw, "Trojans always learn too late."

The affair aroused much comment, all very critical; and I myself felt somewhat bitter that even a few academics among you had nothing better to do in their spare time than to cast slurs on their colleagues' subjects. But I kept in mind that one could not expect the whole crowd of academics to possess wisdom, temperance, and humility; and so I began to dismiss the matter as a triviality. However, since I have been here in Abingdon in attendance at the court of his victorious Majesty [Henry VIII], I have found that the silliness is developing into a form of insanity. For one of the "Trojans," a scholar in his own estimation, a wit of the first water in that of his friends, though slightly deranged in that of anyone observing his actions, *A worrisome* has chosen during Lent to babble in a sermon against not only Greek but *sermon on the* Roman literature, and finally against all polite learning, liberally berating *liberal arts* all the liberal arts.

His whole performance was of a piece. Perhaps such a body of nonsense could not be preached on the basis of any sensible text; in any case, he followed neither the old custom of elucidating a whole passage of Scripture, nor the recent one of expounding some few words of Scripture; instead he elaborated on some stupid British proverbs. So I have no doubt that his frivolous sermon very deeply disturbed those who heard it; since I see that all who have heard fragmentary reports of it are unfavorably impressed.

More reproaches What man in the audience, in whose breast burned even a spark of *the speaker* Christianity, would not groan at the degradation of the royal office of sacred preaching, which gained the world for Christ—above all at the hands of those whose supreme duty it was to protect it with the authority of their office? Who could possibly have devised a more outrageous insult than for an avowed preacher, during the most solemn season of the Church's year, in the presence of a large Christian congregation, in the sanctuary itself, from the elevation of the pulpit (as it were from the throne of Christ), and in view of the Sacred Body of Christ, to turn a Lenten sermon into Bacchanalian ravings? What a look must have been on the faces of the audience, who had come to hear spiritual wisdom, and saw the laughable pantomime he put on in the pulpit! They had expected to listen in reverence to the Word of Life; when they departed, all they could record they had heard was an attack on humane letters and a defamation of the preaching office by a fatuous preacher.

III. Argument It would have been no reproach to secular learning if some good man, *(Confirmatio)* who had retired from the world to monastic life, suddenly returned and

used this speaker's phrases: "much in watchings, much in prayer" or "the path to be trod by those who seek for heaven" or "other matters, like humanistic education, trivial if not a positive hindrance to the spiritual life," or "simple country folk, and the unlettered, flying quicker to heaven," etc.,
5 etc. All this could have been borne from such a man. His simplicity would have been pardoned by his audience. They would have generously admitted his saintliness, and given serious consideration to his piety, devotion, and righteousness. But when they saw a man with the academic ermine over his shoulders, step on to the platform in the midst of a gathering
10 composed solely of academics, and calmly proceed to rant against all humane learning, one would have had to be stone blind not to notice a signal pride and wickedness, a positive hatred of the higher arts. Many must have wondered indeed how such a man could get the idea that he had to preach either about Latin, of which he did not know much, or about the
15 liberal arts, of which he knew less, or about Greek—in which he could not even grunt that it was "all Greek" to him!

If such an abundance of material had been supplied by the seven deadly sins, an altogether suitable theme for sermons, who would have believed him totally inexperienced therein! Though, as a matter of fact, what is it
20 but sloth, when one is in the habit of denouncing rather than of learning that of which one is ignorant? And what is it but hatred, when one defames those who know what one deprecates but does not comprehend? And what is it but supreme pride, when he wishes no kind of knowledge to be prized save what he has falsely persuaded himself that he knows, and
25 when he even—not from modesty, as might be the case with other people—arrogates more praise to himself for his ignorance than for his knowledge?

Now as to the question of humanistic education being secular. No one has ever claimed that a man needed Greek and Latin, or indeed any edu-
30 cation in order to be saved. Still, this education which he calls secular does train the soul in virtue.[2] In any event, few will question that humanistic education is the chief, almost the sole reason why men come to Oxford; children can receive a good education at home from their mothers, all except cultivation and book learning. Moreover, even if men come to Ox-
35 ford to study theology, they do not start with that discipline. They must

More begins his defense of liberal education

2. Daniel Kinney's translation of *animam ad virtutem praeparat* is more accurate here: secular learning "prepares the soul for virtue." See *Complete Works*, vol. 15, p. 139.

Role of philosophy   first study the laws of human nature and conduct,[3] a thing not useless to theologians; without such study they might possibly preach a sermon acceptable to an academic group, without it they would certainly fail to

Poetry, rhetoric reach the common man. And from whom could they acquire such skill
and history praised better than from the poets, orators, and historians?[4]

    Moreover, there are some who through knowledge of things natural

Liberal arts construct a ladder by which to rise to the contemplation of things super-
as a ladder natural; they build a path to theology through philosophy and the liberal arts, which this man condemns as secular; they adorn the queen of heaven with the spoils of the Egyptians![5] This fellow declares that only theology should be studied; but if he admits even that, I don't see how he can accomplish his aim without some knowledge of languages, whether Hebrew or Greek or Latin; unless, of course, the elegant gentleman has convinced himself that there is enough theology written in English or that all theology can be squeezed into the limits of those [late scholastic] "questions" which he likes to pose and answer, for which a modicum of Latin would, I admit, suffice.

Theology demands   But really, I cannot admit that theology, that august queen of heaven,
Latin and Greek can be thus confined. Does she not dwell and abide in Holy Scripture? Does she not pursue her pilgrim way through the cells of the holy Fathers: Augustine and Jerome; Ambrose and Cyprian; Chrysostom, Gregory, Basil, and their like? The study of theology has been solidly based on these now despised expositors of fundamental truth during all the Christian centuries until the invention of these petty and meretricious "questions" which alone are today glibly tossed back and forth. Anyone who boasts that he can understand the works of the Fathers without an uncommon acquaintance with the languages of each and all of them will in his ignorance boast for a long time before the learned trust his judgment.

    But if this foolish preacher pretends that he was not condemning humanistic education in general but only an immoderate thirst for it, I can't see that this desire was such a sin that he had to deal with it in a public assembly, as if it were causing society to rush headlong to ruin. I haven't

---

3. Kinney translates *rerum humanarum prudentia* as "prudence in human affairs" (Ibid.)

4. Compare this list with the one on p. 278. Basil the Great enumerates these same three types of writers, and he gives arguments similar to this paragraph's (cf. the end of section three of "To Young Men, On How They Might Derive Profit from Pagan Literature"). See Marc'hadour's article on Basil and More, esp. pp. 44–45, 51.

5. See Exodus 3:22, Augustine's *On Christian Doctrine* 2.40.60–61, and *Confessions* 7.9.

heard that many have gone so far in such studies that they will soon be overstepping the golden mean. Further, this fellow, just to show how immoderate he could be in a sermon, specifically called students of Greek "heretics," teachers of Greek "chief devils," and pupils in Greek "lesser devils" or, more modestly and facetiously as he thought, "little devils"; and the zeal of this holy man drove him to call by the name of devil one whom everybody knows the Devil himself could hardly bear to see occupy a pulpit. He did everything but name that one [D. Erasmus], as everybody realized just as clearly as they realized the folly of the speaker.

Joking aside—I have no desire to pose as the sole defender of Greek learning; for I know how obvious it must be to scholars of your eminence that the study of Greek is tried and true. To whom is it not obvious that to the Greeks we owe all our precision in the liberal arts generally and in theology particularly; for the Greeks either made the great discoveries themselves or passed them on as part of their heritage. Take philosophy, for example. If you leave out Cicero and Seneca, the Romans wrote their philosophy in Greek or translated it from Greek. *The greatness of the Greeks*

I need hardly mention that the New Testament is in Greek, or that the best New Testament scholars were Greeks and wrote in Greek. I am but repeating the consensus of scholarship when I say: however much was translated of old from Greek, and however much more has been recently and better translated, not half of Greek learning has yet been made available to the West; and, however good the translations have been, the text of the original still remains a surer and more convincing presentation. For that very reason all the Doctors of the Latin Church—Jerome, Augustine, Bede, and a host of others—assiduously gave themselves to learning Greek; and even though many works had already been translated, they were much more accustomed to reading them in the original than are many of our contemporaries who claim to be erudite; nor did they merely learn it themselves, but counseled those among their successors who wanted to be theologians above all to do the same.

So it is not as if I were just giving your Worships good advice about preserving the study of Greek. I am rather exhorting you to do your duty. You should not allow anyone in your university to be frightened away from the study of Greek, either by public assemblies or private inanities, since Greek is a subject required in every place of learning by the Church Universal. Common sense is surely enough to convince you that not all of your number who give themselves to the study of Greek can be block- *More reminds them of their duty* heads; in fact, it is in part from these studies that your university had acquired its pedagogical prestige both at home and abroad.

There seems to be an increasing number of cases where Oxford has benefited from the presence of men nominally studying Greek only, but really taking the whole liberal arts course. It will be a wonder if their enthusiasm for you does not evaporate when they realize that so serious an enterprise is held in such contempt. Just think, too, what they are doing at Cambridge, which you have always outshone; those who are not studying Greek are so moved by common interest in their university that they are actually making large individual contributions to the salary of the Greek professor!

More warns that others are growing unhappy

You see what I mean; and much more could be said to the point by men with better minds than mine. All I am doing is warning you of what others are saying and thinking, not telling you what it behooves you to do. You see much better than I that, if wicked factions are not suppressed at birth, a contagious disease will spread, and the better half be slowly absorbed by the worse, and that outsiders will be forced to take a hand in helping the good and wise among you. Any former student of the university takes its welfare as much to heart as you who are its living members. And I am sure that the Reverend Father in Christ who occupies the See of Canterbury [William Warham], who is the Primate of all our Clergy, and who is also the Chancellor of your university will not fail to do his part. Whether for the clergy's sake or yours, he rightly feels interested in preventing the decay of learning; and learning will perish if the university continues to suffer from the contentions of lazy idiots, and the liberal arts are allowed to be made sport of with impunity. And what about the Reverend Father in Christ, the Cardinal of York [Thomas Wolsey], who is both a patron of learning and himself the most learned of the episcopate? Would he endure patiently if aspersions were cast in your university on the liberal arts and the study of languages? Will he not rather aim the shafts of his learning, virtue, and authority at these witless detractors from the arts?

More invokes their learned king

Last but not least: what of our most Christian King? His sacred Majesty has cultivated all the liberal arts as much as ever a king did; indeed, he possesses greater erudition and judgment than any previous monarch. Will his wisdom and piety suffer him to allow the liberal arts to fail—through the interests of evil and lazy men—in a place where his most illustrious ancestors wished that there be an illustrious seat of letters, a place which is an ancient nursery of learning, whose products have been an ornament not only to England but to the whole Church, a place which possesses so many colleges that have perpetual endowments specially designated for the support of students (in which respect there is no university outside the kingdom that can compare with Oxford), a place in which the aim of all its colleges and the purpose of all its endowments is none other than that a great body of academics, delivered from the necessity of earning their daily bread, might there pursue the liberal arts?

I have no doubt that you yourselves will easily in your wisdom find a way to end this dispute and quiet these stupid factions; that you will see to it not only that all the liberal arts may be free from derision and contempt but that they shall be held in dignity and honor. By such diligence in intellectual pursuits you will reap benefit for yourselves; and it can hardly be said how much you will gain favor with our Illustrious Prince and with the above-mentioned Reverend Fathers in Christ. You will forge an almost miraculous bond between yourselves and myself, who have thought that all this had to be written now in my own hand out of my deep personal affection for you. You know that my services are at the disposal of each and all of you. May God preserve your glorious seat of learning unharmed; and may He grant that it flourish continually in virtue and in all the liberal arts.

Thomas More.

IV. Conclusion (Peroratio)

More is confident of a solution

Conscience and Integrity

Since More is the first writer known to use the English word "integrity,"[1] *and since he consistently appeals to conscience throughout his life, it is important to understand both terms as he did. His most provocative and best known statement, "I die the King's good servant and God's first,"*[2] *underscores More's claim that integrity is possible in political and personal life.*

5

1. *In a letter to his children's teacher, More urged:* "The whole fruit of their [educational] endeavors should consist in the testimony of God and a good conscience. Thus they will be inwardly calm and at peace and neither stirred by praise of flatterers nor stung by the follies of unlearned mockers of learning."[3]

10

2. *More expressed his clearness of conscience in this response to the judges who condemned him:* "I verily trust and shall therefore right heartily pray, that though your lordships have now here in earth been judges to my condemnation, we may yet hereafter in heaven merrily all meet together."[4]

1. See *TMSB*, p. xv, note 13.
2. See *TMSB*, pp. 355, 357.
3. *Selected Letters*, p. 105. See *TMSB*, pp. 198–200.
4. Roper, *Life, TMSB*, p. 61.

3. *While in prison, More wrote:* "The clearness of my conscience has made my heart hop for joy.[5] My case was such in this matter through the clearness of my own conscience that though I might have pain I could not have harm, for a man may in such a case lose his head and have no harm."[6]

4. *Written about More in prison:* "Thus being well and quietly settled in conscience, the security and uprightness of the same so eased and diminished all the griefs and pains of his imprisonment and all his other adversity, that no token or signification of lamenting or sorrow appeared in him, but that in his communication with his daughter, with the Lieutenant and others, he held on his old merry, pleasant talk whosoever occasion served."[7]

5. *On acquiring a calm and clear-sighted mind: In More's view, to achieve serenity and clear sight, one needs a well-cultivated soul that has come to love the "spiritual pleasure . . . of truth." So long as the soul is "overgrown with the barren weeds of carnal pleasures," it will have "no place for the good corn of spiritual pleasure." The whole point is to "keep our minds occupied with good thoughts," for a "wandering mind" is never capable of "wisdom and good manners." Such "diligent remembrance" is well worth the effort it takes, for it is sure to flower in "not a false imagination, but a very true contemplation" of reality as it exists.*[8]

6. *On right imagination and remembrance:* "In the things of the soul, knowledge without remembrance profits little."[9] "I would have people in time of silence take good heed that their minds be occupied with good thoughts, for unoccupied they will never be."[10]

7. *How King Saul loses his calm and clear-sighted mind: In Thomas More's last works, proud King Saul emerges as the recurring example of the danger facing any ruler who does not govern his mind and imagination. Saul was chosen by God*

---

5. That More considered the greatest earthly joy to be a clear conscience, see such passages as *Complete Works,* vol. 1, p. 108, lines 7–8; p. 112, lines 12–13; vol. 12, p. 34–5, lines 26ff

6. *Selected Letters,* p. 235.

7. Harpsfield, *Life of St. Thomas More,* p. 149.

8. *The Last Things, Complete Works,* vol. 1, pp. 132ff.

9. *Ibid.,* p. 138.

10. *Ibid.,* p. 136

and entrusted with the care of Israel, and he began as a just and energetic advocate of Israel's common good. Yet faced with tribulations, Saul became impatient and "murmured, grudged, and mistrusted God." After "boldly framing himself a conscience with a gloss of his own making," he ended up consulting witches, a practice explicitly forbidden by a law that Saul himself had proclaimed.[11]   5

❧

8. *On the importance of attending to conscience, despite weariness and opposition: More warns that, if a leader allows weariness to so grip* "the mind that its strength is sapped and reason gives up the reins, if a [leader] is so overcome by heavy-hearted sleep that he neglects to do what the duty of his office requires . . .—like a cowardly ship's captain who is so disheartened by the   10 furious din of a storm that he deserts the helm, hides away cowering in some cranny, and abandons the ship to the waves—if a [leader] does this, I would certainly not hesitate to juxtapose and compare his sadness with the sadness that leads as [Paul] says, to hell. . . ."[12]

❧

9. *Thomas More on the importance of integrity:* "I considered it my duty to   15 protect the integrity of my reputation. . . . After resigning my office, I waited until the opening of the new term, and, so far, no one has advanced a complaint against my integrity. Either my life has been so spotless or, at any rate, I have been so circumspect that, if my rivals oppose my boasting of the one, they are forced to let me boast of the other. As a matter of fact,   20 the King himself has pronounced on this situation at various times, frequently in private, and twice in public."[13]

11. See esp. *Treatise on the Passion, Complete Works*, vol. 13, pp. 112 and 213.
12. *On the Sadness of Christ, Complete Works*, vol. 14, pp. 263–65.
13. *Selected Letters*, pp. 179–80. See also *TMSB*, pp. 305–7.

On Pride

Pride was a subject of particular interest to Thomas More, as can be seen even in his Utopia. *Because of the confusion about this concept today, it is important to understand More's own conception. The longer selections below are from two of More's last works,* A Dialogue of Comfort against Tribulation *and* Treatise Upon the Passion, *written while he was imprisoned in the Tower of London.*

The Understanding of "Pride" More Inherited:

"Pride [*superbia*] is so called because individuals thereby aim higher [*supra*] than they are. Pride is the appetite for excellence in excess of right reason."[1]

Short Aphorisms from More's Writings

1. Aesop says in a fable that everyone carries a double wallet on his shoulders, and into the one that hangs at his breast he puts other folk's faults and he looks and pores over it often. In the other he puts in all his own and swings it at his back, which he never likes to look in, although others that come behind him cast an eye into it sometimes.[2]

A memorable image

1. Aquinas, II.II.162.a.1.
2. *Dialogue Concerning Heresies, Complete Works,* vol. 6, pp. 295–96.

2. *As Boetheus says:* For one man to be proud that he has rule over oth-er men is much like one mouse being proud to have rule over other mice in a barn.[3]

3. He who sets his delight on the blast of another man's mouth feeds himself but with wind,[4] wherein, be he never so full, he has little substance therein.[5]

4. I never saw a fool yet who thought himself other than wise. . . . If a fool perceives himself a fool, that point is not folly, but a little spark of wit.[6]

5. I counsel every man and woman to beware of even the very least spice of pride, which seems to be the mere delight and liking of ourselves for anything that is in us or outwardly belongs to us.[7]

❧

Pride as an Arrow[8]

For by those words of the psalmist, "the arrow that flies by day," I un-derstand the arrow of pride. And that is something with which the devil tempts a person not during the nighttime of tribulation and adversity, for that time is too disheartening and too fearful for pride, but in the daytime of prosperity, for that time is full of lighthearted vigor and confidence. But surely this worldly prosperity in which one so rejoices, and of which the devil makes one so proud, is very short even for a winter's day. For we be-gin, many of us, poor and cold as can be, and then up we fly like arrows shot straight up into the air. Suddenly we are shot up into the highest, sun-niest realms. But before we can get good and warm there, down we come again to the cold ground, and there we stay stuck. And yet for the short while that we're up on high, Lord, how exhilarated and proud we are. We busily buzz up there like a bumblebee that flies around in the summer, having no idea it will die in the winter. So fare many of us, God help us. For in the short winter's day of worldly wealth and prosperity, this flying arrow from the devil—this high-flying spirit of pride, shot out of the dev-

The high-flying arrow

---

3. *The Correspondence of Sir Thomas More*, pp. 519–20. See *TMSB*, p. 324.

4. Compare this statement with the first four lines of More's "Psalm on Detachment," *TMSB*, p. 171, where he prays that he not "hang upon the blast of men's mouths."

5. *Dialogue of Comfort, Complete Works*, vol. 12, p. 212.

6. Ibid., p. 287.

7. *Treatise on the Passion, Complete Works*, vol. 13, p. 9, and see *TMSB*, p. 219.

8. *Dialogue of Comfort*, modernized by Mary Gottschalk, pp. 158–59; *Complete Works*, vol. 12, pp. 157–58.

il's bow, which pierces the heart all the way through—lifts us up, in our estimation, into the clouds. Thinking we sit on the rainbow, we look down on the world beneath us. Those other poor souls who used to be, perhaps, our friends, we now regard as pitiful little bugs and ants in comparison to
5 our own glorious selves.

Pride's effect on our perceptions

But no matter how high in the clouds this arrow of pride may fly, and no matter how exuberant one may feel while being carried up so high, let us remember that the lightest of these arrows still has a heavy iron head. High as it may fly, therefore, it inevitably has to come down and hit the
10 ground. And sometimes it lands in a not very clean place. The pride turns into shame and disgrace, and then all that glory is gone.

Pride: Its Nature and Manifestations[9]

Good readers, let us here and now, before we go any further, seriously consider this matter and ponder well this fearful point: what horrible peril
15 there is in the pestilent sin of pride; what an abominable sin it is in the sight of God when any creature falls into the delight and liking of itself. This is something which, if continued, will inevitably be followed first by a neglecting of God, then by a scorning of him, and finally (by way of disobedience and rebellion) by a total forsaking of him.

Pride's progression

20 If pride is so infuriating to God that he did not refrain from driving down into hell some noble, high, excellent angels of heaven simply because of their pride, then what nobleman in this wretched world can be so great that he doesn't have great cause to tremble and quake, in every joint in his body, as soon as he feels a high, proud thought once enter into his
25 heart? Surely the greatest of them all will do so if he remembers this terrible warning and threat that God gives in holy Scripture: "Mighty men will be mightily tested" (Wis 6:6). And if the sin of pride is in the sight of God such a terribly bad, unacceptable thing in the person of a great nobleman, who has many reasons to be inclined towards it, then how much more
30 abominable is that foolish pride in a shiftless, low-class bum who has a wallet as penniless as that of any poor peddler, and yet a heart as haughty as that of many a mighty prince! And if it is odious in the sight of God when a woman who is indeed beautiful abuses her beauty by taking a vainglorious pride in it, then how delectable to the devil is that dainty damsel who

9. *Treatise on the Passion, Complete Works,* vol. 13, pp. 7–10.

stands in her own light and takes herself as lovely, and thinks herself well
liked for her elegant forehead, when the young man looking at her notices
A crooked nose more her crooked nose!

And if it is a detestable thing for any of us creatures to rise in pride
upon the thought and consideration of our own character, beauty,   5
strength, intelligence, or education, or any other such kind of thing as by
nature and grace are properly our own, then how much more foolish a
deception is there in that pride by which we worldly folk look up on high
and solemnly esteem ourselves—with a deep disdain of other, far better
people—just for very vain, worldly trifles that properly speaking are not   10
Pride in worldly our own? How proud we are of gold and silver, which are no part of our-
things selves—they're just part of the earth. And by nature they're no better than
the poor copper or tin, nor to our use so profitable as that poor metal,
which makes for us the ploughshare, and horseshoes and horse nails. How
proud so many are of these glittering stones, of which the very brightest,   15
even if it costs you twenty pounds, will never shine half so bright or give
you half so much light as will a poor halfpenny candle. How proudly
many a man looks down on his neighbor because the wool he wears is
finer. And yet fine as it is, a poor sheep wore it on her back before it came
upon his; and all the while that she wore it, regardless of how fine her   20
Just a sheep wool was, she was, by God, still just a sheep. And why should he now be
better than her because of that wool which, though it is his, is yet not so
truly his as it was hers?

But, now, how many men are there who are proud of something that is
not theirs at all? Is there no man who is proud of keeping another man's   25
gate? Another man's horse? Another man's hound or hawk? What a brag-
ging a bear keeper makes with his silver-buttoned belt, for pride of another man's bear! However, why speak of other people's property versus our
own? I can see nothing that, if well considered, anyone can truthfully call
their own. Just as we would characterize as total fools those who are proud   30
of themselves because they strut around in borrowed finery, so may all of
us very well be called fools if we take pride in anything that we have here.
For nothing do we have here that is our very own—not even our own
body. We have borrowed it all from God, and we must yield it all back to
him and send our pitiful soul out naked, no one can tell how soon. "What   35
have you," says Saint Paul, "that you did not receive? If then you received
All is a gift it, why do you boast as if it were not a gift?" (1 Cor 4:7).

All that we ever have, from God we have received—riches, status, au-

thority, beauty, strength, learning, intelligence, body, soul, and all. And almost all these things he has only lent us. For we must depart again from
every last one of these things, except our soul alone. And that, too, we
must give back to God, or else we shall keep it forever with such sorrow
that we would be better off losing it. And as for the misuse of it, and of our
body along with it, and of all the rest of that borrowed ware that we are
now so proud of, we shall yield a very strict account and come to a heavy
reckoning; and many a thousand, body and soul together, will burn in hell
eternally for the foolish pride of that borrowed ware so vaingloriously
boasted of before in the transitory time and short, soon passed life of this
foolish, wretched world. For surely this sin of pride—which is the first of
all sins, the sin begun among the angels in heaven—is the head and root of
all other sins, and the most destructive of them all.

All is on loan

Now, it is not my intention here to explore all the many branches of it,
or to name all the kinds of misfortune that come from it, for that would
take up more time than is appropriate for this present matter. Rather, I
will simply counsel every man and woman to beware of even the very
least speck of it, which seems to me to be the mere delight and liking of
ourselves for anything whatsoever that either is in us or outwardly belongs
to us. Let every one of us watch ourselves very carefully, and let us mark
well when the devil first casts any proud, vain thought into our mind, and
let us immediately make a sign of the cross and thus immediately bless it
out and cast it back at his head. For if we gladly take in one such guest of
his, he will not fail to bring in, soon after, two more—and each one worse
than the previous one (see Mt 12:49).

Pride defined

The Spirit of God well expresses this point in Psalm 12, where the
psalmist notes the perilous progress of proud folk, characterizing them as
"those who say, 'With our tongue we will prevail, our lips are with us; who
is our master?'" They start out, you see, with basically just a vain delight and
pride in the eloquence of their speech; they say they will show it off to
make themselves look good. And in that there would seem to be little harm
other than a fond, foolish vanity—if they went no further. But it is the devil that has brought them to that point first, and he has no intention of allowing them to rest and remain there. Soon he makes them think and say
something further: "Our lips are with us"; in other words, "Our lips are our
own; we have them of ourselves." So, look—at what point are they now?
Do they not now take for their own something that God has lent them and
refuse to acknowledge that it is his? Thus they become thieves unto God.

A final example of pride

And yet, you see, the devil will not leave them there, either. No, he carries them still farther forth, to the very worst point of all. For once they
say that their lips are their own, that they have them of themselves, then
against the truth—which is that they have their lips lent to them by our
Lord, our master—their proud hearts rear up, and they ask, "Who is our   5
master?" And so they deny that they have any master at all. And thus, you
see, beginning with just a vain pride in being praised, they next become
thieves unto God, and finally from thieves they fall into being plain rebel-
The final   lious traitors, and refuse to take God for their God, and fall into the de-
expression of testable pride that Lucifer himself fell into.   10
pride
  Let us therefore, I say, . . . beware of this horrible vice, and resist well
the very first motions of it.

Erasmus on More's Approach to Education

In this letter[1] to his friend Guillaume Budé (1521), Erasmus describes the profound benefits More attributes to his own liberal education. After defending More's decision to give his daughters a liberal education, Erasmus concludes the letter with a reflection on marriage.

ANDERLECHT

c. SEPTEMBER 1521

Erasmus of Rotterdam to His Friend, Guillaume Budé, Greetings.

... More is to be congratulated. He neither aimed at it nor asked for it, but the king has promoted him to a very honorable post, with a salary by no means to be despised: he is his prince's treasurer. This office in England is in the first rank of grandeur and distinction, but is not unduly exposed either to unpopularity or to tedious press of business. He had a rival for it, a fairly influential man who wanted the office so badly that he would not object to holding it at his own costs and charges. But that admirable king gave the clearest proof of his high opinion of More, in that he went so far as to give him a salary when he did not want the post, rather than accept

A notable promotion

5

---

1. *Collected Works of Erasmus*, vol. 8, letter 1233, pp. 294–99.

221

an official who did not need to be paid. Not content with that, this most generous prince has also knighted him, nor can there be any doubt that some day he will honour him with yet greater distinctions when the occasion presents itself; for normally princes show a much greater tendency to promote bachelors. But More is so deeply embedded in the ranks of married men, that not even his wife's death has given him his freedom. For having buried his first wife, who was a girl when he married her, the widower has now taken unto himself a widow.

In the ranks of married men

I am the more delighted for More's sake at this attitude of his prince towards him for this reason, that whatever increase in authority or influence accrues to him, accrues, I believe, to the study of the humanities, of which he is such a keen supporter that, were his resources equal to his wishes, the English would find their gifted minds in no lack of an open-hearted and generous Maecenas. The courts of princes usually behave like the physician who first evacuates the body of the patient entrusted to him and then fills it up and restores its energy; and I do not doubt that our friend More has had some such experience hitherto. How it has gone in your case you know better than I do. And yet gifted men have enjoyed his bounty, in the days when not only was he far from having plenty to give away, he was burdened with debt.

More's support of liberal education

But to be a good scholar himself and give generous support to all other scholars is not the only way in which he honors liberal studies. He takes pains to give his whole household an education in good literature, setting thereby a new precedent which, if I mistake not, will soon be widely followed, so happy is the outcome. He has three daughters, of whom Margaret, the eldest, is already married to a young man who is well off, has a most honorable and modest character, and besides that is no stranger to our literary pursuits. All of them from their earliest years he has had properly and strictly brought up in point of character, and has given them a liberal education. To his three daughters he has added a fourth girl,[2] whom he maintains as a piece of generosity to be a playmate for them. He also has a step-daughter[3] of great beauty and exceptional gifts, married for some years now to a young man not without education and of truly golden character. And he has a son by his first wife,[4] now a boy of about thirteen, who is the youngest of his children.

An example of education in More's house

2. Margaret Giggs.
3. Alice Middleton.
4. John More.

About a year ago, More took it into his head to give me a demonstration of the progress of their education. He told them all to write to me, *Letters for* each of them independently. No subject was supplied them, nor was what *Erasmus* they wrote corrected in any way. When they had shown their drafts to
5 their father for criticism, he told them, as though he took exception to their bad writing, to make a cleaner and more careful copy of the same words; and when they had done that, he did not alter a syllable, but sealed up the letters and sent them off to me. Believe me, my dear Budé, I never saw anything so admirable. In what they said there was nothing foolish or
10 childish, and the language made one feel that they must be making daily progress. This charming group, with the husbands of two of them, he keeps under his own roof. There you never see one of the girls idle, or busied with the trifles that women enjoy; they have a Livy in their hands. They have made such progress that they can read and understand authors
15 of that class without anyone to explain them, unless they come upon some word that might have held up even me or someone like me.

His wife, whose strength lies in mother-wit and experience rather than *In praise of* book-learning, controls the whole institution with remarkable skill, acting *Dame Alice* as a kind of overseer who gives each one her task and sees that she per
20 forms it and allows no idleness or frivolous occupations.

You are wont to complain in your letters from time to time that in your case classical study has acquired a bad name for having brought two bad things into your life, poor health and pecuniary loss. The result of More's activity on the other hand, is to make it acceptable to everyone
25 concerned on every count, for he says he owes to his literary studies his *The benefits of* much better health, his popularity and influence with an excellent prince *liberal education* and all men both friends and strangers, his easier circumstances, his own greater happiness and the happiness he gives his friends, the services he can now render to his country and his relations and kinsfolk, his increased
30 adaptability to court society, to life among the nobility, and to the whole way of life that he now leads, and a greater ease in pleasing heaven. At first liberal studies had a bad name for depriving their devoted adherents of the common touch. There is no journey, no business however voluminous or difficult, that can take the book out of More's hand; and yet it would be
35 hard to find anyone who was more truly a man for all seasons[5] and all

---

5. Erasmus first comments on this phrase, "omnium horarum homo," in the first edition of his *Adages* (1508): "The man who suits himself to seriousness and jesting alike, and whose company is always delightful—that is the man the ancients call 'a man for all hours.'" Robert Whittington

men, who was more ready to oblige, more easily available for meeting, more lively in conversation, or who combined so much real wisdom with such charm of character. The result is that, while only a few days ago a love

Liberal studies now fashionable

of literature was thought to be of no practical or ornamental value, there is now hardly one of our great nobles who would reckon his children worthy of their ancestry if they had no education in liberal studies. Monarchs themselves are thought to lack a good share of the qualities proper to a king if their knowledge of literature leaves much to be desired.

Women and liberal education

Again, scarcely any mortal man was not under the conviction that, for the female sex, education had nothing to offer in the way of either virtue or reputation. Nor was I myself in the old days completely free of this opinion; but More has quite put it out of my head. For two things in particular are perilous to a girl's virtue, idleness and improper amusements, and against both of these the love of literature is a protection. There is no better way to maintain a spotless reputation than faultless behavior, and no woman's chastity is more secure than hers who is chaste by deliberate choice. Not that I disapprove the ideas of those who plan to protect their daughters' honor by teaching them the domestic arts; but nothing so oc-

The love of reading

cupies a girl's whole heart as the love of reading. And besides this advantage, that the mind is kept from pernicious idleness, this is the way to absorb the highest principles, which can both instruct and inspire the mind in the pursuit of virtue. Many have been exposed to the loss of their maidenhead by inexperience and ignorance of the world, before they know what the things are that put that great treasure at risk. Nor do I see why husbands need fear that if they have educated wives they will have wives who are less obedient, unless they are the kind of men who wish to demand from a wife what ought not to be demanded of respectable married women. In my opinion, on the other hand, nothing is more intractable than ignorance. At least, a mind developed and exercised by reading has this advantage, that it can recognize good and just reasons for what they are, and perceive what conduct is proper and what is profitable. Why, the man who has taught her the facts has almost converted her. Besides which,

The marriage of true minds

what makes wedlock delightful and lasting is more the good will between mind and mind than any physical passion, so that far stronger bonds unite those who are joined by mutual affection of minds as well, and a wife has

---

translates this phrase as "a man for all seasons" in his *Vulgaria* (1508). See *Complete Works of Erasmus*, vol 3, p. 304.

A deuout treatise vpon the Pater no=
ster/made fyʒst in latyn by the mooſt fa=
mous doctour mayſter Eraſmus
Roterodamus/ and tourned
in to engliſſhe by a yong
bertuous and well
lerned gentylwoman of .xix.
yere of age.

Title page of Margaret Roper's translation of Erasmus' *A Devout Treatise Upon the Pater Noster* [1525/1531?].

more respect for a husband whom she acknowledges as a teacher also. Devotion will not be less because there is less unreason in it. Personally, I would rather have one talent of pure gold than three contaminated heavily with lead and dross.

We often hear other women returning from church quite ready to say that the preacher gave them a wonderful sermon, and they provide a lively account of his expression. Beyond that, they are quite unable to report what he said or what it was like. These young ladies recount nearly the whole sermon to you in order, though not without some selection; if the preacher let fall anything foolish or irreligious or off the point, as we see not seldom happens nowadays, they know how to make fun of it or ignore it or protest against it. This, and only this, is what listening to a sermon means. One can really enjoy the society of girls like this. I differ profoundly from those who keep a wife for no purpose except physical satisfaction, *Erasmus on wives* for which half-witted females are better fitted. A woman must have intelligence if she is to keep her household up to its duties, to form and mold her children's characters, and meet her husband's needs in every way. Apart from that, when I was talking to More recently, I put the objection that if anything should happen, as the way of all flesh is, he would be the more tormented by grief for the loss of them, inasmuch as he had spent all that effort on their upbringing; and he replied, "If anything inevitable were to happen, I would rather they died educated than uneducated." And I was then reminded of that remark of Phocion, I think it was, who was about to drink the hemlock, and when his wife cried out, "O my husband, you will die an innocent man," his answer was, "What of it, my dear wife? Would you rather I died guilty?". . . .

Farewell.
Erasmus

4

Writings on Government

Opposite

Sir Thomas More (bottom center) stands at the bar in the midst of the Commons. Opposite him sits King Henry VIII in solitary and elevated splendor. To the left of the King are the Bishop of London (Tunstall), who stands holding the roll of his opening speech, and Lord Chancellor Wolsey who is seated with the Archbishop of Canterbury (Warham). To the right are two counselors and a group of the eldest sons of the peers, directly in front of whom is the Garter King of Arms (Sir Thomas Wriothesley). In front of the dais are three earls holding cap of maintenance, baton, and sword. Seated on the woolsacks in the center are the judges (including Sir John More) with recording clerks behind them. The bishops are on the left with the abbots behind; the lords temporal are on the right; and the barons are on the crossbench. This historic Parliament opened on April 15, 1523 at Blackfriars, but Sir Thomas More was presented only on April 18. The artist has conflated the two events, thereby giving Sir Thomas and the Commons an unusual prominence.

On the following left hand page

Holbein's full-length depiction of Henry's frontal stance of "frightening directness" with "firmly knuckled hands" near ready dagger and ostentatious codpiece—a clear "breach of pictorial and gestural etiquette"—was designed as an icon of assertive power and god-like splendor. An explanation of Henry's confrontational stance amidst such a conspicuous display of wealth is suggested by some of the verses that accompanied the original at Whitehall: "To unerring virtue, the presumption of popes has yielded, / And so long as Henry the Eighth carries the scepter in hand / Religion is renewed, and during his reign/ The doctrines of God have begun to be held in his honour." The Whitehall mural was completed in 1537, after the uprisings known as the Pilgrimage of Grace, which ended with Henry's crushing the insurgents and executing the leaders. Around Henry's leg is a garter with the words *Honi soit qui mal y pense* ("Ashamed be he who thinks ill of it"), a motto from that order of chivalry known as the Order of the Garter. Henry wears a "gold-brocaded costume" studded with "squads of pearls and impressive jewels," including "large rubies and other gemstones mounted in typically heavy and ornate gold settings." The silk curtains and the exquisite Turkish carpet contribute to the opulence of the scene. At his death Henry owned more than 800 carpets and sixty manor houses. Although Henry was a trim athlete in his youth, his final suit of armor shows a fifty-four-inch waist and a fifty-seven-inch chest. (See Brooke and Combie's *Henry VIII Revealed: Holbein's Portrait and Its Legacy* [2003], pp. 22, 30–37.)

Sir Thomas More makes his Petition for Free Speech, addressing the
King in Parliament, 1523, as Speaker of the House of Commons.
(See the frontispiece for the original painting from which
this engraving was made.)

Henry VIII in 1537, at age 46. (See p. 228.)

On Dealing with Lions

As Erasmus noted in his famous letter describing More's character, More had a prudent sense of the difficulties involved in public service—especially in the service of a powerful king, as these poems suggest.[1]

"To a Courtier"

You often boast to me that you have the king's ear and often have fun with him, freely and according to your own whims. This is like having fun with tamed lions—often it is harmless, but just as often there is fear of harm. Often he roars in rage for no known reason, and suddenly the fun becomes fatal. The pleasure you get is not safe enough to relieve you of anxiety. For you it is a great pleasure. As for me, let my pleasure be less great—and safe. (*Latin Poems*, #162)

"Fable of the Sick Fox and the Lion"

While a fox lay sick in his narrow den, a smooth-tongued lion took his stand at the entrance. Said he, "Tell me, my friend, don't you feel well? You will soon get well if you let me lick you. You just do not know the power of my tongue." "Your tongue," said the fox, "has healing powers; but the trouble is that such a good tongue has bad neighbors." (*Latin Poems*, #180)

---

1. The poems are from *Complete Works*, vol. 3.2.

"On a Lion and Lysimachus"

While a tamed lion harmlessly licked his trainer, the trainer invited one and all to put themselves in his place. After a long time, when no one among the large crowd of spectators had come forward, brave-hearted Lysimachus leaped up. Said he, "I am brave enough to endure the touch of ₅ the lion's tongue, but his teeth are so close to his tongue that I shall not do it." (*Latin Poems*, #181)

Thomas More to Cromwell[2]

Now after Thomas More resigned his office, Sir Thomas Cromwell (then in the King's high favor) came to Chelsea with a message from the ₁₀ King. After they had fully communed together, Sir Thomas said: "Mr. Cromwell, you have now entered the service of a most noble, wise, and liberal prince; if you will follow my poor advice you shall, in counsel given to his Grace, ever tell him what he ought to do, but never tell him what he is able to do, so shall you show yourself a true faithful servant, and a ₁₅ right worthy Counselor.[3] For if the lion knew his own strength, hard were it for any man to rule him."

2. From Roper's *Life, TMSB.* p. 43.

3. Note what the *Paris Newsletter* records as More's last statement to his judges about good counsel (*TMSB*, p. 355).

Poems on the Human Condition and the Art of Governing

***

As a young man, Thomas More translated poems #27–31 below from Greek to Latin.[1] Poem #32 is his own composition. Like the poems on lions, these poems suggest the depth of More's political thinking on many key subjects, including the bonds connecting members of society, the art of ruling well, the best form of government, and the dangers of ill-governed power. These poems were first published with the 1518 edition of Utopia.

On Two Beggars: One Blind, One Lame

A blind neighbor carries a lame man about; by a skillful[2] combination he borrows eyes and lends feet. (*Latin Poems, #27*)

A blind man carries a lame man around. They manage the situation
5 with skill;[3] the latter lends his eyes, the former his feet. (*Latin Poems, #28*)

A blind man carries a lame man; and so, by a combined effort,[4] one borrows eyes, the other feet. (*Latin Poems, #29*)

---

1. These poems are from *Complete Works*, vol. 3.2. For the Greek originals, see W. R. Paton's edition of *The Greek Anthology*, vol. 3, Cambridge, MA: Loeb Classical Library, 1917. Plato the Younger's Epigram 13 is the model for More's epigrams #27–30; Philippus' or Isidorus' epigram 11 is the model for More's epigram #31.
   2. *skillful*—the Latin term is "arte."
   3. *with skill*—the Latin term is "prudenter."
   4. *by a combined effort*—the Latin phrase is "opera conducit."

A blind man carries a lame man, a heavy but a useful load.[5] He looks
ahead and with his eyes he guides the other's feet. (*Latin Poems, #30*)

Very sad misfortune overtook two unhappy men and cruelly deprived
the one of his eyes, the other of his feet. Their common misery united
them. The lame man rides upon the other. Thus by cooperation[6] they mitigate each other's handicaps. The lame man goes anywhere with the help
of the other's feet, the blind man travels a path determined by the other's
eyes. (*Latin Poems, #31*)

There can be nothing more helpful[7] than a loyal friend, who by his
own efforts assuages your hurts.[8] Two beggars formed an alliance of firm
friendship—a blind man and a lame one. The blind man said to the lame
one, "You must ride upon my shoulders." The latter answered, "You, blind
friend, must find your way by means of my eyes." The love which unites
shuns the castles of proud kings and rules[9] in the humble hut.[10] (*Latin Poems, #32*)

5. *heavy but useful load*—the Latin phrase here is "onus grave sed tamen utile."

6. *cooperation*—the Latin phrase is "communi opera."

7. *helpful*—the Latin term is "utilius."

8. The poem's first line—"Utilius nihil esse potest, quam fidus amicus,"—stresses "utility," a concept that has prominence in Cicero's teaching and (in a different sense) in *Utopia*.

9. *rules*—the Latin is "regnat."

10. The last two lines are: "Alta superborum fugitat penetralia regum, / Inque casa concors paupere regnat amor." "Amor" is given prominent place also in #112 of *Latin Poems*.

Other Poems on Politics

More wrote these poems between 1500 and 1516, when he was between twenty-three and thirty-nine. All are original poems; none are translations based on Greek models (as in the cases of epigrams #27–31 above). They were first published with the 1518 editions of Utopia.[1]

The Difference between a Tyrant and a King

A king who respects the law differs from cruel tyrants thus: a tyrant rules his subjects[2] as slaves; a king thinks of his as his own children. (*Latin Poems,* #109)

That the Tyrant's Life Is Troubled

Great anxiety wears away the waking hours of the mighty tyrant; peace comes at night if it comes at all. But the tyrant does not rest more comfortably on any soft bed than the poor man does on the hard ground. Therefore, tyrant, the happiest part of your life is that in which you willingly become no better than a beggar. (*Latin Poems,* #110)

---

1. These poems are from *Complete Works,* vol. 3.2.
2. *civibus*—which this translation renders as "subjects," but "citizens" is more accurate. See p. 237, note 6.

That the Good King Is a Father Not a Master

A devoted king will never lack children;[3] he is father to the whole kingdom. And so it is that a true king is abundantly blessed in having as many children as he has [citizens]. (*Latin Poems*, #111)

On the Good King and His People

A kingdom in all its parts is like a man; it is held together by natural affection.[4] The king is the head; the people form the other parts. Every citizen the king has he considers a part of his own body (that is why he grieves at the loss of a single one). The people risk themselves to save the king and everyone thinks of him as the head of his own body. (*Latin Poems*, #112)

That the Tyrant While He Sleeps Is No Different from the Commoner

Well then, you madman, it is pride which makes you carry your head so high—because the throng bows to you on bended knee, because the people rise and uncover for you, because you have in your power the life and death of many. But whenever sleep secures your body in inactivity, then, tell me, where is this glory of yours? Then you lie, useless creature, like a lifeless log or like a recent corpse. But if you were not lying protected, like a coward, unseen indoors, your own life would be at the disposal of any man. (*Latin Poems*, #114)

On Kings, Good and Bad

What is a good king? He is a watchdog, guardian of the flock, who by barking keeps the wolves from the sheep. What is the bad king? He is the wolf. (*Latin Poems*, #115)

---

3. The Latin term is "liberos," which can mean "children" or "free men."
4. The Latin sentence is "Totum est unus homo regnum, idque cohaeret amore."

A King Is Protected, Not by a Corps of Guards,
But by His Own Virtues

Not fear (accompanied by hatred), not towering palaces, not wealth wrung from a plundered people protects a king. The stern bodyguard, hired for a pittance, offers no protection, for the guard will serve a new master as he served the old. He will be safe who so rules his people that they judge none other would promote their interests better. (*Latin Poems,* #120)[5]

The Consent of the People Both Bestows and
Withdraws Sovereignty

Any one man who has command of many men owes his authority to those whom he commands; he ought to have command not one instant longer than his [people][6] wish. Why are impotent kings so proud? Because they rule merely on sufferance? (*Latin Poems,* #121)

What Is the Best Form of Government

You ask which governs better, a king or a senate. Neither, if (as is frequently the case) both are bad. But if both are good, then I think that the senate, because of its numbers, is the better and that the greater good lies in numerous good men. Perhaps it is difficult to find a group of good men; even more frequently it is easy for a monarch to be bad. A senate would occupy a position between good and bad; but hardly ever will you have a king who is not either good or bad. An evil senator is influenced by advice from better men than he; but a king is himself the ruler of his advisers. A senator is elected by the people to rule; a king attains this end by being born. In the one case blind chance is supreme; in the other, a reasonable agreement. The one feels that he was made senator by the people; the other feels that the people were created for him so that, of course, he may have subjects to rule.

5. The last sentence is: "Tutus erit, populum qui sic regit, utiliorem / Ut populus nullum censeat esse sibi." For a similar expression of this thought, see *The History of King Richard III, Complete Works,* vol. 2, p. 5, lines 23–27.

6. The translation gives "subjects" here, but this term goes against the "populus" of the title. As Damian Grace points out, "In a 1516 letter to Erasmus [More] quite emphatically rejects the title of subjects as an appropriate designation of the political community" (134). See *Selected Letters,* p. 80.

A king in his first year is always very mild indeed, and so every year the consul will be like a new king. Over a long time a greedy king will gnaw away at his people. If a consul is evil, there is hope of improvement. I am not swayed by the well-known fable which recommends that one endure the well-fed fly lest a hungry one take its place. It is a mistake to believe that a greedy king can be satisfied; such a leech never leaves flesh until it is drained.

But, you say, a serious disagreement impedes a senate's decisions, while no one disagrees with a king. But that is the worse evil of the two, for when there is a difference of opinion about important matters—but say, what started you on this inquiry anyway? Is there anywhere a people upon whom you yourself, by your own decision, can impose either a king or a senate? If this does lie within your power, you are king. Stop considering to whom you may give power. The prior question is whether it would do any good if you could. (*Latin Poems, #198*)

On the King and the Peasant

A forest-bred peasant, more naïve than Faunus or a satyr, came into town. See there! the inhabitants have taken places on either side to fill the avenue, and throughout the city all one could hear was the cry, "The king is coming." The peasant was roused by the strange news and longed to see what the crowd was watching for so eagerly. Suddenly the king rode by, in full view, resplendent with gold, escorted by a large company, and astride a tall horse. Then the crowd really did roar: "Long live the king"; and with rapt expressions they gazed up at the king. The peasant cried out, "Where is the king? Where is the king?" And one of the bystanders replied, "There he is, the one mounted high on that horse over there." The peasant said, "Is that the king? I think you are making fun of me. To me he looks like a man in fancy dress."[7] (*Latin Poems, #201*)

7. "Ille mihi picta veste videtur homo."

On Lust for Power[8]

Among many kings there will be scarcely one, if there is really one,
who is satisfied to have one kingdom. And yet among many kings there
will scarcely be one, if there is really one, who rules a single kingdom
5   well.[9] (*Latin Poems, #243*)

On the Surrender of Tournai to Henry VIII, King of England

Warlike Caesar vanquished you, Tournai,[10] till then unconquered, but
not without disaster to both sides. Henry, a king both mightier and better
than Caesar, has taken you without bloodshed. The king felt that he had
10   gained honor by taking you, and you yourself felt it no less advantageous
to be taken. (*Latin Poems, #244*)

8. "De Cupiditate Regnandi"

9. For similar expressions of this thought, see *Utopia, Complete Works*, vol. 4, p. 57, lines 25–30, p. 89, lines 27–31, and p. 91, lines 14–20; *Dialogue of Comfort, Complete Works*, vol. 12, p. 224, line 28.

10. In September 1513. For Erasmus's criticism of this war, see *CWE*, vol. 5, p. 318, line 1 and note 156.

Thomas More's "Petition for Freedom of Speech"

In 1523, Thomas More was chosen to be Speaker of the House of Commons of Parliament. Very hesitant to accept the post, he asked King Henry VIII to release him from the duty. The king refused his request and, accepting the position, More made a second request to the king: a request for free speech, the first such request ever made and recorded. This historic petition of April 18 follows.[1]

My other humble request, most excellent Prince, is this. Of your commoners here assembled by your high command for your Parliament, a great number have been, in accord with the customary procedure, appointed in the House of Commons to treat and advise on the common affairs among themselves, as a separate group. And, most dear liege Lord, in accord with your prudent advice communicated everywhere by your honorable commands, due diligence has been exercised in sending up to your Highness's court of Parliament the most discreet persons out of every area who were deemed worthy of this office; hence, there can be no doubt that the assembly is a very substantial one, of very wise and politic persons. And yet, most victorious Prince, among so many wise men, not all will be

Purpose of Parliament

Those in Parliament

5

10

---

1. Modernized by Mary Gottschalk. The non-modernized version can be found at *TMSB*, pp. 22–25.

equally wise, and of those who are equally wise, not all will be equally
well-spoken. And often it happens that just as a lot of foolishness is uttered
with ornate and polished speech, so, too, many coarse and rough-spoken
men see deep indeed and give very substantial counsel. Also, in matters of
5 great importance the mind is often so preoccupied with the subject matter
that one thinks more about what to say than about how to say it, for
which reason the wisest and best-spoken man in the country may now
and then, when his mind is engrossed in the subject matter, say something
in such a way that he will later wish he had said it differently, and yet he
10 had no less good will when he spoke it than he has when he would so
gladly change it. And therefore, most gracious Sovereign, considering that
in your high court of Parliament nothing is discussed but weighty and important matters concerning your realm and your own royal estate, many of
your discreet commoners will be hindered from giving their advice and
15 counsel, to the great hindrance of the common affairs, unless every one of
your commoners is utterly discharged of all doubt and fear as to how anything that he happens to say may happen to be taken by your Highness.
And although your well known and proven kindness gives every man
hope, yet such is the seriousness of the matter, such is the reverent dread
20 that the timorous hearts of your natural-born subjects conceive toward
your high Majesty, our most illustrious King and Sovereign, that they cannot be satisfied on this point unless you, in your gracious bounty, remove
the misgivings of their timorous minds and animate and encourage and
reassure them.
25   It may therefore please your most abundant Grace, our most benign
and godly King, to give to all your commoners here assembled your most
gracious permission and allowance for every man freely, without fear of
your dreaded displeasure, to speak his conscience and boldly declare his
advice concerning everything that comes up among us. Whatever any man
30 may happen to say, may it please your noble Majesty, in your inestimable
goodness, to take it all with no offense, interpreting every man's words,
however badly they may be phrased, to proceed nonetheless from a good
zeal toward the profit of your realm and honor of your royal person, the
prosperous condition and preservation of which, most excellent Sover-
35 eign, is the thing which we all, your most humble and loving subjects, according to that most binding duty of our heartfelt allegiance, most highly
desire and pray for.

Reasons freedom of speech is necessary

Reminder of Parliament's purpose and how free speech achieves it

Praises King

Recalls "dread" people have of king

Fear stressed

Conclusion: What is needed

Power of fear

Purpose

Praises King; problem restated

Purpose restated

This painting by Vivian Forbes (*c.* 1927) is outside England's House of Parliament in the "Building of Britain" series in St. Stephen's Hall. It depicts a famous incident that occurred in 1523 while Sir Thomas was Speaker of the House of Commons. The story as told by William Roper in his *Life of Sir Thomas More* (1556) follows. Ten years earlier, in his *History of King Richard III*, More depicted a similar use of silence as a surprising and effective strategy. Twelve years later, More would again use silence as a strategy, this time at the end of his own life.

More Defends the Liberty of the House
William Roper's Account

The following excerpt,[1] taken from William Roper's Life of Sir Thomas More *(1556), tells the story behind Forbes' painting, which captures the climactic moment of confrontation between More as Speaker of the House and Cardinal Wolsey, Chancellor of England. More's rhetorical strategy here—silence—antici-pates his later decision to remain silent on the matter of the King's marriage and the Act of Supremacy whereby Henry was declared head of the Church in England.*

At this Parliament Cardinal Wolsey found himself much grieved with the Burgesses thereof, for that nothing was so soon done or spoken therein but that it was immediately blown abroad in every alehouse. It fortuned at that Parliament a very great subsidy to be demanded, which the Cardi-
5 nal fearing would not pass the Common House, determined for the furtherance thereof to be there personally present himself. Before whose coming, after long debating there, whether it were better but with a few of his lords (as the most opinion of the House was) or with his whole train

The background situation

---

1. The non-modernized version of this text appears on pages 25–27.

More advises the
House
royally to receive him there amongst them. "Masters," quoth Sir Thomas More, "forasmuch as my Lord Cardinal lately, you know well, laid to our charge the lightness of our tongues for things uttered out of this House, it shall not in my mind be amiss with all his pomp to receive him, with his maces, his pillars, his pole-axes, his crosses, his hat, and Great Seal, too—to the intent, if he find the like fault with us hereafter, we may be the bolder from ourselves to lay the blame on those that his Grace bringeth hither with him." Whereunto the House wholly agreeing, he was received accordingly.

Wolsey addresses
the House
Where, after that he had in solemn oration by many reasons proved how necessary it was the demand there moved to be granted, and further showed that less would not serve to maintain the Prince's purpose, he, seeing the company sitting still silent, and thereunto nothing answering, and contrary to his expectation showing in themselves towards his request no towardness of inclination, said unto them: "Masters, you have many wise and learned men among you, and since I am from the King's own person sent hither unto you for the preservation of yourselves and the realm, I think it meet you give me some reasonable answer." Whereat, every man holding his peace, then began he to speak to one Master Marney (after Lord Marney): "How say you," quoth he, "Master Marney?" Who making
All are silent
no answer neither, he severally asked the same question of divers others accounted the wisest of the company.

To whom, when none of them all would give so much as one word, being before agreed, as the custom was, by their Speaker to make answer,
The tension
mounts
"Masters," quoth the Cardinal, "unless it be the manner of your House, as of likelihood it is, by the mouth of your Speaker, whom you have chosen for trusty and wise, as indeed he is, in such cases to utter your minds, here is without doubt a marvelous obstinate silence."

And thereupon he required an answer of Master Speaker, who first
More speaks for
the House
reverently upon his knees excusing the silence of the House, abashed at the presence of so noble a personage, able to amaze the wisest and best learned in a realm, and after by many probable arguments proving that for them to make answer was it neither expedient nor agreeable with the ancient liberty of the House, in conclusion for himself showed that though they had all with their voices trusted him, yet except every one of them could put into his one head all their several wits, he alone in so weighty a matter was unmeet to make his Grace answer.

Whereupon the Cardinal, displeased with Sir Thomas More, that had

not in this Parliament in all things satisfied his desire, suddenly arose and *Wolsey departs in*
departed. *vexation*

And after the Parliament ended, in his gallery at Whitehall in Westminster, uttered unto him his griefs, saying, "Would to God you had been at
5   Rome, Master More, when I made you Speaker." "your Grace not offended, so would I too, my lord," quoth he. And to wind such quarrels out of *More and Wolsey*
the Cardinal's head, he began to talk of that gallery, and said, "I like this *converse later*
gallery of yours, my Lord, much better than your gallery at Hampton
Court." Wherewith so wisely brake he off the Cardinal's displeasant talk
10 that the Cardinal at that present, as it seemed, knew not what more to say
to him. But for the revengement of his displeasure, counseled the King to *Wolsey strikes*
send him ambassador into Spain, commending to his Highness his wis- *back*
dom, learning, and meetness for that voyage; and the difficulty of the cause
considered, none was there, he said, so well able to serve his Grace therein.
15 Which, when the King had broken to Sir Thomas More, and that he had
declared unto his Grace how unfit a journey it was for him, the nature of
the country and disposition of his complexion so disagreeing together that
he should never be likely to do his Grace acceptable service there, knowing right well that if his Grace sent him thither, he should send him to his
20 grave, but showing himself nevertheless ready, according to his duty (all
were it with the loss of his life), to fulfill his Grace's pleasure in that behalf,
the King, allowing well his answer, said unto him, "It is not our meaning,
Master More, to do you hurt, but to do you good would we be glad; we
will this purpose devise upon some other, and employ your service other-
25 wise."

And such entire favor did the King bear him that he made him Chan- *Wolsey foiled*
cellor of the Duchy of Lancaster, upon the death of Sir Richard Wingfield, *again*
who had that office before.

On Private Property, Riches, and Poverty

The following selection[1] provides a striking contrast to the view of private property defended in Utopia *by Raphael Hythlodaeus. The account below is given by Anthony in* The Dialogue of Comfort Against Tribulation *(1534). In this dialogue, old and experienced Anthony is visited by his young and rich nephew Vincent, who urgently requests advice in dealing with immanent violence and persecution. Anthony is commonly thought to represent More since no divergence of opinion has been identified.*

Now, it is true, Nephew, that Christ invited people to follow him by embracing a life of voluntary poverty—by, that is, leaving everything, all at once, for his sake. He recommended this as something freeing a person from the worries of worldly affairs, and from the desire of earthly commodities, so that they might more speedily pursue and attain the state of 5 spiritual perfection with a hungry longing for celestial things. But he never commanded anyone to do this, and certainly not under pain of damnation. Yes, he did say that "whoever of you does not renounce all that he has cannot be my disciple" (Lk 14:33). But what he meant by that is made clear by something else he said just a few sentences before: "If anyone 10

Christ's position clarified

1. *Dialogue of Comfort,* modernized by Mary Gottschalk, pp. 173–76, 177–83. See *Complete Works,* vol. 12, pp. 174–84 for the non-modernized, critical edition of this text.

comes to me and does not hate his own father and mother and wife and children and brothers and sisters, yes, and even his own life, he cannot be my disciple" (Lk 14:26).

Here Christ our Savior clearly means that none can be his disciple unless they love him so far above all their own kinfolk, and even their own life, that for love of him they will, rather than forsake him, forsake all of the above. So by those other words he obviously means that whoever does not renounce and forsake in his own heart, in his own affections, everything he ever has, such that he would rather lose it all, every bit of it, than grievously displease God by holding on to any part of it—that person cannot be his disciple. And that is certainly easy to understand. Christ taught us, after all, to love God above all things, and we do not love God above all things if we keep, contrary to God's pleasure, anything that we have. For we show that we value a thing more than we value God when we are more content to lose God than it. But that everyone should give everything away, or that no one should be rich or even moderately affluent—I find, as I say, no such commandment. There are, as our Savior says, many mansions in the house of his Father (see Jn 14:2), and happy will be anyone who will have the grace to dwell in even the lowest.

Ordering one's various loves

What does one value most?

The Gospel does, indeed, seem to indicate that those who for God's sake patiently suffer penury will in heaven dwell above those who live here in plenty. And not only that, but also that heaven in some kind of way more properly belongs to them, and is more specially prepared for them than it is for the rich. In the Gospel we find Christ counseling rich folk to buy, in a sense, heaven from the poor. He says to the rich, "Make friends for yourselves by means of unrighteous mammon, so that when it fails they may receive you into the eternal habitations" (Lk 16:9).

Poverty and heaven

This superiority of the poor over the rich is, however, simply on the level of poverty versus wealthiness. Presuming that they are both good persons, a rich person may so excel a poor person in some other virtue, or virtues, that in heaven the rich one may be far above the poor one. Proof of this appears clearly in the story of Lazarus and Abraham (see Lk 16:19–31).

Poverty, riches, and virtue

Now, I do not say this with the intention of encouraging rich people to heap up more riches. For the least bit of encouragement is, I'm sure, all they would need—I'm sure very few of them are so proudhearted and obstinate that they wouldn't, with very little exhortation, be most conformable to that counsel! I say it, on the contrary, for those good people to whom God gives both wealth and the intention to use it well, but not the

Advice to the rich intention to give it all away at once. I say it for those who for good reasons wish to keep some of their wealth. I do not want such people to despair of God's favor on account of not doing something that God has neither commanded them nor drawn them by any special calling to do.

The example of Zacchaeus Look at Zacchaeus, who climbed up a tree in his desire to see our Savior. He was filled with gladness and deeply touched with a special grace, to the great profit of his soul, when Christ called out loud to him and said, "Zacchaeus, make haste and come down, for I must stay at your house today" (Lk 19:5). All the people were muttering complaints about this, that Christ would call him and be so familiar with him as to offer, on his own initiative, to come to his house. For they knew he was a senior publican, a chief among the emperor's tax collectors, all of whom were extremely notorious for fraud, extortion, and bribery. In that fellowship Zacchaeus not only had a high rank, but also had grown remarkably rich. And on that account he was judged, by all the people, to be a very sinful, wicked man.

But that was a rash, presumptuous, and blind judgment they made on him, for no one could see his inner disposition and the possibility of a sudden change in it. Zacchaeus, by a prompting from the Spirit of God, and in reproach of all such judgment, immediately proved them all wrong. He showed that with those few words spoken out loud to him, our Lord had so changed his heart that, whatever he had been before, he was then, unbeknownst to them all, suddenly turned good. For in a hurry he came down and gladly received Christ and said, "Behold, Lord, the half of my goods I give to the poor; and if I have defrauded anyone of anything, I restore it fourfold" (Lk 19:8). . . .

I wish to God, Nephew, that every rich Christian with a reputation for being very grand, and (more important, in my opinion) very honest, was *More advice for* both willing and able to do what that little Zacchaeus, that short but great *the rich* publican, said he would do: that is, with less than half his goods recompense everyone he has wronged by four times as much. Indeed, Nephew, I wish such a one would even just barely make the one-time recompense. If he will do that much, then the recipients will be content—I dare promise this on their behalf—to let go of and forget about that thrice-over part. For though this was a very strict point in the old law, Christians must be full of forgiveness and not be in the habit of demanding or even asking for the maximum amount of restitution. (See Ex 22:1, Dt 19:21, and Mt 5:38–41.)

Zacchaeus' promise examined But, now, this is the point I really want to make: Zacchaeus did not promise to give away everything and become a beggar, and neither did he promise to quit his job. Maybe in times past he had not always carried it out in strict compliance with the rule that Saint John the Baptist had given tax collectors: "Collect no more than is appointed you" (Lk 3:13). But just as he might now lawfully use the goods he intended to keep, he might also now lawfully practice his profession by collecting the emperor's taxes in simple compliance with Christ's express commandment, "Render to Caesar the things that are Caesar's" (Mk 12:17), eschewing all extortion and bribery. That our Lord fully approved of his intentions, and that he exacted nothing further from him with regard to his worldly affairs, is clearly indicated in his response: "Today salvation has come to this house, since he is also a son of Abraham" (Lk 19:9).

Zacchaeus keeps his job

Now I'm not forgetting, Nephew, that in effect you've agreed with me, thus far, on this much: that it is possible for a person to be rich without being out of the state of grace, or out of favor with God. You think, however, that though this may have been so in some times and places, it cannot be the case in any time or place like ours, in which there are so many poor people whom one is obliged to help. In such a situation, you think, a person cannot with a clear conscience keep any riches.

Wealth and conscience

Well, Nephew, if that reasoning holds true, then surely there has never been any time or place in this world in which anyone could have kept any wealth without danger of damnation. From, at least, the days of Christ on out to the end of the world, we have the witness of his own word that there never has been nor will be any lack of poor people. He himself said, "You always have the poor with you, and whenever you will, you can do good to them" (Mk 14:7). So, I say, if your reasoning holds true, then I cannot think of or imagine any place or time—from Christ's days till now, or in as long a time before his days, or ever to come after our days—in which anyone could remain rich without risking damnation simply on account of having those riches, regardless of how well they used them.

On the poor

But, Nephew, there have to be people with wealth, because otherwise you'll have, by God, more beggars than there already are, and no one left able to relieve anyone else. For in my mind I feel quite certain of this: that if tomorrow all the money in this country were brought together out of everyone's hands and laid all in one heap, and then divided out equally to everyone, things would be worse on the day after that than they were on the day before. For I suppose that when it was all equally divided among all, the one who had been doing the best would be left little better off than the average beggar is now. Whoever was a beggar before would be so

Reasons for wealth

little enriched by what he received that he would still not be much more than a beggar. Many a rich person, on the other hand, if his riches consisted only of movable assets, would be safe enough from riches for perhaps the rest of his life.

On making a living   People cannot, as you well know, live here in this world unless some individuals provide for many others a means of making a living. Not everyone can have a ship of his own; nor can everyone be a merchant without a stock. Not everyone can have his own plough. But such things, as you well know, must be had by somebody. And who could make a living as a tailor if no one could put in an order to have a garment made? Or as a construction worker, or a carpenter, if no one could finance the building of either a church or a house? Who would be the makers of any kind of cloth if there were no one with the capital needed to put different groups of people to work? A man with only two ducats to his name would most likely be better off if he gave them both away and left himself not a penny, if he lost absolutely everything he had, than if the rich man who puts him to work every week were to lose half of his money; for then the poor man would probably be out of work. The substance of the rich is, indeed, the wellspring of the livelihood of the poor. And so it would go with *The hen and the golden egg* this poor man as it did with the woman in one of Aesop's fables. She had a hen that laid her a golden egg every day. But one day she decided she'd rather have a great many eggs at once, so she killed her hen—and found only one or two eggs inside her. Thus for a few she lost many.

But now, Nephew, to answer your question as to how the rich can possibly with a clear conscience keep any wealth for themselves when they see so many poor people upon whom they could bestow it: They could *A clear conscience possible for the rich* not, indeed, do this with a clear conscience if they were obliged to bestow their wealth upon as many poor people as they possibly could. And we all would, in fact, be so obliged if we were expected to take at face value this command from our Savior: "Give to everyone who begs from you" (Lk 6:30). For you could take this as meaning that all the poor folk you see are so specially committed to your charge alone, by God himself, that you are obliged to keep handing out things, to every beggar who approaches you, as long as there is still a penny in your pocket.

On interpreting Scripture carefully   Actually, Nephew, that saying—like so many other sayings in Scripture, as Saint Augustine points out—needs interpretation. For as Saint Augustine notes, Christ said "Give to everyone who begs from you," but he did not say "Give them everything they beg you for." However, it all really

amounts to the same thing if Christ did mean to bind me by commandment to give something to every person, without exception, who asks me
for something. For by so doing, I would leave myself nothing.

In that same section of the sixth chapter of Saint Luke, our Savior
speaks both of the detachment that we should have from worldly things
and of how we should treat our enemies (see Lk 6:27–30). He tells us to
love our enemies, to give good words in return for evil ones, and not only
to suffer patiently any kind of injury, whether it's the taking away of our
goods or the inflicting on us of some bodily harm, but also to be ready to
suffer twice that amount of injury. And then, over and beyond all that, we
are to do good to those who have done us this harm (see Lk 6:35).

It is in this context that our Lord bids us to give to everyone who asks
of us. He means, therefore, that whatever good we can within reason do   *On doing good*
for a person, we should not refuse to do it, no matter what kind of person   *for others*
this is—even if he's our deadliest enemy. And we especially should do this
when we see that unless we ourselves help this person, there is a real danger that he will die. Thus Saint Paul says, "If your enemy is hungry, feed
him; if he is thirsty, give him drink" (Rom 12:20).

But, now, though I am obliged to meet in some way the needs of every
kind of person, whether friend or foe, Christian or heathen, my obligation
is not the same toward every person, nor toward any one person in every
situation. A difference in circumstances greatly affects the matter. Saint   *Varying*
Paul says, "If anyone does not provide for his relatives, and especially for   *obligations*
his own family, he has disowned the faith and is worse than an unbeliever"
(1 Tm 5:8). Those are ours who belong to our charge either by nature, by
law, or by some commandment of God. In that sense our children, for example, are ours by nature, while the servants in our household are ours by
law. Granted, our children and our servants are not ours to the same extent. However, I would think that if those who are the least ours (that is,
our servants) lack something that they need, we are bound to look after
them and provide what they need. We should see to it, as best we can, that
they do not lack the things that should be serving their needs while they
dwell in our service. It also seems to me that if they fall sick in our service,
and so cannot do the service that we retain them for, we may under no
circumstances then put them out and leave them without hope or consolation, when they are not able to work and to help themselves. For this
would be a most inhuman thing to do.   *Example of a*
Indeed, even if it's just a wayfaring man whom I have received into my   *wayfarer*

house as a guest—if he falls sick there and has no money, I consider myself bound to extend the welcome and rather to go begging about for his relief than to cast him out in that condition, in peril of his life. It makes no difference what it may cost me to keep him. Once God has by such a chance sent him to me, and has matched me with him, I consider myself definitely responsible for him until I can be rightly and decently, without any risk to his life, discharged of that responsibility.

By God's commandment our parents are in our charge, because by nature we are in theirs. As Saint Paul says, it is not the children's part to provide for the parents, but the parents' part to provide for the children (see 2 Cor 12:14). Parents should, that is, provide suitably good education or good occupations by which their children can earn a living with integrity and the favor of God. They should not, however, make provisions for any way of living that, in the eyes of God, their children would be the worse for. On the contrary, if they see by their children's behavior that giving them a lot would make them wicked, the father should then give them a great deal less. But in any case, although nature does not put the parents in the children's charge, it is not only commanded by God but also mandated by the order of nature that the children should both in reverent behavior honor their father and mother and also, when necessary, support them. And yet, as much as God and nature both bind me to the sustenance of my own father, his need may be so little (though it is something), and a stranger's need so great, their needs may be so unequal, that both nature and God would have me relieve that urgent necessity of a stranger—even if it's an enemy of mine and God's too, even if it's a Turk or a Saracen—before relieving a little need that is unlikely to do great harm to my father, and my mother too. And they themselves should be quite content for me to do this.

Example of parents and children

But now, Nephew, apart from cases of such extreme need, the reality of which I can clearly perceive or ascertain for myself, I am not obliged to give to every beggar who asks me for something. I am not obliged to believe every impostor I meet on the street who claims to be very sick. Nor am I obliged to consider all poor folk to be so uniquely committed by God to my charge alone that nobody else should give them anything of theirs until I have first given away everything of mine. I am not obliged to have such an evil opinion of everyone except myself as to think that unless I help, the poor folk will all die at once, since God doesn't now have left in this whole area any more good folk besides me! I may think better of my neighbors and worse of myself than that, and yet stand a good chance of getting to heaven by God's grace.

Closing arguments

On Law and Liberty

Human laws, which More considered to be "the traditions of men," arise as the work of prudent civic leaders concerned for the common good.[1] They provide a "sure and substantial shield" that is absolutely necessary for true freedom and a relatively just society.[2] More recognized an objective law of nature written in the human heart.[3] Even though this law can be known by reason, human beings have free will and, More knew well, all can ignore this law as known by conscience and can follow the "foolish fantasy" of their own imagination—but only for a limited time since conscience always makes itself known. Because of his deep understanding of human nature, More understood clearly that "unlimited power has a tendency to weaken good minds, and that even in the case of very gifted men."[4] For that reason, More recognized that the rule of law must be for everyone, even the king. More says explicitly that no law or set of laws can totally protect the innocent.[5] Therefore, those administering the laws must treat them with the greatest respect—but prudently, as a physician who uses all the means at his disposal to bring about a cure.[6] Laws, like

---

1. *Response to Luther, Complete Works,* vol. 5, p. 281. See Aquinas I–II.91.3 where law is defined as a "dictate of practical reason" and where Cicero is quoted: "Justice has its source in nature; thence certain things came into custom by reason of their utility; afterwards these things which emanated from nature and were approved by custom were sanctioned by fear and reverence for the law."

2. *Dialogue Concerning Heresies, Complete Works,* vol. 6, pp. 262; 368–72, 403–5.

3. Ibid., p. 141.

4. *Latin Poems, Complete Works,* vol. 3.2, p. 105. This statement expresses the same sentiment made popular by Lord Acton: "Power tends to corrupt and absolute power corrupts absolutely" (p. 364).

5. *Dialogue of Salem and Bizance, Complete Works,* vol. 10, pp. 163ff.

6. *Dialogue Concerning Heresies, Complete Works,* vol. 6, p. 261.

medicines, can be applied only by individuals; the justice that results will be propor-
tionate to the prudence, courage, and temperance of those who apply them.

Law alone, therefore, will never be enough to ensure justice. More was convinced
that statesmen will always be needed, good people whose words and good living per-
suasively teach the spirit of the laws.[7] Without diligent statesmen, the thickets of the   5
law could be easily torn down and, then, as Robert Bolt paraphrases More, who
"could stand upright in the winds that would blow?"

In his last work begun before he was imprisoned, More points out that liberty
has always required obedience to law; otherwise, we would forget our status as crea-
tures. While God created us to resemble the Trinity itself, God gave us "precepts and   10
commandments" as a safeguard against pride and as a help to "remember and con-
sider" that we are "but creatures."[8] He also notes that liberty requires diligence in
attending to good counsel—rather than "boldly fram[ing one]self a conscience with a
gloss of [one]'s own making after [one]'s own fantasy."[9] In his interpretation of
Genesis, More poses the provocative question: Why did God not restore Adam and   15
Eve "to the liberty and freedom of their former state . . . in Paradise"?[10] As part of
his response, he points out that in honor and prosperity we cannot know ourselves.[11]
He then goes on to say: "Therefore, to keep him from sin, and especially from pride
the root of all sin, a more base estate was better. And better was it also for him to
have two enemies, that is, the devil and his own sensuality. . . . For the having of   20
both is a cause of double fear, and therefore of double diligence, to set his reason to
keep sure watch to resist them, and for double help to call doubly much upon
almighty God for grace."

On the political level, More points out in his commentary on the Sanhedrin
that "every great council is not always a good council."[12] After elaborating upon   25
their "misused liberty," More offers this prayer: "Gracious God, give me Your grace
so to consider the punishment of that false great council that gathered together
against You, that I be never to Your displeasure partner, nor give my assent to follow
the sinful device of any wicked council."[13]

7. Ibid., p. 142.
8. *Treatise on the Passion, Complete Works*, vol. 13, pp. 12–13.
9. Ibid., p. 112.
10. Ibid., p. 45.
11. Ibid., p. 47, lines 5–7.
12. Ibid., p. 73.
13. Ibid., p. 75.

The Contemplation of Justice, sketch by Colleen Westman of
James E. Fraser's sculpture of 1935.

This sculpture at the entrance of the United States Supreme Court Building shows
Justice contemplating a figure of the human person, with her arm resting upon a
book of law.

1. More on justice for all:

Were it my father on the one side and the devil on the other, his cause being good, the devil should have his right.[14]

❧

2. From More's earliest known poem:

[T]he elusive goods of this perishable world   5
Do not come so readily as they pass away.
Pleasures, praise, homage, all things disappear—
except the love of God, which endures forever.
Therefore, mortals, put no confidence hereafter
in trivialities, no hope in transitory advantage;   10
offer your prayers to the everlasting God,
who will grant us the gift of eternal life.[15]

❧

3. In one of his earliest poems, after a witty debate between Lady Fortune and More, young Thomas puts the choice facing each of us in this challenging way:

Now have I shown you both: choose what you wish,   15
Stately Fortune, or humble Poverty:
That is to say, now lies it in your fist,
To take here bondage, or free liberty.
· · · · ·

Here is why Poverty leads to liberty:

Poverty will nothing take of [Fortune's] gifts, [and]   20
With merry cheer, looks upon the press,[16]
And sees how Fortune's household goes to wreck.
Fast by her stands the wise Socrates. . . .
"I bear," said [the wise one], "all mine with me about."
Wisdom he meant, not Fortune's fickle fees.   25
For nothing he counted his that he might lose.[17]

❧

14. Roper's *Life, TMSB*, p. 36.

15. From More's "Pageant of Life," *Latin Poems, Complete Works*, vol 3.2, #272. This stanza is a prose translation of the Latin.

16. *press*—crowd

17. From More's "Book of Fortune" (1504), *English Poems, Complete Works*, vol. 1, pp. 38–39.

4. *In the last weeks of his life, More wrote this poem after Cromwell visited his cell and promised to restore More's liberty along with his lands and position.*

Eye-flattering Fortune, look you never so fair,
Nor never so pleasantly begin to smile,
As though you would my ruin all repair,
During my life you shall me not beguile.
Trust shall I God, to enter in a while
His haven of heaven ever sure and uniform:
Ever after your calm, look I for a storm.[18]

5. *After he resigned as Lord Chancellor, More wrote the following statement in reply to the seventy-year-old legal scholar Christopher St. German, who had been accusing the Church of causing strife and division in England because of its laws.*

[A]ny laws or statutes already made, be they of the church or the realm, defend them I am content to do if I think them good. But on the other side, if I think them not, although in place and time convenient I would give my advice and counsel to the change, yet to put out books in writing abroad among the people against them—that would I neither do myself nor in so doing commend anyone that does. For if the law were such as were so far against the law of God that it were not possible to stand the man's salvation, then in that case the secret [i.e., private] advice and counsel may become everyone, but the open reproof and refutation thereof may not in my mind well become those that are no more spiritual than I. And surely if the laws may be kept and observed without peril of soul though the change might be to the better: yet out of time and place convenient to put the defects of the laws abroad among the people in writing, and without any surety of the change give people occasion to have the laws in derision, under which they live, namely since he that so shall use to do may sometime mistake the matter, and think the thing not good whereof the change would be worse: that way will I not as thus advised neither use myself nor advise any friend of mine to do.[19]

---

18. "Lewis the Lost Lover" (1535), *English Poems, Complete Works*, vol. 1, p. 45. See *TMSB*, p. 55.
19. *Apology, Complete Works,* vol. 9, pp. 96–97. Compare this view of law with the one expressed in Abraham Lincoln's "Lyceum Address," January 27, 1838.

6. *In book one of his* Utopia, *Thomas More responds to the objection that one ought not enter public service on the grounds that no real good will come of it because of the corruption of politics.*

You must not abandon the ship in a storm because you cannot control the winds. . . . What you cannot turn to good, you must at least make as little bad as you can.[20]

5

20. *Utopia, Complete Works*, vol. 4, pp. 99, 101.

5

Writings on Religion

More's Conception of God

Did More hold a consistent view of God throughout his life? Compare the view expressed in his first published book (pp. 164–70) with these selections written at the end of his life. The first selection is from the most famous of More's "Tower Works," written while a prisoner in the Tower of London, the year before his execution. The second selection consists of the twelve prayers that were interspersed in More's Treatise on the Passion. *The last selections are two psalms which formed part of More's habitual prayer while imprisoned; in brackets are the marginal notes which More wrote in his own hand.*

From *Dialogue of Comfort Against Tribulation* 3.27[1]

ANTHONY: Surely, Nephew, as I said before, when it comes to bearing a loss of worldly goods, and suffering captivity, enslavement, and imprisonment, and gladly sustaining worldly shame, if we would on all of those points deeply ponder the example of our Savior himself, this by itself would be enough to encourage every warm-blooded Christian, whether man or woman, never to refuse to suffer for his sake any or all of those calamities. And now I say the same for a painful death. If only we could and would with due compassion conceive in our minds a right imagination and remembrance of Christ's bitter, painful Passion! Of the many ter-

On bearing suffering

The example of Christ

---

1. Modernized by Mary Gottschalk, pp. 298–301. For the original, see *Complete Works*, vol. 12, pp. 312–15.

rible, bloody strokes that the cruel torturers gave him with rods and whips upon every part of his holy, tender body; of the insulting crown of sharp thorns beaten down upon his holy head, so straight and so deep that on every side his blessed blood issued out and streamed down; of his lovely limbs drawn and stretched out upon the cross, to the intolerable pain of ₅ his already sorely beaten veins and sinews; of him feeling anew, with the cruel stretching and straining, pain far surpassing any cramp, in every part of his blessed body at once. Then, of the big, long nails cruelly driven with hammers through his holy hands and feet; and of him being, in this horrible pain, lifted up and let hang with the weight of his whole body bearing ₁₀ down upon the painful, wounded places so grievously pierced with nails. Of him being put in such torment, with no pity but with many contemptuous insults, and suffered to be pinned and pained for the space of more than three long hours, till he himself willingly gave up to his Father his
Mighty malice holy soul. After which yet, to show the mightiness of their malice even af- ₁₅ ter his holy soul departed, they pierced his holy heart with a sharp spear, at which issued out the holy blood and water whereof his holy sacraments have inestimable secret strength. If we would, I say, remember these things in such a way as I wish to God we would, I really think the consideration of his incomparable kindness could not fail so to inflame our stone-cold ₂₀ hearts and set them on fire with his love that we would find ourselves not merely content but truly glad and desirous to suffer death for the sake of him who so marvelously lovingly did not hesitate to sustain such a far more painful death for our sakes.

I wish to God that we would here and now—if we want to see how ₂₅ shameful are the cold feelings that we return to God for the fervent love and inestimable kindness he has shown us—I wish to God that we would,
The example of I say, just consider what hot affection many of these fleshly lovers have
earthly lovers borne or do bear every day to those upon whom they dote. How many of them have without the least hesitation risked their lives, and how many ₃₀ have willingly lost their lives indeed, without any great kindness shown them before—and afterward, as you well know, there was nothing they could win! And yet in their minds they were contented and satisfied just to know that, by their death, their lover would clearly see how faithfully
On true they had loved. The delight of that idea imprinted in their imagination not ₃₅
remembrance only assuaged but actually outbalanced, to their way of thinking, all their pain. Of these affections, along with the terribly sorrowful effects following upon them, we find proof not only in old written stories, but beyond

that, I think, by everyday experience—in every country, whether Christian or heathen. Is it not, then, a stupendous shame for us to forsake our Savior out of a dread of temporal death, when he willingly suffered such a painful death rather than forsake us? And especially considering, besides all that, the fact that for our suffering he will so lavishly reward us with everlasting wealth?

Oh, if he who is content to die for his love, expecting from her no reward thereafter, but nevertheless going from her by his death—if he might by his death be sure to come to her and dwell with her in delight and pleasure forever after, such a lover would not hesitate to die here for her twice! What cold lovers we must, then, be to God if, rather than die for him once, we will refuse him and forsake him forever, when he not only has died for us but has also provided that if we die here for him, we shall everlastingly in heaven both live and also reign with him. For as Saint Paul says, "If we have died with him, we shall also live with him; if we endure, we shall also reign with him" (1 Tm 2:11–12). We are "heirs of God and fellow heirs with Christ, provided we suffer with him in order that we may also be glorified with him" (Rom 8:17). *Avoiding cold love*

How many Romans, how many noble spirits from many different countries, have willingly given their own lives—suffering great, deadly pains and then very painful deaths—for their countries, expecting to win by their deaths no reward other than worldly renown and fame? Should we, then, shrink from suffering as much for eternal honor and everlasting glory in heaven? The devil even has some heretics who are so obstinate that they will willingly endure a painful death for vainglory. Is it not, then, more than shameful that Christ should see his Catholics forsake his faith rather than suffer the same for heaven and true glory? *The spur of eternal glory*

I wish to God, as I have said many times, that the remembrance of Christ's kindness in suffering his Passion for us, a serious consideration of hell (into which we will fall if we forsake him), and joyful meditation on eternal life in heaven (which we will win if we patiently take this short, temporal death for him) had so deep a place in our hearts as reason dictates that they should, and as I really think they would if we would just make an effort and work for it and pray for it. For then they would take up our minds and carry them off in a whole other direction. You know how a man hurt in a fight will sometimes not feel his wound, or even become aware of it, till later on, when his mind is less preoccupied. He may even lose a hand and not realize it until someone else tells him. Well, so *Thinking on important things* also, to have our minds absorbed in thinking deeply about these other things—Christ's death, hell, and heaven—would very likely diminish or remove from our painful death a good fraction of the feeling of either the fear or the pain. At any rate, I am very sure of this: if we had for Christ just one-fifteenth of the love that he both had and has for us, all the pain of   5 this Turk's persecution could not keep us from him. There would at this day be as many martyrs here in Hungary as in times past there have been in other countries.

From *A Treatise on the Passion:*[2]

For Humble Obedience   10

O glorious blessed Trinity, whose justice has damned to perpetual pain many proud rebellious angels whom your goodness had created to be partners of your eternal glory, because of your tender mercy plant in my heart such meekness that I may by your grace so follow the motion of my good angel and so resist the proud suggestions of those spiteful spirits who   15 fell that I may, through the merits of your bitter passion, be partner of your bliss with those holy spirits who stood and who now, confirmed by your grace, shall stand in glory for ever.

For Resistance to Temptation

Almighty God, who of your infinite goodness did create our first par-   20 ents in the state of innocence, with present wealth and hope of heaven to come till through the devil's deceit their folly fell by sin to wretchedness, by your tender pity of that passion that was paid for their and our redemp- tion, assist me with your gracious help so that to the subtle suggestions of the serpent I never so incline the ears of my heart but that my reason may   25 resist them and master my sensuality and keep me from them.

---

2. No title was given in More's original text to any of the twelve prayers that follow. For the non-modernized form of these prayers, see *A Treatise on the Passion, Complete Works,* vol. 13, pp. 11, 24–25, 49, 52, 65–66, 68, 75, 82, 85, 100, 117, 136.

For Devotion to the Passion

O holy blessed savior Jesus Christ, who willingly did determine to die for man's sake, mollify my hard heart and supple it so by grace that, through tender compassion of thy bitter passion, I may be partner of your
5   holy redemption.

For Ready Response to the Gospel

Good Lord, give us your grace not to read or hear this gospel of your bitter passion with our eyes and our ears in manner of a pastime, but that it may with compassion so sink into our hearts that it may stretch to the
10   everlasting profit of our souls.

For Devotion to the Eucharist

Good Lord, who upon the sacrifice of the paschal lamb did so clearly destroy the first-begotten children of the Egyptians that Pharaoh was thereby forced to let the children of Israel depart out of his bondage, I be-
15   seech you, give me the grace in such faithful wise to receive the very sweet paschal lamb, the very blessed body of our sweet Savior, your son, that [with] the first suggestions of sin killed in my heart by your power, I may safe depart out of the danger of the most cruel Pharaoh, the devil.

For a Happy Death

20   Good Lord, give me the grace so to spend my life that when the day of my death shall come, though I feel pain in my body, I may feel comfort in soul and—with faithful hope of your mercy, in due love towards you and charity towards the world—I may, through your grace, part hence into your glory.

25   ## To Resist Any Wicked Council

Gracious God, give me your grace so to consider the punishment of that false great council that gathered together against you that I never to your displeasure be partner, nor give my assent to follow the sinful device of any wicked council.

To Resist Greed

O my sweet savior Christ—whom your own wicked disciple, entangled with the devil through vile wretched greed, betrayed—inspire, I beseech you, the marvel of your majesty with the love of your goodness, so deep into my heart that, in respect to the least point of your pleasure, my 5 mind may set always this whole wretched world at nought.

For Fervent Love of Christ

O my sweet savior Christ, who in your undeserved love towards mankind so kindly would suffer the painful death of the cross, suffer not me to be cold or lukewarm in love again towards you. 10

For Heaven

Almighty Jesus Christ, who would for our example observe the law that you came to change, and being maker of the whole earth, would have yet no dwelling-house therein, give us your grace so to keep your holy law and so to reckon ourselves for no dwellers but for pilgrims upon earth 15 that we may long and make haste, walking with faith in the way of virtuous works, to come to the glorious country wherein you have bought us inheritance forever with your own precious blood.

For the Humility to Serve

Almighty Jesus, my sweet Savior Christ, who would graciously agree 20 with your own almighty hands to wash the feet of your twelve apostles, not only of the good but of the very traitor too, graciously agree, good Lord, of your excellent goodness, in such wise to wash the foul feet of my affections that I, with meekness and charity for the love of you, never have such pride enter into my heart as to disdain either in friend or foe to de- 25 file my hands with washing of their feet.

For Devotion to the Eucharist

Our most dear savior Christ, who after finishing the old paschal sacrifice instituted the new sacrament of your own blessed body and blood for a memorial of your bitter passion, give us such true faith therein and such fervent devotion thereto that our souls may take fruitful spiritual food thereby.

From Thomas More's *Prayer Book*[3]

Psalm 42

Like the deer that yearns
For running streams,
So my soul is yearning
For you, my God. [Happy is he who can say this from his soul.][4]

5
My soul is thirsting for God,
The God of my life;
When can I enter and see
The face of God?

. . . .

10
These things will I remember
As I pour out my soul:
How I would lead the rejoicing crowd
Into the house of God,
Amid cries of gladness and thanksgiving,

15
The throng wild with joy.

Why are you cast down, my soul,
Why groan within me? [in tribulation]
Hope in God; I will praise him still,

20
My savior and my God.

. . . .

3. See *Thomas More's Prayer Book*, ed. Louis L. Martz and Richard S. Sylvester (Yale UP, 1969), pp. 80, 105.
4. In square brackets are More's marginal annotations.

Psalm 63

O God, you are my God, for you I long;
For you my soul is thirsting.
My body pines for you
Like a dry, weary land without water. [longing for God][5]
So I gaze on you in the sanctuary   5
To see your strength and your glory. [in tribulation
        and fear of death]

For your love is better than life,
My lips will speak your praise.
. . . .
On my bed I remember you.   10
On you I muse through the night
For you have been my help;
In the shadow of your wings I rejoice.
My soul clings to you;
Your right hand holds me fast.[6]   15

5. These marginal notes written by More can be seen in the first illustration on the facing page.

6. More draws a flagged line next to these last two sentences. See the second illustration on the facing page.

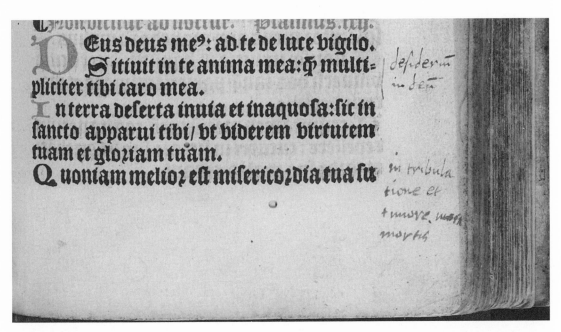

Eus deus me⁹: ad te de luce vigilo.

Sitiuit in te anima mea: ꝓ multi-
pliciter tibi caro mea.

In terra deserta inuia et inaquosa: sic in
sancto apparui tibi/ vt viderem virtutem
tuam et gloriam tuam.

Quoniam melior est misericordia tua sū

desideriū in deū

*in tribula-
tione et
timore mortis
mortis*

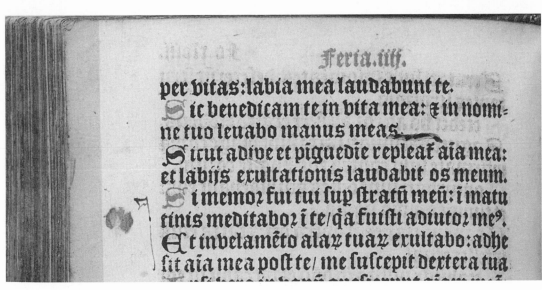

per vitas: labia mea laudabunt te.

Sic benedicam te in vita mea: ꝫ in nomi-
ne tuo leuabo manus meas.

Sicut adipe et pinguedine repleaꝼ aīa mea:
et labijs exultationis laudabit os meum.

Si memor fui tui suꝑ stratū meū: ī matu-
tinis meditabor ī te/ q̄a fuisti adiutor me⁹.

Et inuelamēto alaꝝ tuaꝝ exultabo: adhe-
sit aīa mea post te/ me suscepit dextera tua

Annotations in More's own hand in the margins of Psalm 63, in his *Prayer Book*, pp. 105–106.

Private Judgment and God's Word

In this passage, More discusses the position of "the Messenger," who believes that personal study of Scripture is sufficient and that there is no need for the study of philosophy, commentaries, or the liberal arts except grammar. The Messenger is a college student who is confused by the controversies having to do with Martin Luther and William Tyndale.[1]

From *A Dialogue Concerning Heresies*, 1.22–23, 25:

SIR THOMAS MORE: "And speaking of Scripture, and of the fact that the Church in things necessarily requisite to salvation has the right understanding of holy Scripture, for which I perceive you to be studying the text alone, without attaching much importance to the early fathers' interpretations or to any of the liberal arts (you considering, in fact, all seven, except grammar, to be good for almost nothing), I have such a good opinion of you that I trust that all your study will turn you to good; but to some folk I certainly have seen so much harm come of it that I would never advise anyone else to take that approach to the study of Scripture."

"Why not?" asked he.

The Messenger's manner of reading

5

10

---

1. Modernized by Mary Gottschalk. For the critical edition of this text, see *Complete Works*, vol. 6, pp. 122–32, 152–53.

"Because," I said, "I have known people with right good minds who have set all other learning aside, partly out of laziness, shunning the effort and pain to be sustained in that learning, and partly out of pride, by reason of which they could not endure the refutation that would sometimes *Pride and reading* come to their side in debates. Which dispositions their inward, hidden partiality toward themselves covered and cloaked under the pretexts of simplicity and of good Christian devotion borne to the love of holy Scripture alone. But within a little while after, the damnable spirit of pride that unbeknownst to themselves lurked in their hearts has begun to put out its horns and show itself. For then have they longed under the praise of holy Scripture to show off their own study. Which, to have it seem the more to be esteemed, they have started off with the disparagement and derision of all other disciplines. And because in speaking of such elementary things as all Christians know, they could not seem superior, nor make it appear and be seen that in their study they had accomplished any great mastery, to show themselves therefore extraordinary they set out paradoxes and unfamiliar opinions against the common faith of Christ's entire church. And *Unfamiliar* because they have there the early doctors of the Church against them, they *opinions versus* resort to contempt and disparagement of them, either preferring their *common faith* own foolish glosses to the interpretations of the wise and blessed early fathers or else basing themselves on some words of holy Scripture that seem to speak on their behalf against many more texts that plainly speak against them, without accepting, or even giving ear to, any reasoning or authority of anyone alive or dead, or of the entire church of Christ, that speaks to the contrary. And thus, once by pride persuaded a wrong way, they take *The progress of the* the bridle in their teeth and run forth like a headstrong horse, so that all *proud reader* the world cannot pull them back. And with their sowing of sedition, their *The fruit of* setting forth of errors and heresies, and their spicing of their preaching *sowing sedition* with denunciations of the priesthood and the prelacy for the people's pleasure, they turn many to ruin, including themselves. And then the devil deceives them in their blind inclinations.

"They take for a good zeal for the people, their malicious envy. And for a great virtue their ardent love of preaching, in which they take such great pride because of the people's praise that I think they would preach even if God by his own mouth were to command them the contrary."

"Why should you think so?" he said. "And how can you be sure that you are not misinterpreting their good intentions? Oftentimes it is hard to judge another person's deed that has some appearance of evil, because the

purpose and intent may make it good. So how dangerous is it, then, where
the deed appears good, to judge as bad the thought and intent, which who
can see but God? As Scripture says, 'Only God sees the heart' [1 Samuel
16:7]. And therefore says our Savior, 'Do not judge before the time' [see
Matthew 7:1 and 1 Corinthians 4:5]."   5

"I do not judge," I said, "except upon quite clear and obvious things.
For I am speaking only of those whose erroneous opinions in their
preaching, and whose obstinate pride in the defense of their worldly repu-
tations, well show their attitudes. And some I have seen who, when they

*Perilous preaching
and disobedience* have for their perilous preaching been prohibited by their prelates from   10
preaching, have, that notwithstanding, proceeded on still. And some for the
defense of their disobedience have amended the matter with a heresy,
boldly and stubbornly maintaining that since they had the talent to
preach, therefore they were obliged by God to preach, and no mere human being, nor any law that was made or could be made, had any author-   15
ity to forbid them. And this they thought sufficiently proved by the words
of the Apostle, "We must obey God rather than men" [Acts 5:29]. As
though these men were apostles now specially sent by God to preach
heresies and sow sedition among Christians, just as the true apostles were
indeed sent and commanded by God to preach his true faith to the Jews.   20

New preachers One of this class of this new kind of preacher, when asked why he was going around saying in his sermons that nowadays men did not preach the
Gospel well, answered that he thought this because he did not see the
preachers being persecuted, nor any conflict or commotion arising from
their preaching. Such things, he said and wrote, were the fruits of the   25
Gospel, because Christ said, 'I have not come to bring peace into the
world, but a sword' [Matthew 10:34]. Was this not a pious interpretation,
that because Christ would make a division among infidels, from the remnant of them to win some, therefore these apostles should sow some cockle of dissension among the Christian people whereby Christ might lose   30

*How strife and
persecution grow
among Christians* some of them? For the fruits of conflict among the hearers and of persecution of the preacher cannot easily grow among Christian people except
by the preaching of some unorthodox novelties and the bringing in of
some newfangled heresies for the infection of our old faith.

"One I knew who for all his pertinacity in that opinion (that he could   35
and would and was obliged to preach, any prohibition notwithstanding),
when he was, after all manner of bold and open defense of it, at last reasoned with by a few honorable folk and not only shown the law that runs

contrary to his opinion, which law was made at an ecumenical council, but also convinced by plain authority of holy Scripture that his opinion was erroneous, he so perceived himself satisfied that he meekly acknowledged his error and offered to abjure it and submit himself to penance. But

5   on the next day, when he came out in the public presence of people and saw there many who had often heard him preach, out of his covert pride *An example of* he fell into such an undisguised shame, at the thought of those who had *secret pride* previously held his sermons in high esteem now hearing him go back on his word, that at the first sight of the people he revoked his revocation and

10   said loudly, so that he could well be heard, that his opinion was correct and that he had on the day before been mistaken in that he had confessed it to be wrong. And thus, stubbornly and irrationally, he held his own till the books were shown him again and he himself read them before all the people, and perceived the audience that stood about him to feel and un-

15   derstand the proud foolishness of his defense of his indefensible error. And then, at last, he gave himself up again. Such a secret pride had our spiritual enemy conveyed into the heart of this man, who, I assure you, seemed in all the rest of his outward manner to be as meek and simple a soul as one could have seen in a summer's day.

20   "And some of them do not hesitate to defend themselves with lies and even perjury, and some to stand firm in defense of their errors, or in false denying of their own deeds, to their great danger of being burned, should their judges not show them more mercy than by their malice they deserve. And all this they do because, as they themselves at last confess, they

25   think that if they disavow the holding of heretical beliefs, they will afterward be allowed to preach again. Such a scabby itch of vainglory do they *The itch of* get in their preaching that even should all the world be the worse for it *vainglory* and their own life lie on it, they would still long to be pulpited. And this, I say, is what has become of some who have with contempt of all other

30   learning given themselves to Scripture alone—some who have not in the beginning perceived as such their proclivities toward pride and laziness, but have viewed their vices as devoutness."

     "Would you, then," he said, "condemn that approach to study by which a person has such a great attachment to Scripture alone that, for the

35   delight thereof, he feels little inspiration in anything else, and say that we should lose time in philosophy, the mother of heresies, and leave Scripture alone?"

     "No," I said, "I am not of that mind. There was never anything written

*Scripture
incomparable,
but liberal arts
a gift too*
in this world that is in any way comparable to any part of holy Scripture. And yet I think the liberal arts also to be gifts from God, and not to be thrown away, but worthy to wait and as handmaids to give attendance upon theology. And on this point I am not alone in my thinking. For you will find Saint Jerome, Saint Augustine, Saint Basil, and many of the early 5 doctors of the Church clearly and obviously of the same opinion. And of theology I consider the best part to be contained in holy Scripture. And I say this for him who has the time for it, and who from youth is heading for the priesthood, and who intends to make himself, with God's help, fit for the office of a preacher. However, if any man happens to be starting so 10 late that he will perhaps not have the time for it, or if any young man has that intense an appetite for Scripture that he cannot find it in his heart to read anything else (which propensity one is very fortunate to be given, if

with grace and meekness one guides it well), then I would counsel him to study mainly for the virtuous ordering of his own inclinations, and to use 15 great moderation and temperance in his preaching to others. And in all things to flee the desire of being praised and of showing off knowledge, ever mistrusting his own inclinations, and to live in fear and dread of the devil's subtle deceits and strategies. For though the devil continually lies in wait upon every preacher to reel him into pride if he can, yet his ultimate 20 scheme and proudest triumph consist in the bringing of a person to the worst misuse of that thing that is of its own nature the best. And therefore he makes a great effort, and a great boast if he brings it about, to have a good mind misuse its efforts spent on the study of holy Scripture.

"For the sure avoiding of which, my poor advice would be that in the 25 study of holy Scripture one pay a special attention to the commentaries and other writings of early fathers of the Church. And also that before agreeing with one or another of them, one before all else needs, along with grace and help from God (to be gotten with abstinence and prayer and clean living), to come good and solidly instructed in all the articles 30 and points that the Church believes. These things once being firmly grasped and steadfastly, as undoubtable truths, presupposed, they and reason will then be two good guidelines by which to examine and expound all doubtful texts, since the reader can be sure that no text is to be understood in a way that goes against them both, or against any of the points of 35 the Catholic faith of Christ's church. And therefore if it seems to go against any of them, either the light of natural reason, together with a collating of scriptural texts, will help one find out the truth, or else (which is the safest way) one will perceive the truth in the commentaries of the good early doctors of the Church, to whom God gave the grace of understanding.

"Or, finally, if all that we can either find in others' works or come up with by God's aid from our own reflection cannot suffice to convince us, and some text still seems to us contrary to some point of the Church's faith and belief, then let us, as Saint Augustine says, rest assured that some mistake has been made either by the translator or by the copyist, or, nowadays, by the printer; or, finally, that because of some hindrance or another we are not understanding it aright. And so let us reverently acknowledge our ignorance and side with the faith of the Church and hold fast to it, as to an undoubtable truth, leaving that text to be better perceived when it shall please our Lord with his light to reveal and disclose it. And in this manner shall we take a sure way, one by which we can be sure of one of two things: either to perceive and understand Scripture right, or else, at the very least, never to take it wrong in such a way as might endanger our soul."

Hold fast to the faith of the Church

. . .

"Sir," he said, "I will not deny that this way will do some good. However, I fear that we would probably build up many errors if we were to square our timber and stones by these three measures—others' interpretations, reason, and faith, not that we find in Scripture, but that we bring with us to Scripture.

The Messenger objects: Bringing external measures to Scripture will cause error

"For first, as for the commentators that you speak of, their commentaries tell us either the same tale that the text does, or else another. If they tell me the same one, I believe them only because the text says the same. And if they tell me another, then I believe them not at all, nor at all should I, unless I should believe human beings more than I believe God.

"And as for reason, what greater enemy can you find to faith than is reason, which contradicts faith on every point? And would you then send off to school together those two that can never agree with each other but are ever ready to fight each other and scratch each other's eyes out along the way? It also seems somewhat strange that, when God has quite sufficiently left us in his holy Scripture his doctrine whereby he would have us informed of all such things as he would have us believe and do or leave undone, and has left us Scripture for no other reason than that it should remain to us as the witness of his will, declared to us in writing so that we could not deny that we were informed of it, and there is no other reason

Is not reason an enemy of faith?

why Scripture should be given us but to tell us his pleasure and stir us to fulfill it, we shall now not shape our faith according to Scripture, but first fashion us a faith ourselves and then shape God's Scripture according to that, and make it agree with that. This would indeed be a good, easy way *The example of the slothful mason* for a lazy mason, who is a negligent worker, to make him a carpenter's 5 square and a ruler adaptable to uneven surfaces: that when he does not want to go to the trouble of hewing the stone to the square, he can bend the square to the stone, and so in any event still bring them together."

More defends commentators and reason "As for the early commentators," I said, "they tell you the same tale that the text does, but they tell it to you more plainly, as we will more talk 10 about later. But surely you tricked me just now in selling reason so short, for truly I never would have thought that you would for Scripture like less a wise person than an unreasoning reader. Nor can I see why you should reckon reason for an enemy to faith, unless you reckon everyone for your enemy that is your better and does not hurt you. And in that case, one of 15 your five senses would be an enemy to another—our sense of touch would abhor our sense of sight, because we can see further by four miles than we can feel. How can reason—unless reason is unreasonable—more disdain to hear the truth of any point of faith than to see the fact of many natural phenomena of which reason can no more arrive at the cause than 20 it can in the articles of the faith? But always, for any power that reason has to perceive the cause, she will judge the phenomenon impossible after she proves it true unless she believes her eye to be better than her understanding.

A lodestone "When you see the lodestone draw iron to it, it does not grieve reason 25 to look at this; no, reason takes pleasure in beholding something that surpasses her power to understand. For it is as plainly against the rule of reason that a heavy object should move alone in any direction other than downward, or that any material thing should draw another, as is any article of the faith. Nor ever yet was there a cause assigned by reason that people 30 can perceive as probative except only that it is a hidden property of the stone, which is as much as to say, 'I have no idea what.' And yet, as I say, reason can believe that thing well enough, and not be angry about it or fight against it. And yet all the rules that ever she learned tell her continually that it cannot be." 35

"Yes," he said, "but our own eyes tell us that it can be. And that must *To trust the eyes or the mind?* needs convince us."

"Can we, then, better trust our eyes," I said, "than our mind?"

"Yes, of course," he said. "What can we better trust than our eyes?"

"Our eyes can," I said, "be deceived and think they see what they do not see, if reason gives over its hold. Unless you think the juggler blows those little balls through the goblet's bottom, or in front of your face cuts your belt in twenty pieces and makes it whole again, or puts a knife into his eye and sees never the worse. And turns a plum into a dog's turd in a boy's mouth."

Now it humorously happened that at just that moment one of my servants came to ask whether they should get dinner ready.

"Wait a minute," I said, "let's get some better food first." And at that your friend and I began to laugh.

Laughter before dinner

"Well," I said, "don't make anyone be in any hurry yet for a little while." And so he went on his way half flustered, thinking he had acted or spoken somewhat like a fool, since he was indeed not very sensible, and was prone to do so.

And then I said to your friend, "Now you see that reason is not so proud a dame as you take her for. She sees done in fact by nature what she cannot perceive how, and is quite content with that. She sees a funny fellow deceive her sight and her intellect as well, and she takes it well and in good fun, and is not angry that the juggler will not teach everyone his craft. So do you think, then, that she will take such high offense at God himself, her master and maker, doing what he pleases, and then telling her what, and not telling her how?"

Reason not so proud a dame

"I ask you," I said, "how do you know that our Lord was born of a virgin?"

"Indeed," he said, "by Scripture."

Scripture and faith

"How do you know," I said, "that you should believe Scripture?"

"Indeed," he said, "by faith."

"Why?" I said. "What does faith tell you on this?"

"Faith," he said, "tells me that holy Scripture is true things written by the secret teaching of God."

"And by what means do you know," I said, "that you should believe God?"

"By what means?" he said. "What an absurd question. Every man can well know that."

"That is true," I said, "but is there any horse or any ass that knows that?"

"None," he said, "that I know of, unless Balaam's ass understood any-

Balaam's ass

thing of that. For he spoke like a good rational ass." [See Numbers 22:28–30.]

"If no brute animal can know that," I said, "and every man can, what is the reason why man can and other animals cannot?"

"Indeed," he said, "it is because man has reason and they have none."   5

"Ah, well, then," I said, "one must necessarily, then, have reason in order to be able to tell what one should believe. And so much so must reason *Faith never goes* not resist faith but walk with her, and as her handmaid wait upon her, that *without reason* as much in opposition as you take them to be, faith actually never goes without her. But just as if a maid is allowed to run without restraint, or get   10 besotted, or grow too proud, she will then grow profuse in speech and bandy logic with her masters and behave sometimes as if she were insane, so if reason is allowed to run wild and grow overly arrogant and proud, she will not fail to fall into rebellion against her master's faith. But on the other hand, if she is well brought up and well guided and kept in good tem-   15 per, she will never disobey faith, being in her right mind. And therefore let reason be well guided, for certainly faith never goes without her.

"Now, in the studying of Scripture—in determining the meaning, in considering what you read, in pondering the theses of various commentaries, in putting together and comparing different texts that seem contra-   20 *Reason and* dictory but are not—although I do not deny that grace and God's special *the reading of* help are the great thing here, still he uses as an instrument for that purpose *Scripture* our reason. God helps us to eat also, but yet not without our mouth. And just as the hand becomes the more nimble by the performing of some feats, and the legs and feet the more swift and sure by the habit of going   25 running, and the whole body the more wieldy and healthy by some kind of exercise, so too there is no doubt that by study, effort, and exercise in *Reason quickened* logic, philosophy, and the other liberal arts, reason is strengthened and *by liberal arts* quickened, and judgment, both in those arts and also in orators, laws, and the writings of historians, is much ripened. And although poetry is by   30 many people taken for nothing but painted words, it yet much helps the judgment and, among other things, makes one well equipped with one thing in particular without which all learning is half lame."

"What is that?" he said.

The necessity of a "Indeed," I said, "a good mother wit. And therefore in my opinion   35 *good mother wit* these Lutherans are in a mad frame of mind that would now have all branches of learning save only Scripture clean cast out—things which, if one has the time for them, are to my way of thinking to be taken and had, and with reason brought, as I said before, into the service of theology. And as holy Saint Jerome says [in Epistle 70], 'The Hebrews well despoil the Egyptians when Christ's learned men take out of the pagan writers the riches and learning and wisdom that God gave to them and employ the same in the service of theology about the profit of God's chosen children of Israel, the church of Christ, which he has out of the hard, stony pagans made into children of Abraham.' "

. . .

"And therefore holy Scripture is, as I said, the highest and best learning that anyone can have, if one takes the right way in the learning.

"It is—as a good, holy saint says—so marvelously devised that a mouse could wade in it and an elephant be drowned in it. For there is no man so lowly but that if he will seek his way with the staff of his faith in his hand, and hold that fast and search the way with that, and have the early fathers of the Church also for his guides, going on with a good determination and a humble heart, using reason and refusing no good learning, while calling upon God for wisdom, grace, and help that he may well keep his way and follow his good guides, then he will never fall into danger, but will quite safely wade through and come to such an end of his journey as he would well wish. But assuredly, be he as long as Longinus, if he has a proud heart and puts his trust in his own intelligence (as does anyone, humble as he may appear, who disregards all the early fathers of the Church), that fellow will not fail to sink over the ears and drown. And of all wretches the farthest off-course will he stray who, attaching little importance to the faith of Christ's church, comes to the Scripture of God to investigate and test therein whether the Church believes rightly or not. For he doubts either whether Christ teaches his church truthfully or else whether Christ teaches it at all. And then he doubts whether Christ in his words did tell the truth when he said he would be with his church till the end of the world. And surely the thing that made Arius, Pelagius, Faustus, Manichaeus, Donatus, Helvidius, and the whole pack of the early heretics drown themselves in those damnable heresies was nothing but extreme pride in their learning in Scripture, wherein they followed their own wits and left the common faith of the Catholic Church, preferring their own specious interpretations to the correct, Catholic faith of all of Christ's church, which can never err in any substantial point, any point that God would have us bound to believe. And therefore, to end where we began,

How one may wade through Scripture

How one might drown in Scripture

Heresy and error

Closing summary

whoever will not in the study of Scripture take the points of the Catholic
faith as a standard for interpretation, but, out of misgiving and distrust, will
study Scripture to find out from it whether the faith of the Church is true
or not, such a one cannot fail to fall into worse and far more hazardous errors than anyone can fall into by philosophy, whose reasonings and argu-   5
ments in matters of our faith have nothing like the same authority."

The Two Swords; Heresy and Just War

In this passage[1], More distinguishes the traditional roles of church and state in dealing with "seditious" heresy and with those who use physical violence to disturb a country's peace. When More defended as legitimate the use of force against heretics, he pointed out that his oath of office and the laws of the time required him to do so. Heresy in More's day was not simply what we understand by "heresy" today. Heresy at that time was often accompanied by violence that sought to overthrow flawed but legitimate institutions, as seen in the violence that was occurring throughout Germany. More reported, for example, the slaying of sixty thousand German peasants in the summer of 1525,[2] and he and all the rulers of Europe were concerned that such violence would spread. Given these circumstances, More regularly characterized Luther's and Tyndale's heresies as "seditious."

From *A Dialogue Concerning Heresies*, 4.13–14:

"The fear that these insults and injuries will follow upon such sects and heresies," I said to your friend, "together with the proof that folk have had

---

1. Modernized by Mary Gottschalk. See *Complete Works*, vol. 6, pp. 406–415.

2. See p. 298, *TMSB* and *Complete Works*, vol. 6, p. 369, vol. 8, pp. 126–27. Eventually even Erasmus came to agree (Letter 1670).

of this in some countries, has been the reason that princes and people have
been constrained to punish heresies by terrible death, whereas otherwise
more moderate ways would have been taken to deal with them. And

Why punish therefore I will here to some extent answer the points which you brought
heresy? up at our first meeting, when you said that many people thought it a   5
heartless, uncharitable way taken by the clergy to put those convicted of
heresy sometimes to shame, sometimes to death, and that Christ so much
abhorred all such violence that he did not wish any of his flock to fight in
any way, neither in the defense of themselves nor in that of anyone else,
not so much as in the defense of Christ himself, for which he reproved   10
Saint Peter [see Matthew 26:52], but that we should all live like him in endurance and forbearance, this being so much the case that, as you said, folk
thought that we should not fight in defense of ourselves against the Turks
and infidels. These objections are soon answered.

"For neither do the clergymen do therein any such thing as they are   15
accused of and charged with, nor do the secular authorities either. For al-
The heretics though with good reason they could have, they yet never in fact would
themselves first have resorted so heavily to force and violence against heretics if the vio-
used violence lent cruelty first used by the heretics themselves against good Catholic
folk had not driven good princes to it, for preservation not only of the   20
faith, but also of the peace among their people. For although right after
the death of Christ, at the beginning of the Church, many sects and heresies began (as is well evidenced by the Book of Revelation, written by
Saint John the Evangelist, and by the epistles of the apostle Paul), and after
that, almost continually, various heresies sprang up in various places (as we   25
Earlier approaches plainly see in the history of the Church, by the books of Saint Jerome,
to heresy Saint Augustine, Saint Eusebius, Saint Basil, Saint Ambrose, Saint Gregory
Nazianzen, Saint John Chrysostom, and many other doctors of the
Church), yet in all that time, a long space of many years, there was virtually never any punishment inflicted on those heretics other than refutings   30
and disprovings done in disputations, either oral or written, or condemna-
tions of their opinions by synods and councils, or, finally, excommunication and putting out of Christ's flock; except that sometimes they were
put to silence on pain of forfeiture of a certain amount of money.

"But as I said before, if the heretics had never started with the violence,   35
then even if they had made use of all the ways they could to lure the people by preaching, even if they had thereby done as Luther does now, and as
Mohammed did before—bring into vogue opinions pleasing to the peo-

ple, giving them license for licentiousness—yet if they had left violence alone, good Christian people would perhaps still to this day have used less violence toward them than they do now. And yet heresy well deserves to be punished as severely as any other sin, since there is no sin that more offends God. However, as long as they refrained from violence, there was little violence done to them. And surely although God is able against all persecution to preserve and increase his faith among the people, as he did in the beginning, for all the persecution inflicted by the pagans and the Jews, that is still no reason to expect Christian princes to allow the Catholic Christian people to be oppressed by Turks or by heretics worse than Turks."

Had they left violence alone . . .

"By my soul," said your friend, "I wish that all the world were all agreed to take all violence and compulsion away on all sides, Christian and heathen, and that no one were constrained to believe but as they could be induced to by grace, wisdom, and good words, and then those that would go to God, go in God's name, and those that will go to the devil, the devil go with them."

"Indeed," I said, "and if that were so, I still little doubt that the good seed being sown among the people would as well come up and be strong and able to save itself as the cockle, and that God would always be stronger than the devil. But yet heretics and heathens are two different cases. For in the event that the Turks, Saracens, and pagans were to allow the Christian faith to be peaceably preached among them, and that we Christians were therefore to likewise allow all their religions to be preached among us, and violence taken away by assent on both the sides, I doubt not at all that the Christian faith would much more increase than decline. And although we would find among us those who would for the licentious liberty of those religions draw to the devil, yet so also would we find among them, I have no doubt, many a thousand that would be happy to leave that bestial pleasure and come to the Christian faith, as in the beginning there came to it from the pagans, who lived as hedonistically as the Turks do now. But since violence is used on their side, and Christianity not there allowed to be preached and accepted, those who would now allow that religion to be preached and taught among Christians, and not punish and destroy the doers of that preaching and teaching, are plainly enemies to Christ, since they would be content to allow Christ to lose his worship in many souls on this side, without anyone being won from the other side to take their place.

Differences between heathens and heretics

"But, now, if violence were withdrawn on that side, then this way that you speak of might perhaps be taken between Christendom and Turkey or pagans if the world gave its assent to it and could hold to it in no evil way. *What things we ought most to regard* For since we should nothing so much regard as the honor of God and the spreading of the Christian faith and the winning of people's souls to heaven, we would seem to be dishonoring God if we did not trust that his faith preached among others equally without disturbance would not be able to prosper. And, believing that it would be, we would impair the profit if we were to refuse the condition, when there are many more to be won to Christ on that side than to be lost from him on this side.

"But as for the heretics rising among ourselves and springing from ourselves, they are in no way to be tolerated, but are to be suppressed and overcome at the outset. *No covenant with heresy* For by any covenant with them, Christendom has nothing to win. For as many as we allow to fall to them we lose from Christ. And from all of them we could not win to Christ one the more, even if we won them all home again, because they were our own before. And yet, as I said, for all that, from the beginning they were never by any temporal punishment of their bodies at all harshly treated until they began to be violent themselves.

"We read that in the time of Saint Augustine, the great doctor of the *The example of St. Augustine* Church, the heretics in Africa called the Donatists had recourse to force and violence, robbing, beating, torturing, and killing those that they seized from the true Christian flock, as the Lutherans have done in Germany. For the avoiding whereof, that holy man Saint Augustine, who had for a long time with great patience borne and endured their malice, only writing and preaching in refutation of their errors, and not only had done them no temporal harm but also had hindered and opposed others that would have done it, did yet at last, for the peace of good people, both permit and exhort Count Boniface and others to suppress them with force and threaten them with bodily punishment.[3]

"Which way of acting holy Saint Jerome and other virtuous fathers *St. Jerome and other Fathers on defending peace* have in other places allowed. And since that time there have upon necessity—perceived by great outrages committed against the peace and quiet of

3. See Augustine's "Letter to Count Boniface" (Letter 185, A.D. 417), especially chapters 25–30. Augustine stressed "the doctrine of the peace and unity of Christ" (ch. 15). In this spirit he concluded that "the death penalty was not to be invoked, because Christian moderation was to be observed even toward those unworthy of it, but fines were to be imposed and exile was decreed against their bishops and ministers" (ch. 26). For an example of Augustine's earlier mild treatment of heretics, see Augustine's "Letter to Bishop Januarius" (Letter 88, A.D. 406).

the people in sundry places of Christendom by heretics rising from a small beginning to a strong and unruly multitude—been devised for them many severe punishments, and in particular death by fire, not only in Italy and Germany, but also in Spain and virtually all parts of Christendom. Among which in England, as a good Catholic realm, it has long been punished by death in fire. And especially seeing that in the time of that noble prince of most celebrated memory, King Henry V, when Lord Cobham[4] maintained certain heresies, by that means the number of heretics so grew and increased that within a while, though he himself had fled to Wales, they yet assembled themselves together in a field near London in such a way and in such number that the king and his nobles had to put on armor in order to suppress them, whereupon they were routed and many of them executed; and after that Lord Cobham was taken in Wales and burned in London. Then the king, his nobles, and his people, on considering the great peril and jeopardy that the realm was likely to have fallen in on account of those heresies, made at a parliament very good and substantial provisions, additional to all such as were made before, for counteraction as well as suppression and severe punishment of any such as should be found guilty thereof and left by the clergy to the secular authorities.

The example of Henry V and Lord Cobham

King and Parliament made civil laws against heresy for the sake of peace in the realm

"For here you shall understand that it is not the clergy that endeavors to have them punished by death. It may well be, since we are all human beings and not angels, that some of them may sometimes have too hot a head or an injudicious zeal, or, perhaps, an irascible and cruel heart, by which they may offend God in the selfsame deed whereof they would otherwise have gained great merit. But certainly the intent of the Church law on this is good, reasonable, compassionate, and charitable, and in no way desirous of the death of anyone. For after a first offense the culprit can recant, repudiate by oath all heresies, do such penance for his offense as the bishop assigns him, and in that way be graciously taken back into the favor and graces of Christ's church. But if afterwards he is caught committing the same crime again, then he is put out of the Christian flock by excommunication. And because, his being such, his mingling with Christians would be dangerous, the Church shuns him, and the clergy gives notice of this to the secular authorities—not exhorting the king, or anyone else ei-

The intent of the ecclesiastical laws against heretics

Proper actions taken by the clergy

4. Lord Cobham, or Sir John Oldcastle, who was executed for heresy in 1417. Shakespeare mentions "Oldcastle" in the Epilogue of *2 Henry IV*, and he alludes to that name in *1 Henry IV*, 1.2.41–2. In the original versions of the *Henry IV* plays, he seems to have used Oldcastle instead of Falstaff. See the introduction to the *Henry IV* plays in the Riverside edition of Shakespeare's *Complete Works*.

ther, to kill him or punish him, but in the presence of the civil representative, the clergy not delivers him but leaves him to the secular authorities,
and forsakes him as one excommunicated and removed from the Christian
flock. And though the Church will not lightly or hastily take him back, yet
at the time of his death, upon his request, with indications of repentance,   5
he is absolved and taken back."

. . .

An objection   "Indeed," said your friend, "but as I see it the bishop does as much as
kill him when he leaves him to the secular authorities at such a time and
place as he knows well he will soon be burned."

"I will not here enter into the question," I said, "of whether a priest   10
can for any reason, and if for any, whether then for heresy, legitimately put
or command the putting of anyone to death, either by explicit words or
under the general name of right and justice. In that matter I could not lack
reason, authority, or the example of holy men. But in this matter that we   15
have in hand, it is sufficient that the bishop neither does it nor commands
it. For I think no reasonable person will have it that when the heretic, if he
went at large, would with the spreading of his error infect other folk, the
bishop should have such pity on him that he would, rather than allow oth-
Is punishment   er people to punish his body, allow him to kill other people's souls.   20
inconsistent with   "Indeed," I said, "there are some, as you say, who, out of either a lofty
the counsels of pretended pity or a feigned observance of the counsels of Christ, would
Christ?   have no one punish any heretic, or infidel either, not even if they invaded
us and did us all the harm they possibly could. And of this opinion are
Luther and his followers, who, among their other heresies, hold as an obvi-
Should we resist ous conclusion that it is not permissible for any Christian man to fight   25
the Turk?   against the Turk, or to put up against him any resistance, even if he comes
into Christendom with a big army and tries to destroy everything. For
they say that all Christians are bound by the counsels of Christ, and so
Does Christ forbid they say that we are forbidden to defend ourselves, and that Saint Peter
self-defense?   was, as you mentioned, reproved by our Savior when he struck off   30
Malchus's ear, even though he did it in the defense of his own master and
the most innocent man that ever was. And on top of this they claim, as you
said in the beginning, that since the time that Christian men first resorted
to fighting, Christendom has never increased, but has always diminished
and declined, so that at this day the Turk has very tightly restricted us and   35
brought it in within a very narrow compass, and narrower will make it,
they say, as long as we go around using the sword to defend Christendom.

Which they say should be, as in the beginning it was increased, so now continued and preserved only by patience and martyrdom. Thus holily speak these godly fathers of Luther's sect, endeavoring to procure that no man would resist the Turk, but would let him win everything. And when it should come to that, then they would, so it seems, win everything back by their patience, high virtue, and martyrdom—by which now they cannot manage to resist their bestial sensuality, but break their vows and take to themselves harlots under the name of wives; and where they cannot fight against the Turk, rise up in big bands to fight against their fellow Christians. It takes, I trust, no great genius to perceive whom those who hold that opinion are trying to please. And if the Turk happens to come in, there is little doubt as to whose side they will take, and that Christians are likely to find no Turks as cruel as those people. What an admirable holiness, to abstain out of piety from resisting the Turk, and in the meantime to rise up in rabbles and fight against Christian men, and, as that sect has done, destroy many a good religious house, despoil, maim, and kill many a good, virtuous man, and rob, desecrate, and pull down many a goodly church of Christ.

Defense only by patience and martyrdom?

A perplexity: heretics tolerate heathens but fight fellow Christians

"And now, where they submit as a proof that God is not pleased with battle made against infidels the losses and diminishment suffered by Christendom since that practice began, they behave as once did a sage old father fool in Kent when several upper-class men had some elderly country folk meet with them to think and talk about the restoration of Sandwich Harbor. At that time they started trying to determine, by discussion and by reports made by the old men from around there, what thing had been the reason that so good a harbor had within such a few years so badly deteriorated, and such sands risen, and such shallow sandbars made therewith, that very small vessels now had a lot of trouble coming in at any kind of tide, whereas a few years before, big ships were accustomed to riding without difficulty. And some laid the blame on Goodwin Sands, and some on the lands reclaimed by various owners on the Isle of Thanet out of the Channel, in which the sea used to encompass the isle and bring the vessels around it, and whose course at the ebb used to scour the harbor, whereas now, the sea being shut out from there, the harbor for lack of such course and scouring was choked up with sand. Thus they alleged, different men, different causes. Then one good old father suddenly stood up and said, 'Y'all gentlemen, say every man what he will, I done marked this here thang good as anyone else. And, by God, I know well 'nuff how it gone

The example of Sandwich Harbor

An odd display of reason

bad. For I knowed it when it were good, and I did mark, so I done, when it begun to go bad.' 'And what has hurt it, good father?' said the gentlemen. 'By my faith, sirs,' he said, 'yonder same Tenterden steeple, and nothin' else, that, by the Mass, I wish was a nice big fishin' pole.' 'How has the steeple hurt the harbor, good father?' they said. 'Nah, by our Lady, gentlemen,' he said, 'I cain't well tell y'all how, but I well know it did. For, by God, I knowed it to be a good harbor till that there steeple was built, and, by Mary's Mass, I done marked it well, it never done good since.'

"And thus wisely speak these holy Lutherans who, sowing schisms and seditions among Christian people, lay the loss thereof to the fending off of the Turk's invasion, and the resisting of his malice, when they should rather, if they had any sense in their heads, lay it to the contrary. For when Christian princes did their duty against heretics and infidels, there are histories and monuments enough that witness the manifest aid and help of God in great victories given to good Christian princes by his almighty hand. But, on the other hand, ever since the ambition of Christian rulers who desire each other's dominion set them at war and deadly dissension among themselves, whereby while each of them has aspired to the aggrandizement of his own dominion, they have little cared what came of the common corps of Christendom, God, for the punishing of their inordinate appetites, has withdrawn his help and shown that he cares as little, allowing, while they try to eat one another up, the Turk to prosper and to proceed so far that if their blind passions do not look thereto the sooner, he shall not fail (which our Lord forbid) within a short while to swallow them all. And although Christ forbade Saint Peter, who was a priest and, under Christ himself, prince of Christ's priests, to fight with the temporal sword [see Matthew 26:52] toward the hindrance and resistance of his fruitful Passion, on which depended the salvation of humankind, which propensity our Savior had before that time so severely reproved and rebuked in him as to call him therefore Satan, [see Matthew 16:23] it is nevertheless completely off base to claim that in accord with that example temporal princes should, not with an eye to such spiritual profit but with an allowance of much spiritual harm, let their people be invaded and oppressed by infidels, to their utter undoing, not only temporal, but also, for a great many, perpetual, they being likely of their frailty, for fear of earthly grief and discomfort, to fall from their faith and renounce their baptism. In which danger our Lord would not have anyone deliberately put himself, and for that reason advised his disciples that if they were persecuted in

The Turk prospers because of dissension and ambition among Christian princes

Distinctions drawn between spiritual and temporal princes

Christ's counsel

one city, they should not come forth and foolhardily put themselves in danger of denying Christ because of inability to endure some intolerable tortures, but should instead flee from there to some other place where they could serve him in peace [see Matthew 10:23], till he should allow Importance of

5 them to fall into a predicament from which there was no way to escape, peace and then he would have them like mighty champions stand their ground, where they shall not in such a case fail of his help.

    "Now, although it is true that Christ and his holy apostles exhort Christ's everyone to cultivate patience and endurance, not requiting an evil deed exhortation to

10 or putting up any defense against it, but exercising further sufferance and everyone also returning good for evil, yet neither does this counsel necessarily bind us, against the nature we all have in common, to allow someone to kill us for no reason, nor is it meant to deter us from defending someone whom we see to be innocent and maliciously assaulted and oppressed. In such a

15 case, nature, reason, and God's command bind, first, the ruler to safeguard Obligation to his people at risk of himself, as God taught Moses to know himself bound safeguard and to kill the Egyptian in defense of the Hebrew [see Exodus 2:11–12]. And defend later he binds everyone to help and defend a good and innocent neighbor against the malice and cruelty of the wrongdoer. For as the holy Scripture

20 says, 'He gave commandment to each of them concerning his neighbor' [Sirach 17:14]. God has given everyone charge of his neighbor to keep Love of neighbor him from harm of body and soul as much as may lie in his power [see can necessitate war Leviticus 19:18, Luke 10:27–37, and Romans 15:2].

    "And for that reason, not only excusable but also commendable is that

25 communal war which every people wages in the defense of their country against enemies that would invade it, since every man is fighting not for the defense of himself, out of personal regard for himself, but, out of Christian charity, for the safeguarding and preservation of all the others. Which reasoning, much as it holds true with regard to all battles of de-

30 fense, most especially holds true with regard to the battle by which we defend the Christian countries against the Turks, in that we defend one another from by far the greater danger of loss of worldly possessions, suffering of bodily harm, and perdition of people's souls.

    "And now, if this is legitimate and obligatory also for every private Legitimate and

35 person, how much more so is it for princes and rulers? If on pain of losing obligatory actions their souls they may not knowingly allow it to happen that among the people whom they have in governance, anyone takes away anyone else's horse, then how can they without calling on themselves eternal damna-

tion allow other people, and especially infidels, to come in and disarm and rob and enslave them all? And if they are obliged to provide this defense and cannot do it alone, what madness it would be to say that the people may not help them."

More's Defense of the Clergy

In the following selection, More defends the clergy against attacks which he claims to be slanderous and therefore illegal. He identifies this slander as the strategy that eventually succeeded in destroying the independence of the church in England: beginning with real faults of the clergy, the church's critics grossly exaggerate these and then make up false crimes.

From *The Supplication of Souls* (1529):[1]

For, first, all the misdeeds that any bad priest or friar is guilty of, he accuses all the clergy of them, as intelligently and sensibly as if he were to attribute the misdeeds of some bad lay people to all lay people. But he likes this approach so well that in accusing all priests of the sins of the ones who are undeniably guilty of them, he not only holds them all guilty of the sins against chastity and the hypocritical, worldly lives of those who are bad, but also madly, like a foolish fellow, much more blames them and more earnestly reproves them for the good and honorable lives of those who are good. These he rebukes and abhors because they keep their vows and persevere in chastity. They are, he says, ruiners and destroyers of the realm who are bringing the land back into wilderness by their abstaining from marrying and procreating. Then he aggravates these extreme charges with

On the misdeeds of clergy and laity

1. Modernized by Mary Gottschalk, pp. 85–89, 99–102, 108–10. For the original edition of this text, see *The Supplication of Souls, Complete Works*, vol. 7, pp. 126–30, 139–41, 147–49.

On the malice of accusers

heinous words, specious repetitions, and melodramatic exclamations, calling them "bloodsuckers" drunk with the blood of holy martyrs and saints,
referring here to their condemning of holy heretics. Greedy gluttons, he
calls them, and insatiable whirlpools, because the laity have given them
possessions and give alms to the friars. And all good, virtuous priests and   5
religious he calls "idle holy thieves" because they spend their time in
preaching and prayer.

On the rhetoric of accusers

And then he says, "These are they that make so many sick and suffering
beggars. These are they that make these whores and pimps. These are they
that make these thieves. These are they that make so many idle persons.   10
These are they that corrupt procreation. And these are they that by abstaining from marriage so hinder the procreation of the people that the
whole realm will eventually revert to wilderness unless they get married
before then."

And now, on top of these heinous charges made against all the cler-   15
gy—and made, as every sensible person sees, some very falsely and some
very foolishly—after his grandiose repetitions he begins his bombastic,
melodramatic exclamations, crying out about the "great big bottomless
ocean full of evils" and about the terrible shipwreck of the commonwealth, the removal of the King's kingdom, and the ruin of the King's   20

The attempt to set church and crown at odds

crown. And then, rolling in his rhetoric from figure to figure, he starts in
with a vehement invocation of the King and gives him warning of his
great loss, asking him fervently, "What has become of your sword, your
power, your crown, your dignity?" As though the King had completely lost
his realm expressly for lack of people to reign over, because priests have no   25
wives. And surely the man cannot fail to write with such eloquence, for he
has gathered these splendid flowers out of Luther's garden, almost word for
word, without any more work than just the translating of the Latin into
English.

But to inflame the King's Highness against the Church, he says that the   30
clergy strive for nothing else than to make the King's subjects fall into disobedience and rebellion against His Grace.

More's response

What a likely story! As though the clergy did not know that there is no
other earthly thing that so much keeps themselves in peace, security, and
safety as does the due obedience of the people to the virtuous mind of the   35
prince, whose high goodness would inevitably have much more difficulty
in defending the clergy and keeping the Church in peace if the people fell
into disobedience and rebellion against their prince. And therefore any

child can see that the clergy would never be so mad as to be glad to bring the people into disobedience and rebellion against the prince, since it is by his goodness that they are preserved in peace, and since in any such rebellion of the people they would likely be the first to fall into danger. So nei-
5 ther is there desired by the clergy nor ever will by God's grace happen any such rebellion as the beggars' spokesman and his cohorts, whatever they say, want in the worst way to see.

But this man, in his diatribe against the clergy, dredges up years of yore, going all the way back to King John's days. After expending much effort in
10 the praise and commendation of that good, gracious king, he cries out against the pope of that time, and the clergy of England, and all the lords and all the commoners of the realm, because King John, so he says, made the realm tributary to the pope. Here he is referring, perhaps, to Peter's Pence. But surely all his hot accusation here becomes a very cold story
15 when the truth is known. For the fact is that although there are writers who say that Peter's Pence was granted by King John for the lifting of the interdict that had been laid on England, it actually was paid before King John's great-grandfather was ever born, and of that there is plenty of proof. And if he says, as indeed some writers do say, that King John made England
20 and Ireland tributary to the pope and the Holy See by the granting of a thousand marks, we dare reply that this is definitely untrue.[2] No one in all of Rome either can or ever could show evidence of such a grant, and even if they could, it would be worth absolutely nothing. For never could any king of England give away the realm to the pope, or make the land tribu-
25 tary, even if he wanted to. And no such money is or ever was paid. And as for Peter's Pence, if that is what he means, neither did it make the realm tributary nor was it granted by King John. For before the Norman Conquest it was already being paid to the Holy See, toward the maintenance thereof, but only by way of gratitude and voluntary donations.
30 Now, as for his saying that the pope made Stephen Langton, a traitor to the king, archbishop of Canterbury against the king's will, here he is telling, as we see it, two lies at once. For neither was Langton ever a traitor against the king, as far as we have ever heard, nor did the pope make him an archbishop in any way other than he did anyone else at that time. Lang-
35 ton was properly and canonically chosen as archbishop of Canterbury by

Was England made tributary to Rome? No.

More's correction

Another charge: the example of Archbishop Stephen Langton

---

2. On More's rejection of the pope as feudal lord of England, see the commentary on William Tyndale's *An Answere unto Sir Thomas Mores Dialoge,* pp. 240–41.

the community of monks at Christ's Church in Canterbury, to whom, as the king well knew and never denied, the election of the archbishop at that time belonged. Nor did the king resist his election because of any treason he was charged with. But he was discontented with it. And after the election was over and was confirmed by the pope, he would not for a 5 long time allow him to enjoy the bishopric, because he himself had recommended someone else to the monks, and they had rejected him in favor of Langton. And that it happened as we are telling you, and not as the beggars' spokesman writes for a false foundation for his ranting, you can see not only from several historical accounts but also from several extant 10 documents of the election and confirmation of the said archbishop, as well as of the long litigation and legal action that followed.

Alleged opposition of ecclesiastical and civil jurisdiction

Now he shows himself very angry with the ecclesiastical jurisdiction, which he would anyway wish to be taken completely away, since, he says, it necessarily destroys the civil jurisdiction. Never mind that the good 15 kings of the past have granted it and that the nobles in their times, and the people too, have in fully assembled parliaments confirmed it, and that yet, up to now, blessed be God, everyone has been in too good an agreement to fall into dissension because of the wild words of such a malicious troublemaker. In order to make the clergy hated, he says that they call their ju- 20 risdiction a kingdom. It may please him to use that word, but the truth is that he seldom today sees any clergyman who so calls any ecclesiastical jurisdiction that he exercises.

More on acts of Parliament

Now, where this man uses as a proof thereof that the clergy always mention themselves before the laity, this manner of mentioning comes not 25 from them but from the good disposition and devotion of the laity. So much so that at a parliament, when any acts are drawn up, the words are commonly so couched that the bill says it is enacted first by our sovereign lord the King, and then by the lords ecclesiastical and secular, and then by the commoners assembled in that present parliament. And these bills are 30 often first drafted, submitted, and passed in the House of Commons, where there is not one clergyman present.

Surely the accusers devise to do some good?

. . . But, now, his whole specious line of argument, you know well, would be worth nothing unless he devised some good and wholesome helps against all these evils. It is therefore a wonder to see what judicious 35 solutions he suggests for the great big bottomless ocean of evils; what remedies with which to repair the ruin of the King's crown, to restore and uphold his honor and dignity, to make his sword sharp and strong, and, finally, to save the commonwealth from total shipwreck. You would perhaps think that the man would now devise some good, wholesome laws for help against all these evils. But no, he will do no such thing. For he says he doubts that the King is able to make any law against them, since, he says,

5 the clergy is stronger in the parliament than the King himself. For he reckons that in the higher house the clergy is greater in number and stronger than the laity, and in the House of Commons, he says, all the learned men of the realm except for the King's learned council are paid by the Church to speak for it in the parliament against the King's crown and

10 dignity. And therefore he thinks the King unable to make any law against the misdeeds of the clergy.

This beggars' spokesman wants to come across as a man of great experience and one who has great knowledge of the standard procedure used in the King's parliaments. But then he speaks so sagely of it that from his

15 own wise words it becomes quite evident that he neither has any knowledge of it nor has ever stepped foot in either house.

For as for the higher house, first, the King's own royal person alone more than equals in power all the lords present with him—the ecclesiastical and the secular too. And beyond this, the ecclesiastical lords can never

20 in number exceed the secular lords, but have to be far fewer, if the King so wishes. For His Highness can call there by his writ many more secular lords at his own pleasure.

The accusers are wrong about Parliament

And being what they are, it has never yet been seen that the ecclesiastical lords banded themselves there as a party against the secular lords. But it

25 has been seen that something which the ecclesiastical lords have proposed and have thought reasonable, the secular lords have denied and rejected— one example being the motion made for the legitimation of children born prior to the marriage of their parents. Here, although the reform proposed by the ecclesiastical lords was something that had nothing to do with their

30 own well-being, and although they also cited in support of their position canon law and other ordinances of the Church and the laws of other Christian countries, they yet could not prevail against the secular lords, who brought forward nothing to the contrary but their own wills. In the higher house, the ecclesiastical lords have never yet appeared so strong that

35 they might defeat the secular lords. So, then, how much too feeble they are to win out against them and the King too, whose Highness alone is too strong for them both, and who can by his writ call to his parliament more secular lords whenever he wants.

Relations between ecclesiastical and secular lords

Now, where he says that in the House of Commons all the learned men of the realm except the King's learned council are paid to speak for the clergy, here are two blunders at once. For not all the learned men of the realm are knights or burgesses in the House of Commons, and the King's learned council is not there at all. And therefore it seems that he has heard something from some men who have seen as little as he himself has. And surely if he had ever been in the House of Commons, as some of us have, he would have seen the clergy not gladly spoken for. And we little doubt that you can think of acts and statutes, passed by various parliaments, that are such and were passed in such a way and some of them so recently that you yourselves can see that the clergy either is not the stronger element in the King's parliament or else has no will to compete.

And for a further proof that the King's Highness is not so weak and powerless in his own parliament as this beggars' spokesman so presumptuously tells him he is, His Grace well knows, and so do all his people, that in their own convocations His Grace never in his life devised or desired anything that was ever denied him. And therefore this specious fabrication of this beggars' spokesman, that the King's Highness in his high court of parliament is more weak and feeble than the clergy, is a very feeble ploy.

But, now, since he will have no law drawn up for the remedy of his great complaints, what other solution does he come up with? The solution to all this mess, he says, is nothing other than to let him and other such royal ranters rant at and ridicule the Church and tell the people the priests' misdeeds, and for the wickedness of a part of it, make the entire clergy scorned and hated by all the laity. This, he says, the King must allow if he wants to avoid the ruin of his crown and dignity. And, he says, this will work more efficaciously and be more successful than all the laws that could ever be made, no matter how strong they might be.

Just think, good lords and masters, then you will need no more parliaments! For here is ingeniously found, God be thanked, an easy way to remedy the great big bottomless ocean of evils and save the commonwealth from shipwreck and the King's crown from ruin. It can all be done just by ranting. . . .

Once this charade was played and his beggars' bill so well put into effect, and the beggars had so much less to live on and were so much more numerous, then, surely, just as for the beggars he now writes a bill of complaint to the King's Highness against bishops, abbots, priors, prelates, and priests, so would he then write another bill to the people against mer-

More points out more blunders

More on the king's power

The accuser's proposed solution

Ranting shall achieve all

Merchants, kings, lords in danger next

chants, gentlemen, kings, lords, and princes, complaining that they have everything and saying that they do nothing for it, that they live idly, and that they are commanded in Genesis to live by the labor of their hands in the sweat of their faces, as he says now about the clergy. If they think they will then be in a different position from the one the clergy are in now, they may perhaps be badly deluding themselves. For if they think their case will not be considered entirely the same because they have lands and goods to live on, they must realize that so do the clergy too, and that this is what this beggars' spokesman is complaining about and wants done away with.

Now, some landowners may perhaps suppose that their case will not seem the same as that of the clergy because they think that the clergy have *Lay landowners* their possessions given them for purposes which they do not fulfill, and *are also in danger* that if their possessions happen to be taken from them, it will be done on that basis, and so the lay landowners are out of that danger because, they think, such a cause or basis or perception is lacking and cannot be found with respect to them and their inheritance. Certainly if anyone, whether priest or lay person, has lands in the giving of which has been attached any condition which he has not fulfilled, the giver may with good reason take such advantage of that as the law gives him. But on the other side, whoever would advise princes or lay people to take from the clergy their possessions on the basis of such general allegations as that they do not live as they should, or do not use their possessions well, and would claim that therefore it would be a good deed to take them by force and dispose of *What will follow* them better—we dare boldly say to whoever gives this argument, as now *from the accuser's* does this beggars' spokesman, that we would counsel you to take a good *solution* look at what would follow. For as we said before, if this bill of his were put through, he would not fail to provide you soon after, in a new supplication, plenty of new meritless arguments that would please the people's ears, arguments whereby he would endeavor to have lords' lands and all honest folk's goods confiscated from them by force and distributed among beggars. Of whom there would, by this strategy that he devises, come about such an increase and growth that they could in a hasty, makeshift *More foresees the* way make up a strong party. And as surely as fire always creeps forward and *rise of a strong* tries to turn everything into fire, so will such bold beggars as this one nev- *party* er cease to solicit and procure all that they can—the despoilment and robbery of all who have anything –and to make all people beggars like themselves.

It is all right with us if you do not just take our word for this, because
it has already been proved by those rural Lutherans who revolted in Ger-
The example many. Once stirred up by such seditious books as is this beggars' supplica-
of Germany tion and by such seditious heretics as is he who wrote it, they first attacked
Church prelates. But shortly afterwards they so pressed forward to the sec- 5
ular princes that these had to join forces with those whom they at first had
laughed at seeing put in danger. They hoped to profit by their loss, until
they saw that they were likely to lose along with them. And for all the
punishment inflicted on the rebels, of whom in one summer over sixty
60,000 slain thousand were slain, that fire is still rather covered than quenched, because 10
they let it creep forward so far at first that dissension thereby grew among
the lords themselves, since there can never be lacking some needy, ravenous landowners who are ready to be captains in all such rebellions, such as
Lord Cobham, also called Oldcastle, who was for a time a captain of heretics in England in the days of King Henry V. And surely there would soon 15
More foresees follow some grievous change in the laity should this beggars' spokesman
grievous changes have his malicious supplication against the clergy succeed.

On the Condition of Church and State in England

Toward the end of his life, More wrote in defense of the Church several works similar to the one excerpted above. In so doing, he was accused of showing undue favor to the Church and not recognizing the dissension which the Church had caused in England. More responds to this criticism in his Apology (1533), from which is taken the following account.[1]

From *The Apology of Sir Thomas More,* chapters 11 and 44:

For first, as for my own side, look at my *Dialogue*, my *Supplication of Souls*, and both parts of the *Confutation*, and you will clearly see that I have used with reference to neither the clergy nor the laity any hot, offensive word, and that I have refrained from discussing in particular the faults of
5 either the one group or the other, but have acknowledged that the truth is that neither party is faultless. But then, which is the thing that offends these blessed brethren, I have not moreover refrained from saying this, which I also take for very true: that just as this realm of England has had to this day, God be thanked, as good and as laudable a laity, number for num-

On England's laudable laity and clergy

---

1. Modernized by Mary Gottschalk. See *Complete Works,* vol. 9, pp. 52–54, 144–45.

ber, as has had any other Christian region of its size, so has it also had, number for number, compared with any christened realm of no larger size, as good and as commendable a clergy. Granted, there have never been lacking in either party plenty of such as have always been bad, but their faults have always been their own and not to be imputed to the whole 5 body, either of the clergy or of the laity, saving that there has perhaps been in either party, in some such as by their offices ought to look thereto, some lack of the effort and diligence that they should have shown in the re-

*More's desire
for amendment,
starting with
oneself*

forming of it. I declare always that I would wish that this be amended, and that everyone especially try to amend themselves and accustom themselves 10 to look rather at their own faults than at other people's, and that against those in either party who are found clearly evil and wicked and harmful to the commonwealth, like thieves, murderers, heretics, and other such wretches, the whole corps of the clergy and that of the laity lovingly be of one accord and in agreement, and according to the good ancient laws and 15

*More's vision
of accord and
amendment,
and of their
opposites*

commendable practices long continued in this noble realm, each party it- self endeavor to diligently repress and keep under those evil and ungodly folk that, like sores, scabs, and gangrene, trouble and vex the body, and of all of them to cure those that can be cured, and, for the health of the whole body, to cut and cast off from it the incurably gangrened parts, al- 20 ways observing in the doing thereof such order and fashion as can stand and agree with reason and justice, the king's laws of the realm, God's Scripture, and the laws of Christ's church, ever keeping love and concord between the two principal parties, the clergy and the laity, lest the dregs of both groups, conspiring together and increasing, should little by little 25 grow too strong for both—to which point they might have a good-sized gap and a broad gate by which to get if they could by craft find the means to sever and set asunder the laity to fight against the clergy, and so to let, as it were, the soul and the body quarrel and fight with one another, and while they study nothing else but how the one can grieve the other, the 30 wicked then conspire and agree with one another and set upon the good people of both groups.

    This has to this day been the whole sum of my writing, without any

*More distinguishes
himself from his
adversary*

offensive word used regarding either laity or clergy. And a more mild stance toward all good folk, this other book on the dissension does not 35 have, and also not a more impartial one, as far as I can see, unless he be considered more mild because he puts down his words with much more mildness and restraint when he is saying something about heretics, and shows himself therein more temperate and thereby more discreet than I, and unless he be considered more impartial because the words he uses in rehearsing the faults of the clergy are not in the worst things pointed with partiality toward those members of the clergy that are bad, but are impartially directed and pointed toward the whole body.

. . .

And yet to bring the clergy into the more hatred, and to make the name of the clergy the more odious to the people, this compassionate Pacifier[2] in several places in his book, to appease this dissension therewith, alleges against them that they make big confederacies among themselves to make and maintain a party against the laity and, by such conspiracies and worldly expedients and stiff penalties, to rule the people and punish them and keep them under. And this point he brings in here and there in various places, sometimes with a "some say," and sometimes with a "they say," and sometimes he says it himself. And I really do not know, if he did indeed hate the clergy (as some say he does, and yet I trust he does not), what more hateful thing he could say.

Accusers allege opposition between clergy and laity

What any one kind or sort of people is there in this realm—farmers, craftsmen, merchants, lawyers, judges, knights, lords, or whatever—but that ill-disposed people might start against them a subversive grumbling, throwing around a suspicious babbling about gathering and assembling and whispering and talking and, finally, conspiring together? And yet, when one really thinks about it, all such suspicious babbling put together is not worth a feather.

Who will be safe from seditious talk?

But in several places he harps a great deal on the laws of the Church, as though the ecclesiastical laws which the clergy here have made were a great cause of this dissension. And then several of the laws that he speaks of are not local-church laws made by the clergy here, but the laws in force through the whole of the church of Christ, the making of which cannot be laid to them. Nor are people therefore so irrational that—even if those laws were less good than those that the great wisdom of this Pacifier could devise—they would direct anger about them at our clergy that did not make them, but have been bound to keep them.

Accusations against the laws of the church

And as for defaming them with the charge of misuse of those laws for purposes of cruelty, as he does in his book, there is no great cleverness in

2. More clearly uses this term ironically, since he shows how this "Pacifier" (Christopher St. German) actually seeks the opposite of peace.

the making of that lie. For every fool who wants to can invent the like and allege it of some other folk when he pleases.

On ecclesiastical
assemblies and
constitutions

Now, as for their assemblies and comings together for the making of their local laws and constitutions, for this Pacifier to allege those to be any "confederacies" that should now be a cause of this so recent and sudden grumbling and dissension—that is a very far-fetched idea. For setting aside the discussion of whether those constitutions are as irrational as this Pacifier would have them seem, this thing suffices against him: that there is, I truly think, not one local-church constitution that he speaks of that was made, or to anyone's objection or complaint put in execution, in the time of any of all the prelates that are now living. So how, then, could any of them be any such confederacy or cause of this lately sprung-up dissension?

Convocations or
confederacies?

But I suppose it is those assemblings at their convocations that he calls by the name of confederacies. For unless that is the case, I have no idea what he means by that word. On the other hand, if that is what he means, then, for all that I can see, he is giving a good and wholesome thing an odious and heinous name. For if they assembled more often, and there did the things for which such assemblies of the clergy in every local church through all Christendom from the beginning were instituted and arranged, much more good might have grown thereof than the long disuse can allow us now to perceive.

But in my lifetime, as far as I have heard, and, as I suppose, in a good part of my father's too, they have never come together in convocation except at the request of the king, and at those assemblies they have done very little concerning spiritual things. Whether God has allowed this fact—that they have been in that great, necessary point of their duty so negligent— to grow into a hidden, unperceived cause of dissension and complaint against them, God, whom that negligence has, I fear, sorely offended, knows. But certainly this has to my mind been a somewhat greater fault in the clergy than several of those faults which, under his expression "some say," this Pacifier has in his book made out to be very great.

But certainly if this Pacifier calls those assemblies confederacies, I would not greatly wish to be confederate with them or to be their associate in any such confederacies. For I never yet could assemble with them for any great gain except to come up to their travail, labor, cost, and pain, and tarry and talk, etc., and so get them home again. And therefore people need not greatly complain about or envy them for any such confederacies.

6

More's Last Days

Thomas More's Letter to Erasmus after Resigning as Lord Chancellor

Thomas More resigned as Lord Chancellor on 16 May 1532, the day after Henry VIII pressured the Bishops' Convocation into provisionally accepting the king as head of the spiritual order in England. Despite this bold resistance to Henry's designs, More remained in the King's favor throughout the first part of 1533. But after writing against Henry's chief legal propagandist, Christopher St. German, in April and again in October, and after refusing to attend Anne Boleyn's coronation on 1 June 1533, More not only lost that favor but incurred Henry's wrath. The following letter[1] is this careful lawyer's explanation of his situation eight months before Henry pressed for his arrest. Included with the letter was a public statement literally cut in stone (i.e., on his tombstone, now in Chelsea Old Church, where his wife Jane is buried). In the letter, More gives an account of what occurred since his resignation, and he urges Erasmus to publish this account throughout Europe. In the inscription, as R. W. Chambers explained, More gives a "brief biography" that "summarized the whole meaning of More's career" (22. 24, 233). The epitaph on his wives, which he also appended to this letter, is the last poem he published in his 1518 collection of Latin epigrams (Latin Poem #258, Complete Works, vol. 3.2).

1. *Selected Letters*, #46, pp. 179–83.

Thomas More Sends Greetings to Erasmus of Rotterdam.

. . . Concerning the remark in your earlier letter that you were hesitant about publishing my letter in spite of motives for wanting to have it published, there is no reason, my dear Erasmus, for hesitation on your part.

No reason Some chatterboxes around here began to spread the rumor that I had re-
for delay signed my office unwillingly and that I had kept that detail a secret. So, af- 5
ter making arrangements for the construction of my tomb, I did not hesi-
Why he resigned tate to make, on my Epitaph, a public declaration of the actual facts, to
is public allow anyone a chance to refute them, if he could. As soon as those fellows
noted the Epitaph, since they were unable to deny its truth, they charged
it with being boastful. However, I preferred this charge rather than allow 10
the other rumor take hold, not for any selfish reason, since I do not have a
high regard for what men may say, provided I have the approval of God;
but having written several pamphlets in English in defense of the Faith
His duty to protect against some fellow countrymen who had championed rather perverse
his reputation doctrines, I considered it my duty to protect the integrity of my reputa- 15
tion; and so that you can find out how boastful I was, you will receive a
copy of my Epitaph; you will notice, in reading it, that, out of confidence
in my own position, I do not bait those fellows at all, so as to prevent them
Review of events from making whimsical remarks about me. After resigning my office, I
waited until the opening of the new term, and, so far, no one has advanced 20
a complaint against my integrity. Either my life has been so spotless or, at
any rate, I have been so circumspect that, if my rivals oppose my boasting
of the one, they are forced to let me boast of the other. As a matter of fact,
the King himself has pronounced on this situation at various times, frequently in private, and twice in public. It is embarrassing for me to re- 25
late—but on the occasion of the installation of my most distinguished successor, the King used as his mouthpiece the most illustrious Duke, I mean
The King's the Duke of Norfolk, who is the Lord High Treasurer of England, and he
continued goodwill respectfully ordered the Duke to proclaim publicly that he had unwillingly yielded to my request for resignation; the King, however, was not satis- 30
fied even with that extraordinary manifestation of good will toward me; at
a much later date, he had the same pronouncement repeated, in his presence, at a solemn session of the Lords and Commons, this time using my
successor as his mouthpiece, on the formal occasion of his opening address

to that assembly which, as you know, we call Parliament. Therefore, if you agree, there is no good reason for holding back the publication of my letter. As to the statement in my epitaph that I was a source of trouble for heretics—I wrote that with deep feeling. I find that breed of men ab-
5   solutely loathsome, so much so that, unless they regain their senses, I want to be as hateful to them as anyone can possibly be; for my increasing experience with those men frightens me with the thought of what the world will suffer at their hands. I shall follow your advice and make no reply to the person about whom you wrote, although I have held a lengthy letter
10   in readiness for some time now. My reason for holding back is not that I have any regard for what he, or all of his coworkers, may think or write about me, but because I do not want to be burdened with the obligations of writing replies to outsiders, when I feel the more immediate responsibility of answering our own associates. Best wishes, my dear Erasmus, and
15   a long farewell; the best of luck always.

From my rural home at Chelsea.
Thomas More

Inscription on the Tomb of Thomas More

Thomas More was born in London of respectable, though not distinguished, ancestry; he engaged to some extent in literary matters,[2] and after
20   spending several years of his youth as a pleader in the law courts and after having held the office of judge as an Under-Sheriff in his native city, he was admitted to the Court by the Unconquerable Henry the Eighth, who is the only King to have ever received the unique distinction of meriting the title "Defender of the Faith," a title earned by deeds of sword and pen;
25   he was received at Court, chosen member of the King's Council, knighted, appointed Under-Treasurer and then Chancellor of Lancaster, and finally Chancellor of England by the special favor of his Sovereign. Meanwhile he was elected Speaker of the House of Commons; furthermore, he served as the King's ambassador at various times and in various places, last
30   of all at Cambrai, as an associate and colleague of Cuthbert Tunstal, then

Professional successes

---

2. That More lists his literary engagements first among his life's work seems significant.

Bishop of London and shortly after Bishop of Durham, a man whose
Special mention equal in learning, wisdom, and virtue is seldom seen in the world today. In
of the Peace of that place he witnessed, in the capacity of ambassador, to his great joy, the
Cambrai renewal of a peace treaty between the supreme monarchs of Christendom
and the restoration of a long-desired peace to the world.   5

On More's service   May heaven confirm this peace and make it a lasting one.[3] He so con-
to king and realm ducted himself all through this series of high offices or honors that his Excellent Sovereign found no fault with his service,[4] neither did he make
himself odious to the nobles nor unpleasant to the populace, but he was a
source of trouble to thieves, murderers, and heretics. His father, John   10
More, was a knight and chosen by the King as member of the group of
judges known as the King's Bench; he was an affable man, charming, irre-
proachable, gentle, sympathetic, honest, and upright; though venerable in
age, he was vigorous for a man of his years; after he had lived to see the day
when his son was Chancellor of England, he deemed his sojourn upon   15
On his father earth complete and gladly departed for heaven. The son, all through his father's lifetime, had been compared with him, and was commonly known
as the young More, and so he considered himself to be; but now he felt the
loss of his father, and as he looked upon the four children he had reared
and his eleven grandchildren, he began, in his own mind, to grow old. This   20
feeling was increased by a serious chest ailment, that developed soon after,
as an indication of approaching old age. Now sated with the passing things
On his resignation of this life, he resigned office and, through the unparalleled graciousness of
a most indulgent Sovereign (may God smile favorably upon his enterpris-
es), he at length reached the goal which almost since boyhood had been   25
the object of his longing—to have the last years of his life all to himself, so
that he could gradually retire from the affairs of this world and contem-
plate the eternity of the life to come. Then he arranged for the construction of this tomb for himself, to be a constant reminder of the unrelenting
advance of death, and had the remains of his first wife transferred to this   30
place. That he may not have erected this tomb in vain while still alive, and
that he may not shudder with fear at the thought of encroaching death,
but may go to meet it gladly, with longing for Christ, and that he may find
death not completely a death for himself but rather the gateway to a hap-

---

3. These preceding three lines, which mention peace three times, indicate More's agreement
with the Renaissance humanists' principal concern for a peaceful Christendom.
4. As More indicates in his letter to Erasmus, here is the principal reason he writes and pub-
lishes his own epitaph. See p. 306, lines 1–19.

1udge More S:{.sup}r Tho: Mores Father.

Sir John More, by Hans Holbein, 1526–27

This chalk drawing is another preliminary sketch for the family portrait (see pp. 14–15). In the water-based and oil versions of that painting, 76-year-old Sir John stands out in his scarlet robe, a robe indicating his position as a judge of the King's Bench. The love and respect More had for his father were shown by the deference he showed even while Lord Chancellor and by the care and affection he showed as his father was dying (see p. 37).

pier life, I beg you, kind reader, attend him with your prayers while he still
lives and also when he has done with life.

Epitaph Thereto Attached

On his wives   My beloved wife, Jane, lies here.[5] I, Thomas More, intend that this same
tombe shall be Alice's and mine, too. One of these ladies, my wife in the   5
days of my youth, has made me father of a son and three daughters; the
other has been as devoted to her stepchildren (a rare attainment in a stepmother) as very few mothers are to their own children. The one lived out
her life with me, and the other still lives with me on such terms that I cannot decide whether I did love the one or do love the other more. O, how   10
happily we could have lived all three together if fate and morality permitted. Well, I pray that the grave, that heaven, will bring us together. Thus
death will give what life could not.

5. Jane died in 1511. Thomas married Alice Middleton one month later. See *TMSB*, pp. xxiv, 9.

Thomas More's Account of
His First Interrogation

17 April 1534

Sir Thomas More, after receiving a summons, came before the King's Commis-sioners at the Archbishop of Canterbury's[1] palace at Lambeth on Monday, April 13. He refused to sign the oath, and was delivered to the Abbot of Westminster[2] to be kept as a prisoner. He remained there till Friday, and then was sent prisoner to the Tower of London. Shortly after arriving, he wrote the following letter to his eldest daughter Margaret Roper.[3]

c. 17 APRIL 1534
TOWER OF LONDON

When I was before the Lords at Lambeth,[4] I was the first that was called in, albeit Master Doctor the Vicar of Croydon[5] was come before

---

1. Thomas Cranmer (1489–1506).
2. William Benson.
3. *Selected Letters*, #54, pp. 215–23.
4. More's examiners were Lord Chancellor Audley, Archbishop Cranmer, the Duke of Norfolk (Thomas Howard), and the Duke of Suffolk (Charles Brandon).
5. Rowland Phillips.

me, and divers others. After the cause of my sending for, declared unto me
(whereof I somewhat marveled in my mind, considering that they sent for
no more temporal men but me), I desired the sight of the oath, which they

More examines
the oath and
the Act

showed me under the great seal. Then desired I the sight of the Act of the
Succession, which was delivered me in a printed roll. After which read se-   5
cretly by myself, and the oath considered with the act, I showed unto
them that my purpose was not to put any fault either in the act or any
man that made it, or in the oath or any man that sware it, nor to condemn
the conscience of any other man. But as for myself in good faith my conscience so moved me in the matter that though I would not deny to swear   10
to the succession, yet unto the oath that there was offered me I could not

More refuses
the oath

swear, without the iubarding[6] of my soul to perpetual damnation.[7] And
that if they doubted whether I did refuse the oath only for the grudge of
my conscience, or for any other fantasy, I was ready therein to satisfy them
by mine oath. Which if they trusted not, what should they be the better to   15
give me any oath? And if they trusted that I would therein swear true, then
trusted I that of their goodness they would not move me to swear the oath
that they offered me, perceiving that for to swear it was against my conscience.

Unto this my Lord Chancellor[8] said that they all were sorry to hear me   20

Audley's response
to the refusal

say thus, and see me thus refuse the oath. And they said all that on their
faith I was the very first that ever refused it; which would cause the King's
Highness to conceive great suspicion of me and great indignation toward
me. And therewith they showed me the roll, and let me see the names of
the lords and the commons which had sworn, and subscribed their names   25
already. Which notwithstanding when they saw that I refused to swear the
same myself, not blaming any other man that had sworn, I was in conclusion commanded to go down into the garden, and thereupon I tarried in
the old burned chamber, that looketh into the garden and would not go
down because of the heat. In that time saw I Master Doctor Latimer come   30

Something of a
pageant

into the garden, and there walked he with divers other doctors and chap-
lains of my Lord of Canterbury, and very merry I saw him, for he laughed,
and took one or twain about the neck so handsomely, that if they had
been women, I would have went[9] he had been waxen wanton.[10] After that

6. *iubarding*—risking, jeopardizing
7. See Roper's *Life, TMSB*, p. 51.
8. Sir Thomas Audley (1488–1544).
9. *went*—thought
10. *waxen wanton*—grown unchaste

came Master Doctor Wilson forth from the lords and was with two gentlemen brought by me, and gentlemanly sent straight unto the Tower.
What time my Lord of Rochester[11] was called in before them, that cannot
I tell. But at night I heard that he had been before them, but where he re-
5   mained that night, and so forth till he was sent hither, I never heard. I
heard also that Master Vicar of Croydon, and all the remnant of the priests
of London that were sent for, were sworn, and that they had such favor at
the Council's hand that they were not lingered nor made to dance any
long attendance to their travail and cost, as suitors were sometimes wont
10 to be, but were sped apace to their great comfort so far forth that Master
Vicar of Croydon, either for gladness or for dryness, or else that it might
be seen *(quod ille notus erat pontifici)*[12] went to my Lord's buttery bar and
called for drink, and drank *(valde familiariter).*[13]

When they had played their pageant and were gone out of the place,
15 then was I called in again. And then was it declared unto me what a number had sworn, even since I went inside, gladly, without any sticking.
Wherein I laid no blame in no man, but for my own self answered as be-   *More refuses*
fore. Now as well before as then, they somewhat laid unto me for obstina-   *a second time*
cy, that where as before, sith I refused to swear, I would not declare any
20 special part of that oath that grudged my conscience, and open the cause
wherefore. For thereunto I had said to them, that I feared lest the King's
Highness would as they said take displeasure enough toward me for the
only refusal of the oath. And that if I should open and disclose the causes
why, I should therewith but further exasperate his Highness, which I
25 would in no wise do, but rather would I abide all the danger and harm
that might come toward me, than give his Highness any occasion of further displeasure than the offering of the oath unto me of pure necessity
constrained me. Howbeit when they divers times imputed this to me for
stubbornness and obstinacy that I would neither swear the oath nor yet
30 declare the causes why, I declined thus far toward them that rather than I
would be accounted for obstinate, I would upon the King's gracious license or rather his such commandment had as might be my sufficient warrant that my declaration should not offend his Highness, nor put me in the
danger of any of his statutes, I would be content to declare the causes in
35 writing; and over that to give an oath in the beginning, that if I might find

11. Bishop John Fisher (1469–1535).

12. This alludes to Peter's denial of Christ (John 18:15–16). See Derrett, p. 68.

13. More gives three motives for the Vicar's drink at Archbishop Cranmer's bar. This Latin
phrase ("on very familiar terms") seems to give weight to the third.

those causes by any man in such wise answered as I might think mine own conscience satisfied, I would after that with all mine heart swear the principal oath, too.

To this I was answered that though the King would give me license under his letters patent, yet would it not serve against the statute. Whereto I said that yet if I had them, I would stand unto the trust of his honor at my peril for the remnant. But yet it thinketh me, lo, that if I may not declare the causes without peril, then to leave them undeclared is no obstinacy.

Canterbury questions More

My Lord of Canterbury taking hold upon that that I said, that I condemned not the conscience of them that sware, said unto me that it appeared well that I did not take it for a very sure thing and a certain that I might not lawfully swear it, but rather as a thing uncertain and doubtful. But then (said my Lord) you know for a certainty and a thing without doubt that you be bounden to obey your sovereign lord your King. And therefore are ye bounden to leave off the doubt of your unsure conscience in refusing the oath, and take the sure way in obeying of your prince, and swear it. Now all was it so that in mine own mind methought myself not concluded, yet this argument seemed me suddenly so subtle and namely with such authority coming out of so noble a prelate's mouth, that I could again answer nothing thereto but only that I thought myself I might not well do so, because that in my conscience this was one of the cases in which I was bounden that I should not obey my prince, sith that whatsoever other folk thought in the matter (whose conscience and learning I would not condemn nor take upon me to judge), yet in my conscience

More on his conscience

the truth seemed on the other side. Wherein I had not informed my conscience neither suddenly nor slightly but by long leisure and diligent search for the matter. And of truth if that reason may conclude, than have we a ready way to avoid all perplexities. For in whatsoever matters the doctors stand in great doubt, the King's commandment given upon whither side he list soyleth all the doubts.

Westminster questions More

Then said my Lord of Westminster to me that howsoever the matter seemed unto mine own mind, I had cause to fear that mine own mind was erroneous when I see the great council of the realm determine of my mind the contrary, and that therefore I ought to change my conscience. To that I answered that if there were no more but myself upon my side and the whole Parliament upon the other, I would be sore afraid to lean to mine own mind only against so many. But on the other side, if it so be that

in some things for which I refuse the oath, I have (as I think I have) upon
my part as great a council and a greater too, I am not then bounden to
change my conscience, and confirm it to the council of one realm, against
the general council of Christendom. Upon this Master Secretary (as he
5   that tenderly favoreth me), said and swore a great oath that he had lever
that his own only son (which is of truth a goodly young gentleman, and
shall I trust come to much worship) had lost his head than that I should
thus have refused the oath. For surely the King's Highness would now
conceive a great suspicion against me, and think that the matter of the nun
10 of Canterbury was all contrived by my drift. To which I said that the contrary was true and well known, and whatsoever should mishap me, it lay
not in my power to help it without peril of my soul. Then did my Lord
Chancellor repeat before me my refusal unto Master Secretary, as to him
that was going unto the King's Grace. And in the rehearsing, his Lordship
15 repeated again that I denied not but was content to swear to the succession. Whereunto I said that as for that point, I would be content, so that I
might see my oath in that point so framed in such a manner as might stand
with my conscience.

Then said my Lord: "Marry, Master Secretary mark that too, that he
20 will not swear that neither but under some certain manner." "Verily no,
my Lord," quoth I, "but that I will see it made in such wise first, as I shall
myself see, that I shall neither be forsworn nor swear against my conscience. Surely as to swear to the succession I see no peril, but I thought
and think it reason that to mine own oath I look well myself, and be of
25 counsel also in the fashion, and never intended to swear for a p[i]ece, and
set my hand to the whole oath. Howbeit (as help me God), as touching
the whole oath, I never withdrew any man from it, nor never advised any
to refuse it, nor never put, nor will, any scruple in any man's head, but
leave every man to his own conscience. And methinketh in good faith that
30 so were it good reason that every man should leave me to mine.

Thomas More.

More's conscience and the General Council of Christendom

More's final position

A Dialogue on Conscience[1]

This dialogue, related in the form of letters, was occasioned by real events that occurred on 16 and 17 August 1534. Lord Chancellor Thomas Audley, More's successor, went to More's stepdaughter's home, ostensibly to hunt, but primarily to communicate a message he wanted delivered to his imprisoned friend. Audley was indeed More's friend. He had taken considerable risks to defend Sir Thomas against the wrath of King Henry. Now, however, he wanted More to put a stop to what he considered foolishness. The rest of the story is told in the following two letters. The first was sent by Alice Alington, daughter of More's second wife, to Margaret Roper, More's eldest daughter. The second is a dialogue between Sir Thomas and Margaret, but in Rastell's words, whether this dialogue was "written by Sir Thomas More in his daughter Roper's name or by herself . . . is not certainly known."[2] In this dialogue, Margaret makes her final attempt to persuade her father to sign the oath and to return home. The work has been compared to Plato's Crito, in which the friends of Socrates visit him before his death.

1. Modernized by Mary Gottschalk, pp. 195–218. The original text can be found in *The Correspondence of Sir Thomas More,* ed. Elizabeth Rogers (Princeton University Press, 1947), #205 and 206, pp. 511–32.

2. *The Workes of Sir Thomas More,* p. 1434 (1557 edition).

Letter from Alice Alington to Margaret Roper

17 AUGUST 1534

Sister Roper, with all my heart I give you my regards, thanking you for all your kindness.

The reason I am writing at this time is to let you know that when I got home, within two hours after, my Lord Chancellor came over to hunt a
5 buck in our park—which was to my husband a source of great encouragement, that it would please him to do this. Then, when he had enjoyed himself and killed his deer, he went to spend the night at the home of Sir Thomas Barmeston. The next day, I went to see him there at his request, which I could not say no to, since I thought he asked me with genuine
10 sincerity, and most especially since I wanted to speak to him on behalf of my father.

And when I saw my chance, I did ask him, as humbly as I could, that he would still be, as I have heard it said that he has been, a good lord to my father. And he said that when it came to his being charged with the matter
15 of the nun, things did look very good.[3] But as for this other matter, he marveled that my father is so obstinate in his thinking, when everybody else went ahead with the rest, except only the obstinate bishop [John Fisher] and himself. "And in all honesty," said my Lord, "I am very glad that I have no learning outside of a few of Aesop's fables, of which I shall tell you
20 one. There was a country full of almost nothing but fools. There were only a few who were wise. And they, by their wisdom, knew that there was going to fall a heavy rain which would turn into a fool everyone who got dirtied or wet with it. They, seeing that, made for themselves caves under the ground and stayed there till the rain was all over. Then they came out,
25 thinking to make the fools do what they wanted them to, and rule them as they would. But the fools would have none of that. Despite all this crafty planning, the fools would have the rule themselves. And when the wise men saw that they could not achieve their goal, they wished that they had been in the rain, and dirtied their clothes, with them."

30 When this tale was told, my Lord laughed very delightedly. Then I said to him that for all the delightfulness of his fable I had no doubt that he would be a good lord to my father when he saw his chance. He said, "I

The new Lord Chancellor sends a pointed fable to More

---

3. For Audley's role in preventing More's prosecution in this matter of supposedly listening to treasonous remarks by the Nun of Kent, see Roper's *Life, TMSB*, pp. 44, 49–50.

A second fable offered on conscience would not have your father so scrupulous of conscience." And then he told me another fable, one about a lion, an ass, and a wolf, all going to confession.[4] First the lion confessed that he had devoured all the beasts that he could come by. His confessor absolved him, on the grounds that he was a king and also that it was his nature so to do. Then came the poor ass. He said that he took but one straw out of his master's shoe, for hunger, and that because of this he thought his master had caught a cold. His confessor could not absolve this great trespass, but immediately sent him to the bishop. Then the wolf came and made his confession, and he was strictly commanded not to eat more than a sixpence's worth of food at any one meal. But when the wolf had been on this diet a little while, he grew very hungry. So much so that one day, when he saw come by him a cow with her calf, he said to himself, "I am very hungry and would gladly eat, except that I am bound by my spiritual father. Well, notwithstanding that, my conscience must be my judge. So, then, if that be so, my conscience will be thus: that the cow does now seem to me to be worth but fourpence, and then, if the cow is worth but fourpence, then the calf is worth but twopence." And so the wolf ate both the cow and the calf.

Cleverness and comfort   Now, good sister, has not my Lord told me two clever fables? Actually I liked them not at all, nor did I know what to say, because I was embarrassed by this answer. Anyway, I see no better recourse than to Almighty God, for he is the comforter of all sorrows and will not fail to send his comfort to his servants when they are most in need of it. And so, farewell, my own good sister. Written the Monday after Saint Lawrence, in haste, by

Your sister Dame,
Alice Alington

Letter from Margaret Roper to Alice Alington

AUGUST 1534

The next time I went to see my father after your letter arrived, I thought it both desirable and necessary to show it to him. Desirable, in that he might see thereby the labor of love you undertook for him. And necessary, in that he might perceive thereby that if he stands firm in this

---

4. For Thomas More's later reformulation of this fable, see *TMSB*, pp. 336ff.

scruple of his conscience (as it is at least called by many who are his friends and wise), all his friends that seem most able to do him good either will end up forsaking him or perhaps not actually be able to do him any good at all.

Friends charge
More with
scrupulosity

⁵ And so, the next time I was with him after receiving your letter, first I talked with him a while about his physical ailments, both his chronic chest pains and his recent problems with kidney stones, and also about the cramps that grip him in his legs some nights, and I found by what he said that they were not much worse, but were about the same as before, some-¹⁰ times very bad and sometimes giving him little trouble. At that time I found him not in pain and (as much as one in his situation could be) fair-ly well disposed, once we had said our seven psalms and the litany, to sit and talk and have a good time. So I began first with other things, about how well my mother is holding up and the good attitudes of my brother ¹⁵ and all my sisters, how they are disposing themselves every day more and more to set little by the world and to draw more and more to God, and I told him that his household, his neighbors, and other good friends out there are diligently remembering him in their prayers. And then I added this: "Good Father, I pray to God that their prayers and ours, and your ²⁰ own with them, may procure from God the grace that in this great matter (because of which you are in this trouble, on account of which so also are all of us who love you), you may take, soon, a way that while being pleas-ing to God will also content and please the King—whom you have always found so singularly gracious to you that if you should stubbornly refuse to ²⁵ do what would please him when you could do it without displeasing God (which many great, wise, and very learned men say you could in this thing), it would both be a great blot on your honor, in every wise man's opinion, and, as I myself have heard some say (some that you yourself have always taken for very learned and good), put your soul in danger too. But ³⁰ that point, Father, I will not be so bold as to dispute upon, since I trust in God and your good disposition that you will surely look at that. And your learning I know to be such that I know well you can.

More's physical
ailments

Margaret urges
More to find
a way to take
the oath

The danger to his
honor and soul

"But there is one thing which I and your other loved ones find and perceive out there which needs to be brought to your attention, because ³⁵ otherwise you may, to your great peril, mistakenly hope for less harm (for as for good, I well know that with regard to this matter you are not ex-pecting any in this world) than I am terribly afraid is likely to happen to you. For I assure you, Father, I have recently received a letter from my sister Alington by which I can well see that if you do not change your mind, you are likely to lose all those friends that are able to do you any good. Or that if you do not lose their good wills, you will at least lose the effect of them, for any good that they will be able to do you."

Meg as Eve　　　With this my father smiled at me and said, "What, mistress Eve (as I　5 called you the first time you came), has my daughter Alington played the serpent with you, and with a letter set you at work to come tempt your father again, and for the love that you bear him, labor to make him swear against his conscience, and so send him to the devil?" And after that he *More states his*　looked sad again, and said to me earnestly, "Daughter Margaret, the two of　10 *position*　us have talked of this thing more than two or three times, and the same story, in effect, that you're telling me now, and the same fear too, you have told me twice before. And I have twice answered you, too, that if in this matter it were possible for me to do the thing that might content the King's Grace without God thereby being offended, there is no man who　15 has taken this oath already who has done so more gladly than I would—as he that considers himself more deeply bound to the King's Highness for his most singular bounty, many ways shown and expressed, than all the rest *More on conscience*　of them. But since, my conscience remaining unchanged, I can in no way do it, and since for the instruction of my conscience I have not looked　20 into this matter lightly, but have for many years given it serious study and consideration, and never yet have been able to see or hear anything, nor think I ever will, that could induce my own mind to think otherwise than I do, I have no way out of the bind that God has me in: that I must either mortally displease him or else endure whatever worldly harm he will for　25 my other sins, under name of this thing, let happen to me. Of which (as I have also told you before now) I have, before I came here, not failed to think of and ponder the very worst and absolute most that can possibly happen. And although I know full well my own frailty and the natural *More's trust*　faintness of my own heart, if I had not yet trusted that God would give me　30 strength rather to endure all things than to offend him by blasphemously swearing against my own conscience, you can be very sure I would not have come here. And since in this matter I look only to God, it matters little to me if men call it as it pleases them and say it is not a matter of conscience but just a foolish scruple."　　　　　　　　　　　　　　　　35

　　　At this last word I took advantage of a good opportunity and said to *Meg recounts Lord*　him this: "Really and truly, Father, for my part, neither do I nor could it *Audley's objections*　become me to question either your good disposition or your learning. But

since you speak of what some call only a scruple, I must tell you that, as you will see by my sister's letter, one of the greatest dignitaries in this realm, and a learned man too, and (as I dare say you yourself will think when you find out who he is, and as you have already very effectively
5 proved him) your tender friend and very specially good lord, accounts your problem of conscience in this matter for nothing but a scruple, and you can be sure he says it in good faith and gives no little reason. For he says that whereas you say your conscience moves you to this, all the nobles of this realm, and almost all other men too, are boldly going forth with the
10 contrary, with no hesitation, excepting only yourself and one other man[5]—who is very good, and very learned too, yet I believe few who love you would advise you to rely on his mind alone, against all other men."

And with this I gave him your letter, that he might see that what I said was not something I made up, but was said by this person whom he much
15 loves and highly esteems. Then he read over your letter, and when he came to the end, he began it afresh and read it over again. And he did this in no kind of hurry, but took his time and emphasized every word.

More's careful reading

After that he paused, and then he said this: "Indeed, daughter Margaret, I find my daughter Alington just as I have always found her and, I trust, al-
20 ways will—as naturally watching out for me as you who are my own. Of course, I truly take her for my own too, since I married her mother and have brought her up from childhood as I brought you up, both in other things and in learning, in which, I thank God, she is now finding some fruit. She is bringing up very virtuously and well her own children, of
25 whom God, I thank him, has sent her a good supply. May our Lord safe-guard them and send her much joy of them and of my good son, her gen-tle husband, too, and have mercy on the soul of my other good son, her first husband. I pray daily (please write her so) for them all.

More's love for his step-daughter

"In this matter she has been very much herself, acting wisely and like a
30 true daughter toward me. And at the end of her letter she gives as good counsel as any man with any sense would wish for. God give me the grace to follow it, and God reward her for it.

"Now, daughter Margaret, as for my Lord, I not only think but also have found that he is undoubtedly my exceptionally good lord. And in my
35 other business, concerning the poor nun, as my case was good and blame-less, so in it was he my good lord, and Master Secretary[6] my good master

His gratitude to Audley and Cromwell

5. John Fisher, Bishop of Rochester
6. Thomas Cromwell.

too.[7] For which I shall never cease to pray faithfully for them both. Upon my honor, I pray for them daily as I do for myself. And if at any time it should happen (which I trust in God it never will) that I be found other than a man true to my king, let them never favor me, neither of them. Nor, in truth, could it become them to do so any more than they do.   5

"But in this matter, Meg, to tell the truth between you and me, my Lord's Aesop fables do not greatly move me. But as his Wisdom for his pastime cheerfully told them to my own daughter, so I for my pastime will answer them to you, Meg, another daughter of mine.

Response to the fable about fools and the rain

"The first fable,[8] the one about the rain that washed away the wits of   10
all who stayed outside when it fell, I have often heard before. It was a tale told so often among the King's Council by my Lord Cardinal [Wolsey],

Wolsey's favorite fable

when his Grace was chancellor, that I could not easily forget it. For in truth, in times past, when dissension began to come up between the Emperor and the French king in such a way that they were likely to, and did   15
indeed, go to war, there were in the Council here sometimes different opinions. Some were of the mind that they thought it would be wise for us to sit still and leave them alone. But ever against that way of thinking, my Lord used this fable of those wise men who, because they did not want to be washed with the rain that would make all the people fools, went   20
themselves into caves and hid themselves under the ground. But once the rain had made all the rest fools, and these men came out of their caves wanting to utter their wisdom, the fools agreed together against them and there and then soundly beat them. And so, said his Grace, if we were to be so wise as to sit in peace while the fools fought, they would not fail after-   25
wards to make peace and agree among themselves and eventually all fall upon us.

More's ironic assessment

"I will not dispute his Grace's counsel, and I trust we never made war but as reason would dictate. But yet his telling of this fable did in his day

---

7. Audley and Cromwell both went to great lengths to intercede for More when Henry VIII insisted that More be punished for speaking with the Nun of Kent.

8. See *Utopia, Complete Works,* vol. 4, p. 103, lines 16–23. See also Plato's *Republic* 496d–e, where Socrates compares the philosopher to "a man who has fallen among wild beasts—he will not join in the wickedness of his fellows, but neither is he able singly to resist all their fierce natures, and therefore seeing that he would be of no use to the state or to his friends, and reflecting that he would have to throw away his life without doing any good either to himself or others, he holds his peace, and goes his own way. He is like one who, in the storm of dust and sleet which the driving wind hurries along, retires under the shelter of a wall; and seeing the rest of mankind full of wickedness, he is content, if only he can live his own life and be pure from evil or unrighteousness, and depart in peace and good-will, with bright hopes."

help the King and the realm to spend many a fair penny. But that business is over and his Grace is gone, God rest his soul.

"And therefore I shall come now to this Aesop's fable as my Lord so cheerily laid it out for me. If those wise men, Meg, when the rain was gone and they came outside, where they found all men fools, wished that they too were fools just because they could not rule them, then it would seem that the fools' rain was so severe a shower that even through the ground it sank into their caves and poured down upon their heads and wet them to the skin, and made them more noodleheaded than those that stayed outside. For if they'd had any sense, they might well have seen that if they had been fools too, that would not have sufficed to make them rulers over the other fools, no more than the other fools over them, and that of so many fools, not all could be rulers. Now, when they longed so badly to bear a rule among fools that, so that they could, they would have been glad to lose their good sense and be fools too, the fools' rain had washed them fairly well. Although, to tell the truth, if before the rain came they thought that all the rest would turn into fools, and they were then either so foolish that they wanted to, or so crazy as to think that they would, being so few, rule so many fools, and did not have sense enough to realize that there are none so unruly as they that lack sense and are fools, then these wise men were stark fools before the rain came.

The foolishness of the so-called wise

"Anyway, daughter Roper, whom my Lord takes here for the wise men, and whom he means by the fools, I cannot very well guess; I cannot well read such riddles. For to adapt what Davus says in Terence,[9] 'Non sum Oedipus'—you're quite familiar with this, I may say—I'll make this, '*Non sum Oedipus, sed Morus*' [I am not Oedipus, but More], which name of mine, what it means in Greek,[10] I need not tell you. But I trust my Lord reckons me among the fools, and so I reckon myself, as my name is in Greek. And I find, I thank God, not a few reasons why I should indeed.

More as fool

"But among those that long to be rulers—that is something that certainly God and my own conscience clearly know no man can rightly number and reckon me. And I suppose every other man's conscience can tell him the same, since it is so well known that, of the King's great goodness, I was one of the greatest rulers in this noble realm, and that, at my own great effort, I was by his great goodness discharged. But whomever

More never wished to rule

9. *Andria* 1.2.23.
10. *Morus* in Greek means "fool," and More often joked about his name.

my Lord means the wise men to stand for, and whomever he means by the
fools, and whoever longs for the rule, and whoever longs for none, I beg

Prays that
all wisely rule
themselves

our Lord to make us all so wise as that we may, every one of us here, so
wisely rule ourselves in this time of tears, this vale of misery, this plain
wretched world—in which, as Boethius says,[11] for one man to be proud   5
that he bears rule over other men is much as if one mouse were to be
proud to bear a rule over other mice in a barn—may God, I say, give us

Self-rule required
for heaven

the grace to rule ourselves so wisely here that when we shall depart
posthaste to meet the great Spouse, we shall not be taken asleep and for
lack of light in our lanterns shut out of heaven with the five foolish vir-   10
gins.[12]

Response to the
apocryphal fable of
the lion, the wolf,
and the ass

"The second fable, Margaret, seems not to be Aesop's. Since it has to
do with confession, it would seem to have been invented after Christendom began. For in Greece before Christ's days they did not make use of
confession, no more the people then than the beasts now. And Aesop was a   15
Greek, and died long before Christ was born.

Whom could the
lion represent?

"But so what? Who made up the fable makes little difference. Nor do I
envy Aesop for his getting the credit. But surely it is somewhat too subtle
for me. For whom his Lordship means by the lion and the wolf, the both
of which confessed to destroying and devouring all that they could get   20
their hands on, and one of which enlarged his conscience as he pleased in
the interpretation of his penance, or whom he supposes to be the good,
discerning confessor that imposed on the one a small penance and the

And the
scrupulous ass?

other none at all—none of these things can I tell. But as for the foolish,
scrupulous ass, that had so sore a conscience on account of taking a straw   25
for hunger out of his master's shoe, my Lord's other words about my scruple make clear that his Lordship teasingly meant by that me—signifying
(as it seems by that similitude) that on account of overconscientiousness
and foolishness, my scrupulous conscience is taking for a huge danger to
my soul something that my Lordship thinks would in reality be but a tri-   30
fle: namely, if I were to take this oath. And I well suppose, Margaret, as you
told me just now, that so think many more besides—clergy as well as lay
people—including even some whom, for their learning and their virtue, I
myself hold in not a little esteem. And yet, although I suppose this to be
true, I do not believe very surely even that everyone who says so actually   35

11. *Consolation of Philosophy* 2. Prose 6.
12. See Matthew 25:1–13.

thinks so. But even if they did, daughter, that would not make much difference to me—not even if I should see my Lord of Rochester [Bishop Fisher] say the same and take the oath himself, right in front of me.

"For since you told me just now that those who love me do not think
5 it advisable that, against all other men, I should rely on his mind alone, let *More does not rely* me assure you, daughter, that no more do I. For although it is very true *on his mind alone* that I have him in that reverent an estimation that I reckon not one man in this realm fit to be matched and compared with him in wisdom, learning, and long-proved virtue put together, yet the fact that in this matter I
10 was not led by him appears very well and plainly both in that I refused the oath before it was presented to him and also in that he might have been content to take that oath (as I gathered later by you, when you suggested that I do the same) either to a somewhat further extent or in some other manner than I ever thought of doing. Truly, daughter, I never intend— *More follows his*
15 God being my good lord—to pin my soul to another man's back, not even *own conscience, not* if he's the best man I know who is alive today; for I do not know where he *that of others* might happen to carry it. There is no man living of whom, while he is still living, I can make myself sure. Some might do something for favor, and some might do it for fear, and so they might carry my soul a wrong way.
20 And some might happen to frame themselves a conscience and think that *Malleable* as long as they did it for fear, God would forgive it. And some may perhaps *conscience?* think that they will repent and be absolved of it, and so God will remit it. And some may perhaps be thinking that if they say one thing while thinking the contrary, God more regards their heart than their tongue, and that
25 therefore their oath goes by what they think and not by what they say, as a woman reasoned once. I believe, daughter, you were nearby. But honestly, Margaret, I can use no such ploys in so great a matter.[13] Just as, if my own *More uses no* conscience permitted me to, I would not refrain from doing it even if oth- *such ploys* er men refused to, so also even if others do not refuse to do it, I dare not,
30 my own conscience being against it. If I had, as I told you, looked but lightly into the matter, I would have reason to fear. But by now I have looked into it so much and so long that I intend at the least to have no less regard for my soul than once did a poor honest countryman, named Company, for his."
35 And with this he told me a story—I think I can hardly tell it again to *The tale of* you, because it involves some legal terms and proceedings. But as far as I *"Company," a* *countryman*

13. More refuses to use mental reservation.

can recall, my father's story was this. There is a court that as a matter of course is set up at every fair, to do justice in such things as happen within that fair. This court has a pretty funny name—I can't think of it, but it begins with "pie," and the rest goes, I think, much like the name of a knight that I have met (and you too, I believe, for he has been at my father's often before this, at times when you were there), a fairly tall, dark-complexioned man, his name was Sir William Pounder.[14] But never mind, let the name of the court go for now, or call it, if you want, a court of "pie Sir William Pounder." But look, here was what happened. Once upon a time, at such a *A court at* court held at Bartholomew Fair, there was an escheator[15] from London *Bartholomew Fair* who arrested an outlaw and seized the goods that he had brought into the fair, getting him out of the fair by a trick. The man who was arrested and had his goods seized was a Northerner. By way of friends of his, he caused the escheator at the fair to be arrested upon some charge, I don't know what, and so he was brought before the judge of the court of pie Sir William Pounder, and in the end had to go through a certain proceeding in which he was tried by an inquest[16] of twelve men—a jury, as I remember they call it, or else a perjury.[17]

Now the clothier, through his friendship with the officials, had found the means to have the inquest almost all made up of Northerners who had *The trial of the* had their booths standing there at the fair. Now it came to the last day of *escheator* the trial, in the afternoon. Having heard both parties, and their lawyers, tell their sides of the story at the bar, the twelve men were taken from the courtroom to a place where they could talk and discuss and agree upon the sentence. No, let me get my terms a little more accurate: I believe the judge gives the sentence and the jury's statement is called a verdict. Well, scarcely had they come in together when the Northerners were agreed, and practically all the others too, to convict our London escheator. They thought they needed no more proof that he had done wrong than just the *Company, an* mere name of his occupation. But then there was, as the devil would have *honest fellow on* it, this honest man from another region, the man called Company. And be-
the jury

14. The name Margaret cannot remember is the Court of Piepowder, "a summary court formerly held at fairs and markets to administer justice among itinerant dealers and others temporarily present" *(Oxford English Dictionary)*. The term came from the French *pied-poudreux*, meaning "dusty-footed."

15. *escheator*—government official in charge of confiscating forfeited property

16. *inquest*—jury

17. This lawyer's joke is one bit of internal evidence given by those who argue that Sir Thomas wrote this dialogue and not Meg.

cause the fellow seemed but a fool and sat still and said nothing, they took no account of him, but said, "We are agreed now. Come, let's go give our verdict."

Then, when the poor fellow saw that they were in such a hurry, and that his mind was going not at all the way theirs were (if their minds were going the way they said), he begged them to wait and discuss the matter and give him a reason whereby he might think as they did. When he should do so, he would be glad to go along with them; but otherwise, he said, they must pardon him, for since he had a soul of his own to keep, as did they, he must say as he thought for his, as they must for theirs.

Company objects on the grounds of conscience

When they heard this, they were half angry with him. "What, good fellow," said one of the Northerners, "what's the matter with you? Are there not eleven of us here and you just one, all alone, all the rest of us in agreement? What's holding you back? What is your name, good fellow?" "Sirs," he said, "my name is Company." "Company," they said, "now by your word, good fellow, play then the good companion. Come along with us on that basis; go ahead, just as good company."

The jury members ask him to be a good companion

"I wish to God, good sirs," the man replied, "that there was no more to it than that. But, now, when we depart and come before God, and he sends you to heaven for doing according to your conscience, and me to the devil for doing against mine by going along, at your request here, for the sake of companionship, now, by God, Master Dickenson"—that was the name of one of the Northerners—"if I then say to all of you, 'Sirs, I went once for companionship's sake with you, for which reason I am going now to hell; now it's your turn to play good fellows with me; as I went with you then to keep you good company, so some of you go with me now, to keep me good company,' would you go, Master Dickenson? No, no, by our Lady, nor never a one of you all. And therefore you must excuse me from going along with you unless I can think in the matter as you do. I dare not in such a matter go along for good company. For the passage of my poor soul passes all good company."

Company's response: Will you return the favor later?

And when my father had told me this story, he then said: "I ask you now, good Margaret, to tell me this. Would you wish your poor father, who is at least somewhat learned, to have less regard for the peril of his soul than that honorable unlearned man did for his? I do not meddle, as well you know, with the conscience of any man who has taken the oath, nor do I take it upon myself to be their judge. But now, if they do well and their consciences do not trouble them, if I with my conscience to the con-

More relates the fable to his own position

trary should for companionship's sake go along with them and swear as they do, then when our souls later on shall pass out of this world and stand in judgment at the bar before the high Judge, if he sends them to heaven and me to the devil, because I did as they did, not thinking as they thought, if I should then say (as the good man Company said), 'My old good lords and friends,' naming such-and-such a lord—yes, and perhaps some of the bishops I love best—'I swore because you swore, and went the way that you went; now do the same for me; don't let me go alone; if there be any good fellowship among us, some of you come with me,' upon my

More on this fickle world

honor, Margaret, I may say to you, in confidence, here between the two of us (but let it go no further, I beg you with all my heart), that I find the friendship of this wretched world so fickle that no matter how much entreating and begging I might do, among them all I think I would find not one who would for good fellowship go to the devil with me. And so, by God, Margaret, if you think so too, I suppose it is best that for all the consideration I might have for them, even were they twice as many as they are, I have myself a consideration for my own soul."

"Surely, Father," I said, "without any scruple at all you could be bold enough, I dare say, to swear to that. But, Father, those who think you should not refuse to swear this thing that you see so many—such good men, and so learned—swear before you, do not mean that you should swear in order to bear them fellowship, or go along with them for com-

Why not give credence to one's friends?

panionship's sake. They mean, rather, that the credence that you may reasonably give to their persons on account of those aforesaid qualities should well move you to think the oath such of itself that everyone may well swear it without endangering their soul, if there is not the obstacle of their own private conscience being to the contrary, and that you well ought and have good reason to change your own conscience, conforming your own

Friends want More to conform his conscience

conscience to the conscience of so many others, precisely because they are such as you know they are. And since it is also commanded by a law made by Parliament, they think that you are, under pain of losing your soul, bound to change and reform your conscience, and conform your own, as I said, to other men's."

"Indeed, Margaret," replied my father, "for the part you are playing,

The laws of the land and conscience

you are not doing a bad job. But Margaret, first, as for the law of the land, though everyone born in and inhabiting it is bound to keep it in every case under pain of some temporal punishment, and in many cases also under pain of God's displeasure, still no one is bound to swear that every law is well made, or bound under pain of God's displeasure to perform any point of the law that is actually unlawful. That a law of this kind can happen to be made in any part of Christendom, I suppose no one doubts— the one exception on that point always being a General Council of the whole body of Christendom. Though it may lay down some things better than others, and some things may develop in such a way that by another law they may need to be reformed, yet to institute anything in such a way, to God's displeasure, that it could not lawfully be performed at the time that the law was made, that is something that the Spirit of God that governs his Church has never allowed, nor ever hereafter shall allow, to happen to his whole Catholic Church lawfully gathered together in a General Council. Christ has clearly promised this in Scripture.

The greater authority of General Councils

"Now, should it so happen that in some particular part of Christendom a law is made that is such that because of some part of it, some think that the law of God cannot bear it, and some others think yes—the thing being in such a way in question that through different regions of Christendom some good and intelligent men, both of our own time and before our time, think one way, and some others of like learning and goodness think the contrary—in such a case, those who think against the law neither may swear that the law was lawfully made, their own consciences telling them the contrary, nor are bound under pain of God's displeasure to change their own consciences on that matter. This applies to any particular law made anywhere, other than by a General Council of the Church or by a general faith grown by a universal working of God throughout all Christian nations—no authority other than one of these two (barring special revelation or an express commandment from God). Where the contrary opinions of good and very learned men (as I put to you the case) have cast doubt on what is the correct understanding of Scripture, I cannot see that any other authority may lawfully command and compel anyone to change their own opinion and transfer their own conscience from the one side to the other.

Example of a law in dispute

Local, particular laws cannot compel one to change one's conscience

"For an example of that kind of thing, I have, I believe, before now mentioned to you that whether our Blessed Lady was or was not conceived with original sin was at one time in great question among the great learned men of Christendom. And whether that has yet been determined and defined by any General Council, I do not remember. But this I remember well, that notwithstanding the fact that the feast of her conception was then celebrated in the Church (at least in some places), yet Saint

An example of a dispute among the learned

Bernard—who, as his many books written in honor and praise of our
Lady make clear, was of as devout an affection toward all things tending to
her commendation, that he thought could well be verified or allowed, as
any man then living—yet, I say, that holy, devout man was against that part
of her praise. This shows up very clearly in a letter of his in which he very   5
vehemently and with great reasoning argues against it, and does not ap-
prove of the institution of that feast either. Nor was he alone in this way of
thinking. There were many other very learned men with him, and very
holy men too. Now, there was on the other side the blessed, holy bishop
Saint Anselm, and he not alone either, but many very learned and very vir-   10
tuous men also with him. And the both of them are now holy saints in
heaven, and so are many more that were on either side. And neither side
there was bound to change their opinion for the other, not for any provin-
cial council either.

"But just as after a determination by a well-assembled General Coun-   15
cil, everyone is bound to give credence that way and conform their own
conscience to the determination of the General Council, and all those that
held the contrary before cannot be blamed for that, so too, if before that
determination was made, someone had against his own conscience sworn
Acceptable changes to maintain and defend the other side, that person did not fail to offend   20
of conscience God very grievously. But, indeed, if, on the other hand, a person were on
some issue to take a way all by himself, going by his mind alone, or with
Problematic some few, or with however many, against an evident truth appearing by
conscience the common faith of Christendom, this conscience is very damnable, yes.
Or even if it is not so fully plain and evident, yet if he sees but himself   25
with the far smaller side thinking the one way, against the far larger side—
of people as learned and as good as those who affirm the thing that he
thinks—thinking and affirming the contrary, and these latter folk are such
that he has no good reason not to suppose that in this matter, those who
say they think against his mind are saying this for no reason other than that   30
they think so indeed, then in all truth this is a very good reason why he
should be moved, and yet not compelled, to conform his mind and conscience to theirs.

"But Margaret, for what reasons I refuse the oath, that—as I have often
More's silence said to you—is something I will never tell you, neither you nor anybody   35
else, except if the King's Highness should choose to command me. Which
if his Grace did, I have before now told you how obediently I would respond at such time. But let me assure you, daughter, I have refused it, and

do, for more than one reason. And whatever my reasons for refusing it, of this much I am sure—it is a well-known fact—that of those who have taken it, some of the most learned, before the oath was presented to them, clearly said and affirmed the contrary of some things that they have now sworn to in the oath, and did so then upon their honor and their learning, and not in haste or suddenly, but often and after very diligently exerting themselves to seek and find out the truth."

His friends seem to have changed their positions

"That might be, Father," I said.

"And yet," he said, "since they may see more than they did before, I will not, daughter Margaret, dispute that, nor presume to judge any other person's conscience, which lies in their own heart, far out of my sight. But this I will say: that I myself never heard the reason for their change being any new, further thing found in the words of some authority than, as far as I can tell, they had looked at and, I would suppose, very seriously considered before. Now, of the very same things that they saw before, if some seem otherwise to them now than they did before, I am for their sake a great deal the gladder. But anything that I ever saw before, it still to this day seems to me just as it did. And therefore, even if they may now do otherwise than they might before, still, daughter, I may not.

More holds firm

"Now, as for things that some would perhaps say—such as, that I might with good reason take into less account those people's change, and be less inclined to change my conscience on account of any example of theirs, because their desire to keep the King happy and avoid his indignation, their fear of losing their worldly possessions, in consideration of the discomfort this would cause their relatives and friends, might have made them swear otherwise than they think or else frame their conscience afresh to think otherwise than they thought—any such opinion as this, I will not conceive of them. I have better hope of their goodness than to think that of them. For if such things should have turned them, the same things would likely have made me do the same; for in all honesty, I know few so fainthearted as myself. Therefore I will, Margaret, by my will, think no worse of other folk, in this thing that I do not know, than I find in myself. Rather, as I know well that it is my own conscience that causes me to refuse the oath, so I will trust in God that it was in accord with their conscience that they took the oath and swore.

What others might say of More's friends, though he remains hopeful

"But whereas you think, Margaret, that there are so many more on that side than there are on the side that think in this thing as I think, let me assure you, for your own comfort, that this is a thought you should never

have: that your father is throwing himself away so like a fool that he would
risk the loss of his possessions, and perhaps his body, for no reason having
to do with a danger to his soul, but, rather, is thereby putting his soul at
risk too. To this I will say to you, Margaret, that with respect to some of
my reasons, I have no doubt at all that, even if not in this realm, yet in the   5
rest of Christendom, of all those very learned and virtuous men who are
still living, they are not the smaller part that are of my mind. And besides

*More suspects he
is not alone in his
position*

that, it is, you know, quite possible that some men in this realm, too, think
not so clearly the contrary as, by the oath they have taken, they have
sworn that they think.   10

*Historical support
considered*

"Now, that much I say about those who are still living. But now we go
to those who have died, and who are, I trust, in heaven. I am sure that it is
not the smaller part of them that, all the time that they lived, thought in
some of these things the way that I think now. I am also, Margaret, plenty
sure of this: that of all those holy doctors and saints, who no Christian   15
doubts are long since with God in heaven, whose books we still to this day
can get our hands on, many thought in some of these things as I think
now. I do not say that they all thought so, but certainly so many and of
such a caliber, as well appears in their writings, that I pray that God may
give me the grace that my soul may follow theirs. And still I am not telling   20
you everything, Margaret, that I have for myself in the sure discharge of
my conscience. But in conclusion, daughter Margaret, in this whole thing,
as I have often told you, I do not take it upon myself either to define or to
dispute in these matters, nor do I rebuke or impugn any other man's deed,
nor have I ever written, nor so much as spoken to anyone, any word of   25
criticism about anything that Parliament has passed, nor have I meddled
with the conscience of any man who either thinks or says he thinks contrary to mine. But as concerns my own self, for your comfort I will say,
daughter, to you, that my own conscience on this matter (I condemn no

*More's surety in
his own conscience*

one else's) is such as may well stand with my own salvation—of that I am   30
as sure, Meg, as that God is in heaven. And therefore, as for all the rest—
goods, lands, and life too (if it should come to that)—since this conscience
is sure for me, I truly trust in God that he shall strengthen me to bear the
loss rather than against this conscience to take the oath and put my soul in
peril, since all the reasons I see moving other men to the contrary do not   35
seem to me such that could make any change in my conscience."

*Meg responds by
looking sad*

When he saw me sitting there looking very sad at this—since, I promise
you, sister, my heart was very heavy for the peril of his person, though in all

honesty I have no fear for his soul—he smiled at me and said, "What now, daughter Margaret? What now, mother Eve? Where is your mind now? Is it not musing with some serpent in your breast upon some new line of persuasion by which to offer father Adam the apple yet once again?"

5   "Truly, Father," I said, "I can go no further. I am, as I believe Cressida says in Chaucer, 'come to Dulcarnon, even at my wit's end.'[18] For since in this matter the example of so many wise men cannot move you, I can't see what more I could say, unless I should try to persuade you with the argument that Master Harry Patenson[19] came up with. For one day he came 10   across one of our men, and when he asked where you were, and heard that you were still in the Tower, he actually got angry with you, and said, 'Why? What's wrong with him, that he will not take that oath? Why should he hesitate to take it? I myself have taken it.' And so, in all truthfulness, I can now go no further either, after your taking so many wise men for no ex- 15   ample, unless I should say like Master Harry, 'Why should you refuse to take the oath, Father? For I myself have taken it.'"[20]

Meg's new approach: the Master Harry argument

At this he laughed and said, "That was like Eve too, for she offered Adam no worse fruit than she had eaten herself."

A witty reply

"But yet, Father," I said, "really and truly, I am terribly afraid that this 20   matter will bring you into dreadfully deep trouble. You well know, since I mentioned it to you, that Master Secretary sent you word, as your true friend, to remember that Parliament is still in session."

"Margaret," said my father, "I thank him with all my heart. But as I explained to you then, I have not failed to think about that. And although I 25   know well that if they were to make a law designed to do me any harm, that law could never be lawful, and I trust that God will so keep me in grace that concerning my duty to my king, no man will be able to hurt me without doing me wrong (and then, as I told you, this is like a riddle, a case in which a man may lose his head and not be harmed), and notwith- 30   standing also that I have good hope that God will never allow so good and wise a king to requite in such a way the long service of his true, faithful servant, yet, since there is nothing that couldn't possibly happen, I do not forget in this matter the counsel of Christ in the Gospel, that before beginning to build this castle for the safeguarding of my own soul, I should

More's riddle

18. *Troilus and Criseyde* 3.929–931.

19. Master Harry is the fool or jester depicted in Holbein's sketch of the More family. See *TMSB*, p. 14.

20. As we learn from a marginal note in Rastell's 1557 *The Workes of Sir Thomas More*, Margaret "took the oath with this exception: as far as would stand with the law of God" (p. 1441).

sit and calculate what the cost could be.[21] I counted, Margaret, you can be very sure, during many a restless night, while my wife slept and thought I did too, all the perils that could possibly come upon me. I went so far that I am sure there can come nothing more than what I thought of. And in thinking this through, daughter, I did have a very heavy heart. But yet, I thank our Lord, for all that, I never thought of changing my mind, even should the very worst happen to me that my fear ran upon."

"No, Father," I said, "to think about something that could happen is not the same as to see a thing that will happen, as you would—our Lord save you—if it should go that way. And then you perhaps would think what you do not think now, but by then it might be too late."

"Too late, daughter Margaret?" said my father. "I beg our Lord that if ever I make such a change, it will indeed be too late. For well I know the change could not be good for my soul—that change, I say, that would be caused only by fear. And therefore I pray to God that in this world I never
benefit from such a change. For, however much pain I may have to take here, I at least will on that account have the less to take when I am gone. And even if I now knew for sure that I would afterwards faint and fall and out of fear take the oath, I would still wish to take the pain that comes of refusing at first, for so I would have the better hope of being given the grace to rise again.

"And even though, Margaret, I know well that my wickedness has been such that I know I well deserve for God to let me slip, yet I cannot but trust in his merciful goodness, that as his grace has strengthened me up till now, and has made me content in my heart to lose goods, land, and life too rather than swear against my conscience, and has also put in the King that good and gracious a mind toward me that as yet he has taken from me
nothing but my liberty (by which, so help me God, his Grace has done me such great good, by the spiritual profit that I trust I am taking from it, that among all the great benefits he has heaped so thickly upon me, I reckon upon my faith my imprisonment the very greatest)—I therefore cannot, I say, doubt that by the grace of God, either he shall conserve and keep the King in that gracious intention still to do me no harm, or else, if it be his pleasure that for my other sins I shall suffer things that I seemingly shall not deserve, his grace shall give me the strength to take it docilely, and maybe somewhat gladly too, whereby his high goodness shall—by the merits of his bitter passion joined to, and far surmounting in merit for me,

---

21. Luke 14:28.

all that I can suffer myself—make it serve for release of my pain in purgatory, and over that for increase of some reward in heaven.

"Mistrust him, Meg, I will not, even if I feel myself faint. Yes, and even if *More's trust in*
I should feel my fear rise to the point of overthrowing me, I shall yet re- *God*
5 member how Saint Peter, with a blast of wind, began to sink for his faint
faith, and I shall do as he did—call upon Christ and beg him to help.[22] And
then I trust he shall set his holy hand on me, and in the stormy seas, hold
me up from drowning. Yes, and if he suffers me to play Saint Peter further,
and fall flat on my face and swear and forswear too—which our Lord, for
10 his tender passion, keep me from, and if it does happen, let me lose and
never win anything by—yet afterwards I shall trust that in his goodness he
will look upon me tenderly and compassionately, as he did upon Saint Peter, and make me stand up again and confess the truth of my conscience
afresh and endure here the shame and the harm of my own failing.[23]

15 "And finally, Margaret, this I know well: that except by my own fault he
will not let me be lost. I shall therefore with good hope commit myself
wholly to him. And if he allows me to perish eternally for my failings, then
I still shall serve for a praise of his justice. But in all honesty, Meg, I trust
that his tender pity shall keep my poor soul safe and make me praise his
20 mercy.

"And therefore, my own good daughter, never let your mind be troubled over anything that ever shall happen to me in this world. Nothing can
come but what God wills. And I make myself very sure that whatever that
may be, no matter how bad it seems, it will indeed be the best. And with *All for the best*
25 this, my good child, I beg you with all my heart—you and all your sisters
and my sons too—to be of comfort and service to your good mother, my
wife. And of your good husband's dispositions, I have no doubt whatsoever. Give my regards to them all, and to my good daughter Alington, and to
all my other relatives—sisters, nieces, nephews, in-laws—and all our ser-
30 vants, man, woman, and child, and all my good neighbors and our acquaintances out there. And with all my heart I beg both you and them to *Be merry*
serve God and be merry and rejoice in him. And if anything happens to
me that you would hate to happen, pray to God for me, but do not let
yourself be troubled, as I shall wholeheartedly pray for us all that we may
35 one day meet together in heaven, where we shall make merry forever and
never have trouble again."

22. Matthew 14:30.
23. Matthew 26:69–75 and Luke 22:61.

"Tale of Mother Maud"

On Conscience Again, 1534–1535

One of More's most famous "merry tales," this selection[1] reveals his life-long preference for animal fables. This story appears in More's Dialogue of Comfort Against Tribulation, *and it differs considerably from the story that appeared in* A Dialogue On Conscience.[2] *Why would More eliminate the lion from the first story? and why present a Father Fox character of dubious credibility?*

ANTHONY: When I was a little boy, there was a good old woman who helped my mother take care of us children. We called her Mother Maud— I believe you've heard of her?

VINCENT: Oh, yes, I've heard a lot about her.

ANTHONY: Well, she used to sit by the fire with us children and tell us   5
many childish stories. But as Pliny says that there is almost no book so bad
Silly story, that one cannot find in it something good, so I think there is almost no
serious purpose story so silly that it cannot, in one way or another, serve some serious purpose.

Among the many funny stories she told us, I particularly remember   10
one about an ass and a wolf that once went to confession to a fox. The

---

1. From *A Dialogue of Comfort Against Tribulation*, 2.14. Modernized by Mary Gottschalk, pp. 119–126 of Scepter Edition.

2. See *TMSB*, pp. 316ff.

poor ass, it seems, went to confession during Shrovetide, a day or two before Ash Wednesday, but the wolf would not go to confession till he first
saw Palm Sunday pass by, and then he found some excuse not to do it till
Good Friday.

5   Before the ass said "Bless me, Father," the fox asked him why he had
come for confession so soon, before Lent had even started. The poor beast
answered him that it was for fear of mortal sin; he did not want to lose his
share in any of those special prayers that the priest says during Shrovetide
for those who have already made their confession.

The ass's astonishing scruples

10   Then, in his confession, he mentioned this astonishing scruple that was
eating away at his conscience. He had, one morning, given his master
cause for anger. Before it was time for his master to rise, he had, with his
rude roaring, awakened him from his sleep and thus robbed him of his
rest. With that fault the fox, good and prudent confessor that he was, dealt
15 as follows. He instructed the ass to do this no more, but, instead, to lie
there quietly and go back to sleep like a good son, as it were, until his master was up and ready to go to work. Thus he could be sure not to wake
him up anymore.

    To tell you the poor ass's entire confession would be long, hard work,
20 for everything he did was mortal sin to him, the poor soul was so scrupulous. His wise and wily confessor, however, regarded all these things as the
trifles that they were. And afterwards he swore to the badger that he'd gotten so worn out from sitting so long and listening to this ass that, were it
not for the sake of appearances, he would rather have spent that whole
25 time sitting at breakfast with a good fat goose. But when it came to the
giving of the penance, the fox found that the most serious sin the ass had
confessed was gluttony, and therefore he prudently gave him as his
penance that he should never out of greediness for food either harm or
hinder any other beast in any way—that he should just eat his own food
30 and not look for more.

A wise and wily confessor imposes penance

    Now, as good Mother Maud told it to us, when the wolf went on
Good Friday to confess to Father Reynard[3] (for that was, she said, the fox's
name), this confessor shook at him his big rosary beads (which were almost as big as bowling balls) and asked him why he had come so late. "In-
35 deed, Father Reynard," he said, "I must tell you the truth, for I have come,
as you well know, to do just that. I didn't dare come any sooner for fear

Wolf and fox meet in confession

3. Reynard the Fox was one of the most popular characters in medieval times. He was known
for his wily and unscrupulous ways.

that you would have given me, for my gluttony, the penance of fasting for some part of this Lent."

Father Reynard
on fasting
"Oh, no," said Father Fox, "I'd never be that unreasonable, especially since I myself don't fast for any of it. For I may say to you, son, here in confession, just between the two of us, that it is no commandment of God, this fasting—it's only a human invention. The priests make people fast, they make them worry about the moonlight in the water, they make complete fools out of people, but I guarantee you, son, they'll make no such fool out of me. For I myself eat meat all the way through Lent. However, because I certainly wouldn't want to cause any scandal, I eat it secretly, in my bedroom, out of the sight of all those foolish brethren whose weak, scrupulous consciences would be offended by it. And so I would counsel you to do."

"Indeed, Father Fox," said the wolf, "I already do this as best I can, thank God. For when I go to my meat, I take with me no companions except such sure-footed brethren as are of my own nature. Their consciences are not weak, I can assure you; their stomachs are, in fact, as strong as mine."

"Well, then, no problem," said Father Fox.

But after that the wolf confessed to being such a great plunderer that he sometimes devoured as much meat at one time, and thus spent as much for one meal, as would well have bought enough food to last some poor man, along with his wife and children, almost a whole week. The fox prudently reproved that point in him. He preached to him a discourse on his own practice of temperance, which included, he said, never spending more than sixpence for a meal—actually, not even that much. "For when I bring home a goose," he said, "I don't get it from the butcher's shop, where folk can find them with their feathers already plucked off and can see which is the fattest and then for sixpence choose and buy the best one. No, I get it at the housewife's house, firsthand—she can, you know, afford to sell them at a somewhat cheaper price than the butcher can. True, I don't have the opportunity to see them already plucked, or to stand there and choose them in the light of day; I have to go there at night and just pick one at random, and when I get home I have to do myself all the work of plucking it. But for all that, even it turns out to be just skin and bones and not worth, I think, even fourpence, it sometimes still makes both my lunch and my supper.

Father Reynard
on temperance

"Now, then, as for your living off of plundering, I can find no fault with that. You have lived this way for so long that I don't think you could

do any different. I therefore think it would be foolish of me to forbid you
to go on plundering. To tell the truth, that would even go against my conscience. For I know perfectly well that you've got to live, and that you
know no other way to do so. It therefore stands to reason that you must
live by plundering. Still, you know, too much is too much. Moderation is a
good rule which I can see, from what you've confessed, that you have nev-
er learned to observe. Your penance, therefore, is precisely this: For the rest   *Reynard imposes*
of this year you shall never eat a meal that would cost more than sixpence,   *penance*
as nearly as your conscience can guess the price."

Thus I have related to you, as Mother Maud related them to us, the
confessions of the ass and the wolf. But what now concerns us is the consciences of them both in the actual performing of their penances.

The poor ass, right after his confession, during which he had gotten
very hungry, saw a sow lying with her pigs, all of them well covered up in
new straw. He drew near, thinking about eating some of the straw, but   *The ass performs*
then his scrupulous conscience began to torment him on that matter. His   *his penance*
penance being that he should not, out of greediness for food, do any kind
of harm to any other creature, he thought he must not eat one straw there,
lest for lack of that straw some of those pigs might happen to die from the
cold. So he stayed hungry until someone brought him food. But then,
when he was about to fall to it, he fell into yet another scruple. The
thought came into his mind that he would still be breaking his penance if
he ate any of that, too, since his spiritual father had commanded him that
he should not, in getting food for himself, hinder in any way any other
beast. If he did not eat that food, he thought, then some other beast might
happen to get it, and so by eating it he would perhaps be hindering another. So he just stood there, still fasting, until, after he told someone the reason, his spiritual father came and gave him better instruction. He then cast
off that scruple and properly fell to his food, and was a right honest ass for
many a good day after.

The wolf, on the other hand, when he came out from confession clean   *The wolf performs*
absolved of his sins, set about doing something similar to what a certain   *his penance*
nagging wife, when she came home from confession one day, told her
husband she was going to do. "Cheer up, man," she said, "for today, thanks
be to God, I made a very good confession and got thoroughly absolved, so
now I intend to stop all my old nagging and start over afresh."

VINCENT: Oh, now, uncle, is it fair to tell it that way? I myself heard
her say that, but she said it as a joke, to make her husband laugh.

ANTHONY: Actually, she did seem to mean it halfway as a joke. When she said she would stop all her nagging, there I think she was joking. But

The danger of what she said about beginning it all afresh, that, I'm afraid, her husband
beginning afresh found to be actual fact.

VINCENT: Well, I'm going to tell her what you said, I promise you.

ANTHONY: And then you'll find that I've told you the truth! But   5
whatever she did, this is what the wolf, at least, did do after he cast out in
confession all his old plundering. Hunger then prodded him to go forth

Wolf experiences and, as that nagging wife said, begin it all afresh. Yet a prodding of con-
a dilemma of science pulled and held him back, for he did not want to break his
conscience penance by taking for his meal any prey that could be sold for over six-   10
pence.

Well, it so happened that as he went prowling for some sustenance, he
came to a place where, a few days before, a man had gotten rid of two old
horses that were lean and lame. They were, in fact, so sick that there was
hardly any flesh left on them. One of them, by the time the wolf came by,   15
could hardly stand on his legs, and the other was already dead, his skin
ripped off and carried away. When the wolf suddenly came upon them, he
at first was going to feed upon them and whet his teeth on their bones.
But then he looked around and caught sight of a fair cow in a field, walking with a young calf by her side, and as soon as he saw them, his con-   20

Wolf reasons science began to trouble him about both of those two horses. He sighed
with himself and said to himself, "Alas, wicked wretch that I am, I almost broke my
penance without even realizing it. For yonder dead horse—I've never seen
a dead horse sold in the market, and so I could not guess, to save my sinful
soul, what price I should set on him. But in my conscience I set him far   25
above sixpence, and therefore I dare not meddle with him.

"Now, then, yonder live horse is in all likelihood worth a great deal of
money. For in this country, horses are expensive, especially such gentle
amblers. I see by his pace that he does not trot; in fact, he can barely shift a
foot. Therefore I may not meddle with him, since he far exceeds my six-   30
pence.

"Of cows, however, this country has plenty, while of money it has very

Wolf milks little. Considering, therefore, the abundance of cattle and the scarcity of
the system money, yonder piddling cow seems to me, in my conscience, worth no
more than fourpence, if she's worth even that much. And her calf, now,   35
cannot be worth more than half as much as she is. Since, therefore, the
cow is in my conscience worth but fourpence, my conscience cannot allow me—on pain of sin—to price her calf above twopence. And so the

both of them together don't add up to more than sixpence, and therefore I can eat them both at this one meal without breaking my penance at all." And thereupon he did so, without any scruple of conscience.

If such beasts could speak now, as Mother Maud said they could then, some of them would, I daresay, tell a tale that makes almost as much sense as this one! Actually, if it would not have lessened the impact of old Mother Maud's tale, a shorter version would have sufficed. But as preposterous as this parable is, our purpose is served by the point that it makes: namely, that the "terror of the night" of a somewhat scrupulous conscience, *Lesson on conscience* though it is troublesome and painful to the one who has it (as it was to this poor ass here), is nevertheless not as harmful as a conscience that is overly permissive, that one can adjust to suit one's own fancy, sometimes *The permissive conscience like a belt* pulling it tight and sometimes stretching it out, like a belt, to serve on every side for one's own convenience (as did here the wily wolf).

Now, the latter kind of folk, inasmuch as they manage to stay out of tribulation, have no need of comfort and thus are not our present concern. But those that are in the "terror of the night" of their own scrupulous conscience, let them be very vigilant lest the devil, for weariness of *Advice for the scrupulous* the one, draw them into the other. Let them not flee from Scylla only to be driven into Charybdis. They must do as does a ship coming into a haven in the mouth of which lie hidden rocks under the water on both sides. If they accidentally enter in among those that are on the one side, and they cannot tell how to get out, they must get a reliable, knowledge- *The need for a pilot* able pilot who can steer them away from the rocks on that side without running them into those on the other side—a pilot who can guide them along a middle course. Those stuck in the troublesome fear of their own scrupulous conscience should, I say, submit the rule of their own con- science to the counsel of some good man who can temper his advice ac- cording to the variety and nature of the scruples. Though the scrupulous might themselves be very knowledgeable, let them in this instance adopt the practice that is customary among doctors. For even the most knowl- *The example of a sick doctor* edgeable of doctors will not, when they themselves are sick or injured, put all their trust in themselves. They will, instead, send for colleagues they know to be well qualified, and they will put themselves in their hands, on the basis of several considerations. One of these is fear: they know that in their pain they may greatly exaggerate or completely mistake the import of certain symptoms, and that for the good of one's health it is sometimes better not to know any of the medical facts.

In this very town, I once knew a man who was one of the most knowledgeable, expert, and famous doctors in his field. He accomplished some of the greatest cures for other people. But one time when he himself got seriously sick, I heard his colleagues—every one of whom looked up to him and would, in their own times of sickness, have sought help from him before anyone else—I heard those same colleagues say that for the duration of his own illness, serious as it was, they wished he had known nothing at all about medicine. For he paid such great attention to every possible symptom, and so greatly feared the worst, that his fear sometimes did him much more harm than did the illness itself.

Closing words to the scrupulous   Therefore, as I say, let those afflicted with a scrupulous conscience refrain throughout that time from relying on their own judgment and follow, instead, the counsel of someone else, someone they know to be very knowledgeable and virtuous. Let them do this especially in the confessional; for there, through the grace of the sacrament, God is especially present. Let them not hesitate to quiet their minds and follow the advice they are given there. Let them for a while not think so much about the fearfulness of God's justice, but cheer up at the remembrance of his mercy. Let them persevere in prayer for grace; let them live, and faithfully keep living, in the sure hope of God's help; and then they shall find, without any doubt, that the shield of God's truth shall (as the psalmist said) so completely protect them that they shall not fear this "terror of the night" of scrupulosity, but shall have, instead, a conscience established in good quiet and rest.

More's Interrogation of
2 May 1535

More writes the following letter to Margaret Roper[1] the day after "these fathers of the Charterhouse and Master Reynolds of Sion" were condemned to death for not taking the oath recognizing Henry as Supreme Head of the Church in England. After these monks were sentenced to die, More was interrogated again, and he wrote the following letter as yet another record of the proceedings against him, and of course as a way of allaying his family's fears. A day or two afterwards, on May 4th—on the day and at the very time that the condemned monks were led past More's prison window to be hanged, drawn, and quartered—Meg was permitted to visit her father. Instead of unsettling More, however, this action strengthened him. (See Roper's account of that incident on page 54.)

2 OR 3 MAY 1535
TOWER OF LONDON

Our Lord bless you. My dearly beloved daughter.

I doubt not but by the reason of the Councilors resorting hither, in this time (in which our Lord be their comfort) these fathers of the Charterhouse and Master Reynolds of Sion that be now judged to death for trea-

1. *Selected Letters,* #63, pp. 245–48.

343

son, whose matters and causes I know not, may hap to put you in trouble and fear of mind concerning me, being here prisoner, specially because it is not unlikely but that you have heard that I was brought also before the

*More's reason
for writing*

Council here myself. I have thought it necessary to advertise[2] you of the very truth, to the end that you neither conceive more hope than the mat- 5 ter giveth, lest upon other turn it might grieve your heaviness, nor more grief and fear than the matter giveth of, on the other side. Wherefore shortly you shall understand that on Friday the last day of April in the afternoon, Master Lieutenant came in here unto me, and showed me that Master Secretary would speak with me. Whereupon I shifted my gown 10 and went out with Master Lieutenant into the gallery to him. Where I met many, some known and some unknown in the way. And in conclusion coming into the chamber where his Mastership sat with Master Attorney, Master Solicitor, Master Bedill and Master Doctor Tregonwell, I was offered to sit with them, which in no wise I would. 15

*Interview with
Master Secretary*

Whereupon Master Secretary [Cromwell] showed unto me, that he doubted not, but that I had by such friends as hither had resorted to me seen the new statutes made at the last sitting of the Parliament. Whereunto I answered: "Yes, verily. Howbeit for as much as being there, I have no conversation with any people, I thought it little need for me to bestow 20 much time upon them, and therefore I redelivered the book shortly and the effect of the statutes I never marked nor studied to put in remembrance." Then he asked me whether I had not read the first statute of them, of the King being Head of the Church. Whereunto I answered, "Yes." Then his Mastership declared unto me, that since it was now by act 25 of Parliament ordained that his Highness and his heirs be, and ever right have been, and perpetually should be Supreme Head in the earth of the Church of England under Christ, the King's pleasure was that those of his

*More's opinion
demanded by
the King*

Council there assembled should demand mine opinion, and what my mind was therein. Whereunto I answered that in good faith I had well 30 trusted that the King's Highness would never have commanded any such question to be demanded of me, considering that I ever from the beginning well and truly from time to time declared my mind unto his Highness, and since that time I had, I said, unto your Mastership Master Secretary also, both by mouth and by writing. And now I have in good faith 35 discharged my mind of all such matters, and neither will dispute King's ti-

2. advertise—*inform*

tles nor Pope's, but the King's true faithful subject I am and will be, and
daily I pray for him and for all his, and for you all that are of his honorable
Council, and for all the realm, and otherwise than thus I never intend to
meddle.

5   Whereunto Master Secretary answered that he thought this manner of
answer should not satisfy nor content the King's Highness, but that his
Grace would exact a more full answer. And his Mastership added thereunto, that the King's Highness was a prince not of rigor but of mercy and
pity, and though that he had found obstinacy at some time in any of his
10   subjects, yet when he should find them at another time conformable and
submit themselves, his Grace would show mercy. And that concerning   *The mercy of the*
myself, his Highness would be glad to see me take such conformable ways,   *King*
as I might be abroad in the world again among other men as I have been
before.

15   Whereunto I shortly (after the inward affection of my mind) answered
for a very truth, that I would never meddle in the world again, to have the   *More withdraws*
world given me. And to the remnant of the matter, I answered in effect as   *from politics*
before, showing that I had fully determined with myself neither to study
nor meddle with any matter of this world, but that my whole study should
20   be upon the passion of Christ and mine own passage out of this world.

Upon this I was commanded to go forth for a while, and after called in
again. At which time Master Secretary said unto me that though I was
prisoner and condemned to perpetual prison, yet I was not thereby discharged of mine obedience and allegiance unto the King's Highness. And
25   thereupon demanded me whether I thought that the King's Grace might
exact of me such things as are contained in the statutes and upon like pains
as he might of other men. Whereto I answered that I would not say the
contrary. Whereto he said that likewise as the King's Highness would be
gracious to them that he found conformable, so his Grace would follow
30   the course of his laws toward such as he shall find obstinate. And his Mas-   *Effects of More's*
tership said further that my demeanor in that matter was of a thing that of   *silence*
likelihood made now other men so stifle therein as they be.

Whereto I answered, that I give no man occasion to hold any one
point or the other, nor never gave any man advise or counsel therein one
35   way or other. And for conclusion I could no further go, whatsoever pain
should come thereof. I am, said I, the King's true faithful subject and daily
beadsman and pray for his Highness and all his and all the realm. I do no-   *More defends*
body harm, I say none harm, I think none harm, but wish everybody   *himself as fatihful*
                                                                           subject

good. And if this be not enough to keep a man alive, in good faith, I long
not to live. And I am dying already, and have since I came here been divers
times in the case that I thought to die within one hour, and I thank our
Lord I was never sorry for it, but rather sorry when I saw the pang past.
And therefore my poor body is at the King's pleasure; would God my 5
death might do him good.

After this Master Secretary said: "Well, you find no fault in that statute,
find you any in any of the other statutes after?" Whereto I answered, "Sir,
More's silence   whatsoever thing should seem to me other than good, in any of the
statutes or in that statute either, I would not declare what fault I found, 10
nor speak thereof." Whereunto finally his Mastership said full gently that
of anything that I had spoken, there should none advantage be taken, and
whether he said further that there be none to be taken, I am not well remembered. But he said that report should be made unto the King's High-
Final remarks   ness, and his gracious pleasure known. 15

Whereupon I was delivered again to Master Lieutenant, which was
then called in, and so was I by Master Lieutenant brought again into my
chamber, and here am I yet in such case as I was, neither better nor worse.
That which shall follow lies in the hand of God, whom I beseech to put in
King's Grace's mind that thing that may be to His high pleasure, and in 20
mine, to mind only the weal of my soul, with little regard of my body.

And you with all yours, and my wife and all my children and all our
friends both bodily and ghostly heartily well to fare. And I pray you and all
them, pray for me, and take no thought whatsoever shall happen me. For I
All for the best   verily trust in the goodness of God, seem it never so evil to this world, it 25
shall indeed in another world be for the best.

Your loving father,
Thomas More, Knight.

Thomas More's Final Interrogation

During his final interrogation, reported in this letter to Margaret Roper,[1] More was questioned by the highest-ranking members of King Henry's council: Lord Chancellor Audley, Archbishop Cranmer, Master Secretary Cromwell, Lord Wiltshire (Anne Boleyn's father), and Lord Suffolk (Henry's brother-in-law). The council revealed to More that his example was the "occasion of much grudge and harm in the realm" (p. 348); More revealed to the council that his conscience was sure and that he would not change his stance.

3 JUNE 1535
TOWER OF LONDON

Our Lord bless you and all yours.

For as much, dearly beloved daughter, as it is likely that you either have heard or shortly shall hear that the Council was here this day, and that I was before them, I have thought it necessary to send you word how the matter stands. And verily to be short I perceive little difference between this time and the last, for as far as I can see the whole purpose is either to drive me to say precisely the one way or else precisely the other.

The purpose of the interrogation

---

1. *Selected Letters*, #64, pp. 249–53.

Here sat my Lord of Canterbury, my Lord Chancellor, my Lord of Suffolk, my Lord of Wilshire and Master Secretary. And after my coming,
Master Secretary made rehearsal in what wise he had reported unto the
King's Highness, what had been said by his Grace's Council to me, and
what had been answered by me to them at mine other being before them   5
last. Which thing his Mastership rehearsed in good faith very well, as I acknowledged and confessed and heartily thanked him therefore. Where-
King demands upon he added that the King's Highness was nothing content nor satisfied
that More break with mine answer, but thought that by my demeanor I had been occasion
his silence of much grudge and harm in the realm, and that I had an obstinate mind   10
and an evil toward him and that my duty was being his subject; and so he
had sent them now in his name upon my allegiance to command me to
make a plain and terminate answer whether I thought the statute lawful or
not and that I should either acknowledge and confess it lawful that his
Highness should be Supreme Head of the Church of England or else to   15
utter plainly my malignity.

Whereto I answered that I had no malignity and therefore I could
none utter. And as to the matter, I could none other answer make than I
had before made, which answer his Mastership had there rehearsed. Very
heavy I was that the King's Highness should have any such opinion of me.   20
Howbeit if there were one that had informed his Highness many evil
things of me that were untrue, to which his Highness for the time gave
More's reply credence, I would be very sorry that he should have that opinion of me
the space of one day. Howbeit if I were sure that other should come on
the morrow by whom his Grace should know the truth of my innocence,   25
I should in the meanwhile comfort myself with the consideration of that.
And in like wise now though it be great heaviness to me that his Highness
have such opinion of me for the while, yet have I no remedy to help it, but
More's comfort only to comfort myself with this consideration that I know very well that
the time shall come, when God shall declare my truth toward his Grace   30
before him and all the world. And whereas it might haply seem to be but a
small cause of comfort because I might take harm here first in the meanwhile, I thanked God that my case was such in this matter through the
Calm of conscience clearness of mine own conscience that though I might have pain I could
More's riddle have no harm for a man may in such case lose his head and have no harm.   35
For I was very sure that I had no corrupt affection, but that I had always
from the beginning truly used myself to looking first upon God and next
upon the King, according to the lesson that his Highness taught me at my

first coming to his noble service, the most virtuous lesson that ever prince taught his servant; whose Highness to have of me such opinion is my great heaviness, but I have no means, as I said, to help it but only comfort myself in the meantime with the hope of that joyful day in which my truth to-

5   wards him shall well be known. And in this matter further I could not go nor other answer thereto I could not make.

The King's lesson on principled service

To this it was said by my Lord Chancellor and Master Secretary both that the King might by his laws compel me to make a plain answer there-to, either the one way or the other.

More threatened again

10 Whereunto I answered I would not dispute the King's authority, what his Highness might do in such case, but I said that verily under correction it seemed to me somewhat hard. For if it so were that my conscience gave me against the statutes (wherein how my mind giveth me I make no dec-laration), then I nothing doing nor nothing saying against the statute, it

15 were a very hard thing to compel me to say either precisely with it against my conscience to the loss of my soul, or precisely against it to the destruc-tion of my body.

More on conscience

To this Master Secretary said that I had before this when I was Chan-cellor examined heretics and thieves and other malefactors and gave me a

20 great praise above my deserving in that behalf. And he said that I then, as he thought and at the leastwise Bishops did use to examine heretics, whether they believed the Pope to be the head of the Church and used to compel them to make a precise answer thereto. And why should not then the King, since it is a law made here that his Grace is Head of the Church,

25 here compel men to answer precisely to the law here as they did then concerning the Pope.

Analogy of the heresy interrogation

I answered and said that I protested that I intended not to defend any part or stand in contention; but I said there was a difference between those two cases because at that time, as well here as elsewhere through the corps

30 of Christendom, the Pope's power was recognized for an undoubted thing which seems not like a thing agreed in this realm and the contrary taken for truth in other realms. Whereunto Master Secretary answered that they were as well burned for the denying of that as they be beheaded for deny-ing of this, and therefore as good reason to compel them to make precise

35 answer to the one as to the other.

More argues that the cases are different

Whereto I answered that since in this case a man is not by a law of one realm so bound in his conscience, where there is a law of the whole corps of Christendom to the contrary in matter touching belief, as he is by a law

The new law of one realm vs. the law of Christendom

of the whole corps though there hap to be made in some place a local law
to the contrary, the reasonableness or the unreasonableness in binding a
man to precise answer, standeth not in the respect or difference between
beheading and burning, but because of the difference in charge of conscience, the difference standeth between beheading and hell.   5

Much was there answered unto this both by Master Secretary and my
Lord Chancellor over long to rehearse. And in conclusion they offered me
More asked again an oath by which I should be sworn to make true answer to such things as
to swear should be asked me on the King's behalf, concerning the King's own person.   10

Whereto I answered that verily I never purposed to swear any book
oath more while I lived. Then they said that I was very obstinate if I would
refuse that, for every man doth it in the Star Chamber and everywhere. I
said that was true, but I had not so little foresight that I might well conjec-
ture what should be part of my interrogatory, and as good it was to refuse   15
it at first as afterward.

Whereto my Lord Chancellour answered that he thought I guessed
truth, for I should see them and so they were showed me and they were
but two. The first whether I had seen the statute. The other whether I believed that it were a lawful made statute or not. Whereupon I refused the   20
oath and said further by mouth, that the first I had before confessed, and
Silence to the second I would make none answer.

Which was the end of the communication and I was thereupon sent
away. In the communication before, it was said that it was marveled that I
stuck so much in my conscience while at the uttermost I was not sure   25
The surety of therein. Whereto I said that I was very sure that my own conscience, so in-
More's conscience formed as it is by such diligence as I have so long taken therein, may stand
with mine own salvation. I meddle not with the conscience of them that
think otherwise, every man *suo domino stat et cadit*.[2] I am no man's judge. It
was also said unto me that if I had rather be out of the world as in it, as I   30
had there said, why did I not speak even out plain against the statute. It ap-
On the prospect peared well I was not content to die though I had said so. Whereto I an-
of death swered as the truth is, that I have not been a man of such holy living as I
might be bold to offer myself to death, lest God for my presumption
might suffer me to fall, and therefore I put not myself forward, but draw   35
back. Howbeit if God draw me to it himself, then trust I in his great mercy, that he shall not fail to give me grace and strength.

---

2. Romans 14:4.

In conclusion Master Secretary said that he liked me this day much worse than he did the last time, for then he said he pitied me much and now he thought that I meant not well; but God and I know both that I mean well and so I pray God do by me.

5   I pray you be, you and my other friends, of good cheer whatsoever fall   *Be of good cheer* of me, and take no thought for me but pray for me as I do and shall do for you and all them.

> *Your tender loving father,[3]*
> *Thomas More, Knight.*

3. *tender loving father*—More uses this phrase in his earliest publication to refer to God the Father. See "A Prayer of Pico," *Complete Works*, vol. 1, p. 123, line 11. See *Complete Works*, p. 318, line 20 where More writes of Christ's "tender loving mind." See also *Selected Letters* pp. 223 and 226 where More uses this phrase in his letters to Margaret.

Trial and Execution

The 'Paris Newsletter's' Account,[1]

4 August 1535

On the 1st July 1535, Master Thomas More, Chancellor of England, was brought before the judges and the accusations against him read in his presence. The Chancellor and the Duke of Norfolk turned to him and said, "You, Master More, have gravely erred against the King; nevertheless we hope by his clemency that if you repent and correct your obstinate opinion in which you have so rashly persevered, you will receive pardon." He replied, "My Lords, I thank you very heartily for your good will. I pray God preserve me in my just opinion even to death. As to the accusation against me, I fear words, memory, and judgment would alike fail me to reply to such a length of articles, especially considering my present imprisonment and great infirmity." A chair was then ordered to be placed for him, and he proceeded as follows:

"As to the first article, charging me with having always maliciously opposed the King's second marriage, I will only answer that what I have said has been according to my conscience. I never wished to conceal the truth, and if I had, I should have been a traitor. For this error, if error it should be called, I have been condemned to perpetual imprisonment, which I have

1. This account is taken from *Letters and Papers, Foreign and Domestic, of the Reign of Henry VIII*, vol. 8, #996, with the adjustment noted in the last sentence.

already suffered for fifteen months, and my goods confiscated. For this rea- *More's response to*
son I will only reply to the principal charge against me, that I have in- *the principal*
curred the penalty of the Statute made in the last Parliament since I was in *charge*
prison, by refusing to the King his title of Supreme Head of the Church,
5 in proof of which you allege my reply to the Secretary and Council, that
as I was dead to the world, I did not care to think of such things, but only
of the passion of Christ. I reply that your Statute cannot condemn me to
death for such silence, for neither your Statute nor any laws in the world
punish people except for words or deed,—surely not for keeping silence."
10 To this the King's proctor replied that such silence was a certain proof of
malice intended against the Statute, especially as every faithful subject, on
being questioned about the Statute, was obliged to answer categorically
that the Statute was good and wholesome. "Surely," replied More, "if what
the common law says is true, that he who is silent seems to consent, my si-
15 lence should rather be taken as approval than contempt of your Statute. *More on his*
You say that all good subjects are obliged to reply; but I say that the faith- *conscience*
ful subject is more bound to his conscience and his soul than to anything
else in the world, provided his conscience, like mine, does not raise scandal
or sedition, and I assure you that I have never discovered what is in my
20 conscience to any person living.

"As to the second article, that I have conspired against the Statute by
writing eight letters to the bishop of Rochester, advising him to disobey
it, I could wish these letters had been read in public, but as you say the
Bishop has burnt them, I will tell you the substance of them. Some were
25 about private matters connected with our old friendship. Another was a
reply to one of his asking how I had answered in the Tower to the first examination about the Statute. I said that I had informed my conscience, and
so he also ought to do the same. I swear that this was the tenor of the letters, for which I cannot be condemned by your Statute.

30 "Touching the third article, that when I was examined by the Council,
I answered that your Statute was like a two-edged sword, for he who ap- *The two-edged*
proved it would ruin his soul, and he who contradicted it, his body; and *sword*
that the bishop of Rochester answered similarly, showing that we were
confederates, I reply that I only answered thus conditionally, that if the
35 Statute cut both ways like a two-edged sword, how could a man behave so
as not to incur either danger? I do not know how the Bishop replied, but
if he answered like me, it must have been from the agreement between us
in opinion, but not because we had ever arranged it between us. Be as-

sured I never did or said anything maliciously against the Statute, but it
may be that this has been maliciously reported to the King."

Where does the malice lie?

Then they ordered an usher to summon 12 men according to the custom of the country, and these articles were given to them that they might
judge whether More had maliciously contravened the Statute. After a   5
quarter of an hour's absence they declared him guilty of death, and sentence was pronounced by the Chancellor "selon la lettre de la nouvelle
loy."

More then spoke as follows: "Since I am condemned, and God knows
how, I wish to speak freely of your Statute, for the discharge of my con-   10
science. For the seven years that I have studied the matter, I have not read
in any approved doctor of the Church that a temporal lord could or ought
to be head of the spirituality." The Chancellor interrupting him, said,
"What, More, you wish to be considered wiser and of better conscience
than all the bishops and nobles of the realm?" To this More replied, "My   15
lord, for one bishop of your opinion I have a hundred saints of mine; and
for one parliament of yours, and God knows of what kind, I have all the
General Councils for 1,000 years, and for one kingdom I have France and
all the kingdoms of Christendom." Norfolk told him that now his malice
was clear. More replied, "What I say is necessary for discharge of my con-   20
science and satisfaction of my soul, and to this I call God to witness, the
sole Searcher of human hearts. I say further, that your Statute is ill made,
because you have sworn never to do anything against the Church, which
through all Christendom is one and undivided, and you have no authority,
without the common consent of all Christians, to make a law or Act of   25
Parliament or Council against the union of Christendom. I know well that
the reason why you have condemned me is because I have never been
willing to consent to the King's second marriage; but I hope in the divine
goodness and mercy, that as St. Paul and St. Stephen whom he persecuted
are now friends in Paradise, so we, though differing in this world, shall be   30
united in perfect charity in the other. I pray God to protect the King and
give him good counsel."

More speaks on the Act of Supremacy

An ill made law

More prays for the King

On his way to the Tower one of his daughters, named Margaret,
pushed through the archers and guards, and held him in her embrace some
time without being able to speak. Afterwards More, asking leave of the   35
archers, bade her have patience, for it was God's will, and she had long
known the secret of his heart. After going 10 or 12 steps she returned and
embraced him again, to which he said nothing, except to bid her pray to

God for his soul; and this without tears or change of color. On the Tuesday
following he was beheaded in the open space in front of the Tower. A little
before his death he asked those present to pray to God for him and he
would do the same for them [in the other world.] He then besought them   *Last words*
5   earnestly to pray to God to give the King good counsel, protesting that he
died his good servant, and God's first.[2]

---

2. The translation gives "faithful servant, but God's first" here, even though the French is "qu'il
mouroit son bon serviteur *et* de Dieu premierement" (emphasis added). See the next section of the
TMSB for the significance of these last words.

The Arrest and Supplication of Sir Thomas More, by Antoine Caron, *c.* 1591

Meg breaks through the guards to embrace her father after his trial. (See pages 62 and 344–45.)

Last Words Before
Execution, 6 July 1535

More's famous statement on the scaffold alluded to previous conversations with Henry VIII about conscience and More's service to the King.

❦

"I die the king's good servant, and God's first." (See the original French of the *Paris Newsletter* account, 4 August 1535: ". . . . qu'il mouroit son bon serviteur et de Dieu premierement."[1] In Robert Bolt's *A Man for All Seasons*, More's last words are mistakenly quoted as, "I die the king's good servant, but God's first.")

Here are More's three accounts of the conversations about conscience which he had with King Henry and to which he alluded in that last, brief statement, "I die the king's good servant, and God's first":

❦

I had always, from the beginning [of my service to Henry VIII, in 1518], truly used myself to looking first upon God and next upon the King, according to the lesson that his Highness taught me at my first com-

---

1. For the original French text, see E. V. Hitchcock's edition of Nicholas Harpsfield's *Life and Death of Sir Thomas More* (Oxford UP, 1932), pp. 258–66.

357

ing to his noble service, the most virtuous lesson that ever prince taught
his servant.[2]

>   —"Letter to Margaret," 3 June 1535

His Highness . . . made me [in 1529], as you well know, his Chancellor
of this realm. Soon after, his Grace asked me yet again to look and consid-   5
er his great matter, and well and indifferently to ponder such things as I
should find. . . . And nevertheless he graciously declared unto me that he
would in no wise that I should do or say anything except that I should
perceive my own conscience should serve me, and that I should first look
unto God and after God unto him, which most gracious words was the   10
first lesson also that ever his Grace gave me at my first coming into his noble service.[3]

>   —"Letter to Cromwell," 5 March 1534

For other commandment had I never of his Grace in good faith, saving
that this knot his Highness added thereto that I should therein look first
unto God and after God unto him, which word was also the first that his   15
Grace gave me what time I came first into his noble service and neither a
more indifferent commandment nor a more gracious lesson could there in
my mind never King give counselor or any other servant.[4]

>   —"Letter to Wilson," 1534

---

2. *Selected Letters*, #64, pp. 250–51. See *TMSB*, pp. 348–49.
3. *Selected Letters*, #53, p. 209.
4. *Selected Letters*, #59, p. 229.

Appendices

Chronology of Thomas More's Life

1477[1], Feb 7	Born in London to John and Agnes More
c. 1484–1489	Attends St. Anthony's School, London (7–12)[2]
c. 1489–1491	Page for Archbishop and Chancellor Morton (12–14)
c. 1491–1493	Student at Oxford (14–16)
c. 1493–1495	Pre-law student, New Inn, London (16–18)
1496–c. 1501	Law student, Lincoln's Inn; called to bar (18–23)
1499	Meets Erasmus for the first time (22)
c. 1501–1504	Frequents Charterhouse (Carthusians) (24–27)
c. 1501	Lectures on St. Augustine's *City of God;* begins Greek (24)
c. 1503–1506	Reader at Furnivall's Inn (26–29)
1504	Elected to Parliament (27)
1505	Marries Jane Colt; Margaret born (28)
1506	Studies intensely; visits Coventry; Elizabeth born (29)
1507	Financial secretary of Lincoln's Inn; Cecily born (30)
c. 1508	Visits universities at Paris and Louvain (31)
1509	Member of Mercers' Guild; John born; Henry VIII crowned (32)
1510	Elected to Parliament (33)
1510–1518	Undersheriff of London (33–41)

1. Debate continues on whether More was born in 1477 or 1478. For some of the reasons favoring 1477, see Marc'hadour's article of 1977.

2. More's age at the time.

1511	After Jane's death, marries Alice Middleton; Autumn Reader at Lincoln's Inn (34)
1512	Governor and treasurer of Lincoln's Inn (35)
1513	Henry VIII leads an army against France; to Henry, Erasmus dedicates his translation of Plutarch's essay on flattery (36)
1514	Elected to Doctors' Common; serves on sewers commission (37)
1515	Embassy to Bruges and Antwerp for commerical treaties; Lenten Reader at Lincoln's Inn; refuses royal pension (38)
1516	Continues to study history and political philosophy (39)
1517	Embassy to Calais; counsel to pope's ambassador in England; Evil May Day; Wolsey's Treaty of Universal Peace; Luther's "Ninety-five Theses" (40)
1518	Joins King's service; Master of Requests (41)
1520	Field of Cloth of Gold; peace with France (43)
1521	Knighted; undertreasurer; ambassador to Bruges and Calais; cautions Henry not to exaggerate the pope's secular authority; Margaret marries Roper; Buckingham executed (44)
1522	Gives public oration welcoming Emperor Charles V; serves as Henry's secretary and cautions against war; war with France resumed (45)
1523	Speaker of the House of Commons, proposes free speech; leases Crosby Hall; truce with France; moves to Chelsea (46)
1524	High Steward, Oxford; war with France resumes: "If my head could win [the King] a castle in France, . . . it would not fail to go" (See Roper's *Life*, p. 27) (47)
1525	High Steward, Cambridge; chancellor of Lancaster; Peasants' Revolt; peace treaty with France; Cecily marries Heron; Elizabeth marries Dauncey (48)
1526	Appointed to royal council's subcommittee of four; urges Erasmus to complete writings against Luther; Turks invade Hungary; Tyndale's New Testament secretly distributed (49)
1527	Accompanies Wolsey to France; sack of Rome; Henry consults More about divorce; More's daughters' dispute before Henry; Holbein paints the More family (50)
1528	Tunstall asks More to defend Church in English; Margaret almost dies; More chosen as alternate Master of Revels, Lincoln's Inn; More's three great wishes (see Roper's *Life*, p. 28) (51)
1529	Delegate, Peace of Cambrai; fire at Chelsea; appointed Lord Chancellor; addresses Parliament; John marries Ann Cresacre (52)
1530	More almost dismissed for his opposition to Henry; Cranmer completes his defense of caesaropapism (53)
1531	Henry declared by clergy Supreme Head of the Church in England, "as far as Christ's law allows"; reports universities' approval of royal divorce (March 30) (54)

1532	Counters Cromwell's and St. German's attacks on the clergy; Henry enraged by undiplomatic clerics; Submission of Clergy (May 15); More resigns his office (May 16) (55)
1533	Restraint of Appeals to Rome; England declared an empire (April); Cranmer authorizes royal divorce (May); Anne Boleyn's coronation (June 1); Pope Clement VII condemns the divorce (July); to defend his reputation, More writes to Erasmus (56)
1534	Henry asks for More's indictment (Feb. 21), but the House of Lords refuses three times; More questioned by royal commission (March), interrogated at Lambeth Palace (Apr. 13), and finally imprisoned (illegally) for refusal to take Cromwell's oath regarding the Act of Succession (Apr. 17); Chancellor Audley sends a warning note to More (August) (57)
1535	Margaret visits while monks are led to execution (May 4); More interrogated on May 7, June 3, and June 14; Richard Rich removes writing materials (June 12); More's trial (July 1) and execution (July 6) (58)

Chronology of
Thomas More's Writings

c. 1496–1504	English Poems
1499–1535	Correspondence (Latin and English)
c. 1500	Latin verses to Holt's *Lac Puerorum*
c. 1504	"Letter to John Colet"
1505–1506	Translations of Lucian (published 1506)
1496–1516	Latin Poems (published with 1518 editions of *Utopia*)
1509	"Coronation Ode"
c. 1510	*The Life of John Picus*
1513	Epigrams on Brixius
c. 1513	*The History of King Richard III* (published 1557)
1515	"Letter to Dorp"
1516	*Utopia*
1517–1522	Poem and letters to his children; Letter to Gonell
1518–1520	Letters to Oxford (1518), to a Monk, to Lee (1519), and to Brixius (1520)
c. 1522	*The Four Last Things*
1523	*Responsio ad Lutherum*
1526	"Letter to Bugenhagen" (published 1568)
June 1529	*A Dialogue Concerning Heresies*
Sept 1529	*Supplication of Souls*
May 1531	*A Dialogue Concerning Heresies*, 2nd edition

March 1532	*Confutation of Tyndale's Answer I–III*
Dec 1532	"Letter against Frith" (published December 1533)
Spring 1533	*Confutation of Tyndale IV–VIII*
April 1533	*The Apology of Sir Thomas More*
Oct 1533	*The Debellation of Salem and Bizance*
Dec 1533	*The Answer to a Poisoned Book*
1534	*A Dialogue of Comfort against Tribulation; A Treatise upon the Passion; A Treatise to Receive the Blessed Body; A Dialogue on Conscience*
1534–1535	"Imploring Divine Help against Temptation"; "A Godly Instruction [on How to Treat Those Who Wrong Us]"; "A Godly Meditation [on Detachment]"
1535	*De Tristitia Christi [The Sadness of Christ]* (published 1565)
July 1535	"A Devout Prayer [before Dying]"

Amiens: In 1527 More accompanied Wolsey to complete peace negotiations with France.

Antwerp: More visited this important commercial center in 1515, during his embassy to Bruges. His *Utopia* opens outside its beautiful church.

Barnborough Hall, Yorkshire: As a baby, Ann Cresacre became heir to this estate after her parents died in 1512. More became her guardian and assumed responsibility for her lands until she became of age.

Bruges: More made embassies to this city in 1515 and 1521, primarily to negotiate the trade of wool and cloth between England and Flanders. He was appointed by the King, but was probably nominated by the London merchants. In 1520 he was in the King's retinue for the peace-keeping mission at the Field of Cloth of Gold.

Calais: More went to Calais in 1517 to negotiate with French merchants, and again in 1521 to help Wolsey in peace negotiations between Emperor Charles V and King Francis I.

Cambrai: More considered the 1529 Peace of Cambrai treaty to be the most important achievement of his diplomatic career. It is the only public event he mentions in his epitaph. He rejoiced that peace had finally been restored to Christendom.

Cambridge: More served as High Steward of Cambridge. His friend Bishop John Fisher was its chancellor.

Canterbury: The shrine of St. Thomas Becket was the most popular place of pilgrimage in England. More considered it significant that the date set for his own execution was the eve of Becket's feast. Henry VIII eventually outlawed pilgrimages to this spot. More's head is buried in St. Dunstan's Church in Canterbury.

Coventry: More's sister Elizabeth Rastell lived in this city. On a visit in or about 1506, he met the ignorant friar whom he describes in his "Letter to Dorp." Elizabeth's most famous great grandson would be John Donne.

Lancaster, Duchy of: From 1525 to 1529, More served as chancellor of this territory, which encompassed some forty thousand people.

Louvain: More visited Louvain's university around 1508.

Oxford: More attended Oxford for two years and later served as High Steward. In 1518 he wrote an official letter in defense of Greek studies there.

Paris: More visited the University of Paris around 1508.

Rochester: Here More visited his longtime friend Bishop John Fisher.

Southampton: In 1517 More served as counsel and interpreter for the pope's ambassador in a case involving forfeiture of a papal ship that was docked at Southampton.

Woodstock: More often accompanied Henry's royal retinue to Woodstock, where the King loved to hunt. More was here when news of the great fire at Chelsea reached him, on September 3, 1529.

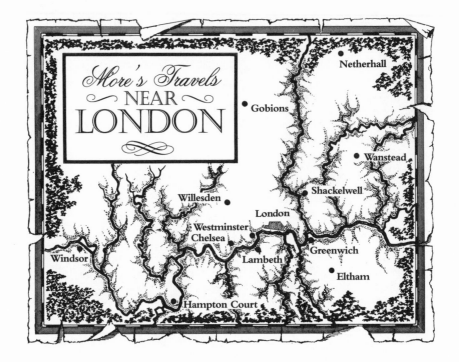

Chelsea: More built his family home on a thiry-four-acre farm, two miles from London. This
location gave him easy access downstream to Westminster Hall, where he did much of
his business, and upstream to Hampton Court.

Eltham, Kent: More surprised Erasmus in 1499 by having him come along for an unan-
nounced visit to Prince Henry at the royal palace. The Ropers had their family estate
here.

Gobions: More's father owned this country estate in North Mimms, Hertfordshire.

Greenwich: The court at Greenwich was one of King Henry's favorites; it was just east of
London, on the Thames.

Hampton Court: Archbishop and Chancellor Wolsey built this magnificent palace in 1514,
and Henry confiscated it in 1529 upon Wolsey's fall. More was often in this palace to do
business with both Wolsey and Henry.

Lambeth Palace: At twelve, More served as page to Archbishop and Chancellor Morton. It
was probably here, at a feast in November 1503, that More delivered the comic poem he
is thought to have written in honor of his father, who had become a sergeant-at-law, and
his maternal grandfather, who had been elected sheriff of London. Later, More would
come to this place to see William Warham, Archbishop of Canterbury and former Lord
Chancellor of England. Just prior to his imprisonment, More was interrogated in this
palace by Cranmer, Cromwell, Audley, and Benson.

Netherhall: More's wife Jane Colt, one of eighteen children, lived on this country estate in
Essex.

Shackelwell, Hackney: More became responsible for this magnificent manor and all of its
lands when he became the guardian of Giles Heron, in 1523. After More's death, Heron

was accused by a disgruntled former tenant of having "mumble[d] certain words touching the King" in the parlor of Shackelwell; he was imprisoned in 1539 and executed in 1540.

Wanstead: This was another estate owned by Giles Heron, a property that Richard Rich acquired after Heron's execution.

Westminster: Here the English Parliament began, and here More practiced law. He served in the Parliament of 1504, which met in the Chapter House of Westminster Abbey. He met with Wolsey frequently at Whitehall; here, during that famous confrontation of 1523, he tactfully broke off the Cardinal's "displeasant talk" by complimenting him on his beautiful gallery. More was tried and found guilty in Westminster Hall.

Willesden: Giles Alington, husband of Alice (More's stepdaugher), owned an estate near this town. In 1525 a double wedding took place in Alington's private chapel: Elizabeth More married William Dauncey, and Cecily More married Giles Heron.

Willesden, St. Mary: This shrine dates back to the tenth century. More walked the seven miles to make his pilgrimage there.

Windsor: At this castle, built as a fortress by William the Conqueror, More served at Henry's court.

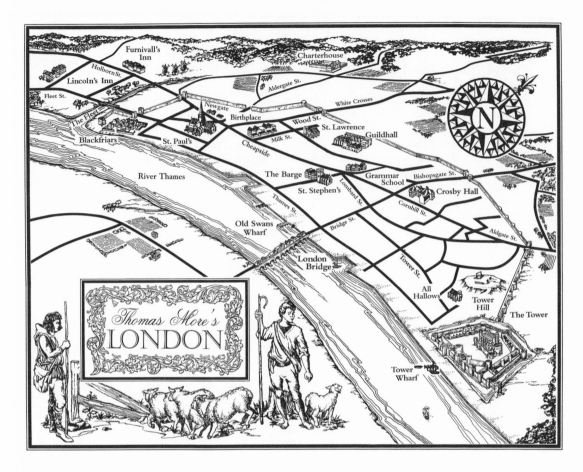

All Hallows Church: More regularly made pilgrimages, always on foot, in and around London. He visited the famous Marian shrine at this church, which was near the Tower.

The Barge: More's first home, where all his children were born, was called "The Barge." This was in an attractive part of London, on Bucklersbury Street, and was aromatic because of the many spice dealers in the area.

Blackfriars: When Parliament met here in 1523, More served as Speaker of the House of Commons. In his opening address, More argued for freedom of speech—the first such appeal ever recorded.

Charterhouse: While studying law, More attached himself to this strict Carthusian monastery to receive spiritual formation. It was Henry II who originally invited the Carthusians to come into England—as part of his reparation for the murder of Thomas Becket in 1170.

Crosby Hall: More bought the lease of this magnificent home in 1523 (Richard III had been a previous resident), but shortly afterwards sold it to his good friend Antonio Bonvisi. In 1910 the great hall of this estate was moved to Chelsea.

Furnivall's Inn: More taught law at this school from 1503 to 1506.

Guildhall: More served as under-sheriff and handled a great deal of city business in this grand municipal center.

Lincoln's Inn: Both Thomas and his father studied law at this inn of court and remained active there throughout their careers.

London Bridge: Both Thomas and his father served on commissions charged with the maintenance of London Bridge. The head of Thomas More was displayed here just after his execution.

Milk Street: More's birth place. Milk Street was a prosperous residential area off the busy commercial district of the city. Sir John More lived here for most of his life; the exact location of his home is no longer known.

Old Swan's Wharf: After his trial at Westminster on July 1, 1535, More landed at this wharf and then walked along lower Thames Street to the Tower.

St. Anthony's School: The school More attended as a child. Just north of Threadneedle Street, St. Anthony's was among the best grammar schools in London.

St. Lawrence Jewry, Church of: This was the Mores' parish church, where young Thomas lectured on Augustine's *City of God*.

St. Paul's Cathedral: More's good friend and spiritual advisor Fr. John Colet was dean of this cathedral.

St. Stephen's, Walbrook: While More lived at The Barge, this was his parish church. It was here that he buried Jane, that he married Alice, and that Margaret married William Roper.

The Tower: More was imprisoned in the Bell Tower of this fortress for more than a year before his public execution on Tower Hill. His body is buried in the Chapel of St. Peter ad Vincula.

Tower Wharf: Margaret's last meeting with her father occurred at this spot.

Study Outline—Roper's 'Life of Sir Thomas More'

Personal Life

Henry's "Great Matter"

More as Lord Chancellor

In Retirement

Imprisonment

Trial and Execution

Works Cited

Ackroyd, Peter. *Thomas More.* London: Chatto & Windus, 1998.

Acton, Lord John. *Essays on Freedom and Power by Lord Acton.* Ed. Gertrude Himmelfarb. Glencoe, IL: The Free P, 1948.

Adams, Robert P. *The Better Part of Valor: More, Erasmus, Colet, and Vives on Humanism, War, and Peace,* Seattle: U of Washington P, 1962.

Allen, Ward. "Speculations on St. Thomas More's Use of Hesychius." *Philological Quarterly* 46.2 (April 1967): 156–66.

Aquinas, Thomas. *Summa Theologica.* Trans. Fathers of the English Dominican Province. Westminster, MD: Christian Classics, 1981.

Aristotle. *Basic Works of Aristotle.* Trans. W. D. Ross. Ed. Richard McKeon. New York: Random House, 1941.

Augustine. *Letters.* Volumes 18 and 30 of *The Fathers of the Church.* Trans. Sr. Wilfrid Parsons. New York, 1953, 1955.

Bolt, Robert. *A Man for All Seasons: A Play in Two Acts.* New York: Vintage Books, 1990.

Boyle, Marjorie O'Rourke. *Rhetoric and Reform: Erasmus' Civil Dispute with Luther.* Cambridge, MA: Harvard UP, 1983.

Bradshaw, Brendan. "The Christian Humanism of Erasmus." *Journal of Theological Studies.* N.S. 33.2 (Oct. 1982): 411–447.

———. "The Controversial Sir Thomas More." *Journal of Ecclesiastical History* 36 (1985): 535–569.

Brooke, C. F. Tucker (ed). *The Shakespeare Apocrypha.* Oxford: Oxford UP, 1908.

Brooke, Xanthe and David Combie. *Henry VIII Revealed: Holbein's Portrait and Its Legacy.* London: Paul Holberton Publishing, 2003.

Butler, John R. *The Quest for Becket's Bones: The Mystery of the Relics of St. Thomas Becket of Canterbury.* New Haven, CT: Yale UP, 1995.

Campbell, Lorne, Margaret Mann Phillips, Hubertus Schulte Herbrüggen, and J. B. Trapp. "Quentin Matsys, Desiderius Erasmus, Pieter Gillis and Thomas More." *The Burlington Magazine,* Nov. 1978: 716–25.

Candido, Joseph and Charles Forker. "Wit, Wisdom, and Theatricality in *The Book of Sir Thomas More,*" *Shakespeare Studies* 13 (1980), 85–86.

Chambers, R. W. *The Place of St. Thomas More in English Literature and History.* New York: Haskell House, 1964.

Derrett, J. Duncan M. "The Trial of Sir Thomas More." *English Historical Review* 79 (1964): 449–77.

———. "Two Dicta of More's." *Moreana,* no. 8 (November 1965): 67–72.

Donne, John. *Biathanotos.* Ed. Ernest Sullivan. U of Delaware P and Toronto Associated P, 1984.

Elton, G. R. *Studies in Tudor and Stuart Politics and Government.* Vols. 1:129–72, 3:344–55, 4:144–160. Campridge UP, 1974–92.

Erasmus, Desiderius. *Collected Works of Erasmus.* [*CWE*]. Toronto: University of Toronto Press, 1974–[still in progress].

———. *Erasmi epistolae* [EE]. Ed. P. S. Allen et al. 12 vols. Oxford UP, 1906–55.

———. "Marriage." In *Colloquies,* vol. 39 of *CWE.* Trans. Craig R. Thompson. Toronto: University of Toronto Press, 1997.

Fox, Alistair. "Humanism." *Reassessing the Henrician Age: Humanism, Politics and Reform 1500–1550*: 9–73. Ed. Alistair Fox and John Guy. Oxford: Basil Blackwell, 1986.

———. "Thomas More's Controversial Writings and His View of the Renaissance." *Parergon* 11 (1975): 41–48.

———. "Thomas More's *Dialogue* and the *Book of the Tales of Caunterbury*: 'Good Mother Wit' and Creative Imitation." *Familiar Colloquy: Essays Presented to Arthur Edward Barker*: 15–24. Ed. Patricia Bruckmann. Canada: Oberon P, 1978.

Grace, Damian. "Subjects or Citizens? *Populi* and *cives* in More's *Epigrammata.*" *Moreana* no. 97 (March 1988): 133–36.

Greg, W. W. *The Book of Sir Thomas More.* Malone Society Reprints. Oxford, Eng: Oxford UP, 1911.

Guy, John. *Thomas More.* New York: Oxford UP, 2000.

———. *Tudor England.* Oxford UP, 1988.

Hall, Edward. *Lives of the Kings: Henry VIII.* Vol. 1. London: T. C. and E. C. Jack, 1904.

Hankins, James. "Humanism and the Origins of Modern Political Thought." *The Cambridge Companion to Renaissance Humanism*: 118–141. Ed. Jill Kraye. Cambridge UP, 1996.

Harpsfield, Nicholas, and William Roper. *Lives of Saint Thomas More.* Ed. E. E. Reynolds. New York: Everyman's Library, 1963.

———. *The Life and Death of Sir Thomas Moore, Knight.* Ed. Elsie V. Hitchcock. London: Oxford UP, 1932.

Hasting, Margaret. "Sir Thomas More: Maker of English Law?" In *Essential Articles for the Study of Thomas More*: 104–118. Ed. Germain Marc'hadour and Richard S. Sylvester. Hamden, CN: Archon Books, 1977.

Hergrüggen, H. Schulte. "Seven New Letters from Thomas More." *Moreana,* no. 103 (1990): 49–66.

Heywood, John. *The Plays of John Heywood.* Ed. Richard Axton and Peter Happe. (Cambridge, UK: D.S. Brewer, 1991).

Hillerbrand, Hans J., ed. *Erasmus and His Age: Selected Letters.* New York: Harper & Row, 1970.

Holinshed, Raphael. *Chronicles.* In six volumes. London, 1807.

Horace. *Odes.* Trans. David Ferry. New York: Farrar, Straus, and Giroux, 1997.

———. *The Odes and Epodes.* Trans. C. E. Bennett. Cambridge: Harvard UP, 1914.

Howard-Hill, T.H. (ed.) *Shakespeare and Sir Thomas More: Essays on the Play and Its Shakespearean Interest.* New York: Cambridge UP, 1989.

Jonson, Ben. *Ben Jonson.* 11 vol. Ed. C. H. Herford and Percy Simpson. Oxford: Clarenden P, 1925.

Kinney, Daniel. "Christian Wisdom and Secular Learning." *In Defence of Humanism: Letter to Martin Dorp, Letter to the University of Oxford, Letter to Edward Lee, Letter to a Monk, with a New Text and Translation of Historia Richardi Tertii*. Vol. 15 of *The Yale Edition of the Complete Works of St. Thomas More*: xlvi–lxxi. Ed. Daniel Kinney. New Haven: Yale UP, 1986.

Kristeller, Paul O. "Thomas More as a Renaissance Humanist." *Moreana,* no 65 (June 1980): 5–22.

Letters and Papers, Foreign and Domestic, of the Reign of Henry VIII. Ed. J. S. Brewer, James Gairdner, and R. H. Brodie. 21 vols. London: Longmans and Co., 1862–1932.

Lewi, Angela. *The Thomas More Family Group.* London: Her Majesty's Stationery Office, 1974.

Lewis, Lesley. *The Thomas More Family Group Portraits After Holbein.* Leominster, Eng.: Gracewing, 1998.

Logan, George M. "*Utopia* and Renaissance Humanism." *The Meaning of More's* Utopia: 254–70. Princeton UP, 1983.

Marc'hadour, Germain. "Basil the Great and Thomas More." *Moreana* no. 111–112 (Nov. 1992): 43–54.

———. "Thomas More's Birth: 1477 or 1478?" *Moreana* no. 53 (March 1977): 5–10.

———. "Thomas More in Emulation and Defense of Erasmus." *Erasmus of Rotterdam: The Man and the Scholar*. 203–14. Ed J. S. Weiland and W. Frijhoff. Leiden: E. J. Brill, 1988.

Marius, Richard. "Thomas More and the Renaissance." *Thomas More: A Biography*: 64–78. NY: Alfred A. Knopf, 1984.

Martz, Louis L. *Thomas More: The Search for the Inner Man.* New Haven, CN: Yale UP, 1990.

McConica, James. "The Patrimony of Thomas More." *History and Imagination: Essays in Honor of H. R. Trevor-Roper.* 56–71. Ed. Hugh Lloyd-Jones, Valerie Pearl, and Blair Worden. New York: Holmes & Meier Publishers, 1981.

McCutcheon, Elizabeth. "Margaret More Roper." *Women Writers of the Renaissance and Reformation*: 449–400. Ed. Katharina M. Wilson. Athens & London: U of Georgia P, 1987.

———. "Sir Thomas More." *Dictionary of Literary Biography,* vol. 136. Detroit, MI: Gale Research Co., 1994: 235–54.

———. "Thomas More." *Tudor England: An Encyclopedia.* Garland, 2001: 496–99.

McMillin, Scott. *The Book of Sir Thomas More*: A Theatrical View," *Modern Philology* 68 (1970).

Miller, Clarence H. "Thomas More's Letters to Frans Van Cranevelt." *Moreana,* no. 117 (1994): 3–66.

Moorman, F. W. "Plays of Uncertain Authorship Attributed to Shakespeare." *The Cambridge History of English Literature,* vol. 5: 236–258. Ed. A. P. Waller and Sir A. W. Ward. Cambridge UP, 1950.

More, Thomas. *The Correspondence of Sir Thomas More.* Ed. Elizabeth F. Rogers. Princeton, NJ: Princeton UP, 1947.

———. *A Dialogue of Comfort Against Tribulation.* Rendered in modern English by Mary Gottschalk. Princeton, NJ: Scepter Publishers, 1998.

———. *A Dialogue on Conscience*. In *The Four Last Things, The Supplication of Souls, A Dialogue on Conscience*. Rendered in modern English by Mary Gottschalk. Princeton, NJ: Scepter Publishers, 2002.

———. *The Four Last Things, The Supplication of Souls, A Dialogue on Conscience*. Modernized by Mary Gottschalk. Princeton, NJ: Scepter Publishers, 2002.

———. "Letter to Antonio Bonvisi." Trans. Elizabeth McCutcheon. *Moreana,* nos. 71–72 (Nov. 1981): 55–6.

———. *Selected Letters.* Trans. Elizabeth F. Rogers. New Haven, CN: Yale UP, 1961.

————. *Thomas More's Prayer Book*. Ed. Louis L. Martz and Richard S. Sylvester. New Haven, CN:Yale UP, 1969.

————. [CW]. *The Yale Edition of the Complete Works of St. Thomas More*. New Haven, CN: Yale UP, 1963–1997.

CW 1   *English Poems, Life of Pico, The Last Things*. Ed. Anthony S. G. Edwards, Katherine Gardiner Rogers, and Clarence H. Miller, 1997.

CW 2   *The History of King Richard III*. Ed. Richard S. Sylvester. 1963.

CW 3.1 *Translations of Lucian*. Ed. Craig R. Thompson. 1974.

CW 3.2 *The Latin Poems*. Ed. Clarence H. Miller, Leicester Bradner, Charles A. Lynch, and Revilo P. Oliver. 1984.

CW 4   *Utopia*. Ed. Edward Surtz and J. H. Hexter. 1965.

CW 5   *Responsio ad Lutherum* Ed. John M. Headley. 1969.

CW 6   *A Dialogue Concerning Heresies*. Ed. Thomas Lawler, Germain Marc'hadour, and Richard C. Marius. 1981.

CW 7   *Letter to Bugenhagen, Supplication of Souls, Letter against Frith*. Ed. Frank Manley, Germain Marc'hadour, Richard C. Marius, and Clarence H. Miller. 1990.

CW 8   *The Confutation of Tyndale's Answer*. Ed. Louis A. Schuster, Richard C. Marius, James P. Lusardi, and Richard J. Schoeck. 1973.

CW 9   *The Apology of Sir Thomas More*. Ed. J. B. Trapp. 1979.

CW 10   *The Debellation of Salem and Bizance*. Ed. John Guy, Ralph Keen, Clarence H. Miller, and Ruth McGugan. 1987.

CW 11   *The Answer to a Poisoned Book*. Ed. Stephen M. Foley and Clarence H. Miller. 1985.

CW 12   *A Dialogue of Comfort against Tribulation*. Ed. Louis L. Martz and Frank Manley. 1976.

CW 13   *A Treatise upon the Passion*. Ed. Garry E. Haupt. 1976.

CW 14   *De Tristitia Christi*. Ed. Clarence H. Miller. 1976.

CW 15   *In Defense of Humanism*. Ed. Daniel Kinney. 1986.

Munday, Anthony, and others. *Sir Thomas More*. Ed. Vittorio Gabrieli and Giorgio Melchiori. New York: Manchester UP, 1990.

————. *Sir Thomas More*. Ed. John Shirley. Canterbury: H. J. Goulden, Ltd. [1939].

Nauert, Charles G. *Humanism and the Culture of Renaissance Europe*. Cambridge UP, 1995.

Neil, J. E. "The Commons' Privilege of Free Speech in Parliament." *Historical Studies of the English Parliament*. Vol. 2, 1399–1603: 147–176. Ed. E. B. Fryde and Edward Miller. Cambridge UP, 1970.

Nelson, William. "Thomas More, Grammarian and Orator." *PMLA* 58 (1943): 337–52.

Nichols, Francis M. (Trans.) *The Epistles of Erasmus*, Vol. 1. NY: Russell & Russell, 1962.

Norrington, Ruth. *The Household of Sir Thomas More*. Buckinghamshire, Eng: The Kylin Press, 1985.

Plato. *Republic*. Trans. Benjamin Jowett. New York, 1901.

Plutarch. *Essays*. Trans. Robert Waterfield. London: Penguin Books, 1992.

————. *Moralia*. Vol. 6. Trans. W. C. Helmbold. Ed. T. E. Page, E. Cappas, W. H. D. Rouse, A. Post, and E. H. Warmington. Cambridge, MA: Harvard UP, 1957.

Pole, Reginald. *Pole's Defense of the Unity of the Church*. Westminster, MD: The Newman P, 1965.

Reynolds, E. E. *The Trial of St. Thomas More*. New York: P. J. Kennedy & Sons, 1964.

Roper, William, and Nicholas Harpsfield. *Lives of Saint Thomas More*. Ed. E. E. Reynolds. New York: Everyman's Library, 1963.

Seneca. *Moral and Political Essays.* Ed. and trans. John M. Cooper and J. F. Procopé. Cambridge: Cambridge UP, 1995.

———. *Hippolyta.* Trans. Frank Miller. Loeb Classical Library (*Seneca*, vol. 8). Cambridge, Mass.: Harvard UP, 1979.

———. *Oedipus.* Trans. Frank Miller. Loeb Classical Library (*Seneca*, vol. 8). Cambridge, Mass.: Harvard UP, 1979.

Shakespeare, William. *The Norton Shakespeare.* Ed. Walter Cohen, Stephen Greenblatt, Jean E. Howard, and Katharine Eisaman Maus. New York: W. W. Norton, 1997.

———. *The Oxford Shakespeare* (2nd edition). Ed, John Jowet, William Montgomery, Gary Taylor, and Stanley Wells. New York: Oxford UP, 1999.

———. *The Riverside Shakespeare* (2nd edition). Ed. Herschel Baker, G. Blakemore Evans, and J. J. M. Tobin. Boston: Houghton Mifflin Co., 1997.

Skinner, Quentin. *Liberty Before Liberalism.* Cambridge UP, 1998.

———. "Political Philosophy." *Cambridge History of Renaissance Philosophy:* 412–52. Ed. Charles Schmitt and Quentin Skinner. Cambridge UP, 1988.

———. "*Utopia* and the Critique of Humanism" in *The Foundations of Modern Political Thought*, vol. 1: 255–262. London: Cambridge UP, 1978.

Stapleton, Thomas. *The Life of Sir Thomas More.* New York: Fordham UP, 1966.

Sylvester, Richard S. "Thomas More: Humanist in Action." *Medieval and Renaissance Studies,* no. 1: 125–136. Ed. O. B. Hardison, Jr. Chapel Hill: U of North Carolina P, 1966. Reprinted in *Essential Articles for the Study of Thomas More:* 462–69. Hamden, CT: Archon Books, 1977.

Tyndale, William. *An Answere unto Sir Thomas Mores Dialoge.* Ed. Anne M. O'Donnell and Jared Wicks. Washington, DC: Catholic U of America P 2000.

Wegemer, Gerard. "The Civic Humanism of Thomas More: Why Law Has Prominence over Rhetoric." *Ben Jonson Journal* 7 (2000): 187–198.

———. *Thomas More: A Portrait of Courage.* Princeton, NJ: Scepter Publishers, 1995.

———. *Thomas More on Statesmanship.* Washington, DC: Catholic U of America P, 1996.

Index

Becket, St. Thomas *(cont.)*
1162; Archbishop of Canterbury, 1162–1170), 63, 366–67, 370
Bede, St., 209
Benson, William (Abbot of Westminster), 311, 314–15
Bernard, St., 330
Betts, George, 74–77; in *Sir Thomas More*, 72, 87, 89, 92–94, 104
Betts, Ralph, the clown, in *Sir Thomas More*, 72, 87–90, 92, 97, 101–3
Biathanotos, 68
Bible. *See* individual books of Bible
Blackfriars, 33, 228, 370
Boethius, xiv, 15(ill), 202, 324; pride and, 215–16; *Consolation of Philosophy,* xiv, 15(ill), 202n3, 324n11
Boleyn, Anne (Queen of England, 1533–36), 32, 33, 40, 51; coronation of, 43–44, 305; fall of, 52
Boleyn, Thomas (Earl of Wiltshire; father of Anne Boleyn), 46, 46n66, 347, 348
Bolt, Robert, 254; *A Man for All Seasons*, xiii, xxx, 357
Boniface, 284
Bonvisi, Antonio: Henry VIII's disfavor towards, 182; TM's friendship with, xviii, 182–84; TM's imprisonment and, 182; TM's letter to, 182–84
The Book of Fortune (CW 1), 256
Boyle, Marjarie O'Rourke, xxviiin89,
Bradshaw, Brandon, xvin21, xxx n98
Brandon, Charles (Duke of Suffolk; Henry VIII's brother–in–law), 311n4; TM's interrogation and, 347, 348
Brooke, C. F. Tucker, 67
Brooke, Xanthe, 228
Bucklersbury (The Barge), TM's home at, 3, 20, 370
BudÈ, Guillaume, TM's letter to, 221–25
Bruges, 362, 366

Caesar, 185, 239
Cambrai, xxv, 34, 307–8, 362, 366
Cambrai, Peace of, xxv, 307–8
Cambridge University, xvi, 27–28, 40, 210
Campeggio, Cardinal Lorenzo, 33
Candido, Joseph, 67–68
candor: criticism vs., 191–94; effective, 192; friendship and, 189–94; self-love and, 189
Canterbury, Archbishops of. *See* Cranmer, Thomas; Morton, John; Warham, William
Caron, Antoine, 356(ill)

Carthusian Order. *See* Charterhouse
Castor, 160
Catesby, the steward, in *Sir Thomas More*, 72, 133, 147–48
Catholic Church: authority of, xxvii; divine right of kings and, xviii; in England, 257, 291; faith of, 275, 279–80; General Council of, 329; independence of, 291; kings and, 292; laws of, 257, 301–2; Scripture and, 270; state and, 281, 299–302
Caveler, in *Sir Thomas More*, 72, 74, 76
Chambers, R. W., xiii, 305
charity. *See* virtue
Charles V (Holy Roman Emperor, 1519–1556), xxvii, 27–28, 31, 65
Charterhouse, London (Carthusian monastery), xxi, 19, 54, 343, 361
Charybdis, 341
Chaucer, Geoffrey, 333
Chelsea, TM's home in: and barn-burning, 180, 367; move to, 362; in *Roper's Life*, 27–28, 41, 43, 49–50, 55, 232; in *Sir Thomas More*, 70–71, 131, 133, 136, 143, 144n54, 146, 153
Chettle, Henry, xxxi, 67
children, parental obligation to, 252. *See also* education.
chivalry, xvi–xviii, 228
Cholmley, Roger, in *Sir Thomas More*, 73, 85–86
Christ. *See* Jesus Christ
Christ Church College (Oxford), xx
Christendom: and General Councils, 60–61, 315, 329–30, 332, 339, 349, 354; law of, 329, 349; TM's desires for, xviii, 28–29, 33, 48, 50, 72, 93n13, 284–88, 302, 308, 366
"The Christian English Cicero," xvi
Christian humanism. *See* humanism
Christian Job, TM as, 180
"Christian Socrates," TM as, xiv, 316
Chronicles. See Holinshed
Chrysostom, St. John, 208, 282
church–state relations, xviii, 288, 291–302. *See also* Parliament, clergy
Cicero, xvi, xxi, xxii, xxxii, 209; on law and justice, 253n1; *De Officiis*, xxii
citizens: government and, xix–xx; subjects vs., xvii, 235n2, 236, 237n6
city life, 176–77
City of God (De Civitate Dei). See Augustine
Clement, John, 65
Clement, Margaret Giggs (adopted daughter of TM), 14(ill), 65, 222
Clement VII (pope, 1523–34), 363
clergy: faults of, 291–92; Henry VIII and, 296;

A Thomas More Source Book was designed and composed in Bembo with Cataneo

display type by Kachergis Book Design, Pittsboro, North Carolina; and printed on 60-pound

Glatfelter Natural and bound by Thomson-Shore, Inc., Dexter, Michigan.